D0609797

THE ECONOMICS OF
FINANCIAL MARKETS

THE ECONOMICS OF FINANCIAL MARKETS

Hendrik S. Houthakker
and Peter J. Williamson

NATIONAL UNIVERSITY
LIBRARY   SAN DIEGO

New York   Oxford
OXFORD UNIVERSITY PRESS
1996

Oxford University Press

Oxford   New York

Athens   Auckland   Bangkok   Bogota   Bombay
Buenos Aires   Calcutta   Cape Town   Dar es Salaam
Delhi   Florence   Hong Kong   Istanbul   Karachi
Kuala Lumpur   Madras   Madrid   Melbourne
Mexico City   Nairobi   Paris   Singapore
Taipei   Tokyo   Toronto

and associated companies in
Berlin   Ibadan

Copyright © 1996 by Oxford University Press, Inc.

Published by Oxford University Press, Inc.,
198 Madison Avenue, New York, New York 10016

Oxford is a registered trademark of Oxford University Press

All rights reserved. No part of this publication may be reproduced,
stored in a retrieval system, or transmitted, in any form or by any means,
electronic, mechanical, photocopying, recording, or otherwise
without the prior permission of Oxford University Press.

Library of Congress Cataloging-in-Publication Data
Houthakker, Hendrik S.
The economics of financial markets / Hendrick S. Houthakker and
Peter J. Williamson.
p.   cm.
Includes bibliographical references.
ISBN 0-19-504407-X
1. Capital market.   2. Capital market—United States.   3. Stock
—exchange.   4. Futures market.   I. Williamson, Peter J.   II. Title.
HG4523.H68   1995
332.63′2′0973—dc20   94-3949

1 3 5 7 9 8 6 4 2

Printed in the United States of America
on acid-free paper

Preface

Does economics have anything useful to say about the financial markets? The fact that most large financial firms employ sizable staffs of economists indicates that it does. During the last three decades the study of these markets has been transformed by a number of eminent scholars, several of whom subsequently received the Nobel prize in economics. The most illuminating of their contributions were the statement of the Efficient Market Hypothesis in its various forms, of the Capital Assets Pricing Model, and of options pricing theory. These subjects are taken up in Chapters 5, 6, and 8, respectively. In addition, Chapter 2 draws in part on Irving Fisher's theory of interest rates, Chapter 4 on Markowitz's analysis of portfolio selection, and Chapter 7 on Tobin's comparison of asset values and Porter's ideas on business strategy, while Chapter 10 owes much to Working's insights into futures trading. This academic work has had a significant impact on the actual operation of financial markets.

Although we have tried to do justice to these various ideas, we have not treated them as dogmas. By referring to empirical evidence as much as possible, we have sought to give readers a critical understanding of their validity. In the same spirit we have devoted considerable attention to certain institutional details. Thus we have stressed the importance of transaction costs, which are often assumed to be zero in theoretical analyses. Without explicit consideration of transaction costs it is difficult, for example, to understand the standardization that is characteristic of successful financial markets. Some knowledge of institutional details is also necessary for an intelligent perusal of the financial press.

Another feature of this book is the frequent presentation of statistical data in tables or graphs. These serve not only to give readers a sense of proportion but also to acquaint them with possible sources for any research they may wish to undertake themselves. We believe that some of these statistics cannot be easily found elsewhere.

For the sake of truth in advertising we should also make it clear that this is not a "get rich quick" book. Indeed the Efficient Market Hypothesis, to which we subscribe with some qualifications, implies that there is no royal road to riches in the financial markets: their secret is that there is no secret. We believe that studying our work will have a positive payoff, though perhaps more in income from employment than in capital gains. Thanks in part to the infusion of economics, the financial sector has grown rapidly in recent years, and our intention is to help those who wish to participate in its further growth.

This book has its origin in an undergraduate lecture course entitled "Securities, Options and Futures" that Houthakker taught once a year starting in 1980. Designed as an elective for economics majors, the course consistently attracted a sizable enrollment, which suggests that it filled a need. Its purpose was to make students with a background in microeconomics and macroeconomics—but with only modest knowledge of mathematics—aware of the light shed by the theoretical contributions just mentioned on the financial markets.

Since there was no book that covered all these topics on a suitable level, Williamson transformed the notes taken by Robert Jones in the early 1980s into a preliminary text, adding much new material in the process. This text went through many revisions and extensions. We are grateful to a succession of teaching fellows—especially to Bruce Darringer, Stephen Grenadier, Jennifer van Heeckeren, Gordon Phillips, Judith Ruud, and Eduard Sprokholt—for helpful suggestions and to Herbert Addison of the Oxford University Press for his encouragement and patience. The first author also has learned much from his colleagues on the board of the New York Futures Exchange, particularly from John Phelan and Lewis Horowitz.

Harvard University   H.S.H.
INSEAD, The European Institute of Business Administration   P.J.W.
November 1995

Contents

THE ECONOMICS OF
FINANCIAL MARKETS

1

Introduction

1.1 WHAT THIS BOOK IS ABOUT

When you pick up a copy of the *Wall Street Journal* or London's leading financial daily, the *Financial Times,* you see only the tip of an iceberg. Underneath lie the millions of individual transactions that move the prices of different financial instruments, create and destroy fortunes, spawn new instruments, and retire old ones. It is relatively easy to discover *what* has happened as a result of all this activity. In fact, with the help of electronics many of us can watch it happening minute by minute. But have you ever asked, how is this change happening, and why? Take a look at the newspaper headlines from a typical working day and try it:

- General Motors Corp. reported a fourth quarter loss of $651.8 billion and a world record-breaking $23.5 billion deficit for the year. Investors boosted the company's stock to $40.50, up $1.25 per share, or 3%.
- Schering-Plough, the U.S. drugs and health care company, has authorized the repurchase of an additional $500 million of its common shares. The news prompted Moody's Investors Service, the U.S. rating agency, to cut the group's long-term debt ratings.
- The opening of trading in Eastman Kodak was delayed due to an early imbalance on the sell side.
- Inflation slide sends equities forward.
- Depressed dividend yield on stocks no longer seen as a warning sign.
- Tokyo—The Nikkei closed moderately higher. Traders said prices moved forward just before the close in technical trading linked to options activity.
- London—News of better than expected public debt repayment figures

prompted switching to long-dated paper and a flattening of the yield curve.

- Chicago—Prices of near-term grain and soybean futures ended nearly unchanged on Monday, but more distant wheat deliveries rose.
- New York—A burst of program trading lifts equity prices toward the close.
- Washington—The Federal Reserve Bank of New York attributed a rash of squeezes in the Treasury bond market in 1992 primarily to natural forces.

This book examines and explains many of the processes at work behind these types of headlines. It discusses in detail each of the main financial markets; those in equities (also called shares or stocks), bonds, foreign currencies, options, and futures contracts. We examine the variety of objects being traded (known collectively as financial instruments), the pricing of these instruments, and the types of transactions occurring in each market. Some of our discussion is primarily descriptive, helping the reader master the jargon of financial markets and understand the different institutional players. Throughout this book, however, we draw on economic analysis to explain not only "what" and "how" but also "why."

Take the example of news of lower inflation producing a rally in the stock market. In Chapter 2 we deal with the crucial first link in this chain of events. We examine the way in which macroeconomic developments, such as changes in Gross Domestic Product (GDP) growth or inflation, influence the supply and demand for financial assets and the price of money (i.e., its nominal and real interest rate). We also outline the ways in which government fiscal and monetary policies impact the financial markets, an increasingly important topic given the pervasive influence of large government budget deficits in the United States and many other countries.

Consider the Schering-Plough repurchase of $500 million worth of its common shares. This action changes the supply of its securities on the market. Because of the interrelationships between the securities supplied by a single issuer, the announcement of a share repurchase also influenced the opinion of Moody's (a rating agency) on the Schering-Plough bonds already outstanding. These are aspects of the *supply side* of the securities markets discussed in Chapter 3. There we explore the characteristics and relative importance of different securities including government securities, municipal bonds, corporate equities and senior debt, junk bonds, convertibles, mutual fund shares, and claims on financial institutions, as well as the ways in which the supply of each changes over time.

The supply of securities also changes when a government repays some of its national debt. However, the fact that, according to the *Financial Times*, such a repayment by the British government prompted switching to longer-dated paper also reflected the behavior of demand from investors. This *demand side* of the financial markets is the topic of Chapter 4. Three important factors driving demand are covered in detail: the time value of money, attitudes toward risk, and the possibility of reducing risk by holding a diversified portfolio of investments. Economic analysis plays a central role in helping us progress beyond vague notions of investor attitudes to a more quantitative approach to demand behavior. This approach allows us to develop the links between demand and interest rates on bonds of different maturities or rates of return on financial instruments with different risk profiles.

The financial markets discussed in this book are generally highly competitive: Information flows rapidly and different volumes of instruments can change hands more or less continuously with little friction. But the efficiency and smooth working of these markets is not an accident; their structures and procedures have been designed to achieve these goals. Even then they sometimes temporarily fail. In the *Wall Street Journal* quotation about the delayed opening of trading in Eastman Kodak shares, the market for these shares was suffering from a bout of indigestion that had to be remedied.

In Chapter 5 we explain how the New York Stock Exchange (NYSE) and some of the world's other most important markets for securities work to promote smooth and efficient trading. Equally important, we analyze the implications of the way financial markets operate for the kinds of information that are likely to be rewarded with higher profits. After all, one won't get rich by telling the market what it already knows.

Having discussed the supply and demand for securities and the organization of the financial markets in which they are exchanged, we then tackle the issue of security prices in Chapter 6. We begin with one of the largest and best-known categories of financial instruments: equities. What is the relationship between the dividends paid and expected by holders of a stock and its price on the exchange? Why might it be that the *Wall Street Journal* observed: "Depressed dividend yields no longer seen as a warning sign"? How does the market price of a stock with a particular risk and expected return vary with the return expected on others?

To answer these kinds of questions we call again on economic analysis. From the previous list of newspaper headlines, General Motors reported world-record losses but its share price rose by 3%. This rise may have reflected expectations among a majority of investors that the company's results would shortly improve. But how might one go about analyzing whether the majority's sentiments are correct? How much is GM's stock really worth on the basis of the cash and profits it is likely to generate in the future? Techniques of *security analysis* designed to help answer these questions are the subject of Chapter 7. We begin by examining the implications of market efficiency for the possible returns to be gained from security analysis. We explain how to analyze the intrinsic value of a corporate equity taking into account the responsiveness of the company's performance to economic growth, the structure of its industry, and its sources of competitive advantage. The insights to be gained by proper analysis of a company's financial statements are explained. Finally we assess the uses and pitfalls of various shortcuts to security valuation including the uses of price-earnings ratios and Tobin's q ratio.

The report that "the prices of stocks in Tokyo rose because of technical trading linked to options activity" is just one example of the important role that options now play in the world's financial markets. As we discuss in Chapter 8, options contracts have long been a familiar part of everyday life. When you guarantee a hotel reservation against a credit card, you are actually buying a form of option. But it is only recently that options have come to be widely traded as financial instruments. We discuss the most important types of option contracts now available and the possibilities for creating an even wider range of different investment positions by combining various options contracts or mixing options and equities. Some of the main models for valuing options are presented, and we explore the lessons of options theory for valuing convertible bonds and stocks themselves.

Terms such as *March soybean futures* and even *stock index futures* refer to a part of the financial markets that remains a mystery even to many investors who have long traded actively in stocks and bonds. But during the 1980s a number of futures markets, especially financial futures, grew much faster than other types of securities trading. In the United States, financial futures trading alone now involves well over 100 million contracts per year. Futures contracts are a class of instruments that no serious student or practitioner of the financial markets can afford to ignore. In Chapter 9 we explain the basic elements of a futures contract and the terminology used to describe the different futures positions and their relationship to the underlying assets. We then discuss the organization of futures markets and the different categories of traders.

How futures are priced and their relationship to the current market price (known as the *spot price*) is covered in Chapter 10. We explore different determinants of prices of both commodity futures (contracts based on a tangible commodity) and financial futures (those based on another financial instrument or index). After looking at the role of futures in "program trading" and the realities of so-called portfolio insurance through the use of futures and options—a concept that was put to the test by the "Black Monday" crash of 1987—we conclude by discussing futures as an investment.

When investment performance is mediocre, more than one investor or analyst has probably dreamt of creating a "squeeze" or even of "cornering" a financial market so as to exercise monopoly power in what are usually highly competitive markets. In an operation that was later described as "beyond greed," a syndicate of investors in the silver markets tried to do just that. Distortions caused by artificial squeezes or corners can force legitimate investors and speculators into unfair bankruptcy, undermine confidence in the trading system, and destroy its liquidity. In these cases *regulation* is called for to maintain fair competition and efficiency in the financial markets. At the same time, the authorities must avoid cumbersome regulations that would hamper legitimate trading or close markets unnecessarily. As the final headline from the list illustrates, there can be debate about whether certain market behavior is a "natural" consequence of healthy competition or reflects attempts by a few parties to control the market for their advantage. Likewise, there are questions as to whether or not particular trading rules would achieve their ultimate objectives even if followed to the letter. Nonetheless, regulation, which also serves to diminish the risk of fraud, is a daily fact of life for participants in financial markets. In Chapter 11 we therefore discuss how the regulatory processes work, what they have set out to achieve, and how well they have performed.

Starting from a macroeconomic perspective on the financial markets, each successive chapter therefore fills in a piece of the jigsaw puzzle: the drivers of supply and demand for financial instruments; how these forces come together to determine the prices of stocks and bonds; the operation of securities markets both in the United States and across the globe; and the opportunities to improve investment returns through security analysis. We then examine the increasingly important markets for options and futures. We describe how these markets work and analyze the forces determining prices and generating profits and losses for the different players involved.

We hope that the reader who finishes this book and then picks up the *Wall Street Journal* or the *Financial Times* will be able to look beyond the headlines to assess the real implications of each story with the help of economic analysis. Our purpose does not end there, however. The financial markets provide an abundance of object lessons for those with some training in economics. Not the least of the markets' fascinations is that they are constantly being innovated and thus challenge the insight of those who follow them, whether from the inside or the outside. In many countries, in fact, the financial markets are among the most dynamic sectors of the economy.

1.2 FINANCIAL MARKETS AND FINANCIAL INSTRUMENTS DEFINED

In its original meaning, a market is a small area, say a city square or a specially designated building, where buyers and sellers gather. Names such as Haymarket Square in Boston recall this history. A market in this narrow sense is herein referred to as a *central trading place*.

In economics the word *market* usually has a wider meaning. We speak, for instance, of the U.S. labor market, yet there is no single place where employers and workers get together to conclude employment contracts. Similarly we speak of the capital market as if it were a single market, though in fact it consists of a large number of submarkets, each dealing with particular financial instruments and often without a central trading place.

This book is mostly concerned with markets in the narrow, historical sense. The stock exchanges and the futures markets are important examples; in both the physical proximity of buyers and sellers (possibly represented by middlemen) is essential to the trading process. We only refer occasionally to such abstract notions as the capital market as a whole.

The discussion, however, is not confined to central trading places such as the New York Stock Exchange and the Chicago Board of Trade. There are other important financial markets (notably those in government bonds, in foreign currencies, and in over-the-counter stocks) that do not have central trading places yet share many features with markets in the narrow sense. In the markets just mentioned, buyers and sellers do not gather in one spot, but they keep in constant touch by telephone, telex, and other devices. Competition in these spatially dispersed markets can be just as intense as in those with central trading places, and it is the intensity of competition that really matters. *Financial markets* are accordingly defined as highly competitive markets in financial instruments.

By *financial instruments* we mean readily negotiable claims. A *bond* is a claim on the interest and principal promised by the issuer of the bond. A *share* in a corporation is a claim on any dividends that the corporation may pay in the future, and on the residual value in case it is liquidated. A *futures contract* (defined in Chapter 9; see also Chapter 10) is a claim on certain quantities of the commodity or security underlying the contract. An *option* (discussed in Chapter 8) is also a claim, but the buyer does not have to exercise it. Since futures and options differ in essential ways from equities and bonds, and are traded in different markets, they may be called *derived* financial instruments, or *derivatives* for short.

In accordance with common usage, the term *security* is reserved for equities, bonds, and certain similar financial instruments (discussed in Chapter 3). In this book, therefore, we deal with three broad classes of financial instruments: securities (particularly equities and bonds of various types; see Chapters 3–7), options, and futures.

In our definition of financial instruments, *ready negotiability* means that the owner of the claim in question can sell it without undue delay at a price that is close to the price at which he or she could buy the same claim. It is important to note that a highly competitive market is not one in which there is a single price for every item traded.[1] On the contrary, in such a market—and also in many less competitive markets—there are normally two prices: the *bid price,* at which someone is willing to buy the item, and the *offer price* (or asking price), at which someone is willing to sell it.[2] The difference between the bid price and the offer price is known as the *bid-ask spread.* A small bid-ask spread is the hallmark of a highly competitive market; thus we see that the definitions of financial markets and of financial instruments are mirror images of each other. What constitutes a "small" bid-ask spread is somewhat arbitrary; a spread of less than 1% may be considered small, but a spread of 5% or more certainly is not.

The bid-ask spread is not the only component of the cost of buying and selling. In addition, there are usually commissions and other fees payable by the buyer and/or seller. Both buyer and seller may spend some of their time on the transaction. For a market to be highly competitive, these other costs, which need not be the same for all participants, must also be small.

By no means do all claims satisfy the criterion of ready negotiability. If you have lent money to your destitute cousin, you may have a hard time finding someone willing to buy this claim at face value (or anywhere near it), so it is not a financial instrument in the sense used in this book. Many corporate shares are not readily negotiable, either; in the United States there are literally millions of corporations,[3] but no more than about 6,000 different shares are regularly traded on stock exchanges and other competitive markets. Your corner drugstore, or even your doctor, may well be a corporation, but there is no ready market for their shares. Corporations of this type are sometimes described as *closely held;* typically the stockholders (if there is more than one) all belong to one family. Such corporations are generally small, though a few are in the billion-dollar range. In the aggregate, closely held corporations account for a large part of the corporate sector, but since trading in their shares is infrequent at best, we are mostly concerned with *listed* firms, whose shares are traded in competitive markets, particularly the stock exchanges and the over-the-counter market.

1.3 BASIC CONCEPTS OF ACCOUNTING

In the study of financial markets one of the main tools is accounting, including both private and national accounting. A full treatment of this subject is beyond the scope of this book, but a brief discussion is needed to grasp the economic meaning (or lack of it) of accounting statements, which are all too often accepted at face value.* In the equity markets, for instance, much attention is paid to corporate earnings, yet it will be shown that published earnings reports can be quite misleading.

To understand accounting it is first of all necessary to distinguish between *stocks* and *flows*.[4] A factory building or a retail store is a stock because it does not depend on the units (days, years, etc.) in which time is measured. The value of the store, for example, could be $1 million, not $1 million per week. A firm's sales and profits, by contrast, are flows; to be meaningful they must be expressed in terms of a time interval, such as a quarter or a year. Thus a firm may have sales of $10 million *per year*. In accounting, therefore, we find two kinds of statements: stock statements and flow statements. The only stock statement needed for present purposes is the balance sheet, which will be discussed first; after that we shall consider two kinds of flow statements: the cash flow statement and the income statement.

In this section all stock and flow statements are assumed to refer to firms. These statements can also be used for individuals, and indeed you may find it instructive to calculate them for yourself. In Chapter 2 we provide accounting statements for various aggregates such as an entire country or the corporate sector of an economy.

---

*Parts of this section will be familiar to readers with previous knowledge of accounting, but they may find it worthwhile to at least skim through it.

1.3.1 The Balance Sheet

The balance sheet of a firm may be thought of as a snapshot showing its financial condition at a certain point of time. Another important distinction must now be made, namely between assets and liabilities. *Assets* are what the firm owns, *liabilities* are what it owes. The difference between a firm's total assets and its total liabilities is its *net worth,* also called the *value* of the firm. A simplified example of a firm's balance sheet is presented in Table 1.1.

The categories listed under assets and liabilities are typical for a manufacturing firm and do not call for comment at this point. Some of the dollar figures attached to these categories, however, need a closer look. The most straightforward item is Cash, which includes currency and readily available deposits at banks. Its money value is obvious, provided the currency and deposits actually exist—a question to be decided by the firm's auditors. Other uncontroversial items are Accounts Payable (that is, payable to the firm's suppliers) and Bank Loans. The only comment relevant to Accounts Receivable (from the firm's customers) is that some adjustment must be made for claims that may be uncollectable.

For Land and Plant and Equipment, more difficult problems emerge. Recall that the purpose of a balance sheet is to shed light on the *value* of the firm, which may be defined more precisely as the amount a buyer would pay for the firm as a whole. Suppose the firm owns a parcel of land that cost $25 million when it was acquired 20 years ago but is now worth $50 million.[5] Which of these figures should be used on the balance sheet? To an economist the answer

Table 1.1   Balance Sheet as of the End of 1993
and 1994
(millions of dollars)

	1993	1994
ASSETS		
Cash	75	95
Accounts Receivable	200	190
Land	150	150
Plant and Equipment	600	620
Inventories	150	130
TOTAL ASSETS	1175	1185
LIABILITIES		
Bank Loans	300	200
Accounts Payable	100	150
Mortgages and Bonds	550	530
TOTAL LIABILITIES	950	880
NET WORTH	225	305

is clear: a potential buyer of the firm would not be interested in the historical cost of the land but only in its current value of $50 million. Nevertheless, that is not what would be entered on the balance sheet published by most firms with the approval of their auditors; there we would find the land valued at its historical cost of $25 million.

Thus we encounter a major obstacle in interpreting conventional accounting, which has its own rules and is only remotely connected with economics. A firm's auditors will not approve its balance sheet and other financial statements unless they agree with Generally Accepted Accounting Principles (GAAP). These principles are primarily designed to prevent fraud, not to provide economic insight. This is why they stress easily ascertainable facts, such as historical cost, and frown upon the estimates often needed to use current values. The full implications of GAAP become clearer in the context of the profit-and-loss statement discussed in the next subsection. In the meantime, it should be made clear that the statements used as examples in this section are all assumed to satisfy GAAP.

Returning to Table 1.1, consider further the category of assets, Plant and Equipment. The buildings, machinery, and vehicles in this category gradually lose their usefulness because of wear and tear, obsolescence, and exposure to the weather until they can no longer be used profitably. Although some of these effects can be offset by maintenance and repairs, it is usually necessary to set aside funds for replacement. This procedure is called *depreciation* and will affect the balance sheet figure. The general rule is that the balance sheet should show the depreciated value of plant and equipment.

How much is set aside for depreciation will again depend on the method of accounting. Under GAAP a truck that originally cost $30,000 and has an expected life of 5 years should be depreciated in such a way that after 5 years only the salvage value (if any) appears on the balance sheet.[6] The difficulty with this approach is that after 5 years, due to inflation and other factors, trucks may cost more than they did initially, so that the accumulated depreciation will not be sufficient to trade in the old truck for a new one.

It would clearly be more prudent to calculate depreciation on the basis of replacement cost instead of historical cost. Whenever the current cost of an asset rises, depreciation would then be increased to provide enough money for ultimate replacement; in the rare cases where the current cost falls over time—computers are a case in point—depreciation could be reduced. When discussing the income statements some further ramifications of changes in current cost will be pointed out. (see Section 1.3.3).

The final category of assets is Inventories, which usually consist of raw materials (to be used as inputs in future production), finished (but as yet unsold) products, and work in progress (such as a ship under construction, provided it is still owned by the shipbuilder). Raw materials, in particular, are subject to considerable price fluctuation, and once more it is the current cost that matters from the economic point of view, whereas GAAP would normally stick to the historical cost.[7]

On the liabilities side, the only item remaining for discussion is Mortgages and Bonds. Under GAAP they would be shown at face value, which is normally the amount to be repaid when they are due. However, if the bonds are traded in the market, as they are likely to be for sizable corporations, their prices will vary over time. It could be argued that bonds should be valued at the market price if it is less than the face value, since the debtor could buy back the bonds at that price. Since corporations do not often trade in their own bonds, and since entering them at less than face value might raise doubts about the debtor's commitment to repay them in full, there is a case for not valuing bonds at market prices.

To complete the discussion of Table 1.1 a few words should be said about net worth. On an actual balance sheet for a corporation net worth is often broken down further into the *nominal value* of the shares and a remainder called *surplus*. This breakdown is not very meaningful because the surplus also belongs to the shareholders; in any case the nominal value (also called par value) of a share has little economic significance because corporate shares, unlike bonds, cannot be redeemed at this value.[8]

The final question we must ask about Table 1.1 is whether it really gives an adequate picture of the firm's value in the sense defined earlier. We have seen that it may not do so under GAAP, but is replacement cost accounting the whole answer? In general it is not because it does not include some important items that a potential buyer of the firm would consider. One of these is technology, especially if it is supported by patents. Although the value of patents is sometimes difficult to estimate, they certainly have to be recognized if they are present. An even more shadowy item is "goodwill," which represents the firm's success in establishing steady relations with its customers by advertising and the like. It is clear, for instance, that such brand names as Coca-Cola and Macintosh give their respective firms a value beyond the tangible assets and liabilities included in the table. For simplicity's sake, however, these "intangible" assets are not shown here.

1.3.2 The Cash Flow Statement

We now proceed to the flow statements, the most straightforward of which is the *cash flow statement*. As the name implies, it represents inflows and outflows of cash and these can be determined unambiguously. In some corporate reports this statement appears under the heading "Sources and Uses of Funds."

The principal distinction made in Table 1.2 is between current items and capital items. *Current items* affect the balance sheet only through the cash balance, whereas *capital items* affect the specific assets and liabilities directly.[9] Apart from this distinction, it must be borne in mind that all items are shown as inflows and outflows of cash, regardless of their economic interpretation.

A few comments on the entries in the table may be helpful. The first current item, Sales, refers to sales of output produced during the year, not to sales from

Table 1.2   Cash Flow Statement for the Year 1994
(millions of dollars)

CURRENT ITEMS		
1	Sales	4000
2	Cost of Goods Sold	−3000
3	GROSS OPERATING PROFIT (1+2)	1000
4	Overhead Expenses	−250
5	Interest Paid	−80
6	Research & Development	−50
7	NET OPERATING PROFIT BEFORE TAX (3+4+5+6)	620
8	Taxes Paid (less refunds)	−300
9	NET OPERATING PROFIT AFTER TAX (7+8)	320
10	Dividends Paid	−100
11	NET CURRENT CASH FLOW (9+10)	220
CAPITAL ITEMS		
12	Net Purchases of Land	0
13	Net Purchases of Plant and Equipment	−80
14	Change in Inventories	20
15	NET PURCHASES OF REAL ASSETS (12+13+14)	−60
16	Net Increase in Accounts Payable	50
17	Net Decrease in Accounts Receivable	10
18	Net Increase in Bank Loans	−100
19	Net Increase in Mortgages and Bonds	−20
20	NET CHANGE IN CLAIMS AND LIABILITIES (16+17+18+19)	−60
21	Net Issue of Equities	−80
22	NET CASH FLOW IN FINANCIAL ITEMS (20+21)	−140
23	NET CASH FLOW IN ALL CAPITAL ITEMS (15+22)	−200
24	NET TOTAL CASH FLOW (11+22)	20

preexisting inventories or to sales of assets and securities. The Cost of Goods Sold represents expenses specifically related to the production of particular products, such as the wages of production workers, raw materials, and consumption of energy. Overhead Expenses include the salaries of managers and other employees (for instance secretaries and janitors) whose work is not attributable to particular products; it may also include advertising. The Interest Paid is obviously related to the bank loans, mortgages, and bonds encountered on the balance sheet.[10]

Among the capital items, Net Purchases of Plant and Equipment refers to investment in new buildings, machinery, and so on, less the proceeds of any such assets that were sold. The Change in Inventories gives rise to a positive cash flow if inventories are reduced and to a negative flow if they are increased; as mentioned earlier, changes in inventories are not included in the current item "sales." A Net Increase in Accounts Payable, if positive, is a source of funds and hence a positive cash flow, and the same is true of a Net Decrease in Accounts Receivable. As regards Net Issue of Equities, this clearly results in a

Table 1.3   Income Statement for the Year
1994
(millions of dollars)

1	Net Operating Profit before Tax[a]	620
2	Depreciation[b]	60
3	INCOME BEFORE TAX $(1-2)$	560
4	Taxes Paid (net of refunds)[c]	300
5	INCOME AFTER TAX $(3-4)$	260
6	Dividents[d]	100
7	Retained Earnings $(5-6)$	160

[a]Cash flow item 7.

[b]On plant and equipment.

[c]Cash flow item 8.

[d]Cash flow item 10.

positive cash flow if it is positive; in Table 1.2, however, it is negative and therefore corresponds to net purchases by the firm of its own shares.

1.3.3 The Income Statement

While the cash flow statement may be viewed as the core of a firm's system of accounts, it does not cover everything. Thus the attentive reader will have noticed the absence of depreciation, which is not a cash item. Moreover, the cash-flow statement is not what actual or potential shareholders are primarily interested in.[11] Their first concern is likely to be the *income statement,* which does include depreciation but otherwise is derived from the cash flow statement. An example of an income statement is given in Table 1.3, which should be self-explanatory.

Recall at this point that all statements are assumed to be on a historical cost basis. The difficulties this causes for depreciation have already been discussed in Section 1.3.1. We saw there that, in an inflationary environment, depreciation according to GAAP is likely to fall short of what is required to keep capital intact.[12] Replacement cost accounting actually has further consequences for the income statement that cannot be pursued here in detail: if assets are revalued in line with current prices there will be capital gains (or, more rarely, losses) for which additional lines are needed on the income statement. This will become clearer in Chapter 2, where we discuss aggregate accounting (see especially Section 2.2.3).

To conclude the section on accounting, it is necessary to deal briefly with the relation between the balance sheet and the two flow statements. Taking Plant and Equipment as an example, we see on the balance sheet a value of $600 million for the end of 1993 and of $620 million for the end of 1994; the difference represents net purchases of $80 million (line 13 of the cash-flow statement) less depreciation of $60 million (line 2 of the income statement). The differences

Table 1.4 Reconciliation of the Income
Statement with the Balance Sheets
(millions of dollars)

1	NET WORTH AT END OF 1993	225
2	Retained Earnings in 1994	160
3	Net Issue of Equities in 1994	−80
4	NET WORTH AT END OF 1994 (1+2+3)	305

in cash between the two balance sheets agree with the final item of the cash flow statement. A reconciliation of net worth is given in Table 1.4, which shows that (at least under GAAP) changes in net worth can be reduced to two factors: retained earnings and net issue of equities. The reader is encouraged to verify why, in the final analysis, only these two factors matter.

1.4 SOURCES OF INFORMATION

There are abundant sources of information on the financial markets. Every day the *Wall Street Journal* and the better general newspapers contain pages and pages of data. Those who need still more can sometimes find additional facts in the *Investor's Business Daily* or, for international markets, in the *Financial Times*. Newspapers are not very convenient for research purposes, and market data in machine-readable form can be obtained from the Center for Research in Security Prices (known more crisply as CRISP) at the University of Chicago and from a number of private firms. The principal stock and futures exchanges also publish detailed statistical yearbooks. In addition to reference books such as *Moody's Industrials,* Compustat is the main source of machine-readable financial data on listed corporations.

The very abundance of financial data is itself a problem; to make sense of them one needs theories, several of which can be found in later chapters of this book and in numerous other texts on finance or investments. There are also many books of the "get-rich-quick" variety; the frugal shopper can often pick these up on the remainder tables for a dollar or less, which is approximately what they are worth. No doubt fortunes can be made in the financial markets, but those who have succeeded are rarely if ever able to explain how they did it.

2

The Place of Financial
Markets in the Economy

In this chapter we deploy some of the frameworks and concepts of macroeconomics to explore the place of financial markets in the economy. We also introduce a few important questions, such as how interest rates are determined, that are elaborated upon in later chapters. One of the main tools of analysis is provided by the National Income and Product Accounts (NIPA), which extend the accounting concepts developed in Chapter 1 to the economy as a whole. These accounts are combined with the Flow of Funds accounts into a framework for describing supply and demand in the securities markets. We then use this framework to discuss the effects of monetary and fiscal policy and of inflation, particularly on interest rates.

2.1 REAL ASSETS AND FINANCIAL CLAIMS

Anyone who has observed the response of the financial markets to rumors concerning changes in the monetary policy of the Federal Reserve Board, and to news of unexpected changes in Gross Domestic Product or inflation, will appreciate the importance of understanding the influence of macroeconomic developments on the pricing of securities. Conversely, large changes in share prices (such as occurred on "Black Monday" in October, 1987) often raise concern about their possible effect on the economy at large.

The purpose of this and the following sections is, therefore, to outline a framework for describing the interrelations between changes in overall economic activity, monetary and fiscal policy, and shifts in the international balance of payments on the one hand, and security prices on the other hand. We begin with some basic notions of capital, saving, and real capital formation.

Underlying the operation of any economy is a stock of real (as distinct from financial) capital in the form of land and natural resources, buildings, inventories, productive equipment, consumer durables, and public infrastructure such as highways and schools. In addition to these tangible assets there are various "intangible" (but nonetheless real) assets, specifically human capital and the organizational systems built up by firms,[1] governments, and nonprofit entities in the course of their past activities.

In some cases these assets represent direct saving and investment by those who employ them, such as the homeowner's equity in his or her dwelling or a farmer's investment in the fertility of his land. More commonly, however, an asset embodies the savings of individuals other than those who employ that asset directly; these savings are made available to owners of real assets through the *credit mechanism,* of which the financial markets are a major component. Examples include the home partly purchased with mortgage funds and the plant and equipment employed by a corporation and financed by equities and various forms of debt. By relying on credit, households and firms can acquire assets without waiting until they have accumulated all the funds needed to buy them.

In any economy based on private property, therefore, the existence of a productive asset is frequently associated with some form of credit: There is a financial liability on the part of the owner and a financial claim elsewhere in the economy. The specifics of the financial contracts that relate the credit to the assets will depend on the nature of the service generated by the asset, its productive life, and other factors. There will consequently be many kinds of financial contracts differing in their risk, return, and maturity characteristics (see Chapter 3). If these contracts are financial instruments, as defined in Chapter 1, they will be traded in financial markets. The ownership of shares in a corporation does not constitute credit in the strict sense of the word, but it gives rise to financial instruments that are readily negotiable in the case of the larger corporations and are similar in most respects to instruments arising from credit.

The broad pattern of real assets and financial claims underlying a country's economy is set out in Table 2.1. Each column represents the aggregate portfolio of real assets and liabilities held by the individual entities that make up a major economic sector. The coverage of three of these sectors (households, nonfinancial business, and government) is clear, but the other two require a word of explanation. The private financial sector includes banks, savings institutions, pension funds, insurance companies, security brokers and dealers, consumer finance companies, mutual funds, and money market funds. The foreign sector, sometimes described as the "Rest of the World," enters to the extent that it has assets in or liabilities to the country concerned. In general, financial claims are not listed if the corresponding liabilities are within the same sector; in other words, only "net" claims appear in the table.

At any instant in time, each sector, as well as the economy as a whole, must satisfy the basic balance sheet identity:

Real Assets + Financial Assets = Liabilities + Net Worth.

Table 2.1   The Structure of Assets ($+$) and Liabilities ($-$)

	Personal[a]	Business[b]	Finance[c]	Government	ROW[d]	Net
REAL ASSETS						
Land[e]	+	+	+	+	+	+
Dwellings	+	+	0	+	0	+
Consumer durables	+	0	0	0	0	+
Business fixed assets	0	+	+	0	0	+
Inventories	+	+	0	+	0	+
Public infrastructure	0	0	0	+	0	+
Human capital	+	0	0	0	0	+
Other intangibles	+	+	+	+	0	+
FINANCIAL ASSETS AND						
LIABILITIES						
Gold[f]	0	0	0	+	−	0
Currency	+	+	+	−	+	0
Bank deposits	+	+	−	+	−/+	0
Pension funds[g]	+	0	−	−	0	0
Mortgages	−	−	+	+	0	0
Consumer loans	−	+	+	+	0	0
Equities[h]	+	−	−	+	+	0
Business loans	+	−	+	+	−/+	0
Corporate bonds	+	−	−	0	+	0
Government bonds[i]	+	+	+	−	+	0
Unpaid taxes[j]	−	−	−	+	0	0
Bank reserves	0	0	+	−	0	0
Net claims on ROW[d]	+/−	+/−	+/−	+/−	−/+	0
NET WORTH	+	0	0	+/−	+/−	+

[a]Households, personal trusts, and private nonprofit institutions.

[b]Nonfinancial only.

[c]Private only; the monetary authorities and federally sponsored agencies are considered part of the government.

[d]Rest of the World.

[e]Includes natural resources.

[f]Including official reserves of foreign exchange and claims on the International Monetary Fund and similar organizations.

[g]Including life insurance; in both cases the reserves of these financial institutions are considered to belong to the ultimate beneficiaries.

[h]Including equity in unincorporated business.

[i]Including treasury bills and other short-term obligations.

[j]Less refunds, normally less than taxes due.

The business and financial sectors are considered to belong to their ultimate owners: the shareholders in the case of corporations, and the proprietors or partners in the case of unincorporated firms. Consequently these two sectors are shown with zero net worth in Table 2.1.[2] Among the private sectors, only households have a positive net worth. In principle one could also argue that the government belongs to the people, but for various reasons that idea is difficult to implement statistically. Since the government debt normally exceeds the value of its tangible and financial assets, it appears with a negative net worth, while the debt itself shows up as an asset of the household sector. The net worth of the Rest of the World reflects the balance of foreign claims and liabilities, and may be of either sign.

Finally it will be noticed that although the financial items (unlike the real assets) always add up to zero, this is true only because the Rest of the World is included as a sector. As the reader can easily verify, the net worth of the country as a whole equals the value of its real assets plus its net claims (which may be negative) on the Rest of the World. These net international claims are discussed in Section 2.1.2.

2.1.1 Balance Sheets for the U.S. Economy

The ideas expressed in Table 2.1 have to a large extent been implemented by the Federal Reserve Board in a publication with the same title as this section.[3] Drawing in part on estimates from the U.S. Department of Commerce, the Board has assembled data on the tangible assets of three private sectors (households, nonfinancial business, and private financial institutions) and combined these with its existing statistics on the stock of financial assets and liabilities. Although incomplete—intangible assets are missing, and so are the government sector and the Rest of the World—the result is an illuminating overview of the U.S. economy.

A condensation of these data for the end of 1993 is presented as Table 2.2. Tangible assets (except land and inventories) are valued at their current cost (essentially the same as replacement cost)—that is, what it would cost at that time to produce exactly the same assets—rather than the historical cost at which they were originally produced. As shown in Chapter 1, from the economic point of view historical cost belongs to the category of bygones that are bygones. Nevertheless it should be realized that these values could not be obtained by adding the corresponding items on the balance sheets published by individual firms, which generally reflect historical cost.[4] Land, inventories, and financial claims are in principle valued at their market price, though this may not be true for all items.

Looking first at private tangible assets, you see that in the household sector real estate accounted for more than half of the total.[5] In the business sector land and plant and equipment were the largest items; the dwellings listed there are typically apartment buildings. Private financial institutions owned relatively few tangible assets.

Among the financial claims, money, which includes savings deposits and the like, accounted for about one-third of the net financial assets of households. Not surprisingly, money so defined was also a large liability of the financial sector. Another important category of financial assets in the household sector was its equity in noncorporate business, although it was not as large as the market value of corporate equities held by that sector. The two equity items together accounted for about one-quarter of household net worth.[6] Claims on pension funds and life insurance companies were also a large household asset;

these institutions invest mostly in corporate and federal securities, in mortgages, and, to a lesser extent, in commercial real estate. The household sector owned few corporate bonds, which were largely held by financial institutions. Although its holdings of government securities were still relatively minor, they increased rapidly in recent years because of favorable yields on the long-term issues.

Table 2.2 Assets and Liabilities of Major Private Sectors, End of 1993 (trillions of dollars)

	Personal[a]	Business[b]	Financial[c]
TANGIBLE ASSETS			
Land[d]	2.9	1.2	0.1
Dwellings	4.3	1.4	0.0
Consumer durables	2.3	4.7	0.5
Plant and eqipment	0.5[j]	1.1	0.0
Inventories			
TOTAL	10.0	8.4	0.6
NET FINANCIAL ASSETS AND			
LIABILITIES			
Money[e]	3.1	0.8	−3.8
Pension funds[f]	5.4	−0.1	−5.1
Mortgages	−2.8	−1.1	2.2
Corporate equities	4.1[k]	0.0[l]	1.8[m]
Other equity[g]	2.4	0.0[l]	0.0[l]
Corporate bonds[h]	0.2	−1.2	1.0
Government securities	1.1	0.1	3.6
Miscellaneous items[i]	−0.4	−0.5	1.0
TOTAL	13.1	−2.1[l]	0.7[l]
NET WORTH	23.0	6.3[l]	1.3[l]

[a]Households, personal trusts, and private nonprofit organizations.

[b]Nonfinancial only; includes farms and unincorporated business.

[c]Private only; includes mutual funds.

[d]Includes natural resources.

[e]Including all types of bank deposits and money market funds

[f]Including life insurance; the reserves of pension funds and life insurance companies are considered to belong to the ultimate beneficiaries.

[g]Equity in unincorporated business.

[h]Including commercial paper and foreign bonds.

[i]Including consumer, trade and security credit, and bank loans.

[j]Owned by private nonprofit organizations.

[k]At market value. Includes all mutual funds (including bond funds).

[l]Equity in the sector's own firms is not deducted as a liability.

[m]Represents the sector's holdings of corporate equities less the value of mutual fund shares. Preceding footnote also applies.

Source: Board of Governors of the Federal Reserve System, *Balance Sheets for the U.S. Economy 1945–93,* September 1994.

Both households and business had considerable net liabilities in the form of mortgages. Some of these mortgages were held by government agencies such as the Federal Housing Administration. Since the government is not included in Table 2.2 because the data are incomplete, mortgage liabilities are less than the mortgage assets shown. It should also be borne in mind that the rest of the world is omitted as well.

The treatment of corporate and noncorporate equities in Table 2.2, which differs from that in Table 2.1, needs some explanation. These equities appear as an asset of the household sector but not as a liability of the other two private sectors. The reason is that the net worth of a corporation, as shown in Chapter 1, is the difference between its total assets and its total liabilities to third parties; thus the table indicates a total net worth of the business and financial sectors of $7.6 trillion ($7.6t for short), compared to equity holdings (of households and financial institutions) valued at $4.1t.[7] This means, in effect, that the market valued business assets at less than their reproduction cost.[8] To sidestep this problem, equity is not considered a liability of the business and financial sectors.

The total net worth of the three private sectors, therefore, cannot be obtained simply by adding the figures in the bottom row of the table. In fact there is no unique answer to this question. If the market is assumed to value business assets correctly and the government is ignored, then total private net worth is equal to the net worth of the personal sector.[9] If reproduction cost is used as the valuation method, then the market value of corporate equities should be deducted from the stated net worth of the business and financial sectors, and the three net worth figures can then be summed to give total private net worth on a consolidated basis; an adjustment for foreign shareholdings is also needed.

As a final observation, the exclusion of the government sector from Table 2.2 has important consequences. Among the assets of the three private sectors are government securities, but the corresponding liability does not appear. Barro (1974), in an influential article entitled "Are Government Bonds Net Wealth?", has persuasively answered his own question in the negative. His basic reason is that government obligations represent future tax liabilities of which prudent individuals should take account in calculating their net worth. This does not necessarily mean that these obligations should be deducted in toto from private net worth, since the government also has considerable assets. There are no official estimates of the value of government assets, so the government's net worth is uncertain. We have to recognize that the national net worth is unknown and that it is not the same as the private net worth.

2.1.2 The International Investment Position
of the United States

Both business and government have long been involved in the rest of the world, but the extent of their involvement has increased greatly in recent years. Until the early 1980s the United States had net claims on the rest of the world, which

Table 2.3 U.S. and Foreign Assets Outstanding
(billions of dollars, end of year)

	1980	1985	1990	1993
FOREIGN ASSETS OWNED BY U.S. RESIDENTS	673	884	1390	1497
of which:				
Direct investment abroad	404	425	633	716
Corporate equities and bonds	68	225	225	501
U.S. ASSETS OWNED BY FOREIGNERS	394	769	1657	2129
of which:				
U.S. government securities	136	241	502	743
Corporate equities and bonds	56	252	439	613
Direct investment in United States	126	231	468	517
U.S. NET FOREIGN ASSETS	279	115	−267	−633

Source: Board of Governors of the Federal Reserve System, *Balance Sheets for the U.S. Economy 1945–93*,
September 20, 1994.

meant that the value of foreign assets held by U.S. residents (including the government) exceeded the value of U.S. assets held by foreigners. As Table 2.3 shows, there has been a drastic change in recent years.

Although U.S.-owned foreign assets increased significantly, foreign-owned U.S. assets increased much more, and the net asset position of the United States with respect to the rest of the world became strongly negative. The value of foreign-held corporate equities and corporate bonds rose more than tenfold between 1980 and 1990, much more than the percentage increase in U.S. holdings of foreign corporate securities. The same pattern is found in direct investment. Foreign holdings of U.S. government securities also rose substantially. The trends in assets shown in Table 2.3 are to a large extent a reflection of the trends in the balance of payments discussed in Section 2.2.4.

To put the negative net asset position of the United States in perspective, it should be compared with the net worth figures of Table 2.2. At the end of 1993 that position amounts to less than 3% of household net worth, hardly an alarming ratio. What is disturbing about the figures in Table 2.3 is not so much the present situation as the rapidity with which it has deteriorated: In the course of 13 years the United States changed from the world's large creditor to the world's largest debtor. More to the point in this book, however, is the observation that through their holdings of American government and corporate securities foreigners have become a major presence in American financial markets, just as American investors have long been in foreign markets.

2.1.3 The Distribution of Financial Assets

It is also interesting to know that, assuming there were about 93.5 million households at the end of 1993, the average net worth per household was about

$190,000. Needless to say the distribution underlying this average was very un-equal.[10] A handful of households owned as much as a billion dollars each, while a great many had zero or negative net worth.[11] Moreover the bulk of the house-holds with positive net worth had most of their assets in the form of real estate and pension claims, rather than in financial instruments as defined earlier.

The ownership of financial instruments, in fact, is concentrated among the wealthy. In 1976, the latest year for which such estimates are available, the wealthiest 1% of all persons in the United States held 18% of all assets, but they held 46% of the corporate stock, 30% of the bonds, and 37% of other debt instruments. On the other hand, they owned only 13% of the real estate, 11% of the cash, and 7% of the life insurance. Among the assets held by the top 1%, corporate stock accounted for 29% of the total, as compared to 11% for the population at large.[12]

More recent data, though not entirely comparable to those just cited, shed further light on the distribution of financial asset holdings. In 1984, according to a government survey, only 20% of all households owned stocks and mutual fund shares, but this fraction was as high as 66% for households whose net worth exceeded $500,000 and 49% for households with monthly incomes over $4,000.[13] Among households with a monthly income below $2,000, only 10% owned shares. The distribution of interest-earning assets such as bonds and money market funds (but excluding checking accounts) was similarly unequal.

These statistics may suggest that in the United States the idea of "people's capitalism," according to which most of the population would be directly in-volved in the major financial markets, is far from being realized.[14] It should be remembered, however, that many people who do not own stocks or bonds di-rectly nevertheless have an indirect interest through pension funds or life insur-ance policies that are invested in those instruments.

2.2 A FRAMEWORK FOR MACROECONOMIC ANALYSIS OF FLOWS

So far we have looked at balance sheets, which give a snapshot of the situation on a particular date. The assets and liabilities on these balance sheets are in a continual state of flux because, among other things:

- The monetary authorities alter the supply of money
- The government sector runs a surplus or a deficit, thus changing the supply of government obligations
- New capital is created
- Most existing capital assets—land is an exception—depreciate
- New types of claims are introduced[15]
- The population and the labor force change in size and composition
- Various changes occur in the rest of the world

· The nonfinancial sectors adjust their balance sheets according to economic conditions

These portfolio adjustments in turn determine the supply and demand for securities and are therefore essential to the study of financial markets. To understand these changes you need to look at the flows, as distinct form the stocks, in an economy. This distinction is ultimately based on a similar one in microeconomic accounting (particularly of business firms), where the balance sheet covers stocks and the profit-and-loss statement covers flows.

2.2.1 The National Accounts

The best-known system of macroeconomic flow statistics is the National Accounts (known officially as the National Income and Product Accounts, or NIPAs), with which the reader is assumed to have at least a nodding acquaintance. Recall that the National Accounts present two main aggregates:

1. *Gross Domestic Product,*[16] which is the market value of all goods and services produced during a period; it is divided into four components: private consumption expenditures, gross private domestic investment, government purchases of goods and services, and net exports. GDP is available not only in current prices but also in constant prices (that is, with an adjustment for inflation); in the latter form it provides the most comprehensive measure of economic activity.
2. *National Income,* which is the sum of all factor payments (wages and salaries, dividends, profits of unincorporated enterprises, interest, and rent).

Of special importance to the financial markets are the National Accounts data on saving and investment. The economic function of these markets is, among other things, to help channel savings into profitable use (particularly in capital formation) and to help finance capital formation by attracting savings. "Investment," in the national accounting context, is the formation of real capital, not the buying of financial instruments; in fact, financial instruments as such do not appear in these accounts. Since this dual meaning of the word "investment" is a source of confusion, we occasionally use the term "(real) capital formation" where appropriate, but it is difficult to do so consistently because national accounting terminology is widely used. The NIPAs assume that investment, in the sense of capital formation, is undertaken only by the business sector.[17]

The meaning of *saving* in the NIPAs depends on the sector where it occurs:

· In the *household sector* saving is simply the difference between personal income after taxes and consumers' outlays.
· The profits of *unincorporated business firms* (partnerships and sole proprietorships) are attributed to the households that own them, and the only savings of this sector are therefore the amount these firms set aside for the

replacement of their capital assets, known technically as *capital consumption allowances*.

· In the *corporate business sector*, saving equals retained earnings (that is, income after dividends and taxes) plus capital consumption allowances, which are called "depreciation" in Chapter 1.

· For the *government sector* (including state and local), saving—negative in recent years—is the difference between current receipts (mostly taxes) and expenditures (purchases of goods and services plus transfer payments).

· From the U.S. point of view, saving by the *rest of the world* equals net U.S. imports of goods and services.[18]

For recent years the flow of saving and investment in the United States is summarized in Table 2.4. Note that the business sector does the bulk of the gross saving, mostly in the form of capital consumption allowances. During the middle 1980s, the savings of the household sector were more than offset by the dissaving of the federal government, and this was also true in 1993. As a per-

Table 2.4 Gross U.S. Saving and Investment
(billions of dollars)

	1980	1985	1990	1993
Personal[a]	137	125	170	193
Noncorporate business:				
Depreciation[b]	122	169	235	261
Corporate business:				
Depreciation[b]	181	269	394	437
Undistributed profits	38	103	63	91
Gross private saving	478	665	861	1003[d]
Government:				
Federal	−61	−197	−164	−241
State and local	27	65	25	26
GROSS SAVING	445	534	723	708
as % of National Income	16.3	15.6	16.1	13.8
Gross private domestic investment	437	643	809	882
Net foreign investment	13	−114	−79	−92
GROSS INVESTMENT	450	529	730	790
as % of GDP[c]	16.5	13.2	13.2	12.5
Statistical discrepancy	5	−5	8	2

[a]Households, personal trusts, and nonprofit organizations.

[b]Includes the capital consumption adjustment. Undistributed profits include the inventory valuation adjustment.

[c]GNP in 1980 and 1985.

[d]Includes wage accruals less disbursements.

Source: Survey of Current Business, July 1994 and earlier issues.

centage of National Income, gross saving has not shown any significant trend between 1980 and 1990 despite large federal deficits.

Note also that total saving is almost equal to investment; the difference is due to the "statistical discrepancy," which is a (rather inadequate) measure of the inaccuracies in the National Accounts. Total gross investment (including net foreign investment) as a percentage of GNP declined significantly during the 1980s and early 1990s. This decline is often held responsible for the relatively slow increase in productivity in recent years, though it may not be the only cause.

Many items in the National Accounts—specifically GDP and its components but not National Income—are published both in current prices and in the prices of some benchmark year (currently 1992, but until recently 1987). This feature provides various price indexes, which are the most comprehensive ones available for the American economy. The simplest of these is known as the *GDP deflator*, calculated by dividing GDP at constant prices into GDP at current prices. Another is the *GDP fixed-weight price index;* it is considered more meaningful than the deflator because the latter is influenced by changes in the relative importance of consumption, capital formation, and the other components of GDP.

In view of the central importance of inflation in the analysis of security prices we present a chart of the annual rate of inflation measured by percentage changes in the index or deflator. Figure 2.1 shows not only the GNP deflator[19] but also the more familiar Consumer Price Index (CPI) for urban consumers.

Five principal conclusions can be drawn from Figure 2.1:

1. Without exception, inflation has been positive since 1960 (and also, we may add, in nearly all earlier years since World War II).
2. Inflation has been quite variable throughout the period shown.
3. The two most recent peaks in inflation were associated with the "oil shocks" of 1973–1974 and 1979; similarly, the dip in 1986 reflected a temporary collapse of the price of crude oil.
4. In the early 1990s inflation came close to the low rate prevailing in the early 1960s.
5. There is not much difference between changes in the GDP deflator and changes in the CPI, but the latter, which covers only part of GDP, is distinctly more volatile.
6. Changes in the CPI tend to precede changes in the deflator by a short time interval.
7. Economic theories of inflation will be discussed in Section 2.4.1.

The *growth rate* of the economy is at least as important as the inflation rate because of its effects on the welfare of consumers and on the profitability of firms. It is also closely watched by participants in the financial markets, though perhaps more because of its presumed impact on inflation than for its own sake.[20] Customarily measured by the percentage change in GDP at constant prices, it is made public every quarter, with monthly revisions as more of the underlying data become available. Although these quarterly numbers are indis-

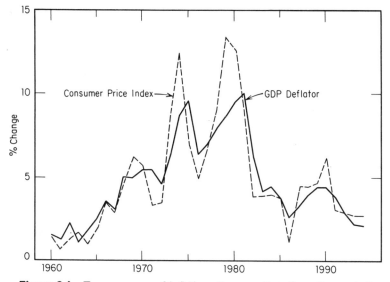

Figure 2.1   Two measures of inflation. *Source:*   Data from *Economic Report of the President,* February 1995, tables B-3 and B-63.

pensable in assessing short-run developments in the economy, we shall consider only changes from year to year.

The solid line in Figure 2.2 shows the annual growth rate of real GDP from 1960 through 1992. The well-known pattern of booms lasting several years, punctuated by shorter recessions, is clearly discernible. The 1970s stand out as a very disturbed period, as they did in the preceding chart. Economic performance in the 1980s was much better—in fact the boom of that decade was the longest on record—but the following recovery has gathered considerable strength. On the average, growth since 1960 has been around 3%.

Figure 2.2 also shows changes in the related concept of "output per hour" (that is, GDP per hour worked in the business sector of the economy), often referred to as "productivity". This is actually a rather loose use of the term; productivity is more properly defined as the ratio of output to the aggregate of all inputs, whereas output per hour (OPH) reflects only labor inputs without adjustment for the quality of labor.[21] Despite this defect, output per hour is of interest because it clarifies fluctuations in growth rates to some extent.

Changes in OPH tend to "lead" changes in GDP. Typically, OPH increases markedly at the end of a recession, when firms are able to produce more output without hiring more labor. During booms the growth of OPH tends to decline as employment rises strongly while output rises at an approximately constant rate. Therefore, OPH is worth watching as a predictor of future GDP. Although we cannot show it here, a rise in OPH may also have a favorable effect on inflation and corporate profits.

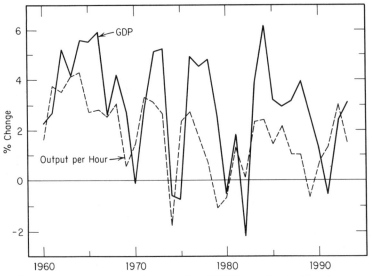

Figure 2.2   Annual growth rates of real GDP and of output per hour.
Source: Data from *Economic Report of the President,* January 1993, tables B-1 and B-45; updated from *Economic Indicators,* August 1993.

2.2.2 The Flow of Funds Accounts

Another system of macroeconomic flow statistics, the Flow of Funds (FOF) accounts, is particularly oriented toward financial institutions and markets, so it is directly relevant to our subject matter. Published quarterly by the Federal Reserve Board, these accounts shed light on the linkages between macroeconomic trends and the securities markets. While relying on the National Accounts for macroeconomic data, the Flow of Funds contains a great deal of additional information, some of which provides a check on the National Accounts.

Originally this system was designed as a matrix (that is, a table arranged in rows and columns) describing the financial flows between different sectors of the economy.[22] The present usefulness of the Flow of Funds resides less in the matrix than in the more detailed tables covering particular sectors and particular types of financial instruments (see Chapter 3). By way of introduction we give another example in Table 2.5; it refers to the household sector and provides further perspective on personal saving.

The table has two main parts, gross saving and gross investment. The first part includes net saving (that is, gross saving less depreciation), the concept most economists have in mind when they talk about saving without further clarification. The NIPA concept of personal saving, encountered in the preceding section, also refers to net savings. Both the National Accounts and the Flow of Funds derive net saving as the difference between disposable income and consumption. In the Flow of

Table 2.5   Saving and Investment of the Personal Sector[a]
(billions of dollars)

	1980	1985	1990	1993	1994
Disposable personal income	1918	2943	4051	4689	4960
−Personal outlays[b]	1781	2754	3881	4496	4756
=Personal saving (NIPA)[c]	137	190	170	193	204
+Adjustments to income[d]	35	73	92	110	116
+Net durables[e]	33	96	90	89	100
=Net saving (Flow of Funds)	206	358	352	392	420
+Capital consumption[f]	244	340	494	583	634
=GROSS SAVING	450	697	846	974	1054
GROSS INVESTMENT	448	743	935	990	1067
Capital expenditures[g]	343	538	697	809	898
residential construction	113	162	192	250	261
consumer durables	219	353	468	538	591
Net acquisition of financial assets	233	527	465	497	526
deposits at financial inst.[h]	153	125	72	−21	44
U.S. govt. securities	33	15	127	5	359
other fixed interest[i]	5	147	30	−6	19
mutual fund shares	1	76	38	187	77
other corporate equities	−11	−111	−22	−33	−89
pension funds[j]	119	282	191	344	134
noncorporate equity	−77	−59	−28	−10	−45
miscellaneous assets	12	52	57	31	27
Net increase in liabilities	128	321	227	316	357
home mortgages	96	161	179	178	186
other liabilities	32	154	48	138	171
Statistical discrepancy[k]	−6	−46	−89	−16	−13

[a]Includes nonprofit organizations.

[b]Personal consumption expenditures plus interest paid by consumers to business and net personal transfers to foreigners (from the National Accounts).

[c]Corresponds to the first line of Table 2.4.

[d]Credits from government insurance.

[e]Expenditures on consumer durables less depreciation.

[f]Depreciation of dwellings, durables, and nonprofit capital goods.

[g]Net of sales. Includes capital expenditures of nonprofit organizations.

[h]Includes currency.

[i]Includes municipal and corporate bonds as well as montgages.

[j]Includes the increase in life insurance reserves.

[k]Gross saving minus gross investment.

Source: Federal Reserve, Release Z.1, March 8, 1995.

Funds, however, income and consumption are defined somewhat differently; as a result, the FOF estimate of saving varies from the NIPA estimate.

As to income, the FOF increases it by an item (capital gain dividends) that is not found in the NIPAs at all.[23] Although not large in relation to income, this item is sizable in relation to saving. The difference between the two agencies in the treatment of consumption is more important both conceptually and quantitatively. The FOF considers consumers' expenditure on durable goods to be investment (in the sense of capital formation). This view requires an allowance for depreciation on the stock of durables. Unlike the National Accounts, moreover, the FOF keeps owner-occupied dwellings in the household sector, thus avoiding the artifact of treating homeowners as businessmen who pay rent to themselves.

The end result of all this is that the Flow of Funds usually comes up with higher—sometimes much higher—estimates for net saving than do the National Accounts. In recent years there has been much concern about the decline in the personal savings rate (the ratio of net saving to disposable personal income), but in the FOF there is little evidence of such a decline.[24]

So much for net saving. Nothing further needs to be said about gross saving, which corresponds to the funds available from the household sector for investment. The most distinctive contribution of the Flow of Funds is in the gross investment part of Table 2.5, where we see what the sector did with the available funds. Most of these went into real capital formation (dwellings and durables). The remainder was used for net acquisition of financial assets and is of particular interest for the analysis of financial markets. Note, for instance, that households were net sellers of corporate equities other than mutual funds during the years shown in the table, as indeed they have been for the last three decades.[25] Household purchases of mutual funds have generally not been large enough to offset these sales of corporate shares. Apart from large increases in bank deposits, households did much of their financial investment through pension funds and life insurance, which in turn (not shown in the table) have, by and large, bought the corporate shares sold by households.[26] As noted already, in the last few years the household sector has bought large amounts of U.S. government bonds.

Leaving further study of Table 2.5 to the reader, we now tie up a loose end by connecting the balance sheet data of Section 2.2 with the flow data just discussed. This is similar to the reconciliation between the stock and flow data undertaken at the end of the accounting section in Chapter 1.

2.2.3 The Relation between Stocks and Flows

It is clear that data on the stock of assets, such as those in Table 2.2, cannot be independent of data on the flow of the same assets, such as those in Table 2.5. If the household sector held $3.3t of money at the end of 1989 and $3.1t at the end of 1988, then there must have been a flow of $0.2t during 1988. But this conclusion holds only because the price of money is always the same; it need not hold if prices have changed. For any asset other than money, the difference between the beginning and ending stock depends not only on the flow but also on any changes in value that may have occurred during the period.

In fact, an accurate allocation of the change in stock into a flow component and a revaluation component would be a virtually impossible task in the case of

Table 2.6 Asset Revaluations for the Household Sector (billions of dollars)

	1980	1985	1990	1993
Dwellings	143	47	91	148
Corporate equities	252	381	−111	343
Equity in unincorporated business	297	98	−25	28
Pension fund reserves[a]	40	91	−82	169
TOTAL REVALUATIONS[b]	851	654	−168	728
Disposable personal income	1953	2943	4051	4689
Total revaluation as % of DPI	44	22	−4	16
Net worth	9666	13938	19059	23027
Total revaluations as % of NW	9	5	−1	3

[a] Includes life insurance.

[b] Includes certain assets not listed separately. Excludes land holdings, where the change in value cannot be decomposed into revaluation and net purchases. Also excludes government and corporate bonds, for which no revaluations are calculated.

Source: Federal Reserve, Release C.9, September 20, 1994.

equities and other assets whose prices vary incessantly.[27] Although any actual allocation must therefore be approximate, the result would still be of interest because it would shed light on the magnitude of capital gains and losses. The main reason for wanting to know about gains and losses is that, according to some theories, consumers' expenditure—the main component of GDP—is affected by them.

Let us see, then, what revaluations are implied by statistics such as those in Table 2.2. This is done for the household sector in Table 2.6, for a few major types of assets and for all relevant assets combined; personal disposable income is included for comparison. The table shows that revaluations were quite variable from year to year, both in their total and their composition. The general though irregular rise in equity prices was a major source of capital gains. These capital gains were large enough to have a potential effect on consumption, but such an effect has not been conclusively demonstrated.

2.2.4 International Transactions

As shown in Section 2.1.2, the U.S. economy in general, and the financial markets in particular, have become increasingly integrated into the world economy. It is therefore necessary to pay attention to financial flows to and from the Rest of the World. Table 2.7 shows certain aggregates from the National Accounts. In this table receipts from foreigners are by definition equal to payments to foreigners; this is accomplished by including the balancing item (Net Foreign Investment) in payments to foreigners. It is equivalent to the *Balance on Current Account,* as it is known in international economics,[28] which in turn is defined to be equal (with the opposite sign) to the *Balance on Capital Account.* The differ-

Table 2.7 Summary of International Transactions
(billions of dollars)

	1980	1985	1990	1993
RECEIPTS FROM FOREIGNERS	361	399	726	796
Merchandise exports	226	222	399	461
Factor income	81	97	169	137
Other services	53	80	158	198
PAYMENTS TO FOREIGNERS	361	399	726	796
Merchandise imports	249	343	509	592
Factor income	47	82	147	132
Other services	45	74	120	132
Transfers (net)	9	17	29	32
NET FOREIGN INVESTMENT	12	−118	−79	−92
Memo: Trade balance	−23	−121	−110	−131
Balance on invisibles	33	−16	31	39

Source: Survey of Current Business, July 1994 and earlier July issues.

ence between merchandise exports and merchandise imports is called the *trade balance,* while the difference between the other components of the Balance on Current Account is sometimes referred to as the *balance on invisible items.*

Neither the current-account nor the capital-account balance can be legitimately regarded as the cause of the other. Thus a country can have a current-account deficit—and consequently a capital-account surplus—because its exports do not sell well enough to pay for its imports, but the same pattern can emerge if its securities are more attractive to foreigners than foreign securities are to the country's residents. During the 1980s the U.S. government had to borrow heavily because of a budget deficit. As explained in Section 2.3.2, this tended to make U.S. interest rates high relative to those prevailing in certain other countries, particularly Japan. The Japanese therefore bought large amounts of American government and private securities and acquired the dollars needed to pay for these securities by running a merchandise surplus. No doubt this is not the whole story, but it should be noted that unless a country can finance a budget deficit by private domestic saving, it will necessarily have a current-account deficit.[29] In other words, the role of the financial markets in international transactions is not necessarily passive, as popular and official indignation about the Japanese trade surplus tends to assume. One reason the Japanese do not buy as much of our products as we would like is that they buy so much of our securities.

2.2.5 Exchange Rates

To gain further insight into the data in Table 2.7 we must look at the exchange rate of the dollar in terms of other currencies. Since the foreign exchange mar-

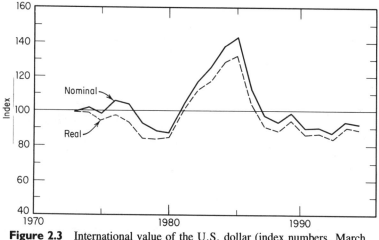

Figure 2.3   International value of the U.S. dollar (index numbers, March
1973 = 100). *Source:*   Data from *Economic Report of the President,* February 1995, table B-12.

kets are among the most active financial markets, and since other financial markets (such as the equity markets) are increasingly influenced by developments in
exchange rates, a simplified discussion of this complicated subject may be helpful in any case. It is complicated because, as is often the case in economics,
everything affects everything else. Instead of attempting a formal analysis, which
may be found in any good text on international economics, we shall argue mostly
from examples.

To begin with, Figure 2.3 presents two measures of the international value
of the dollar. There are so many bilateral exchange rates that it is convenient to
use index numbers. The particular indexes shown here reflect the weighted value
of the dollar in terms of the currencies of ten industrial countries, the weights
being based on the trade between the U.S. and each of these countries. The first
measure (called "nominal") takes the exchange rates as they are quoted; the
second (called "real") includes an adjustment for inflation here and in each other
country.[30] These indexes are not comprehensive, since they exclude such important trading partners as Mexico and China. Nevertheless they give a more
accurate picture than the few bilateral exchange rates—particularly the dollar-
yen and the dollar-mark rates—that receive most attention in the financial press
even though they can be quite misleading.

The period covered by Figure 2.3 starts in 1973, when the present regime
of floating exchange rates was established. Until 1971 exchange rates were fixed,
except for infrequent devaluations or revaluations. After a brief interval of transition, the major countries agreed to let supply and demand determine exchange
rates, but they reserved the right to intervene. The present regime can therefore
be described as "managed floating."

From Figure 2.3 we see considerable variation in the international value of the dollar, but the overall trend was slightly downward.[31] This trend is somewhat more pronounced in the real index, indicating that on balance the ten other countries had more inflation than the United States and that the deterioration was not due to excessive inflation here.

Let us now try to interpret some of the more conspicuous developments. Exchange rates influence the trade balance through the demand for imports in the country of destination and the supply of exports in the country of origin. Thus if the dollar is expensive in other countries, the demand for American exports is discouraged and so is the supply of exports from the United States. As a result, the American trade balance tends to becomes smaller (or more negative), generally after a delay of one or two years. The demand for imports also depends on the overall level of economic activity in the importing country, as measured by its GDP; when GDP rises (everything else remaining the same), the demand for imports also rises. Some of the service components of the current account behave in a similar manner: when the dollar is down, we see more Japanese tourists in the Harvard yard and fewer Americans on the Eiffel Tower.

International movements of capital are sensitive to the rates of return prevailing in different countries. When German securities yield more than British securities, some capital will flow from Britain to Germany, and borrowers (or issuers of equities) will seek funds in Britain rather than in Germany. Such capital movements are to some extent deterred by exchange rate risk, but we shall see in Chapters 9 and 10 that this risk can be hedged. In addition, some capital movements are speculative (that is, they are made in anticipation of a favorable movement in the exchange rate). At times such speculation may involve large sums and force intervention by central banks.

An important difference between current-account and capital-account transactions is that the former respond much more slowly to changes in their basic determinants than the latter. Capital moves with little or no delay, but flows of goods and services adjust only with a lag. Since by definition the current-account balance is the opposite of the capital-account balance, the exchange rate has to be at a level that will bring about this equality. Because of the delayed response of the current-account balance, short-run variations in exchange rates are dominated by capital movements. In the longer run the current-account balance has an important effect on exchange rates.

Going back to Figure 2.3, we notice a pronounced rise in the dollar index during the first half of the 1980s, followed by an even more pronounced fall in the second half and a much smaller and irregular decline thereafter. The initial appreciation appears to have been due mostly to the rise in U.S. interest rates shown in Figure 2.4. Nominal interest rates increased due to a large budget deficit and a restrictive monetary policy (see Figure 2.5), but this monetary policy also reduced the inflation rate. The net result was that investing in the United States became very attractive, while borrowing here became correspondingly less attractive. So much capital flowed in that the negative effect on the current-account balance was more than offset, at least temporarily, and the external value of the dollar rose.

In due course, as shown in Table 2.7, the U.S. current-account balance did adjust to the appreciation of the dollar. It had been positive in 1980, but by 1985 it had become negative. When interest rates receded to more normal levels in the second half of the 1980s, the current-account deficit started to weigh more heavily on the dollar and the preceding appreciation was reversed.[32]

During the first half of the 1990s the dollar index remained under slight downward pressure, in part because the current account continued to be in deficit. The underlying problem is that private saving in the United States is not large enough to overcome the government deficit, so capital must be attracted from abroad. It could be attracted by offering higher interest rates, but that might jeopardize domestic prosperity. In effect, therefore, the needed foreign capital is attracted by making the dollar cheaper.

The perceptive reader may wonder how long such a policy—never stated explicitly—can be sustained. This important question is outside the scope of this book, but we can say that a continuing budget deficit, even if it is modest in relation to GDP, raises a danger of instability in the currency markets. Unless this deficit can be drastically reduced, the best hope of avoiding instability is the improvement in the U.S. current account that the depreciation will sooner or later bring about.

2.3 THE RATE OF INTEREST

So far we have been occupied with a framework that arranges stocks and flows of real and financial assets in a systematic way. At present this framework has little room, however, for the prices of these assets.[33] There is no lack of other sources for asset prices; they are used in following chapters as needed, but not here. At this point, rather, we turn to a preliminary theory of asset prices, changing from a largely descriptive approach to a more analytical one that will enable us to deal with macroeconomic issues important to the financial markets.

Important issues are rarely simple. Analysis implies dividing complicated issues into more basic problems that may not be of obvious interest in themselves. It is necessary to start by abstracting from certain features of the real world and to reintroduce them at a later stage.

2.3.1 The Rate of Interest in a Barter Economy

We have already shown that there are numerous kinds of financial instruments, discussed fully in the next chapter, but our introduction to asset pricing begins by assuming there is only one, which may be thought of as a medium-term bond. In the simplified economy considered in this section, the firms are not incorporated, so there are no shares. These firms produce two goods: a consumption good bought only by households (called "bread" for short), and a capital good ("ovens") bought only by other firms. There is no money, and hence no scope for monetary policy; instead, the consumption good itself serves as the standard of value. The only bond, therefore, is denominated in bread; it is initially issued at its face value of 100 loaves of bread, and if the interest rate is $r\%$, the owner of each bond is paid r loaves of bread per year until the bond is redeemed at its face value.

In this economy, credit is extended by buying and selling the standard bond. The buyers are households, to whom the bonds are a source of income and a device for structuring their consumption optimally over their lifetime. The sellers are firms, who use the bonds to buy the capital good.[34] The question is, what determines the rate of interest?

To answer this question, let us first look at the firms that issue the bonds in order to buy ovens. They will do so only if the increase in their output resulting from owning an additional oven is worth at least as much, on an annual basis, as the interest they must pay on the bond; in fact, they will issue bonds and buy ovens up to the point where the marginal product of the oven, expressed in terms of bread, equals the rate of interest r.

A household that purchases a bond gives up the bread it could consume now in return for a series of interest payments in subsequent years and a lump-sum payment of 100 loaves when the bond is redeemed. It may seem that the higher the rate of interest, the more bonds a household with a given labor income is willing to buy, but that is not necessarily true. For one thing, it becomes increasingly unattractive to sacrifice present consumption for future consumption as the former approaches the subsistence level. More importantly, a household has a finite life, and there is much evidence that this so-called life-cycle consideration has a decisive influence on the desire to save, which is what purchasing a bond amounts to. A higher r means that less needs to be saved now to permit a specified level of consumption in some future period (say, after retirement). The effect of the interest rate on saving, consequently, may theoretically be of either sign, and empirical research has not found it to be significantly different from zero.

If so, the demand for bonds in our simplified economy is inelastic[35] and *the rate of interest is determined exclusively by the marginal productivity of capital.* If the marginal productivity is high (that is, if for some reason, such as population growth, firms find themselves short of ovens), r will be high, and conversely.[36] This important conclusion, of course, reflects the simplifying assumptions made in this section, but we shall show that it carries over to some extent to more realistic circumstances.

2.3.2 Government Borrowing

Primitive though this economy is, it can also be used to shed some light on the effects of fiscal policy. Suppose a government spends only on its employees, who are paid in bread as are private employees. To avoid unnecessary complications, suppose the government's revenue is derived entirely from lump-sum taxes that do not interfere with any marginal conditions. As long as the government's budget is balanced, its existence does not affect anything said so far.

Now suppose the government decides to hire more workers without arranging for additional revenue. It will then have to issue bonds, which are assumed to be just like the bonds already outstanding. What will this do the rate of interest? Firms, as before, sell bonds up to the point where the interest rate equals the marginal productivity of capital. Households buy bonds in accordance with their income. If that income remains unchanged, the number of bonds outstanding would not change either; the interest rate would clearly have to rise so as to make room for the government borrowing, and a corresponding amount of the real capital formation by firms would be "crowded out."[37]

Actually, the income of the household sector will not remain the same, for two reasons: (1) The interest payments on the new bonds acquired by the sector will be higher than it was on the old bonds that are redeemed; and (2) the hiring of more government employees may increase employment. Depending on the magnitude of these effects, less investment will have to be crowded out. Conceivably, if unemployment were large enough to start with, no investment would be crowded out at all, and the government borrowing would not lead to any increase in interest rates. To put it in a different way, there will be crowding out of real capital formation only if there is crowding out of labor.

The preceding analysis may seem straightforward, but it has been questioned on the ground that a bond-financed government deficit must sooner or later be repaid from increased tax revenues, and that taxpayers will consequently save more in anticipation of these future taxes. If so, no additional employment would be created and the interest rate would not move.[38] Since there does not appear to be much empirical support for this objection, we mention it only because it is sometimes comes up in current debates over the large federal deficit in the United States.

2.3.3 Introducing Money: Nominal and Real Interest Rates

When money is introduced into the barter economy just discussed, it is no longer necessary to limit the number of goods. It remains convenient to assume there is only one bond (sold by firms and bought by households), but that bond is now denominated and pays interest in money. The main difficulty created by monetization is that the value of money in terms of goods (or its reciprocal, the general price level) need not be constant. The question where the money comes from is left aside until later; all that needs to be assumed at this point is the existence of some degree of uncertainty about the future value of money.

Given this uncertainty, borrowers and lenders will learn to distinguish between the *nominal* interest rate, expressed in money terms, and the *real* rate, expressed in terms of the goods they buy or sell. When there is inflation, the nominal rate will exceed the real rate, which is the one that matters to them; indeed, the real rate can easily be negative if inflation is severe enough. Borrowers know that if inflation continues the principal and interest they must pay will represent less in terms of real goods and services; even if they had to increase their total dollar payments, they would still find the entire transaction (borrowing to invest in the capital good) worth their while. Competition will then force them to pay a real interest rate equal to the marginal productivity of capital.

Lenders are in a slightly different position. No doubt they would like to be compensated for the loss of purchasing power on each dollar they receive back, but under the assumptions made earlier their supply of bonds is interest-inelastic as long as the interest rate (which now must mean the real rate) is positive. They must therefore rely on competition among borrowers to obtain the real rate.

It is also clear that what matters is the inflation expected to prevail *until the financial instrument is liquidated:* When the loan is repaid, the uncertainty about the value of the principal is removed. If the instrument has a short life (say, one month), there will not be much uncertainty about the value of money since the rate of inflation rarely changes drastically from one month to the next. An allowance for inflation should still be made, but it will not be as uncertain as in the case of long-term bonds where those involved have to estimate the rate of inflation over the next 20 or 30 years.

This line of reasoning leads to the following relationship between interest rates and inflation, essentially as first proposed by Irving Fisher in his *Theory of Interest:*

$$i = r + I_e.$$

In words: the nominal (observed) interest rate i equals the underlying real rate r (based, under our current assumptions, on the marginal productivity of capital) plus the expected rate of inflation I_e from the present to the redemption of the loan. The last term represents an allowance for the expected decline in purchasing power of the dollars in which the loan is repaid. The subscript in I_e reminds us that the future rate of inflation is unknown, so it is the expected rate that matters.

The assumptions underlying Fisher's theorem are much more general than the highly special ones we have maintained so far. In particular, the theorem does not require that there is only one bond, no equities, and no meaningful government, so we abandon these assumptions at this point. This will make it possible to make some remarks about the performance of Fisher's theorem in the real world.

For this purpose it is desirable and customary to eliminate one troublesome feature of the equation, namely the reference to expectations. While theoretically relevant, expectations are difficult to measure and they make the theorem into something of a tautology. It is more interesting to know whether in retrospect nominal interest rates have reflected *actual* inflation in the way envisaged by Fisher.

One test is to compare countries with different inflation rates. In the late 1980s Germany had inflation rates close to zero; the United States, Canada, and the United Kingdom had moderate inflation (say, around 5% per year), while much higher inflation rates were found in certain developing countries, particularly in South America.[39] On the whole, interest rates, to the extent they can be made comparable, are in agreement with this pattern: The implied real rates are much less different than the nominal rates.

Another test involves comparison of nominal interest rates on medium-term bonds over time for a single country. Historically, the real rate of interest after allowance for *actual* inflation has averaged in the range of 2% to 4% per annum. Inflation in the United States, meanwhile, has ranged between −1% and +13% per annum since the end of the Korean War. According to Fisher's equation, nominal interest rates should adjust to reflect the sum of the two.

Interestingly, however, if we plot the real return investors in a highly liquid, default-free security such as U.S. Treasury bonds actually received over the past 40 years (see Figure 2.4), we observe substantial variation, from real rates that are markedly negative (generally in periods of high inflation) to positive real rates significantly greater than 1% or 2% (usually during periods of low inflation or deflation). The high real rates of the 1980s may also be linked to the large federal deficit, in accordance with the argument of the previous section.

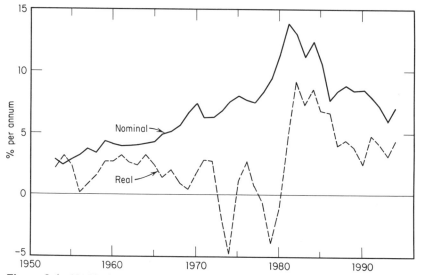

Figure 2.4   Nominal and real interest rates. *Note:*   Both interest rates refer to a (notional) Treasury bond with a constant maturity of 10 years. The rate of inflation, not shown separately, is measured by the December-to-December change in the Consumer Price Index. *Source:*   Data from *Economic Report of the President,* February 1995, tables B-63 and B-72.

To sum up: While the Fisher equation explains a sizable part of the correlation between nominal interest rates and inflation, significant departures from it do occur, largely because nominal rates seem to be relatively insensitive to short-term variations in the inflation rate. Part of the explanation of this phenomenon may be that inflationary expectations, an important theoretical determinant of nominal interest rates, respond to changes in the actual rate of inflation only after a substantial lag. Another part may be that the real rate is not constant because of changes in the marginal productivity of capital, also in accordance with the theoretical model.[40] All this needs further investigation, but on balance it appears that the Fisher equation needs to be taken seriously. It is of special importance in understanding monetary policy, the subject of the next section.

Finally, we emphasize that the Fisher equation applies only to debt, such as bonds and mortgages. It does not apply to equities, which represent ownership rather than debt. The main reason, more fully developed in Chapter 6, is that in the aggregate dividends tend to be roughly proportional to nominal National Income, thus providing a more or less automatic adjustment for inflation.

2.4 MONETARY AND FISCAL POLICY

We are now ready to take up some macroeconomic issues that are of great concern to the financial markets. The first of these is the effect of monetary policy, one of the two principal methods by which the government tries to affect the state of the economy. In the United States, monetary policy is entrusted to the Board of Governors of the Federal Reserve System.[41] Actually, basic decisions on monetary policy are made every three weeks by the Open Market Committee, which consists of the seven governors of the system together with the presidents of five of the twelve regional Federal Reserve banks. Since the Committee does not disclose its decisions immediately, much speculation in the financial markets centers on what it has decided or will decide in the future. Sometimes the Committee authorizes the Board or its chairman to make policy adjustments between meetings.

2.4.1 The Supply of Money

The main business of the Federal Reserve is to control the growth of the money stock. The terms "money stock" and its synonym "money supply" are often used loosely, and a list of definitions is needed at this point:

- The *monetary base* equals currency outside banks plus commercial banks' demand deposits at the Federal Reserve.
- *M1* equals the monetary base plus demand deposits at commercial banks, travelers' checks, and other checkable deposits.
- *M2* equals M1 plus savings and small time deposits, shares in most money market funds,[42] and certain short-term financial instruments.

- *M3* equals M2 plus large time deposits and certain other short-term instruments.
- *L* equals all liquid assets, including M3, Treasury bills, savings bonds, and commercial paper.

The Open Market Committee periodically sets target ranges for the growth rate of these concepts and for a related concept, total private debt. The announced ranges for 1985, for instance, included 4% to 7% per year for M1, 6% to 9% for M2, and 6% to 9.5% for M3. More recently, target ranges for M1 have not been set. In reality, however, it is difficult enough to keep one of these concepts within its range, let alone two or more at the same time.[43] When there is a conflict, the Federal Reserve has in recent years tended to give priority to M2.

Why is the money stock important? This question, discussed more fully in the following text, goes to the heart of recent controversies in macroeconomics. The Keynesians, who dominated policy discussion until some 20 years ago, held that the money supply served only to determine interest rates, and that interest rates did not matter much outside the financial sector. The Fed's task, in their view, was confined to controlling interest rates.

The monetarists, on the other hand, considered the money stock to be the main determinant of nominal GDP (that is, GDP without adjustment for inflation). In an influential book, Friedman and Schwartz (1963) showed that historically there had been a fairly close correlation between M2 and GNP. Later Andersen and Jordan (1968) and Sims (1972) demonstrated that the direction of causality did in fact go from the money stock to GNP, not the other way around as some Keynesians had argued. These researchers also showed that fiscal policy had much less effect on GNP than Keynesian analysis predicted.

To illustrate the Friedman–Schwartz findings, using recent data, Figure 2.5 presents percentage changes in M2 and in domestic final sales.[44] The change in M2 refers to the year preceding the one to which the other variables refers; thus the change in M2 from 1988 to 1989 is related to the change in domestic final sales from 1989 to 1990. This means that the money supply affects domestic demand with a sizable lag.[45]

Figure 2.5 shows a high correlation between the two variables in the first half of the period covered. It is also clear, however, that during the 1980s the correlation became much weaker. The monetarist relation based on M2 may be in need of reconsideration; however, a recent study by Feldstein and Stock (1994) tends to support Friedman's theory.[46] It is interesting to note that in the early 1990s, when the economy recovered from a recession despite very slow growth in M2, there was a considerable increase in M1.

Keynesians and monetarists also differ in their explanation of inflation. Most Keynesians relate inflation to such "real" factors as the unemployment rate and other indicators of idle productive capacity. According to that view, embodied in the "Phillips curve," the general price level will rise in proportion to the strain

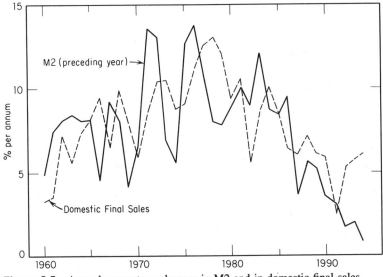

Figure 2.5   Annual percentage changes in M2 and in domestic final sales,
1960–1994. *Source:*   Calculated from *Economic Report of the
President,* February 1995, tables B-1 and B-68.

that aggregate demand puts on the economy's capacity to produce. They also attribute much importance to developments in particular commodities such as oil and grains. Monetarists, by contrast, emphasize that inflation cannot continue for any length of time without an increase in the money supply, since firms and households would otherwise find themselves short of liquidity.[47]

The "stagflation" (a combination of high unemployment, inflation, and low growth) that emerged in the early 1970s provided a crucial experiment, and the verdict of informed public opinion went in favor of the monetarists. The sharp reduction in inflation achieved by the monetarist policy adopted in 1979 consolidated this victory.[48] Although monetarist views are still far from universal among academic economists, the Federal Reserve became more and more monetarist during the 1970s; it adopted the growth targets for the money stock described earlier, and allowed most interest rates to be set by supply and demand. The resulting volatility further convinced the financial markets that the money stock was important, though this conviction is no longer universal. In any case, we must go more deeply into the process through which monetary policy operates.

For this purpose we focus on M1 as already defined.[49] Both currency and checkable deposits are subject to some control by the monetary authorities, but in practice they are mostly concerned with deposits, which account for most of M1. These deposits, of course, are liabilities of banks and are normally covered by bank assets (principally loans and other short-term investments). If the owner of a demand deposit wants to draw on it, whether by check or in cash, the bank needs liquid assets with which to execute the transaction; most of its earning assets are too illiquid to be used for this purpose.

These liquid assets are known as the bank's *reserves* and consist of its currency holdings (the so-called vault cash) and its demand deposits at a Federal Reserve bank. The reserves held by commercial banks against demand deposits and various other liabilities are the key to control of the money stock by the Federal Reserve System. Since neither form of reserves pays interest and their purchasing power is eroded by inflation, commercial banks will keep them as low as possible. The Fed can use this fact in two ways: It can change the reserves actually held by commercial banks, and it can alter the required ratio between a particular class of liabilities and the reserves held against that class.

The first of these methods, known as *open market policy,* is used frequently, indeed almost continuously. To change the overall size of bank reserves, the Fed buys or sells financial instruments (particularly Treasury bills) to or from the banks. Thus if a bank buys T-bills from the Fed, it pays for them by drawing on its demand deposit at the Fed, thereby increasing its earning assets but reducing its reserves. Conversely, the Fed can increase bank reserves by buying T-bills from commercial banks.[50]

The second type of control over the money stock, by a change in *reserve requirements,* is exercised more rarely and usually signals a major change in monetary policy. Reserve requirements have to be handled gingerly because the Fed is also responsible for maintaining the commercial banks in sound financial condition; if the requirement is set too low, banks might be tempted to grant unduly risky loans. Whatever the method adopted, a change in reserves or reserve requirements induces the commercial banks to adjust their liabilities.[51]

Actually, banks adjust their liabilities mostly by adjusting their assets. When a bank provides a loan, for instance, it usually does so by giving the borrower a deposit against which he or she can write checks. The recipients of these checks will in turn deposit them in their bank accounts. In fact, monetary theory tells us that every loan creates a deposit. Thus, controlling the money stock is largely equivalent to controlling the volume of bank credit.

2.4.2 The Demand for Money

Having now analyzed the supply of money, we turn to the demand side. The willingness of individuals and business firms to hold assets in the form of money depends primarily on (1) the use they expect to make of it and (2) its opportunity cost.[52]

As to the use of money, a major component of money holdings is known as *transaction balances,* since they reflect the transactions that the holder expects to make in the near future. A wage-earner, for instance, receives wages once a week and uses them for consumption during the week. If consumption is spread evenly over the week, his or her money holdings will average one-half of weekly consumption. Similarly, many business firms receive and disburse money all the time, but the inflow and outflow do not necessarily match in any short period of time, so money must be held to prevent a temporary suspension of operations for lack of cash. Again, the firm's transaction balance will be roughly proportional to the money value of the firm's transactions.

In addition to their transaction balances, households and firms may hold money for emergencies, or to be prepared for such favorable opportunities as may present themselves. These *precautionary balances,* however, are inherently more flexible than transaction balances, and can be adjusted to the opportunity cost of holding money; if that cost is high, less money will be held. The reason is that, even in these days of "NOW accounts," money balances normally earn lower rates of return than other investments.

When aggregated over all households and firms, the demand for money is written as a function of two variables: an indicator of the money value of transactions (usually nominal GDP) and an indicator of the relevant interest rate (usually a short-term rate such as the one for Treasury bills). The exact specification must also pay due attention to time lags since the adjustment of money holdings to these variables is not instantaneous.

Now suppose that the central bank increases the money stock at a time when the private sector had already adjusted its money holdings to the prevailing interest rate. Some households and/or business firms will therefore find themselves with more money than they wish to hold at that rate. They will attempt to reduce their money holdings by exchanging money or bank deposits for financial investments, consumer goods, plant and equipment, and inventories. This attempt is bound to fail,because it merely transfers the excess money from one holder to another. The private sector as a whole cannot cut its total money holdings. As individuals bid for assets in an attempt to reduce their money balances, however, the prices of these assets are forced up, causing their yields as a percentage of the purchase price to fall. This process continues until the yields on nonmoney assets fall sufficiently to make it worthwhile to hold the enlarged money stock. Viewed in terms of the Flow of Funds framework, the process allows the Federal Reserve, by causing an expansion of the money supply, to provide an additional source of funds to the private sector. Total private sector sources thus exceeded total private sector uses, causing interest rates to decline.

The establishment of a new equilibrium is aided by another factor: To the extent that increased liquidity leads to increased consumption and real capital formation, the demand for transaction balances will also rise, so the interest rate does not have to carry the full burden of adjustment. This is so regardless of whether the increases in consumption and capital formation result from higher quantities of higher prices.

Just how much prices of different types of assets (and their yields) are affected depends on the degree of substitutability between them in individual portfolios. The prices and yields of assets that are poor substitutes for money will generally be less influenced by changes in the money supply than those of assets that are closely substitutable for money in terms of risk and liquidity. Thus the yield on Treasury bills will be highly sensitive to changes in the money stock, while the price and yield on real estate, which is a poor substitute for money, will be influenced much less. Other assets, such as equities and long-term bonds, will be somewhere in between.

Nevertheless, since virtually all assets are substitutable among each other to some extent, the impact of monetary policy is quite pervasive. It is hardly surprising, therefore, that participants in many different financial markets are alert to anticipated and announced charges in the rate of growth of the money stock. The Federal Reserve Board (or in other countries, the central bank) is aware of these repercussions as it influences the money stock via its open market operations, changes in the bank reserve ratio, and the discount rate, though it cannot be certain of the magnitudes involved. Money supply is also determined, in part, by the behavior of financial institutions (especially banks) through the process of credit creation. That process is not our primary focus here; the interested reader is directed to the excellent explanations in Goodhart (1975) or Mishkin (1995).

2.4.3 The Objectives of Monetary Policy

So far we have examined the effects of monetary policy; now we must ask what the central bank is trying to accomplish. In most countries the goal is steady, noninflationary growth of the economy with a high level of employment; the balance of payment may also be an important consideration. Within this general statement there is room for differences in emphasis, some countries being more averse to inflation or unemployment than others.[53]

In the United States and many other countries, moderate economic growth and a tolerable level of unemployment can probably be maintained (aside from occasional mild recessions) if real long-term interest rates and inflation are both kept below 5%. It would be even better if both were lower, but central banks have learned not to be too ambitious. Although monetary authorities, as we have seen, have considerable leverage over short-term interest rates, they cannot push them down too far without reviving inflation, which in due course will be reflected in higher nominal rates (see Section 2.3.3). Central bankers, in fact, must keep Fisher's equation constantly in mind; their power to set interest rates is much more limited than is commonly believed.

For the same reason, central banks cannot reasonably aim to prevent all economic downturns. No doubt even a mild recession can cause considerable distress in terms of unemployment and bankruptcies, but it also serves to correct distortions created by the preceding boom.[54] It is more important to prevent a recession from getting out of hand than to prevent it altogether. In practice this means allowing short-term interest rates to fall moderately when the economy shows signs of weakness but not to create excess liquidity that would sow the seed for subsequent inflation.

The normal reduction of interest rates in a recession, incidentally, has another important consequence. Holders of bills and bonds welcome bad news about the economy because lower interest rates raise the value of their investments. To some extent this seemingly perverse reaction also applies to the stock market, which (as explained in Chapter 6) tends to go up when interest rates go down. A partial offset to this effect, however, is the adverse impact of poor economic conditions on corporate earnings and dividends.

In an open economy—and even the United States, with its huge domestic market, is now an open economy—the central bank will also be concerned about the balance of international payments, though it is not always clear how this concern translates into actual policy. Under the present regime of floating exchange rates, an external deficit need not lead to a more restrictive monetary policy, as was the case under the preceding system of fixed exchange rates; instead, the currency can simply be allowed to depreciate (or appreciate, in case of a surplus). Between 1980 and 1985, the U.S. dollar rose sharply, only to lose almost half its external value (by some calculations) in the 7 years since then; none of this had a detectable effect on Federal Reserve policy. In most other industrial countries, monetary policy also appears to be governed primarily by domestic considerations.[55]

2.4.4 Fiscal Policy and the Government Budget

Fiscal policy consists of those actions by the government that change the size and composition of public expenditures and the revenue from taxation. Many changes in expenditures or revenues, it should be noted, have nothing to do with fiscal policy thus defined; tax receipts, for example, will rise when the economy is booming even if tax rates remain the same. A change in tax rates does constitute an exercise in fiscal policy.

The government surplus or deficit affects the securities markets through two main channels. The first follows from the fact that a surplus or deficit in the public sector normally alters the supply of government securities to the rest of the economy; it may also affect the size of the liquid assets held by the government. This condition is true whether or not the change in the budget balance results from fiscal policy actions. The second set of impacts arises because fiscal policy may alter the level of economic activity in the private sector, thus shifting the balance between sources and uses of funds within the economy as a whole.

The use of fiscal policy to influence the economy was popular from the 1930s until the 1970s but has recently been deemphasized as attention shifts to monetary policy. The first channel just mentioned, however, is more important than ever because of the persistence of large federal deficits. As shown in Table 2.4, the government deficit is not entirely offset by private domestic savings and is in effect being financed by the Rest of the World. This does not mean that foreigners are buying all the Treasury bonds for which there is no domestic demand, although, in fact, considerable amounts of bonds have been sold abroad. On the whole, the Rest of the World has preferred to invest its dollar earnings in other assets, such as corporate shares, foreign-owned factories, and real estate.

It was shown earlier that government borrowing tends to raise interest rates unless it results in an increase in GDP large enough to create an offsetting demand for bonds. It is not yet clear what the effect of the large budget deficits in recent years has been. There may have been some favorable effect on GDP, but probably not enough to leave interest rates unaffected. On the contrary, the historically high level of real long-term interest rates during most of the 1980s and the early 1990s (well over 4% on Treasury bonds in 1995) suggests that federal deficits crowded out some domestic capital formation.

We conclude with a brief discussion of the interaction between fiscal and monetary policy. It is brief because in most industrial countries (including the United States) this interaction is minimal. The Federal Reserve is under no obligation to assist the financing of the federal deficit by keeping interest rates low; we know by now that any attempt to do so would be self-defeating because of the resulting inflation. Since the Fed conducts its open-market operations mostly in Treasury bills, it may be said to give some indirect support through the large portfolio of T-bills it holds for that purpose, but this is of minor importance. The Fed does not normally deal in Treasury bonds at all, nor does it normally give credit to the federal government directly. Such direct credit, tantamount to financing the government deficit by printing money, is a major source of inflation in certain developing countries.

3

The Supply of Securities

As in the economic analysis of any market, our interest in the supply of securities stems first from its role, along with demand, in determining the market prices and, hence, the yields attached to various securities. In the case of asset markets, an assessment of the supplier is especially important because the value a buyer derives from an asset generally continues to depend on the supplier's performance even after the initial exchange has taken place. Take the purchase of a new automobile, for example. Even though you may own the car outright when you drive it from the showroom, the supplier's future performance can still be crucial to its value, particularly when you need spare parts or repairs under the guarantee.

The purchase of a security (typically a bond or a corporate share) is an extreme case of this general characteristic of assets since the physical item exchanged has little or no intrinsic value. Apart from its potential as a decorative wall hanging, virtually all of its value depends on the supplier's future behavior. Financial claims vary, however, in the extent to which their value is ultimately exposed to poor supplier performance. A mortgage, for example, is relatively unexposed, given that the mortgagee is prevented from disposing of the underlying asset or markedly altering it without the prior consent of the mortgage holder.[1] The value of common stock in a corporation, by contrast, is strongly affected by the actions of its managers and directors. This basic feature is shared by all securities to some degree.

It should be clear from these examples what is meant by the "supplier" of a security. It is not the investor from whom it was purchased. His or her identity is usually unknown to the buyer as a result of trading through an impersonal market such as the New York Stock Exchange. Once a legal title to the security has been established the buyer needs to know nothing more about the previous owner, who is discharged from further responsibility (except in case of fraud or misrepresentation). The more crucial actor is the ultimate supplier: the firm, individual, financial institution, or government agency against whom the security is issued. This ultimate supplier is called the *issuer* of the security.

In this chapter we examine the supply of securities both in terms of the contractual characteristics of each main type and the way in which the actual performance of each is influenced by the behavior of issuers.

3.1 GENERAL CHARACTERISTICS OF SECURITIES

There are four key dimensions across which securities vary:

1. The dollar value of the anticipated return
2. The timing of these returns, including the time (if any) at which the principal is expected to be repaid
3. Their risk characteristics
4. Their negotiability

Each of these may be influenced by the issuer's actions. The return on a corporate share, for example, varies with the profitability of the company. Profit will depend on the firm's new investment or product strategy decisions; it may also vary with general economic conditions, such as the growth of real GNP and the rate of inflation, that are beyond the firm's control. A company can alter the negotiability (also known as *liquidity*) of its securities by applying for a listing on a stock exchange, by having them delisted, or by arranging for them to be traded in some other competitive market. Issuers of securities also influence the volume of securities with particular characteristics supplied to the market in response to changes in price or other economic variables, in the same way as suppliers of goods and services do. Supply may be increased through new issues or reduced by retirement or repurchase. Similarly, the maturity of a corporate bond is altered when the firm chooses to exercise a call provision (discussed in Section 3.4.3) or goes into bankruptcy.

In examining these processes our emphasis is on *securities*, defined in Chapter 1 as readily negotiable primary financial instruments. These are bonds issued by sizable corporations and governments, and corporate shares, but not the derivatives (options and futures) based on them. We also discuss, though more briefly, the supply of a number of other financial instruments, such as negotiable certificates of deposit issued by banks and mortgage-backed securities, as well as nontraded loans and deposits with financial institutions.

3.2 THE SUPPLY OF GOVERNMENT SECURITIES

Government agencies at all levels from federal to local are major issuers of securities to the financial markets. Indeed, their importance has continued to increase in the recent era of substantial deficit spending, the bulk of which is financed through issue of public debt.[2]

3.2.1 Federal Government Obligations

In the United States the largest single issuer of securities is the federal government. While its offerings encompass a range of different types of claims, they all share two basic features. First, because of the federal government's ultimate ability either to levy enough taxes or to print enough money to meet its obligations, its securities are regarded as being free of *default risk*. We shall therefore call them *default-free*. This designation does not mean, however, that U.S. government securities are "risk-free" in a broader and more meaningful sense of the term. An investor who purchases a long maturity bond with fixed coupon rate, for example, is exposed to the considerable risk that interest rates will rise, either leaving him or her locked into a low yielding asset or involving a capital loss if the bond were sold on the market; this *price risk* is common to all securities.[3] There is also the very real possibility that the value of an investor's return on the bond will be eaten away by inflation so that the real rate of return is risky even though the nominal rate and principal are guaranteed. This *exposure* may be called *inflation risk* (see Section 3.2.4).

The second feature shared by most U.S. government securities is ready negotiability. Of the total stock of federal government debt in the hands of the private sector, about 85% is in the form of marketable securities, which can be freely exchanged between the original purchaser and all subsequent holders. The markets in these securities are highly competitive.[4] The only important exceptions are U.S. Savings Bonds and certain bonds issued to foreign governments.

Given that the federal government is restricted to the issue of debt instruments, its securities differ primarily in their maturity characteristics. By offering a range of securities with different maturities, the government can obtain funds from different segments of the market.[5] Four main classes of securities are offered by the federal government: Treasury bills, Treasury bonds, Treasury notes, and savings bonds.

1. *Treasury bills* are issued with maturities of 13 weeks (91 days), 26 weeks, or 1 year, generally in denominations of $10,000 and up.[6] New "T-bills," as they are known in the markets, are offered to the public by auction, generally each Monday for 13- and 26-week bills, monthly in the case of notes, and quarterly for long-term bonds.[7] Since they are "bearer" securities (i.e., possession of the instrument is accepted as proof of ownership), they are readily negotiable.

2. *Treasury notes* come next in the maturity spectrum of federal government securities. They are issued for a life of between 1 and 7 years. Unlike T-bills, notes carry an annual coupon rate, set so the notes are originally intended for sale at par (i.e., face value), which ranges from a minimum denomination of $1,000 upward.[8]

Notes are also actively traded. In the financial pages of any good newspaper,

Treasury notes and other obligations are listed by maturity date and coupon rate, usually quoting a bid and ask price per $100 par value of bonds. This figure is customarily but confusingly reported in fractions of $1/32$ of a dollar. The newspaper will also give the *yield,* which is the return (coupon plus the value of any discount) netted by buying at the current ask price and holding the note until maturity.

3. *Treasury bonds* are generally issued for the purpose of long-term financing at maturities between 7 and 30 years. Some bonds, however, are *callable* at the option of the Treasury (i.e., it can repay the principal at its discretion and stop paying interest) in the final 5 to 10 years prior to maturity. Otherwise, they differ from notes only in that they are issued for longer terms.

4. *Savings bonds* constitute the final major class of federal government securities. These are offered only to individuals and certain nonprofit organizations. Both "discount" and "coupon" series have been issued, but as we have already noted, these bonds are neither tradable in the market nor privately negotiable, and they are therefore not financial instruments as defined in Chapter 1.

In the last few years the boundaries between the first three classes of Treasury securities have become less distinct as a result of the introduction of *zero-coupon bonds,* which, like T-bills, pay no interest and therefore trade at a discount prior to maturity. The owner of a large portfolio of ordinary long-term bonds can assemble the coupons from different bonds that are payable at the same date into a new security whose principal is payable at a certain date but that has no coupons. The principal of different bonds maturing on the same date can be similarly assembled. This operation, known as "stripping," was originally performed by private security firms who issued securities based on stripped Treasury bonds and notes, but zero-coupon bonds have also been issued occasionally by the Treasury itself. They have become widely popular, particularly among holders of Individual Retirement Accounts (IRAs) and Keogh accounts (basically IRAs for the self-employed), and Treasury securities are now regularly traded in stripped form. These "Treasury strips" mature on the fifteenth day of the second month of every quarter in the next 30 years.[9]

Since Treasury obligations (except for savings bonds) differ only in their maturity, the relation between yield and maturity is fairly clear-cut and important for many purposes. This relation is conventionally expressed in the *yield curve,* charted for three different time periods in Figure 3.1. Starting with the most recent data, we see that the yield was lowest for the shortest maturity shown (1 year) and rose steadily for the longer maturities. This relationship was also true in 1985, when the entire curve was at a higher level than in 1991. The pattern for 1985 and 1991 corresponds to a "normal" yield curve, such as is found most of the time. In 1980, by contrast, the yield curve was "inverted": The short maturities yielded more than the distant ones. The reasons for these diverse patterns are discussed in Chapter 4, where it will also be argued that the type of yield curve shown in Figure 3.1 is not very meaningful.

In addition to the Treasury obligations listed above, there are bonds issued by federal agencies other than the Treasury; examples are the Federal National

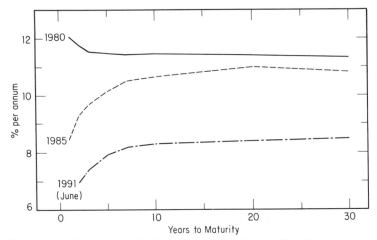

Figure 3.1   Yield curves for federal securities. *Note:*   The yields are
for "constant maturities," which means that they are interpolated
from the quotations for actual notes and bonds of similar maturity.
The yield for 20-year bonds is not given in the source and has also
been interpolated. *Source:*   Data from *Federal Reserve Bulletin,* September 1991 and earlier issues, table A23.

Mortgage Association and the Tennessee Valley Authority. Some of these are
guaranteed by the Treasury, but even so they generally yield slightly more than
similar Treasury bonds because agency issues are not as readily negotiable and
because reliance on the Treasury guarantee may involve a delay.

3.2.2 Municipal Bonds

The other major source of government bonds are those issued by states, counties,
cities and towns, school districts, and other special authorities such as sewer
districts. They are collectively known as "municipals" in the United States. It is
a long-standing federal policy that the interest earned on these securities shall be
exempt from federal income tax.[10] Municipals, which are also referred to as
"tax-exempt" bonds, are therefore particularly attractive to individuals who face
high marginal tax rates. For an individual in the 33% tax bracket, for instance,
a 6% municipal bond produces as much after-tax interest as a 9% taxable bond.

   While granting this tax privilege, the federal government does not guarantee
municipals against default. The individual authority must therefore back these
bonds with its own revenue generating power. They must issue either General Obligation Bonds (G.O.'s), where an authority with theoretically unlimited taxing
power pledges to collect the necessary revenue to meet its obligations on these
bonds (a pledge called "full faith and credit"), or Revenue Bonds, which are entitled to access only the revenues of a specific project (such as a turnpike or a port).

Because municipal bonds are not default-free, prudent investors want to know how secure each bond is. This information is provided by rating agencies, discussed more fully in connection with corporate bonds (see Section 3.3). Most municipal bonds enjoy high ratings, indicating a low risk of default. The exceptions arise in cases where the market or rating agency believe that an authority has an excessive quantity of debt compared with its realistic (rather than theoretical) revenue base. In fact, defaults have been rare since the Great Depression, although some have occurred.[11]

3.2.3 Bonds of Foreign Governments and International Organizations

Residents of one country may own bonds issued by the government of another country, but these are not default-free to their owners. Like the U.S. government, a foreign government can satisfy its domestic creditors, at least in nominal terms, by levying additional taxes or printing more money. This merely means that the government in question can always come up with the domestic currency. If the bonds are denominated in another currency (for instance, if Sweden issues bonds denominated in U.S. dollars), that is not enough to rule out default on externally held bonds since the debtor may not be able to obtain the foreign currency. Furthermore, the owner of foreign bonds that are denominated in some currency other than the owner's will have an exchange-rate risk (i.e., the currency in which the bond is denominated may be worth less in terms of the holder's own currency than when the bond was acquired). Nevertheless government bonds are often held by nonresidents; thus a sizable part of the U.S. government debt is now in the hands of private Japanese investors.[12]

Bonds issued by international organizations, such as the World Bank, are similar in their characteristics. The World Bank (officially known as the International Bank for Reconstruction and Development) has made it a practice to issue bonds in many different currencies. The risk of default on these bonds is not zero, but because of the close financial links between the bank and its shareholders (that is, the member countries), it is close to zero.

3.2.4 Index-Linked Bonds

As shown in Section 2.4.3, ordinary fixed-interest government securities are subject to inflation risk. This condition is the main reason for describing them as "default-free" rather than "risk-free." To achieve greater freedom from risk, such securities must offer protection against inflation, which can be accomplished by linking payments of interest and principal to a general price index such as the CPI. Thus a 3% index-linked bond with a face value of $1,000 would entitle the holder to an annual interest not of $30 but of $30 multiplied by the value of the CPI at the time the interest is due, and similarly for the principal. The interest rate of 3% would then be a real rate, not a nominal rate.

Although index-linked bonds have often been advocated, the U.S. Treasury has traditionally opposed them. In the official view, it appears, inflation is no more than a temporary problem, to be counteracted by appropriate monetary and fiscal policies instead of being accommodated. Figure 2.1 showed that inflation has persisted despite these pious intentions. Many other countries have adopted a more pragmatic attitude. In countries with high inflation, for instance in South America, government bonds without indexing are virtually nonexistent; the few that survive are literally not worth the paper they are printed on. Some countries with more moderate inflation have also responded to the demand for truly risk-free investments.

One of these countries is the United Kingdom. According to the *Financial Times,* the leading British financial daily, the yield on index-linked bonds in mid-February 1991 was about 4%.[13] The yield on comparable nonindexed bonds was around 10%, implying an expected inflation rate of about 6%. The actual inflation rate at that time was about 9%, so a considerable reduction of inflation was anticipated and has in fact occurred since then.

3.3 CORPORATE FINANCIAL POLICY

The activities of virtually all business enterprises require the firm to maintain a portfolio of assets. As described in Chapter 1, these may be in the form of physical plant, cash, and bank deposits required to facilitate transactions, or inventories and work in progress. In the case of smaller unincorporated enterprises and private companies, the funds required may come directly from the accumulated savings of owners, or perhaps from bank loans. As they grow, however, most firms sooner or later approach the securities markets for additional capital with which to finance their assets.

The mix of securities supplied to the markets depends on the financial policy of firms. It is convenient to distinguish three key decision areas:

1. The optimal mix of debt versus equity
2. The desirable maturity structure of debt
3. The preferred source of debt funds (e.g., corporate bonds versus banks or finance companies)

The ultimate objective is to minimize the total cost of funds required to finance any given level of assets. In a more general analysis, not attempted here, the assets themselves would also be treated as variables.

Debt instruments have a simple but compelling attraction for the firm: They often are a cheaper source of funds than equity. This is the reality for two reasons. First, the interest expense on debt is deductible from the corporate income tax, whereas dividends on shares are not. Second, because debt holders have priority over shareholders in the allocation of the firm's earnings, and because they are promised a stable rate of return in the form of interest, the firm is often able to raise debt at a lower expected return than it would have to offer on equity.

Another consideration limits the usefulness of equity financing from the viewpoint of management. The shareholders are the ultimate owners of a corporation. They elect the board of directors, which in turn has the power to hire and fire executives. Most of the time the shareholders, especially if they are numerous and individually small, do not exercise their power; indeed many of them do not even bother to vote at the annual meeting required by law. In those circumstances, control of the corporation effectively resides in a small number of large shareholders, who are likely to be closely associated with management but who need not have a majority of the shares. Occasionally, however, the shareholders do matter, namely when there is danger of a corporate takeover (see Section 3.4.2). The management of a corporation often feels more secure if there are not too many shares in public hands. Bondholders do not vote (except if the firm goes bankrupt) and are therefore harmless as far as management is concerned.

Why, then, do firms not finance themselves with 99.9% debt instead of the average of only 38%, which we shall soon observe in the aggregate data?[14] The answer lies in the fact that the more debt a firm issues relative to its total assets, the more its long-run survival is put at risk.[15] This answer follows from the constraint that if the firm fails to repay any part of the total interest or principal payment due on its debt during any year, all its debt immediately become repayable and debt holders have the right to force the firm into liquidation in order to recover their funds.

Prospective holders of the firm's shares and bonds, as well as prospective lenders such as banks, recognize the increasing risk of bankruptcy as the ratio of debt to equity in a corporate balance sheet rises. A firm must therefore offer a higher rate of return on its securities the more debt it issues against its assets. Indeed, certain lenders may be unwilling to buy a firm's securities at any price if in their opinion the firm has too much debt already, or if its credit is not well established; this can be a serious problem for new firms.

More expensive funds reduce the value of the firm. Up to a point, however, this effect is outweighed by the inherently lower cost of debt. The general relationship between the value of a firm and its debt-equity ratio is therefore of the form shown in Figure 3.2. Supplying more debt increases a firm's value so long as the chance of bankruptcy is relatively low.

Within this context it should be noted that, given unchanged risk preferences, a more volatile economy (and hence more variable corporate profitability) will require firms to reduce their debt ratios, supplying more equity to the securities markets. The more volatile the corporate earnings, the greater the likelihood of inability to meet committed interest payments on any given level of debt.

In practice, of course, bankruptcies will occur, so that we should look not only at the claim of each class of securities on the debtor's income but also at the rights attached to each type of security under liquidation. While some of the

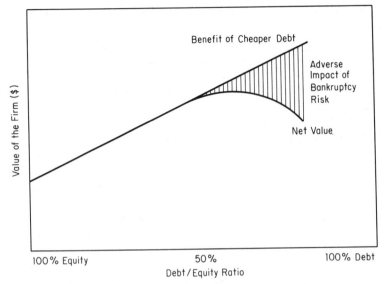

Figure 3.2 Debt policy and a firm's market value

details may vary depending on the precise terms under which debt is issued, a typical ranking of liabilities is shown in Table 3.1. The liquidating agent's fees, accrued wages owed to employees, and unpaid taxes have the first claims on assets, ahead of other creditors. Holders of mortgages or other debt secured by a specific asset as collateral, however, have the right to liquidate that asset in order to recover their due.

Next, creditors such as holders of corporate debentures, who are secured on the general assets of the firm, must be paid in full (assuming there are sufficient assets). Unsecured creditors, including trade creditors or holders of unsecured notes, then have first claim on what remains, followed by the holders of subordinated debt. The residual is then distributed pro rata to preferred and common stockholders.[16]

Table 3.2 lists the classifications used by the two leading bond rating agencies in the United States: Moody's Investors Service and Standard & Poor's.[17] The table also shows the average yield for each rating class as of early 1991. Within the "investment" category the yields were not greatly different, but they rose steeply as the rating got worse.

Returning to the firm's decision making process, once the optimal level of debt financing is determined, the company must decide what maturity structure is best suited to its purposes. This choice is influenced by two opposing forces. On the one hand—assuming the yield curve to be "normal" as defined in Section 3.2.1—short-term securities are generally a cheaper source of funds for the firm than those with longer maturities. Not only do they usually carry a lower interest rate, as shown by the yield curve, but also they offer greater flexibility in match-

Table 3.1 Ranking of Corporate Liabilities under Bankruptcy

FIRST

Liquidator's fees

Accrued wages and employee benefits

Taxes

Mortgages and other debts secured on particular assets

First ranking debentures

Lower ranking debentures

Unsecured notes

Trade creditors

Preferred shares

Subordinated debt

Common shares

LAST

The lower the ranking, the greater the probability that all or part of the original investment made in the security will be lost. In the case of corporate bonds, various rating agencies publish assessments of the risk of loss due to bankruptcy associated with particular bonds.

Table 3.2 Bond Rating Categories of Two Agencies and Corresponding Yields

Category	Moody's	Standard & Poor's	Yield[a]
Investment grades	Aaa	AAA	8.7
	Aa	AA	8.8
	A	A	9.4
Medium grades	Baa	BBB	10.1
	Ba	BB	12.0
	B	B	17.7
Speculative bonds	Caa	CCC	
	Ca	CC	35.0[c]
	C	C[b]	
Bonds in default[d]	—	D	[e]

[a] Average yield on Standard & Poor's rating. We are indebted to Kirk Ott for these estimates, which refer to February 1991.

[b] Payment of principal or interest in arrears.

[c] Approximate average yield of bonds rated C, CC and CCC by Standard & Poor's.

[d] Income bonds on which no interest is currently being paid.

[e] Not meaningful.

Table 3.3 Aggregate Balance Sheets of U.S. Nonfinancial Corporate Business (trillions of dollars or percentage[a] at end of year)

	1967		1977		1987		1993	
	$	%	$	%	$	%	$	%
AT CURRENT COST								
Fixed assets[b]	0.6	56	1.8	60	3.9	57	4.0	52
Inventories	0.2	15	0.4	14	0.8	12	1.0	13
Liquid assets	0.1	6	0.1	5	0.6	9	0.9	12
Other assets	0.2	23	0.6	21	1.5	22	1.8	23
TOTAL ASSETS	1.0	100	2.7	100	6.8	100	7.7	100
Bonds	0.1	12	0.3	11	1.0	15	1.3	17
Bank loans	0.1	7	0.2	5	0.6	9	0.5	6
Other liabilities	0.2	21	0.5	16	1.3	19	2.1	27
TOTAL LIABILITIES	0.4	41	1.0	32	2.9	43	3.9	51
NET WORTH	0.6	59	1.8	68	3.9	57	3.8	49
MARKET VALUE[c]	0.7		0.7		2.2		5.1	
at % of net worth		107		37		57		136
AT HISTORICAL COST								
Fixed assets[b]	0.4		1.0		2.5		3.3	
Inventories	0.2		0.4		0.7		0.9	
Total assets[d]	0.9		2.2		5.3		7.0	
Net worth	0.5		1.2		2.4		3.1	
Market value as % of net worth		135		61		92		165

[a] Percentage of total assets (at current cost) unless noted otherwise. Percentages were calculated from unrounded dollar amounts.

[b] Plant and equipment, residential structures and land.

[c] Market value of corresponding equities; includes small amount for corporate farms, which are excluded from balance sheet data.

[d] Including financial assets.

Source: Federal Reserve Board, *Balance Sheets of the U.S. Economy* (Release C.9), September 20, 1994.

ing borrowings with the changing need for funds, so that the firm can avoid paying for unwanted capital when its financing needs decline.

On the other hand, the use of short-term securities to finance illiquid assets requires the firm to "roll over" (refinance) its debt at frequent intervals regardless of the state of the capital markets. It is thus exposed to a risk of high interest rates and other unfavorable terms in periods of tight credit. These may also be periods when some supposedly liquid assets (particularly inventories and accounts receivable) turn out to be not so liquid after all.

These considerations have led many companies to aim at achieving a match between the maturities of their assets and liabilities. Long-term funding (equities and bonds) is used to support fixed assets and working capital, which tend to grow along a fairly stable long-run trendline, though perhaps with some discrete "jumps" when major new investments are made. The cyclical requirement for funds to finance fluctuations in inventories, accounts receivable, and cash requirements related to sales is met with short-term securities and bank credit.

3.3.1 Empirical Evidence

An indication of where firms end up in the pursuit of their financial objectives is given by the average balance sheet structure of U.S. nonfinancial corporations, as derived from the Federal Reserve's aggregate data and reported for selected years in Table 3.3. The table is divided in two parts. In the top part tangible assets are valued at "current cost" (essentially equal to replacement cost), which is most meaningful from the economic point of view; as shown in Chapter 1, replacement cost is what interests anyone considering the takeover of a corporation. In the lower part, assets are valued at "historical cost" (i.e., at what they cost when they were originally acquired, less depreciation), emphasized by conventional accounting practices. For financial assets and liabilities the distinction between current and historical cost is generally of little significance.

Considering first the current cost data, we see that in 1993 net worth, also known as shareholders' equity, was about 49% of total assets, significantly less than in the earlier years shown. In general, the equity originates from net sales of shares, from retained earnings, and from increases in the nominal value of fixed assets due mostly to inflation. The liabilities consisted largely of bonds, trade debt, bank loans, and mortgages.[18]

The top part of Table 3.3 shows that in the late 1970s shareholders' equity financed an unusually high percentage of corporations' total assets. By 1987 the ratio of net worth to total assets had returned to the ratio prevailing in 1967 (and also, by and large, in earlier years). One may perhaps infer that corporations had thus corrected a temporary imbalance in the structure of their liabilities. As is shown in Section 3.4.1, they did so mostly by repurchasing their own shares, thereby taking advantage of the low ratio of the market value of these shares to their theoretical value implicit in the balance sheet.[19] The stock market, according to this argument, had grossly undervalued the equities of nonfinancial corporations in the late 1970s and early 1980s; this undervaluation had not been fully eliminated by the end of 1987, when the market value was still only 57% of net worth. By the end of 1993 the market value exceeded net worth at current cost by a considerable margin (see also Figure 3.3). Remember, however, that the aggregate balance sheet at current cost reflects a number of debatable assumptions made by the statisticians at the Federal Reserve and the U.S. Department of Commerce. The omission of intangible assets (patents, goodwill, etc.) is a serious limitation of the published balance sheets.

The historical cost data in the bottom half of Table 3.3 present a rather different picture. The figures for fixed assets, in particular, are much lower than their counterparts at current cost. As a result, net worth is significantly lower at historical cost than at current cost. Instead of the undervaluation of equities

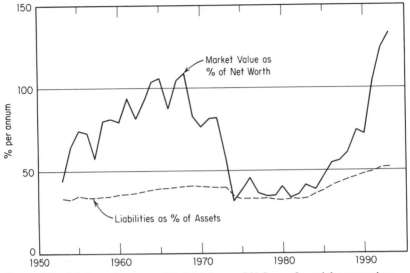

Figure 3.3   Market valuation and indebtedness of U.S. nonfinancial corporations. *Note:* Data from Federal Reserve Board, *Balance Sheets of the U.S. Economy* (Release C.9), September 20, 1994.

pointed out in the preceding paragraph, there now appears a marked overvaluation in 1967 and 1993, though not in 1977 and 1987. Which of these contrasting interpretations should we believe? The current-cost calculation has the backing of economic theory, but that does not imply it is believed by the market. If the current-cost approach is correct, the market value of equities should have moved closer to the underlying net worth, as indeed it had done with a vengeance by 1993. Needless to say, one such observation is not conclusive, and the problem is discussed further in Chapter 6.

It is also of interest that net worth is a much smaller fraction of total assets in the private financial sector of the economy than in the nonfinancial sector. According to the same source as was used for Table 3.3, the total assets of private financial institutions at the end of 1991 were $13 trillion and their net worth was only $1 trillion. Moreover, the ratio of net worth to total assets has tended to shrink in recent years, again in contrast to the other sector.

The Flow of Funds Accounts provide a very detailed breakdown, both of sectors and of transactions. An example that provides some perspective on recent developments in the financial markets is the "Sector Statement of Saving and Investment" for nonfinancial corporate business, shown (again in condensed form) for some recent years as Table 3.4.

We see that in 1980 and 1993 corporations issued a relatively small amount of equities but in the other years they bought back their own equities on a large scale. In fact, corporations were net purchasers of their own equities from the latter part of 1983 through the first quarter of 1991, a phenomenon to which we

Table 3.4 Saving and Investment of Nonfinancial Corporate Business[a]
(billions of dollars)

	1980	1985	1990	1993	1994
Profits before tax	181	166	231	293	356
− Tax accruals	67	70	93	117	142
− Dividends[b]	45	74	117	159	158
= Earnings retained in U.S.	69	22	21	18	55
+ Foreign earnings[c]	19	20	43	51	35
+ Depreciation charges	173	256	327	358	379
+ Valuation adjustments[d]	− 61	44	22	36	33
= GROSS SAVING	200	352	412	462	502
Net change in financial assets	97	83	86	83	127
− Net equities issued	10	− 85	− 63	22	− 41
− Net borrowing[e]	121	198	167	73	119
= NET FINANCIAL INVESTMENT	− 34	− 31	− 39	− 12	− 33
+ Real investment	256	375	403	440	522
= GROSS INVESTMENT	222	344	365	428	489
Sector discrepancy	− 23	8	47	34	13

[a]Excluding farm corporations.

[b]Less earnings received from abroad.

[c]Earnings retained abroad.

[d]The Inventory Valuation Adjustment changes inventories from historical to current cost; the Capital Consumption Adjustment does the same for depreciation charges.

[e]Including foreign direct investment in the United States.

Source: Federal Reserve, *Flow of Funds Accounts* (Release Z.1), March 8, 1995, and earlier issues.

return in Section 3.4.1. As a result, they had to borrow heavily, because they also had to finance real investment and were acquiring other financial assets on a large scale. When repurchases of shares came to a temporary end in the early 1990s, borrowing declined sharply. This is the most striking development revealed, but the attentive reader will notice much else of interest, including the increasing tendency of these corporations to keep their earnings abroad (presumably because the dollar tended to fall from 1985 on).[20]

3.4 THE SUPPLY OF CORPORATE SECURITIES

The preceding theoretical discussion suggests that a cost-benefit calculation for different types of securities, in conjunction with the firm's funding requirements and the risk of bankruptcy, leads most companies of significant size to issue a range of securities. These include:

- *Common stock,* which has last claim on earnings and assets but stands to benefit from higher profits in successful years and to bear the risk of lower or negative profits in unsuccessful years. The common stockholders are the owners of the corporations and elect the board of directors at the annual meeting. In the United States, corporations generally have only one class of common stock, but in other countries they may have more than one class with different claims to dividends or different voting rights.

· *Preferred shares,* which claim a predetermined dividend ahead of common stockholders if sufficient earnings are available after payment of interest, but no more than their fixed dividend in successful years. They may be either *cumulative preferred,* in which case unpaid claims on past dividends will cumulate until funds are available, or *noncumulative,* in which case shortfalls are not carried forward to better years. Since the noncumulative variety is open to abuse—a firm may conceivably juggle its reported earnings so as to show an insufficient amount for preferred dividends—most preferred shares issued in recent years are cumulative.

· Various forms of fixed-interest *corporate debt* with first claim on earnings and in most cases an enhanced ranking under bankruptcy. These include first and second ranking debentures, unsecured notes, and subordinated debt, with a wide range of maturities (usually varying between 5 and 20 years) designed to match the pattern of funding requirements over time. In addition, large corporations sometimes issue *commercial paper* (also known as "open market paper"), short-term IOUs that are sold directly to investors. Except for being subject to default risk, commercial paper is similar to Treasury bills. The interest rate on such paper is higher than the T-bill rate but lower than the prime rate charged by banks on loans to their best customers.

· *Mortgages* and other liabilities with claims on a specific asset, such as the firm's land and buildings or a particular piece of equipment, again usually with fixed interest payments. These are augmented by short-term borrowing from banks or other financial institutions, and indirect financing by means of leasing arrangements.

3.4.1 Corporate Equities

As with its products, a firm may alter the volume of securities it is supplying to the market at any time. In the case of equities this change may be accomplished in four main ways: through flotation of new shares, rights issues, stock splits (and the related methods of bonus issues or stock dividends), or share repurchase.

When a corporation is initially established, its charter specifies the number of shares it is authorized to issue, generally at a stated par value.[21] These shares only acquire economic significance, however, when they are actually issued. Stock may be issued privately to individuals connected with the company or its officers, or by public offering. In the latter case the shares must be registered with the Securities and Exchange Commission (SEC) and a prospectus must be made available (see Chapter 11). The prospectus must disclose at least the legal minimum of information about the corporation's current and proposed activities, its existing assets and liabilities, its directors and their beneficial interests, and so on.

Provided it has sufficient authorized capital and is not under any legal injunction, a corporation may issue shares at any time.[22] However, the statutory requirements (and, in the case of listed shares, the rules of the stock exchanges) mean that the transactions costs involved are usually significant. Since a high proportion of those costs is independent of the size of the issue, most companies issue new shares infrequently and in large parcels.[23] Once newly issued shares have been subscribed and the funds collected from investors, they become permanent capital.

As the corporation continues in business and retains part of its earnings, its share price will typically rise above the original par value at which the shares were initially bought by the founders. Any issue of new shares will therefore be made at a price that includes a premium over the par value, reflecting the greater worth of a share in the established company. This premium rewards the initial stockholders for their successful initiative.

Most public issues are underwritten by investment bankers[24] who, for a percentage of the final value, guarantee that the corporation will receive an agreed amount from the issue. If some of the offered securities remain unsold after a specified period, the underwriters are forced to absorb them temporarily into their own portfolios to make up the cash shortfall; the market price is then likely to fall below the issue price. Less frequently, the issue will not be underwritten, but the investment banker will operate on a "best efforts" basis for a lower fee. Certain investment bankers, the "venture capitalists," specialize in the shares of newly established firms, which they may keep in their portfolio until the conditions for a public offering appear favorable.

Instead of offering its shares to all comers, a firm may choose to sell new equity to its existing shareholders by means of a *rights issue*. In this case, each existing shareholder receives the right to purchase a number of new shares in proportion to his or her current holding. Thus a "1 for 4" rights issue would allow a shareholder to purchase one additional share for every four currently held. Since companies wish to ensure that a new issue is successfully subscribed, the new shares are offered at a price below the current market value, indeed below the price expected to prevail after the shares have been "diluted" by the new issue.[25] If the issuing firm has judged the market correctly, the "rights" will therefore have a money value and they will be traded as a separate security until they expire.

An investor who exercises the rights in full will maintain the same proportion of voting shares as before the issue. Alternatively, an investor who does not wish to subscribe can sell the rights in the market as a compensation for the fall in the stock's price resulting from dilution. Depending on how well the issue is received (i.e., on whether it attracts many new buyers) he or she may also realize a capital gain or loss.

Corporations can also alter the number of their shares outstanding by *stock dividends,* also described more appealingly as "bonus issues." When the generous corporation of which you are a shareholder "pays" a stock dividend (say, one new share for every twenty currently held), it may be premature to break out the champagne. Because the firm's net worth and earnings potential are unaffected, it may be argued that the same total value is now divided among more units of stock so that each is worth less—another example of dilution.

Nevertheless, many respectable corporations do declare regular or occasional stock dividends. In doing so they usually leave the cash dividend per share unchanged; consequently each shareholder collects a larger payout. If so, champagne may be in order after all. In many cases, declaring a stock dividend is merely an indirect way of increasing the cash dividend. It is convenient and customary to keep cash dividends at a round figure (such as 60 cents) per share, and stock dividends introduce flexibility without going into odd figures. By adopting a stated policy of periodic (say, annual) stock dividends, a corporation in effect promises its shareholders a steady rise in cash dividends.

Another frequently used way of increasing the number of shares is through a *stock split.* Thus if shares are split 2 for 1, each shareholder receives two new shares for one existing share held. Less common is a reverse split (1 for 2, for instance), which reduces the number of shares outstanding.

One motive for declaring a stock split is to increase the demand for shares by adjusting the price per share downward into a more desirable trading range. Shares are normally traded in "round lots" of 100; transaction costs per share are larger for "odd lots" of smaller size. If the price per share is high, the round lot may be too expensive for small investors, and trading may lack liquidity. A reverse split, by contrast, may be undertaken to remove the unfavorable image often associated with low-value shares, which in extreme cases are called "penny stocks." Some executives also argue that stock splits (and to a lesser extent stock dividends) send a positive signal to investors about the firm's prospective growth, thereby increasing the total market value of the firm.

Several researchers have examined the effects of actual splits. The basic method, known as an "event study," is to estimate the "normal" path of a stock's price on the assumption that, except for the split, the price would have maintained its historic relation to a general index of share prices. This path is then compared with the actual movement in prices around the time the split takes place.

An influential paper by Fama and others (1969) using this approach failed to find any significant change in the market value of the firm following a split or stock dividend. Over the period immediately prior to a split, however, stocks on average gave an abnormally high return. The probable explanation is that management tended to split the stock only after it had risen strongly. More recent studies have reached similar conclusions. On the question of liquidity, Copeland (1979) found that after a split transactions costs tended, if anything, to increase as a percentage of value, and that the turnover of the shares (the volume traded divided by the number of outstanding shares) often fell following a split.

The final method a corporation may use to alter the supply of its securities is to *repurchase* them. As shown in Table 3.5, nonfinancial corporations have on balance repurchased their shares on a large scale in recent years. Share repurchase may be undertaken either by the corporation buying its own shares in the open market or by a tender offer in which it offers a stated price for all shares tendered to it prior to a closing date or until its desired quota is reached.

Companies that have accumulated cash and lack promising investment opportunities within the firm may decide to repurchase some of their shares as a way of giving investors a return in the form of capital gains rather than dividends. Alternatively, the management may regard its shares as currently underpriced and signals this to the market by offering to purchase them for cash, in the hope that the market will react by increasing the price. Yet another motive, discussed more fully in Section 3.4.2, is fear on the part of management that the corporation will be taken over by unfriendly investors, who may replace the incumbent managers and directors with their own appointees.[26] In any of these cases the repurchase results in a decline in the total assets held by the firm and a reduction in the supply of its shares to the market; unless the company has surplus cash, it will also lead to an increase in debt.

Table 3.5   Net Issues and Purchases of Corporate Equities (billions of dollars)

	1980	1985	1990	1993	1994
ISSUING SECTORS[a]					
Nonfinancial	10.4	− 84.5	− 63.0	21.3	− 40.9
Financial[b]	2.1	15.8	10.0	38.2	28.6
Foreign	2.4	3.7	7.4	60.6	43.9
TOTAL	14.9	− 65.0	− 45.6	120.1	31.6
PURCHASING SECTORS[c]					
Households[d]	− 12.3	− 124.0	− 21.2	− 83.7	− 109.4
Financial[b]	24.8	44.3	− 22.8	65.6	17.4
Mutual funds[e]	− 1.8	10.3	14.4	128.8	122.7
Foreign	4.2	4.4	− 16.0	20.5	0.9
TOTAL	14.9	− 65.0	− 45.6	120.1	31.6
OPEN-END MUTUAL FUNDS					
Shares issued	3.5	88.7	65.3	316.8	128.5
Purchased by households[d]	1.7	81.9	47.4	231.8	91.7

[a]Excluding open-end mutual funds.

[b]Banks, insurance companies, real estate investment trusts, brokers and dealers, and closed-end funds; does not include open-end mutual funds.

[c]Excluding purchases of mutual fund shares.

[d]Including bank personal trusts after 1980.

[e]Net purchases by open-end mutual funds of primary equity issues (see text).

Source: Federal Reserve, release Z.1, March 8, 1995, and earlier issues.

The Flow of Funds accounts include statements showing the net supply and demand for specific types of financial instruments. Comparison of these statements over time indicates not only variations in the size of net issues of each class of financial instrument (i.e., the net amount of new securities coming onto the market in a year) but also changes in the identity of the purchasers. Table 3.5 makes such a comparison for corporate equities for selected years from 1980 through 1994.

The three parts of this table reflect a distinction between primary and secondary equities. Primary equities are issued by firms as an incidental part of their main business, which may be manufacturing, banking, retailing, or whatever; secondary equities, by contrast, are issued by mutual funds, whose main business is precisely the selling of their own shares. As is explained more fully in Section 3.5, the principal assets of a mutual fund are the primary securities (stocks and bonds) of other companies, against which they issue their own shares. The distinction between primary and secondary equities is necessary to avoid double counting.

As noted in Section 3.3.1, net equity issues can be negative, as they were in most of the 1980s and 1990s, particularly for nonfinancial corporations. The household sector has been a net seller of primary equities in every year since 1961, though in many years these net sales have been wholly or partly offset by net purchases of mutual fund shares. The financial sector (excluding mutual funds), on the other hand, has usually been a net buyer of equities; so, except in a few years, has been the rest of the world. During the stock market boom that crested in August 1987, therefore, the public was taking profits while the financial sector and the rest of the world continued to buy. This behavior casts doubt on the belief, widespread among financial "experts," that the public is usually wrong and the experts usually right.

The massive net repurchases of equities in recent years, incidentally, shed new light on the role of the stock market in the economy. It used to be thought that its main economic function is to aid in the financing of investment by creating a liquid market in which new share issues can be readily absorbed. Recently, however, nonfinancial corporations have on balance used the stock market not to sell their own shares but buy them back. Admittedly this may be a temporary phenomenon, but it helps to explain why the spectacular crash of 1987—at least as severe as the notorious crash of 1929—had so little impact on the economy as a whole.

Repurchases by corporations aside, households have in effect been selling primary equities to the financial sector (which in this context essentially means pension funds, life insurance companies, and mutual funds) for many years. As shown in Table 3.4, a large part of household saving takes the form of acquiring claims on these same institutional investors. One possible interpretation of this interchange is that households have gained more confidence in the management of equity investments by professional investors as compared to their own. Another interpretation—not necessarily inconsistent with the previous one—is that there are significant economies of scale in investment management, so that institutions can do it more cheaply than individuals.

3.4.2 Corporate Takeovers

Reference was just made to management's fear of a hostile takeover. Attempts to gain control of a company by buying a sufficient number of shares are nothing new, but they appear to have become more common and are often dramatic enough to make headlines in the newspapers, especially when they involve many billions of dollars. The incumbent executives typically denounce the would-be "raiders" to the shareholders in terms of righteous indignation, accusing them of financial irresponsibility, intentions to "loot" the company by selling off assets, "sheer greed," and other violations of business ethics. The shareholders generally adopt a more relaxed attitude as they watch share prices soar during the battle for corporate control.

A variety of tactics can be employed by the incumbents in the course of this battle. Not infrequently they take the raiders to court for alleged infractions of the securities or antitrust laws. They may also prevail on state legislatures to enact "anti-takeover" legislation.[27] Another approach is to find a "white knight," a friendly third party willing to give financial support to the incumbents. If these tactics appear likely to succeed, the raiders can sometimes be persuaded to sell their accumulated shares to the incumbents at a profit, a practice known as "greenmail." The attacking side has fewer options; its main tactic is to raise the price at which they will buy shares.

The disinterested observer of these striking episodes should remember, first of all, that a corporation belongs to its shareholders, not to management. Those who attempt to gain control of a company must bid more than the prevailing market price, and they would not do so unless they consider its shares to be undervalued. This assessment usually means that they expect to obtain a higher return from the company's assets than the existing management, either by using these assets more profitably or by selling them to other firms. Takeovers, therefore, may lead to greater efficiency, and that is the main argument against making them too difficult by legislation or otherwise.[28]

Several studies in the finance literature on the actual effects of takeovers (most recently by Roll, 1986) suggest that existing shareholders nearly always gain, but that the raiders on average do no better than break even; in other words, the latter tend to pay a fair price. This evidence supports the theoretical notion that takeovers promote efficiency.

3.4.3 Corporate Bonds

We turn now to corporate actions that influence the market supply of bonds. New bonds are generally issued against a trust indenture or trust deed, a legal agreement in which the corporation promises an independent trustee to comply with provisions regarding the payment of interest, disposal of assets, issue of additional bonds, and notification of changes in the firm's financial position. The trustee represents the bondholders when there is a default.

Bonds may be issued in two ways that are about equally important. In a *private placement,* a broker or investment banker seeks out one or more buyers for the new issue and arranges a direct trade between issuer and investor. A *public offering* is usually underwritten in the way previously described for shares.

The supply of corporate bonds may be reduced either by repayment on maturity, by repurchase in the open market, or by redeeming them prior to that time under a *call provision* in the bond indenture. Not all bonds are callable, but in the many cases where a call provision exists, it enables the firm to replace debt issued during periods of high interest rates with cheaper sources of funds when rates become more favorable. A call provision is an example of an option (see Chapter 8).

Clearly, call provisions reduce investors' opportunities for capital gains on high-yielding bonds when interest rates decline. In order to sell callable bonds, therefore, the issuer must offer some mix of higher yield and call protection. The latter may take the form of a promise in the indenture that the bonds will not be called before a certain time, or the specification of a penalty to be paid over the face value if the bond is called.

3.4.4 Junk Bonds

Until the early 1980s underwriters would not normally support a public bond offering unless the bonds were of investment grade (see Table 3.2), implying a low risk of default. If a bond had a low grade that was the result of unfavorable developments subsequent to the original issue, the bonds were known as "fallen angels." A study by Hickman (1958) suggested that such bonds tended to be undervalued by the market; in other words, that too much weight was given to the risk of default.[29] When the implications of this study were belatedly realized on Wall Street it became more common to make initial offerings of bonds with a lower grade and, needless to say, a higher yield. These are usually called "junk bonds," though the underwriters prefer the more appetizing term "high-yield bonds." Such bonds may also have a lower priority than other bonds in case of liquidation, though they would still rank ahead of common stock.

The emergence of junk bonds has enlarged the financing menu for corporations, already discussed at the beginning of Section 3.4. As a source of funds they probably compete mostly with new equity issues, which managers often considered undesirable because they endanger corporate control and because dividends, unlike interest, are not tax-deductible to the paying corporation. At first, most junk bonds were issued to facilitate corporate takeovers (see Section 3.4.2), but the financial advantages of issuing junk bonds have been increasingly understood by well-entrenched managements as well. It appears that the changing balance between new shares issued and shares repurchased (noted at several points in this chapter) may be due, at least in part, to the new financing opportunities afforded by junk bonds.

In assessing the performance of junk bonds as a financial instrument it should be borne in mind that they became popular when general economic conditions were unusually favorable. The previous recession bottomed out in late 1982; until 1990 the economy saw fairly steady growth; inflation was kept under control; corporate profits were rising. A severe test for junk bonds was provided by the most recent recession, which ended in 1992. A sharp fall in corporate profits could have caused widespread defaults on junk bonds and discredited the entire concept.[30] Corporate profits did fall somewhat and there were a number of defaults, but they were not on a massive scale. Although it is still too early for a definitive verdict on junk bonds, the evidence to date suggests that on the whole they weathered the recession of 1990–1991 fairly well. In fact, several new issues of junk bonds in 1992 and 1993 were well received by the market.

A default, incidentally, does not necessarily mean that all is lost. Even though a company runs out of cash, it may still have assets that can be sold to pay something—sometimes all it owes—to bondholders. It is not yet known whether the total return on the junk bonds issued during the 1980s (including the high interest paid initially and the subsequent losses on defaulted issues) was high enough to reward investors for the obvious risks they knowingly undertook in buying these low-rated securities, but there is little doubt that most holders of junk bonds came out well despite some anxious moments.

3.4.5 Convertible Securities

Various "hybrid" securities are also issued by the corporate sector, the most important of these being convertible securities. In the case of *convertible bonds,* the company issues a standard long-term bond at a fixed coupon rate, attached to which is an option[31] permitting the holder to exchange each bond for a specific number of shares of common stock. In some instances, the bond may only be converted during a specific period; for example, not prior to 2 years following the original issue of the bond, nor after 10 years have elapsed. Alternatively, the "conversion ratio," that is, the number of shares per $1,000 of bonds redeemed, may decrease after some point to encourage early conversion, or the agreement may include a call provision which allows the company to force conversion after a certain date.

Convertible bonds therefore usually amount to a delayed issue of equity. As such, they may offer several advantages to the company. The first flows from the fact that the option to convert is worth something to the investor because if the share price rises sufficiently, there will be a profit to be made in the exchange. A conversion ratio set at 20 shares per $1,000 of bonds, for instance, effectively gives the holder the right to buy shares from the company at a prices of $50 per share. If 3 years hence the share is trading at $60, the investor makes a handsome return in addition to the value of the coupon payments on the bond during the interim. It is precisely because this option is valuable that the investor will be prepared to accept a somewhat lower coupon rate on the original bond.

By issuing convertibles, therefore, a company can cut its cost of financing in the short run.[32] A possible further advantage to the issuing corporation (or at least to its management) is that existing control is not diluted in the short run. A group of major shareholders can thus effectively increase the equity base of the firm without the immediate threat to their voting control that a substantial new equity issue might entail.

In addition to convertible bonds, *convertible preferred shares* with analogous provisions are also issued by some firms. In that case, preferred shares may be exchanged for common shares at a price specified in advance.[33]

3.4.6 Partnership Units and Business Taxation

In recent years a new type of corporate security has been introduced that does not fit into any of the above categories. Before we describe it, an overview of the tax treatment of business firms will be helpful.[34] We saw in Chapter 2 that there are two main classes of firms: corporations and unincorporated enterprises. The latter class can be divided further into sole proprietorships and partnerships.

Sole proprietorships are firms with a single owner who receives all the profits, bears all the losses, and is personally liable for the firm's debts. The owner pays income tax on the profits and may take a deduction (subject to certain limitations) for the losses. There are no other federal taxes on such firms, which are typically small.

Partnerships are basically similar in their tax status to sole proprietorships. The main difference is that there is more than one owner. Profits and losses are divided among the owners according to a formula agreed upon when the partnership was set up. In the simplest type of partnership, however, each partner is personally liable for *all* the firm's debts. The partners pay income tax on their share of the profits and may be able to deduct their share of the losses. The partnership as such is not subject to federal tax.

In a more complicated form of partnership there are two classes of partners, general and limited. The division of profits and losses is again determined by the initial agreement, but here only the general partners are fully liable for the firm's debts; the limited partners cannot lose more than their investment. The general partner or partners—there may be one or more—usually manage the firm. The tax treatment is again similar to that of sole proprietorships.

Turning now to corporations there are again two subspecies. Small corporations, as defined by the Internal Revenue Code, are essentially treated as partnerships; that is to say, the corporation as such is not taxed but the shareholders pay income tax on any dividends they receive. Such corporations are also known as "Subchapter S" corporations after the part of the tax code that deals with them.

The larger corporations that do not qualify for Subchapter S are of principal interest in a book on financial markets. Those whose shares are traded on exchanges or over the counter belong to this second subspecies. Unlike all the firms discussed so far, they are taxed directly through the corporate income tax. In addition, the shareholders pay the individual income tax on any dividends they receive, but there is no deduction for any losses reported by the corporation. Consequently, corporate profits are subject to double taxation: once at the corporate level and again (assuming dividends are paid) at the individual level.[35]

Evidently large corporations have a strong incentive to avoid this double taxation, since doing so would make their equities more attractive. In the 1980s a legal way of avoiding double taxation was found. A few listed corporations—we have identified only about a dozen—organized partnerships to hold a portion of their common stock.[36] The general partner is the corporation itself, and the limited partners are the holders of "partnerships units," who take the place of the common stockholders. These units trade just like ordinary equities. The corporation still pays the corporate tax on its share (as the general partner) of the profits, but the limited partners pay only the individual income tax on the dividends they collect.

The dividend yield on the currently listed partnership units is generally much higher than the typical yield on common shares issued by otherwise similar corporations. Indeed, it is close to the typical return on junk bonds—between 9 and 11% in early 1995. The history of these units is too short to determine if the risk is also comparable to the risk on junk bonds. However, the interest rate on bonds is fixed, whereas the dividends on partnership units may rise or fall over time. The merits of these units as an investment, and as a source of funds for the issuers, need further investigation.

As mentioned already, the number of firms with listed partnership units is small. From 1987 on, new partnership arrangements have not been permitted, and the existing ones will lose their tax exemption in 1997, at which time they will presumably disappear. The main reason for discussing them is the opportunity to deal briefly with an example of the way business taxation can impact the supply of securities.

3.5 MUTUAL FUND SHARES

Mutual funds are not ultimate suppliers of securities in quite the same way as corporations or governments. They pool existing securities and then issue their own shares against this portfolio. In this fashion they generate securities with risk-return characteristics that individuals may be unable to reproduce; more specifically, they provide diversification. Because of high transactions costs and lack of information, there are limits on the diversification that an individual investor, particularly if her portfolio is small, can achieve. An annual management fee and often also an initial sales fee are charged for this service.[37]

In the past, mutual funds invested mostly in equities, but in recent years funds specializing in bonds (federal, municipal, or corporate) have become prominent. In the United States there are now thousands of mutual funds, on which data are published every day in the financial press. All of them can be divided into two main categories depending on their supply characteristics: open-end funds and closed-end funds.

The most numerous funds are in the *open-end* category.[38] Here the management stands ready to redeem an investor's share on demand at a price (known as Net Asset Value, or NAV) equal to the market value of the underlying assets. The management is also empowered to issue new shares at any time at the NAV in the case of so-called no-load funds. New shares are issued at a premium to cover marketing costs in the case of "load" funds.[39] This premium or sales charge is typically 8.5%, so the buyer has an immediate loss if she changes her mind. Consequently load funds are not suitable for in-and-out traders. By buying and selling the underlying securities, the fund manager keeps assets in balance with the outstanding shares. At the end of 1991, open-end mutual funds had total financial assets of $478b, of which 39% was invested in equities and most of the remainder in government and corporate bonds.

In a *closed-end fund,* the management has no obligation to redeem an investor's shares or to sell additional shares to the public. At any time, the fund has a portfolio of securities against which it has issued a fixed number of shares. Most closed-end funds may, however, make new issues or repurchases of their own shares to and from the market at the manager's discretion. Such funds, which unlike open-end funds are listed on a stock exchange or over the counter, are usually quoted at a discount to Net Asset Value. It does not follow, as is sometimes maintained, that this feature makes them a good buy; the discount merely reflects the management fee, which is deducted from the payments to shareholders. When a closed-end fund is organized, its shares are typically offered at NAV, but in most cases these shares develop a discount sooner or later. Buying a closed-end fund at its initial public offering is evidently a risky proposition.

Closed-end funds generally pay out earnings from dividends and interest, along with net realized capital gains, to shareholders.[40] In open-end funds, the accrued earnings and capital gains are usually credited to shareholders in the form of additional shares in the fund.

As mentioned earlier, the principal service provided by mutual funds is diversification. That, however, is not how they present themselves to the investing public. There is often an explicit or implicit claim that the fund's management has special skill in selecting good investments. Several studies testing this claim have been conducted, and their results are overwhelmingly negative.[41] Despite their reliance on sophisticated analysis, many funds perform no better than the stock market averages. In any finite period of time, of course, some funds do better than others, and there are always a few that improve on the averages, but their performance appears to be due more to luck than to skill.

This disconcerting observation has led to the creation of *index funds,* whose portfolio is composed in approximately the same proportions as a market average such as the Standard & Poor 500.[42] These funds have no need for highly paid analysts, so their expenses are modest. Their performance is necessarily close to the chosen average. Although index funds have grown in importance, most mutual funds still pursue the will-o'-the-wisp of above-average performance.

Mutual funds (particularly the open-end variety) can also be categorized by their stated investment objectives. Income funds, as the name implies, promise their shareholders relatively large dividends, while growth funds aim at capital gains. Index funds, of course, are somewhere between these two extremes. So-called value funds try to select companies that are undervalued by the market. Large fund managers usually operate a family of funds that cover the spectrum from income to growth.

There are also funds that specialize in particular industries or particular countries. The latter are known as country funds and (if they are of the closed-end type) may have large premiums over Net Asset Value when the country in question makes it difficult for individual foreign investors to buy equities on their own. Country funds have proliferated for two reasons: More and more countries are relying on private corporations to stimulate their economic development, and investors have become increasingly interested in diversifying their investments internationally rather than in just one country.

One of the minor difficulties in understanding the financial markets is that the same word is sometimes used with more than one meaning; the meaning has to be inferred from the context in which it is used. Mutual funds provide an example. The management of an open-end fund will occasionally decide to "close" it, which does *not* mean that it is turned into a closed-end fund. Closing an open-end fund means, instead, that no new shares are an offer to investors.[43] This is most likely to occur in highly specialized funds, particularly those that invest only in a small country or in a small industry. The typical reason for closing an open-end fund is that the managers, faced with a large inflow of money, cannot find attractive investment opportunities within the fund's scope. Usually, after a lapse of a few months or so, the fund is "reopened."

The closing of an open-end fund raises an economic problem of some interest. Once the fund is closed, no new money comes in, but for a variety of reasons some existing shareholders are likely to sell. Consequently, the fund has a net outflow of money, forcing the managers to sell some of their investments. If the fund has sizable holdings in a small country or industry, these sales may in turn depress the price of the remaining investments. This argument suggests that closing a fund may have an adverse effect on the Net Asset Value, but this tentative conclusion needs empirical verification.

There is no analogue to "closing" in the case of a closed-end fund, whose managers are not constrained by inflows or outflows of money. However, there is another action that may change the status of a closed-end fund. We saw that sooner or later such a fund tends to trade at a discount to NAV. If the discount becomes large (say more than 15%), the shareholders may decide to turn the closed-end fund into an open-end fund, which normally trades at NAV. In the process the management is likely to be fired, and this is one reason why conversions from closed-end to open-end status are infrequent. The managers tend to oppose the conversion and rely on their own holdings, and those of their associates, to block it. Nevertheless, the possibility of conversion serves as a check on possible mismanagement of a closed-end fund. It is also possible that a fund trading at a large discount will be taken over by a better managed closed-end fund.

3.5.1 Money Market Funds

Technically, money market funds are also open-end mutual funds, but the close resemblance of their shares to bank deposits places them in a special category that is kept separate in the statistics. In money market funds (MMFs) the pooled assets against which shares are issued consist of short-term financial instruments such as Treasury bills, commercial paper, and certificates of deposit. Since the prices of short-term securities fluctuate less than those of stocks and bonds, MMF managers attempt to keep the Net Asset Value underlying each share constant, customarily at $1.00 per share.[44]

To the shareholders, therefore, claims on an MMF are "like money in the bank." This impression is greatly reinforced by the fact that they can draw checks on their holdings, or more precisely on an unaffiliated bank where the fund has an account. Although an MMF is not itself a bank, most shareholders would be hard put to tell the difference.[45]

The advantage enjoyed by MMFs is that, not being subject to the same regulations as banks, they can offer higher interest rates. During the monetary upheavals of the early 1980s some MMFs paid nearly 20%, whereas banks could then pay no more than 5% on their best checking accounts. As a result, holdings in MMFs soared from $4 billion at the end of 1977 to $220 billion five years later. Since then, falling interest rates have made the MMFs less competitive and shareholdings have grown at a more moderate rate, but they remain substantial with assets of $540 billion at the end of 1994.

3.6 MORTGAGES AND MORTGAGE-BACKED SECURITIES

Mortgages (i.e., loans secured by real estate) have long been the main securities supplied to the market by the household sector. They usually have maturities of around 25 years and provide for equal monthly payments that include both interest and reductions of principal. As shown in Section 2.4, nonfinancial business is also a significant issuer of mortgages. The interest rate on a mortgage is usually fixed, but because of recent volatility variable-rate mortgages have become more common. In this type of mortgage the interest rate is revised from time to time by reference to some index of market rates. Many mortgages are redeemed in full prior to maturity, in much the same way as a company redeems a callable bond.

Since mortgages are tied to specific parcels of real estate, they are not readily negotiable. To overcome this defect, various types of *mortgage-backed securities* have been introduced. These are generated by pooling mortgages that have been insured by a third party—most often the federal government—against default; mortgage-backed bonds are then issued against this pool. Major issuers include the now private, but originally government-owned, Federal National Mortgage Association (known as Fannie Mae) and two federal agencies: the Government National Mortgage Association (Ginnie Mae) and the Federal Home Loan Mortgage Corporation (Freddie Mac).

Although they take a variety of forms, most mortgage-backed bonds (in some cases called "participation certificates" or "pass-throughs") are issued for periods similar to the mortgages that underlie them and carry an interest rate equivalent to the weighted average of the mortgages that make up the pool. The holder of the bond then receives this rate plus a share in the principal repayment made by the issuer of the original mortgage, usually on a monthly basis. The majority of mortgage-backed bonds have fixed coupon rates, although more recently some variable-rate mortgage-backed securities have been issued, based on pools of variable rate mortgage instruments.

The main difficulty, paradoxically, in pooling individual mortgages is not so much the risk of default (assuming there is adequate collateral), but the risk of prepayment. If a mortgage carries a high rate of interest, the borrower is likely to prepay it as soon as possible, thus forcing the issuer of a mortgage-backed security to find other (and presumably less attractive) mortgages in which to invest, or to pay off some of the securities. This is why mortgage-backed securities with a high coupon rate are often not quoted at a correspondingly high price: Their expected life is short. Various schemes to overcome this difficulty have been proposed.

A recent variation on mortgage-backed securities are known as "asset-backed." Here the collateral consists not of real estate but of such assets as accounts receivable (particularly on credit cards). They exemplify the never-ending search for new financial instruments.

3.7 CLAIMS ON FINANCIAL INSTITUTIONS

The wide range of demand and time deposit accounts available at financial institutions (including commercial banks, Savings and Loan Associations, Credit Unions, and money market funds) is an important channel through which funds flow from ultimate savers to those investing in real assets. The majority of these do not give rise to negotiable securities. Nevertheless, there are some important exceptions. Mortgage loans, as has been noted, can be "securitized" (i.e., transformed into financial instruments). Other examples include certificates of deposit (including Eurodollar CDs), commercial paper, and bankers' acceptances.

Certificates of Deposit are issued in units ranging usually from $5,000 to $100,000. They are evidence of title to a time deposit at a bank, frequently with a maturity of 30 or 90 days. Their standardized characteristics make these certificates readily negotiable, and an active market has developed. Their credit standing is equal to that of the bank at which the underlying deposit is held; part of the deposit may be covered by the Federal Deposit Insurance Corporation (FDIC).

Eurodollar Certificates of Deposit differ from those just discussed in that they are issued by banks in other countries yet are denominated in U.S. dollars.[46] More generally, the term *Eurocurrencies* refers to CDs issued by a bank in a currency different from its own; thus a Eurosterling CD, denominated in British pounds, may be issued by a Swiss or Japanese bank. Until recently, American banks were not allowed to offer deposits denominated in foreign currencies to U.S. residents, but this prohibition has now been removed. Actually, the abolition of exchange controls in many industrial countries has made the distinction between domestic and Eurodollar CDs largely irrelevant.

The market in such CDs has assumed enormous dimensions since it emerged in the late 1950s, to the point where banks in all important countries are now effectively part of one international short-term capital market. Because this highly competitive market is centered in London, the interest rate at which Euro-CDs can be sold is known as LIBOR, short for London Interbank Offered Rate. That rate, which is quoted for 1 month, 3 months, and so on, serves as a basis for calculating interest rates on bank loans around the world, so that a borrower may be charged "one and a half per cent over LIBOR."

The term *commercial paper,* or open market paper, refers to short-term promissory notes of standard size issued by large corporations and financial institutions, including the holding companies by which many banks are owned. Typical of the large issuers is the General Motors Acceptance Corporation, which finances automobile purchases. The notes are issued on a discount rather than a fixed-interest basis. In some cases they are "accepted" by a bank, which, for a fee, agrees to repay the holder on maturity in the event of default by the issuing corporation, thus creating a *banker's acceptance.* Both types are usually issued to finance short-term cyclical working capital requirements.

While a significant quantity of commercial paper is outstanding in the United States, not all of it is readily negotiable. In some other countries (notably the United Kingdom), "commercial bills" or "bank accepted bills of exchange," as they are called there, form the main instrument traded in the short-term money markets, but that is not the case here.

Some of the factors governing the supply of deposits and financial instruments by banks have already been discussed in Chapter 2. The discussion of corporate financial policy in Section 3.4 is to a large extent also relevant to financial institutions, the principal difference being that the latter have few fixed assets or inventories. Accordingly, their main business is finding the most profitable combination of financial assets and liabilities. This topic is outside our scope.

To conclude this section, we return to a financial market, already mentioned in Section 2.5, that is of great importance to banks but in which their customers do not participate: the *Federal Funds* market, in which commercial banks buy and sell deposits at Federal Reserve Banks. These deposits, it will be remembered, constitute the bulk of the liquid assets backing their liabilities. Trading in the Federal Funds market enables individual banks to match their required reserves fairly closely with daily fluctuations in their liabilities.[47]

By their nature, Federal Funds are financial instruments with a very short maturity, generally overnight. They are at one extreme of the maturity spectrum.[48] Like all fixed-interest instruments, their price is quoted in terms of an annual rate of interest. This rate sometimes changes drastically from one day to the next, or even within the day. Since the daily surpluses or deficits of individual banks tend to cancel out in the aggregate, fluctuations in the Federal Funds rate usually reflect open-market operations by the Federal Reserve. In fact, the daily intervention of the Fed (as opposed to its growth targets for the money supply) is geared largely to the Federal Funds rate, which in turn has an effect on other short-term interest rates because it represents the marginal cost of liquid assets to the commercial banks.

4

The Demand for Securities

Chapter 3 examined securities from the issuer's point of view. Now it is the purchaser's turn. We present a framework, based on economic theory, for analyzing why individuals and other investors are interested in the various types of financial instruments described earlier. Why, for instance, would an individual consider owning government bonds? Why would a pension fund be interested in owning equities? Such questions can be made more precise by replacing the word "why" with "under what conditions."

In this chapter we show that the willingness of an investor to hold a particular security depends on two sets of characteristics: those of the investor and those of the security. The principal characteristics of securities—particularly the time pattern of returns, the risk of default, and the negotiability—are discussed in the Chapter 3. How to characterize the behavior of individual investors is the topic here.

There are two fundamental reasons why individuals demand securities either directly or through some form of financial intermediary such as a mutual or pension fund. The first is that their pattern of income over time differs from their desired sequence of consumption. By holding financial assets, the pattern of cash receipts can be rearranged so as to synchronize it with the pattern of spending needs.[1] Investment in securities as a means of providing for retirement or saving for the purchase of an automobile are common examples. Each purpose requires a different timing of investment, return, and redemption of principal. One major group of attributes of interest to those demanding securities, therefore, are those relating to timing: the maturity and liquidity characteristics of a security as well as the degree to which it offers opportunities for regular withdrawal of cash or reinvestment.

The second major reason for demanding securities stems from the desire to increase total dollar wealth. Sometimes this reflects an "aggressive" attempt to increase individual net worth through successful speculation. For other investors it is essentially a "defensive" attempt to maintain the purchasing power of their savings in the face of rising prices. These different objectives, and the different degrees of risk aversion that underlie them, give rise to variations in demand for securities according to their risk and expected return characteristics.

In this chapter we begin by examining the underpinnings of demand for securities in terms of these three basic attributes: time characteristics, expected return, and risk. The remainder of the chapter is devoted to what might be termed the "portfolio complication." Here we introduce a concept that will appear a number of times throughout this book because it has revolutionized thinking about the evaluation of securities since the late 1950s. It centers on the realization that the correct measure of one of the most important attributes of a security, namely its risk, will differ depending on whether it is viewed in isolation or as part of a portfolio. Since this is the case, we need to consider the structure of an investor's entire portfolio even to define the relevant attributes of a security. Portfolio relationships therefore become the key to understanding securities demand.

4.1 THE TIME DIMENSION

In Chapter 2 we examined some of the macroeconomic relationships involving the demand for securities, mostly at the empirical level. It is now time to explore the microeconomic theory relevant to that demand. The focus is on a problem that is important to most people, namely, saving for retirement. This objective is also important for the financial markets because it is a major source of funds, either directly from individual investors or indirectly through pension funds or life insurance companies.[2] Uncertainty is disregarded in this section; it is taken up in Section 4.2.

4.1.1 A Case in Microeconomics: Saving for Retirement

To keep the exposition simple, take the case of an individual (Adam) who starts his working life on his twenty-fifth birthday. He considers his remaining life in terms of two periods: the first being his working years (assumed to be fixed at 40), and the second a period of retirement of unknown length. Uncertainty about the length of the retirement period can in principle be eliminated by buying an *annuity*. This is a contract, usually made with a life insurance company, under which the individual pays a lump sum immediately and in exchange receives a fixed amount per year or month as long as he or she lives.[3] We suppose, therefore, that on his sixty-sixth birthday (when he retires) Adam buys an annuity

that provides a fixed income per year until his death. The possibility that Adam
wants to leave an inheritance to his dependents, or a charitable bequest, is disregarded; so are other complications such as taxation, inflation, and contractual
saving (e.g., through an employer's pension fund).

During his working life Adam is assumed to earn a fixed amount of $20,000
per year, payable at the beginning of each year. In the present context, the basic
decision Adam has to make is how much of his earnings he will consume during
his working life, the balance being saved for consumption in retirement. This
choice can be analyzed by means of the *utility function,* one of the main tools of
microeconomics. The utility function serves to represent an individual's preferences for various alternatives. Thus if x and y are two levels of wealth, and $u(x)$
and $u(y)$ are the utility levels associated with them, then $u(x) > u(y)$ means that
the individual prefers x over y.[4]

With his savings Adam purchases securities whose annual return r is assumed to be certain and constant over time. An investment of $1 now will be
worth $\$(1+r)$ one year from now, and $\$(1+r)^{40}$ in 40 years. Thus if Adam
saves an amount of s_t in year t of his working life (where t runs from 1 through
40), then his accumulated savings on his sixty-sixth birthday will be

$$A = s_1(1+r)^{40} + s_2(1+r)^{39} + \ldots + s_{40}(1+r).$$

With these accumulated savings Adam buys an annuity that will pay cA at the
beginning of each year until he dies.[5] The fraction c, which is supposed to be
known in advance, depends on the rate of interest and Adam's life expectancy
at age 66.

We now introduce a further simplification, namely, that Adam saves the
same amount each year. Since it was earlier postulated that his earnings remain
constant during his working life, this is not implausible; the question whether it
is optimal cannot be addressed here. Algebraically this means $s_t = s$ for all t, and
the displayed equation becomes

$$A = s\{(1+r)^{40} + (1+r)^{39} + \ldots + (1+r)\}$$
$$= s(1+r)\{1 + (1+r) + (1+r)^2 + \ldots + (1+r)^{39}\}.$$

The expression in braces on the second line is a geometric series whose sum can
be found in elementary algebra texts:

$$\sum_{t=0}^{39} (1+r)^t = \frac{(1+r)^{40} - 1}{r}.$$

For instance, with $r = .05$ (corresponding to an annual interest rate of 5%)
the sum amounts to 120.8, meaning that a person who saves $1 per year will
have $120.80 after 39 years. Of this total, $40 is original investment and $80.80
is accumulated interest. From the penultimate equation we then see that on his

sixty-sixth birthday Adam's savings of $\$s$ per year will have produced assets (A) of $(1.05)(120.8)s = 126.84s$ dollars.

So far the value of s has not been specified. We need one additional item of information to discuss s meaningfully. This item is the constant c, which determines annual annuity payments from a given purchase price A. Suppose $c = 0.1$, which means that the annual payments are 10% of the purchase price. It follows that these annual payments equal $\$12.684s$. Thus, annual savings of $\$2,000$ would imply annual annuity receipts of $\$25,368$, more than Adam earned during his working years. Depending on his utility function this may be the pattern he prefers. It should be borne in mind, however, that after retirement there is no further need for saving under our assumptions, so all of the $\$25,368$ is available for consumption compared to $\$18,000$ (earnings less savings) during Adam's working years.

It is of interest to explore an alternative lifetime pattern, in which consumption is constant throughout. Putting annual earning for convenience equal to y, we then find that $y - s = 12.684s$, which implies $s = 0.073y$, or savings are 7.3% of earnings. Despite the many simplifying hypotheses, this is not an implausible figure. With his assumed earnings of $\$20,000$ Adam would then save $\$1,460$ during each working year, leaving $\$18,540$ for consumption. The reader can also verify that is approximately equal to consumption during retirement, the small discrepancy being attributable to round-off errors.

What we have developed is a bare-bones application of the "life-cycle" theory of saving. This theory is mostly due to Franco Modigliani, who later received a Nobel prize for his work. It has important implications for the individual's demand for securities.[6] Since most saving for retirement involves a long-term commitment, the theory clearly points to investment in long-term securities such as equities and long-term bonds. In this connection, recall the yield curve mentioned in the Chapter 3—and reconsidered later in the present one—according to which short-term bonds normally yield less than long-term bonds. A person who is planning for retirement would not normally be interested in short-term securities. We already know, however, that there are many types of securities, each with their own price, rate of return, and other characteristics. The next issue to address, therefore, is the relationship between rate of return and security prices.

4.1.2 Present Value and Duration

In the preceding section we did discuss the allocation of savings between alternative investment opportunities, nor shall we do so here. We can say, however, that in order to be willing to invest in a particular security, Adam would require a total rate of return of r per annum. What price would he then be willing to pay for a security that returns $\$F_1$ in year 1, $\$F_2$ in year 2, and so on for 5 years with return of the principal invested Π on maturity? Ignoring the risk for the present, the answer is the "present value" of that security, calculated as follows:

$$PV = \frac{F_1}{1+r} + \frac{F_2}{(1+r)^2} + \frac{F_3}{(1+r)^3} + \frac{F_4}{(1+r)^4} + \frac{F_5 + \Pi}{(1+r)^5}.$$

The present value (PV) formula reflects the fact that a return in the future, which can only be used or reinvested when it is received, is worth less than a return now. Hence future returns must be "discounted" by the required rate of return. The value we place on future returns (payoffs) by this process is equal to the amount we would have to invest now at the required rate r in order to generate that payoff in the future.

More generally, if the required rate of return is allowed to vary over time, the general form of the PV formula becomes

$$PV = \frac{F_1}{(1+r_1)} + \frac{F_2}{(1+r_1)(1+r_2)} + \frac{F_3}{(1+r_1)(1+r_2)(1+r_3)} + \cdots$$
$$+ \frac{F_n + \Pi}{(1+r_1)(1+r_2) \cdots (1+r_n)}.$$

Alternatively, the dollar payoffs and the required rate of return may both be constant but continue into perpetuity. Using the formula for the sum of an infinite geometric series, the present value then turns out be simply

$$PV = F/r.$$

Thus a preferred stock in a top-rated company (i.e., one whose risk of default is negligible) paying $2.00 per year would have a present value of $40 if the required interest rate is 5%.

Let us now relate this PV concept to some other specific types of securities. Recall that the PV is equal to the current price we should be willing to pay. Consider, then, a $1,000 bond issued with an annual coupon rate of r_c and a maturity of 3 years. Its PV is

$$PV_B = 1,000 \left\{ \frac{r_c}{(1+r)} + \frac{r_c}{(1+r)^2} + \frac{(1+r_c)}{(1+r)^3} \right\}.$$

The required rate of return in this case must be equal to the rate available on new issues of an equivalent bond. On the day of this bond's issue, therefore, r is equal to the coupon rate r_c, so the PV becomes:

$$PV_B = 1000 \{ r/(1+r) + r/(1+r)^2 + (1+r)/(1+r)^3 \}.$$

By performing a little algebra, the reader can be convinced that the bond's PV on its day of issue is equal to its face value, as one would expect. Next, suppose that bond rates rise immediately after the issue. If our bond has a coupon of 10% and rates rose to 15%, its PV would then be:

$$PV_B = \frac{100}{1.15} + \frac{100}{1.15^2} + \frac{1100}{1.15^3} = \$887.21.$$

In other words, a rise in bond rates causes the price of outstanding bonds to fall, and the holder to suffer a consequent capital loss. Conversely, declining bond rates produce a capital gain on existing bonds. It should also be clear that the longer the bond's maturity, the more its price will be influenced (r appears more times and with higher power in the denominator of the PV formula the longer is the maturity). In this sense, therefore, longer bonds have a higher risk than short bonds.

In fact, however, the simple "term" of the bond (i.e., its years to maturity) is not always the relevant measure of maturity for pricing purposes. Consider the case of two bonds each with 10 years to maturity; one is a "coupon" bond paying 10% interest per annum and the other a "zero-coupon" bond (see Section 3.2.1) paying only the principal at maturity. Will the price of one be more strongly affected by changes in interest rates than the other?

The answer is clearly "yes" because some of the coupon bond's return comes in the early periods, hence this part of its value is in effect "short-term" despite the long maturity of the overall bond, and so is less influenced by interest rate changes. To account for these differences a statistic known as *duration* is computed. In contrast to simple maturity it provides a measure of the true "timing attributes" of a bond.

Duration is calculated by taking the maturity of each payment the bond returns to its holder (e.g., the maturity of the second annual interest payment is 2 years) and multiplying it by the percentage of the bond's present value paid out at that maturity. It is thus a weighted average of the different maturities represented by the coupon and principal repayments associated with the bond. More formally:

$$DUR = FV \frac{r_c \sum_{t=1}^{n} \{t/(1+r)^t\} + n/(1+r)^n}{PV},$$

where DUR is the duration, FV the face value, PV the present value, and t time in periods (years if interest is annual, quarters if it is quarterly, etc.). The final value of DUR is thus a "corrected" maturity with the same periodicity as t, usually years.

Shares, of course, also have important time-related attributes. The price an investor is willing to pay for a share may be expressed in terms of the following present value calculation:

$$PV_s = div_1/(1+r_0) + div_2/(1+r_0)^2 + div_3/(1+r_0)^3 + \ldots + (div_n + P_n)/(1+r_0)^n,$$

where div_i is the dividend paid in each time period, Π_n the market value of the share at the end of the investor's desired "holding period" or investment horizon, and r_0 the required rate of return.[7]

A great deal of care must be taken in the interpretation of this formula.[8] Superficially, it might appear that an increase in the current dividend payout will necessarily cause the share price to rise. In fact, such an assertion is often completely unjustified because the size of future dividend payments (div_2, div_3, etc.) will depend on the rate at which earnings grow. So long as the firm has profitable[9] investment opportunities open to it, the more earnings it retains and reinvests, the faster its future earnings will grow, and the larger will be its potential for future dividends. Paying out higher dividends now reduces the funds available for reinvestment. Current dividends therefore tend to reduce the unit value of the firm's shares in the periods following the payout. If these funds are not replaced from other sources, or if alternative sources come at higher cost, the total value of the firm's shares may fall.

These interactions become more transparent when we write out the present value formula for a share in full, rather than the summarized form given above:

$$PV_S = \frac{d_1(e_1 A_1)}{1+r_0} + \frac{d_2(e_2 A_2)}{(1+r_0)^2} + \cdots + \frac{d_n(e_n A_n)}{(1+r_0)^n},$$

where d_t = the dividend payout ratio (i.e., dividends over earnings) in period t; e = the rate of return the firm earns on its assets; and A = total assets per share.

Now assets per share in the future will depend on current retained earnings and the amount of funds raised externally in the financial markets through the issue of new securities by the firm. Thus

$$A_2 = A_1 + RE_1 + NI_1,$$

where RE = earnings per share retained in the period and NI = new funds raised externally and invested (per share) in the period. Therefore

$$PV_S = \frac{(d_1 e_1 A_1)}{1+r_0} + \frac{d_2(e_2 A_1 + RE_1 + NI_1)}{(1+r_0)^2} + \cdots + \frac{d_n(e_n A_{n-1} + RE_{n-1} + NI_{n-1})}{(1+r_0)^n}$$
$$+ \frac{P_n}{(1+r_0)^n}.$$

Suppose, then, that we compare the shares of two firms that are identical except that one (firm X) pays all of its first year's earnings out as a dividend and the other (firm Y) does not pay a first-year dividend at all. Neither raises any new capital, and they are both liquidated at the book value of their assets at the end of 2 years. The respective present values of a share in each are then

$$PV_X = 1(e_1)\frac{A_1}{(1+r_0)} + d_2(e_2)\frac{(A_1 + 0 + 0)}{(1+r_0)^2} + \frac{A_1}{(1+r_0)^2}.$$

$$PV_Y = 0(e_1)\frac{A_1}{(1+r_0)} + d_2(e_2)\frac{(A_1 + e_1 A_1)}{(1+r_0)^2} + A_1 + e_1\frac{A_1}{(1+r_0)^2}.$$

Since the amount of retained earnings in firm Y is $RE_1 e_1 A_1$, the difference in present value per share is

$$PV_X - PV_Y = \frac{e_1 A_1}{1 + r_0} - \frac{d_2 e_2 e_1 A_1}{(1 + r_0)^2} - \frac{e_1 A_1}{(1 + r_0)^2}.$$

Now $d_2 = 1$ in both cases, since the firms are liquidated at the end of the second year, thus:

$$PV_X - PV_Y = (1 + r_0) e_1 A_1 - e_2 e_1 A_1 - e_1 \frac{A_1}{(1 + r_0)^2}$$

$$= r_0 e_1 A_1 - e_2 e_1 \frac{A_1}{(1 + r_0)^2}$$

$$= (r_0 - e_2) e_1 \frac{A_1}{(1 + r_0)^2},$$

an expression that will be negative so long as $e_2 > r$.

In other words, the current value of a share in the firm with the higher dividend payout is less than the firm with no dividend payout so long as its rate of return on assets exceeds the minimum required rate of return r. This condition defines "profitable" opportunities for reinvestment. A firm that has such profitable opportunities available to it will increase the unit price of its share the higher the percentage of earnings it retains. For example, IBM and Xerox, which did not pay any dividends at all for a number of years after their formation, still enjoyed strong increases in their share prices because both had opportunities for reinvestment at very attractive expected returns. Consider the intuition: As an investor, would you rather that these companies paid out the funds in dividends or reinvested them in their high-yielding industries?

Perhaps contrary to your intuition, the answer is actually that, except for the transactions cost and personal taxation implications, you should not really care. The reason is quite simple: If the firm retains its earnings, then the price of your existing shares will rise. If, instead, they pay out their earnings in dividends and issue more shares to finance their investment needs, the price of your existing shares will not rise as much, but you can use those dividends to purchase more shares. In each case, the value of your investment increases by the same amount.

This observation leads to a very significant conclusion—namely, that the timing of a firm's earnings matters for its present value but the timing of its dividend payments does not (provided it has profitable investment opportunities). We illustrate with the following example.

Suppose a firm has a present value of $100 million and 10 million shares outstanding, and it decides to pay out $10 million in dividends. The share price will therefore fall from $10 before the dividend has been paid to $9 after the dividend payment, given that its total present value is now only $90 million. The holder of 90 shares would then have a total of $810 worth of shares and cash. This compares with $900 worth of shares before the dividend.

To maintain its total assets, however, the firm must issue $10 million worth of new shares at the market value of $9 each. If you then use your dividend to purchase 10 additional shares, your holding will increase to 100 shares at $9 each, maintaining the total value of your investment at its original $900. According to this argument, then, it makes no difference whether the company pays a dividend and issues more shares, or retains its earnings, so long as the sum total assets are being supported under both options.

In practice, however, there are three reasons why the value of your investment may in fact change and hence the firm's dividend policy may alter the attractiveness of its shares to you, the investor. The first reason stems from the taxation implications. In most countries, including the United States, the rate of personal taxation on long-term capital gains has often been less than that on dividends.[10] In the case of securities held directly, therefore, a stock with high retention of earnings would then be preferred to one with high dividend payout on taxation grounds. If this were true for a majority of investors, demand for low dividend payout stocks would increase, causing their prices to rise relative to high payout stocks. Some investors, however, notably life insurance offices and pension funds, are taxed on capital gains but not on dividends. As a result, the overall response of demand to different dividend payout levels is unclear. Obviously the dividend payout characteristics will affect the particular "clientele" of investors attracted to a stock, but the net effect on its price is uncertain.

The second reason concerns the potential effect of transactions costs. On one level, the company with a high payout policy faces costs (often quite substantial) of mounting the issue of new securities necessary to maintain an asset level equivalent to that of the low payout company (including legal and underwriting fees). This extra cost, in turn, reduces the total value of the firm and hence its shares. In addition, the investor may face various costs in handling the dividends and resubscribing the proceeds to a new issue, or buying additional shares to maintain the total investment on the open market. Transactions costs on both sides, therefore, reduce the demand for high payout shares. On the other hand, to the extent that investors seek a regular income from their securities, payment of dividends might reduce an investor's transactions costs by avoiding the necessity to sell a portion of the shares at regular intervals so as to provide the desired cash flow.

The third reason pertains to the possible "information content" of dividends. In this connection it is often argued that the declaration of an increased dividend provides positive information to the market about a company's performance and the managers' confidence in its future. To the extent that investors did not previously recognize the firm's success, the demand for its shares and, hence, their price might be expected to rise in response to this dividend "signal." While this argument is often raised, it is not altogether convincing. For one reason, as noted earlier in this section, an increased dividend payout may signal the lack of profitable new opportunities in which to invest earnings, rather than successful performance.

Overall, therefore, while a number of complications do exist, it seems that our basic conclusions regarding the "time attributes" of shares remain fairly robust—that is, while the timing of a firm's earnings pattern is a crucial attribute in the determination of demand for and price of its shares, the timing of its dividend payments are of considerably less, possibly even little, relevance as an attribute of the share.

4.1.3 The Calculation of Yields on Zero-Coupon Bonds

Until now, all the formulas presented have been in terms of years, which is to say they assume "discrete" time intervals. This assumption limits the usefulness of the formulas because it makes it difficult to calculate the present value or the return on a Treasury bill that matures 68 days from now.[11] For many purposes it is easier to operate with "continuous" time rather than with discrete intervals. This approach requires a little more mathematics, but the resulting gain in simplicity makes the work worthwhile.

The key concept in the continuous-time approach is exponential growth or decline. Elementary calculus tells us that if

$$y(t) = ae^{bt}, \tag{4.1}$$

where t is time as before, then

$$\frac{y'(t)}{y}(t) = b. \tag{4.2}$$

Here $y'(t)$ is the derivative or rate of change (over time) of y, and the whole left-hand side of Equation (4.2) may be interpreted as the "proportionate rate of change," which has the value b irrespective of time. It is quite possible for b to be negative, indicating decline rather than growth. We shall see in a moment that b is closely related to the rate of interest, which can also be negative.[12] It should be clear that Equation (4.1) can be written

$$\log y(t) = \log a + bt, \tag{4.3}$$

where the logarithm is understood to be "natural" (that is, with $e = 2.71828 \ldots$ as base). Since natural logarithms are available on most calculators, the last equation is convenient for numerical applications. Equation (4.3) implies that if y is observed at two different times then

$$\log y(t_2) - \log y(t_1) = b\{t_2 - t_1\}. \tag{4.4}$$

As an illustration we consider the yield on zero-coupon bonds, a category that includes Treasury bills (as explained in Chapter 3).[13] Suppose a T-bill maturing 68 days from now is quoted at 98; what is its yield? More precisely, at what annual interest rate does a sum of $980 have to grow so as to become $1,000 in 68 days?[14] To answer this question, we first calculate that 68 days is 0.1863 years, and that $\log(1000) - \log(980) = 6.9078 - 6.8876 = 0.0202$. Equation (4.4) can then be solved for b by dividing 0.1863 into 0.0202, the solution being 0.1084. This number is not yet the annual interest rate we seek; it is merely a proportionate rate of change that is independent of the time unit.

The annual interest rate can be calculated by considering the growth of y over a finite period of time, in this case 1 year. In Equation (4.4) put $t_1 = 0$ and $t_2 = 1$, thus obtaining the change in $\log(y)$. Taking exponentials and dividing by y, we get the proportionate increase or decrease in y over 1 year, which is the annual interest rate on T-bills:

$$r_T = \frac{y(1) - y(0)}{y(0)} = e^b - 1. \tag{4.5}$$

In the current example this means $r_T = 0.1145$, not very different from b. Thus a T-bill maturing in 68 days and priced at 98 has a yield of 11.45%.

At this point a warning is in order. The reader who looks up the yield on a T-bill or other zero-coupon bond in the newspaper may well find a figure that is slightly different from the one calculated by our method. Indeed, if he looks at a second newspaper he may find yet another figure. It appears that several ways of calculating yields are in use, all of them based on special (and usually unstated) assumptions and producing somewhat different results. The method presented here, recommended also by the more sophisticated texts on finance, does not depend on any special assumptions. In the following section it is applied to a comparison of the yield on zero-coupon bonds of varying maturity.

4.1.4 The Term Structure of Interest Rates

In Chapter 3 we presented "yield curves" for Treasury obligations of different maturities. The relation between yield and maturity expressed by such curves is known as the *term structure*. Based on Federal Reserve estimates, the curves of Chapter 3 reflected the prices quoted for coupon bonds. A Treasury coupon bond, as shown in Chapter 3, is a stream of payments scheduled every 6 months until the bond is redeemed. It is therefore equivalent to a bundle of zero-coupon bonds maturing at differing times, all but one of which represent interest while the remaining ones represent the principal.

In Section 4.1.3 a method for calculating yields was applied to a zero-coupon bond. The question arises whether this method can also be applied to a coupon bond, and the answer—except in certain special cases of little interest—is "no." The method consists of determining a constant growth rate that will lead from the initial investment to the ultimate payoff. In general there is no constant growth rate for a sequence of zero-coupon bonds maturing at different times; instead there will usually be a different growth rate for each maturity, and any attempt to average these growth rates in some fashion is inherently arbitrary.

This may seem a serious drawback of the continuous-time approach of Section 4.1.3, but actually it agrees with reality. At the end of that section we referred to the special assumptions made in calculating yields on coupon bonds.

One such assumption is that interest receipts are reinvested in the bond itself; this assumption implies, among other things, that an 8% coupon bond due in 20 years and trading at par (100% of the face value) has a yield of 8%. This implication may at first seem eminently plausible, but actually it is nearly always false because of the term structure, which says that yield depends on maturity. In general, when interest is received on a coupon bond it cannot be reinvested in the same bond at the same interest rate, because at that time the bond is no longer a 20-year bond but one of shorter maturity.[15] If the yield curve is "normal"—that is, upward sloping—the yield upon reinvestment will be less than 8%; if the curve is "inverted," the yield will be more. It is only when the yield curve is completely flat that the special assumption just analyzed is valid; this is the uninteresting exception alluded to earlier and subsequently acknowledged by such qualifiers as "generally" or "nearly always."

Thus we are led to conclude that the most meaningful yields are those on zero-coupon bonds.[16] The conventional yield curves for coupon bonds presented in Chapter 3 are, strictly speaking, incorrect and should be replaced by those calculated from the prices of zero-coupon bonds. Until recently this calculation was difficult because price quotations on "zeros" were hard to obtain.[17] Now such quotations are published daily in financial newspapers, and they are used for three recent dates given in Figure 4.1.

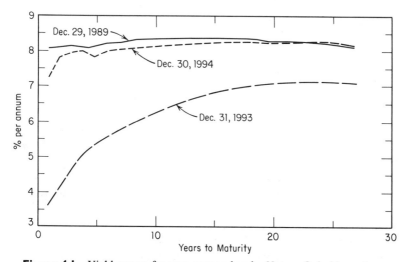

Figure 4.1 Yield curves for zero-coupon bonds. *Note:* Only November maturities are shown. *Source:* Calculated from prices in the *Wall Street Journal* (Annual Review in first issues of 1990, 1994, and 1995) using the method given in Section 4.1.3. For the earliest date, the prices reflected last trades; for the later dates, they are averages of bid and ask prices. The yields given in the source were not used because they appear to have been calculated by different methods.

The patterns revealed by Figure 4.1 are not greatly different from those shown in Chapter 3 for coupon bonds. The earliest yield curve, somewhat jagged because it reflects actual trades that are not necessarily simultaneous, is slightly inverted but close to being flat. The curve for the end of 1993 shows a marked difference between the yields on short and long maturities, at least up to about 20 years from the present; the yields for very distant maturities are lower again.[18] Note also that at the end of 1993 the nearby maturities had a much lower yield than at the previous date, but that the long-term yields did not change as much. Thus the 1993 curve was much steeper than the 1989 and 1994 curves, which reflected tight monetary policy; the 1993 curve exhibits a "normal" pattern.

4.2 THE RISK DIMENSION

Many investors have traditionally thought of risk only as a characteristic of the so called "speculative securities" such as shares or futures contracts. In fact, risk is a characteristic of virtually every type of investment available in the market. Even a checking deposit with a federally insured bank involves a risk, the risk that the real purchasing power of that deposit will be eroded by an uncertain rate of inflation.

Such a pervasive element in the demand or securities clearly requires explicit recognition in our analysis. To make this possible, however, we need some way of satisfactorily quantifying the risk such that it can be manipulated along with other measurable parameters such as interest rates or securities prices. We achieve this quantification by expressing risk in terms of probability theory.*

4.2.1 The Measurement of Risk

To begin with, we need a method for analyzing risk. Such a method is provided by probability theory, which may be described as the mathematics of uncertainty. Probability theory had its origin in the study of games of chance, but it was soon applied to more important topics[19] and is now used in virtually every field of science.

The basic concept is the probability of one outcome in the context of a given set of possible outcomes. Thus, if a fair die is thrown there are six possible outcomes, and the probability of getting a "three" is one in six. In this simple case the six outcomes may be called "elemental" in the sense that they cannot be easily explained in terms of more basic causes.[20] The calculus of probabilities is especially concerned with "composite" outcomes, such as getting an even number of points with one throw, or two "threes" in two successive throws. These composite outcomes are combinations of elemental outcomes.[21] The calculus of probabilities provides rules, which need not concern us here, for deriving the probabilities of composite outcomes from those of elemental outcomes.

---

*Readers familiar with elementary probability theory may skip the next section.

In the study of risk we are especially concerned with outcomes that have numerical values, the *outcome values* for short. Usually these outcome values will be positive or negative amounts of money. An outcome value is a random variable, an ordinary variable whose values corresponds a certain probability. Thus, in throwing a fair die the probability attached to each of the elemental outcome values 1, 2, . . . 6 is one-sixth, but if the die were not fair, the probabilities would be different. In any case, the probabilities must satisfy two conditions: They must be nonnegative and if they are summed over all elemental outcomes their sum must be one.

Suppose you bet $10, double or nothing, on the toss of a fair coin. There are clearly two possible outcomes: Either you lose $10 (the probability of which is 50%, the chance of your chosen side facing down) or you win $10 in addition to the return of your $10 original stake (again with probability of 50%). If you continued to enter such a wager with everyone you met, how much would you expect to take away with you at the end of the day?

The answer is, of course, $10.[22] This result can be shown mathematically by taking the expected value (*EV*) of the wager, which is equal to the sum of all possible outcomes (in dollars), each multiplied by its respective probability.[23] In this case we have: $EV = \$20 \times 0.5 + \$0 \times 0.5 = \$10$.

The idea of a random variable is central to probability theory. Closely related is the concept of a *probability distribution,* which is a function $\mathrm{Prob}(x)$ defining the probability p corresponding to each outcome value x. In the examples used so far there is only a finite number of x's, but it is often more interesting to consider a continuum of possible outcomes. For instance, the temperature at noon tomorrow may be considered a continuous random variable. The probability distribution for a continuum of outcomes is defined in much the same way as it was in the case of a finite number of outcomes.[24] The outcomes x whose probability is defined by $\mathrm{Prob}(x)$ need not be elemental, but they must be mutually exclusive and exhaustive.

From any sample of observations, or from any given probability distribution, certain important numbers called *descriptive constants* can be calculated. The best known descriptive constant is the *mean* or *expected value,* defined as the sum of the numerical values (outcome values) of all possible mutually exclusive outcomes each multiplied by its probability, or by its relative frequency in the case of a sample. Consider a lottery in which each ticket has a 1% probability of winning the only prize of $500. There are only two mutually exclusive outcomes, with numerical values of 500 and 0, respectively.[25] The expected value of the ticket is

$$m_1(x) = 0.01 \times \$500 + 0.99 \times \$0 = \$5.00. \qquad (4.6)$$

The reader is encouraged to verify that in the dice-throwing example the expected value is 3.5.

The mean belongs to a class of descriptive constants known as *moments;* in fact, it is sometimes called the first moment and the preceding notation reflects this terminology.[26] The second moment differs from the first only in that the outcome values in the first—but not the probabilities—are squared. Thus, for the lottery we get

$$m_2(x) = 0.01 \times 500^2 + 0.99 \times 0^2 = 2500. \tag{4.7}$$

It will be seen that the second moment is the expected value of x^2.

A related concept, the *variance,* is actually more useful. To calculate it, each of the outcome values in Equation (4.7) is first reduced by the mean.[27] Consequently

$$\text{var}(x) = 0.01 \times (500 - 5)^2 + 0.99 \times (0 - 5)^2 = 2475.25. \tag{4.8}$$

As is shown in every beginning statistics textbook, the variance can be more easily computed from the formula

$$\text{var}(x) = m_2(x) - \{m_1(x)\}^2. \tag{4.9}$$

Finding the variance in the dice-throwing example is again left as an exercise.

The variance is important as a measure of the *dispersion* of the outcome values. We can see why this is so by looking at a case where all the outcome values are the same, which obviously implies that each is equal to the mean so that the variance is zero. In the lottery example the outcome values are very different and the variance is many times larger than the mean.

Strictly speaking, though, the mean and the variance are not comparable because they do not have the same dimension (dollars for the mean, dollars squared for the variance). This defect can be overcome by taking the square root of the variance to obtain the *standard deviation,* usually denoted by σ. In the lottery example, σ is about 49.75, still much larger than the mean. In the dice-throwing case, on the other hand, σ is about 1.71, less than half the mean. However, the means in the two examples are different. To ensure comparability, it is customary to divide the standard deviation by the mean; the result is called the *coefficient of variation.* The respective values for the two examples are 9.95 and 0.49.

Since the coefficient of variation does not depend on the units of measurement, it is the simplest indicator of the relative riskiness of different investment prospects. By this criterion, the lottery is about twenty times riskier than throwing dice. Of course, the lottery used as an example was hypothetical, but actual lotteries probably have even larger coefficients of variation, especially if they include "megabuck" prizes. It should also be pointed out that so far nothing has been said about the cost of participating in these games of chance.

There are also moments beyond the second, of which we at present consider only the third. By now it should be clear that the third moment is calculated by raising the outcome values to the third power, and that it is desirable to subtract the mean from the outcome values. The result is called the third moment "around the mean" and indicates the asymmetry, or *skewness,* of the probabilities of the elemental outcomes. In throwing dice, for instance, favorable outcomes (those above the mean) are just as likely as unfavorable ones; the outcomes therefore have symmetric probabilities and the third moment around the mean is zero, as the reader may like to verify.

By contrast, the outcomes of the assumed lottery are highly skewed: a small probability of winning the prize and a large probability of getting nothing. The third moment around the mean is approximately equal to 9.85.[28] Because this value is greater than zero, the distribution of the outcomes is said to be "positively skewed"; negative skewness could mean a small probability of a very unfavorable outcome and a large probability of an outcome whose value is slightly above the mean. An example is owning an uninsured house, where the unfavorable outcome corresponds to a fire.

4.2.2 Bivariate Distributions

So far we have considered only one random variable at a time. In the analysis of risk it is often desirable to consider more than one random variable, for instance tomorrow's prices of two securities. The definition of a probability distribution can easily be extended to the case of two or more random variables; when there are two, for instance, we write $\text{Prob}(x, y)$, where $\text{Prob}(x, y)$ is a *bivariate* probability distribution.

One may think of a bivariate distribution as a univariate distribution in which the outcomes are all possible (and mutually exclusive) combinations of the outcomes in each random variable separately. Consider an individual who owns two tickets in the same lottery. There are now three outcomes with positive probabilities: Ticket no. 1 wins the prize $(x=500, y=0)$, ticket no. 2 wins $(x=0, y=500)$, and neither ticket wins $(x=y=0)$.[29] From the elemental outcomes, of which there are 100 as before, it is clear that

$$\text{Prob}(500,0) \doteq 01, \qquad \text{Prob}(0,500) \doteq 01, \qquad \text{Prob}(0,0) \doteq 98. \qquad (4.10)$$

The expected value of ticket no. 1 is given by

$$(m_1)(x) = \text{Prob}(500,0) \times \$500 + \text{Prob}(0,500) \times \$0 + \text{Prob}(0,0) \times \$0$$
$$= \$5.00, \qquad (4.11)$$

just as in Equation (4.6). It can easily be verified that $m_1(y)$ also equals $5.00.

When there are two or more variables, the relations between them are obviously of interest. The *covariance,* a concept that has no counterpart in univariate distributions but also belongs to the class of moments, can often be used to describe these relations. It is defined as the expected value of the product of two random variables, each of them reduced by its respective mean (just as for the variance.) In formula:

$$\text{cov}(x, y) = m_1\{x - m_1(x)\} \times \{y - m_1(y)\}. \qquad (4.12)$$

Applying this formula to the lottery example we get

$$
\begin{aligned}
\text{cov}(x,y) &= \text{Prob}(500,0) \times 495 \times (-5) + \text{Prob}(0,500) \times (-5) \times 495 \\
&\quad + \text{Prob}(0,0) \times (-5) \times (-5) \\
&= 0.01 \times (-2475) + 0.01 \times (-2475) + 0.98 \times 25 \\
&= -25.
\end{aligned}
\tag{4.13}
$$

Since the covariance, like the variance, depends on the unit of measurement, it is again desirable to introduce a dimensionless counterpart. This is the *correlation coefficient,* defined by

$$
\text{corr}(x,y) = \frac{\text{cov}(x,y)}{\sqrt{\text{var}(x)\text{var}(y)}}
\tag{4.14}
$$

The variance of x in the lottery example was calculated in Equation (4.8), and in this case var(y) obviously has the same value. Therefore

$$
\text{corr}(x,y) = -25/2475.25 = -0.0101.
\tag{4.15}
$$

The negative correlation reflects the fact that ticket no. 1 and ticket no. 2 compete for the same prize, but the correlation is very small because neither ticket has much chance of winning.[30]

Using the idea of a probability distribution and its related moments, it is then possible to define the risk of a wager relative to this expected value. If we have a 100% probability of achieving an outcome very close to the expected value, then the wager has a low risk. The larger the range of possible outcomes and the more dispersed across these possibilities the probability becomes, the greater is the total risk. A simple illustration is provided in Figure 4.2. Both investments have an expected value of zero (in other words, on average they

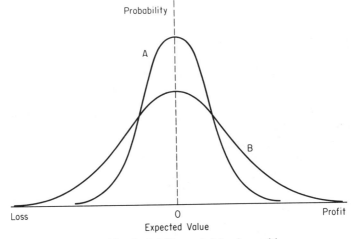

Figure 4.2 Probability and risk of securities

will both break even), but the risk of B (the investment with a much greater dispersion of probable outcomes) is considerably higher than that of A.

Let us now take one more step toward reality. Suppose that the expected values of the two investments are unequal so you are faced with deciding how much you would be willing to pay for either of the two securities C and D shown in Figure 4.3.

Security D has some attractive possibilities for high profits and a higher expected value. At the same time, it has a long tail of sizable potential losses from which the investor in security C is protected. On the other hand, while the return on security C is less volatile, it has a lower expected value.

Many real world investment decisions are like the one shown in Figure 4.3. A higher expected return often comes only at the expense of higher risk and vice versa. What we require, therefore, is some way of measuring the rate of trade-off which an investor considers acceptable; that is, how much extra expected return is required to render an investor willing to accept an additional unit of risk? The major body of work that has proved useful in tackling this problem is the theory of expected utility.

4.2.3 Expected Utility

The roots of the expected utility theory go back as least as far as Czarist Russia and its passion for gambling, to a puzzle that has become known as the "St. Petersburg Paradox." The problem was as follows. Suppose you are offered $2 if heads comes up on the first toss of a fair coin, $4 for two heads in a row, $8 for three heads in a sequence, $16 for four heads, and so on. You are permitted to keep your winnings on all previous throws. However you are "knocked out"

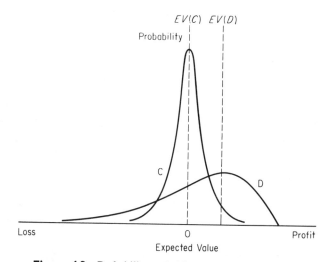

Figure 4.3 Probability and risk—unequal expected values

of the game the first time tails comes up. How much would you be willing to pay to have the opportunity to play this game?

As a starting point, let us look at the expected value of the St. Petersburg game for an arbitrary number of throws:

$$EV = \frac{1}{2} \times 2 + \frac{1}{4} \times 2^2 + \frac{1}{8} \times 2^3 + \ldots + \frac{1}{2^n} \times 2^n.$$

The probability of three heads in a row, for instance, is $(\frac{1}{2} \times \frac{1}{2} \times \frac{1}{2})$ for a payoff of 2^3. Evaluating the expression as n goes to infinity we get $EV = 1 + 1 + 1 + \ldots = \infty$. Not surprisingly, there are few takers, even in a gambling community, at an infinite price, yet that is the expected value of the game.

The paradox can be resolved by observing that for most individuals the marginal utility they derive from an additional \$1 of wealth declines as their total wealth increases. Put another way, \$1 means more to you when you have only \$10 to your name than it would if you were already a millionaire.

Consider throw number 21 in the St. Petersburg game. Its expected value is \$1, but would you pay an extra \$1 now for the chance to win approximately \$2 million with a probability of $(\frac{1}{2,000,000})$ when you might be "knocked out" on the first throw and it has already cost you a great deal to play? The answer for most people is "no"; they may be willing to pay something but not as much as \$1 extra.

Clearly, to take this into account we need to calculate the expected value of the utilities of the possible payoffs, not just their dollar values: in other words the expected utility:

$$EU = \frac{1}{2}U(2) + \frac{1}{4}U(4) + \ldots + \frac{1}{2^n}U(2^n),$$

where $U(x)$ represents the utility of a payoff of \$x.

Now a new question poses itself: What is the appropriate utility function to use? Utility functions fall into three main categories depending on the behavior of marginal utility as wealth increases. These are illustrated in Figure 4.4.

Diminishing marginal utility of wealth (i.e., each additional dollar of wealth provides less additional utility than its predecessor) is associated with risk aversion. Constant marginal utility of wealth means that the investor is risk-neutral, while increasing marginal utility of wealth is associated with risk-loving behavior.

A risk-neutral investor will be prepared to purchase a share in a risky investment at its expected value. Risk averters will only purchase a risky investment at a discount below its expected value because the associated risk has a negative utility that offsets some of the positive worth of the expected return. Risk lovers, on the other hand, will be willing to pay more than the expected value in order to have the chance to participate in a risky venture.

It is possible, of course, that any individual will exhibit all three of these attitudes toward risk over different ranges of wealth. Friedman and Savage (1948), for example, pointed out that it is common for a single individual to buy both lottery tickets and insurance. Since the institution running the lottery takes a percentage of the total pool, lottery tickets cost more than their objective ex-

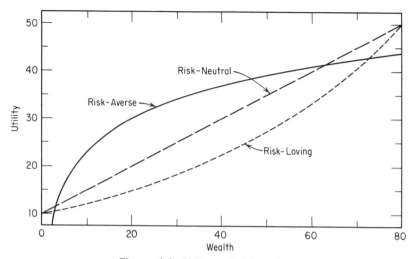

Figure 4.4 Utility and risk preference

pected value. Their purchase, then, may be an example of risk-loving behavior.[31] Yet the same individuals who buy lottery tickets clearly show risk aversion when they insure themselves against a potential loss from fire instead of simply accepting the uninsured expected value.

It appears, therefore, that when the size of the loss relative to total wealth is small and the possible winning large (even at a very low probability), many people act as risk lovers. Conversely, when the potential loss of total wealth is large, even at relatively small probability (such as a household fire), people are risk-averse.

An alternative explanation is that although people are generally risk-averse across the entire wealth range, they believe that the probability of winning in the case of a lottery (i.e., their subjective probability) is much higher than the objective odds. In this case the "expected value," based on subjective probability, is actually above the cost of the ticket and hence their behavior is consistent with risk aversion.

In any case, since risk-averse behavior is the most common trait observed in practice, it is the main focus of attention in the analysis that follows. We should begin, therefore, by defining it with slightly more precision. As we have seen, an individual is defined as risk-averse if he or she is willing to pay less for a risky investment than its expected value (assuming probabilities can be objectively determined and are equal to the investor's subjective probabilities). The maximum amount an individual is prepared to pay for a risky investment, in turn, should be such that the utility of the cash given up in purchasing the security is just equal to the expected utility that that security provides. In other words, the dollar value of a security is equal to the dollar value of its expected utility.

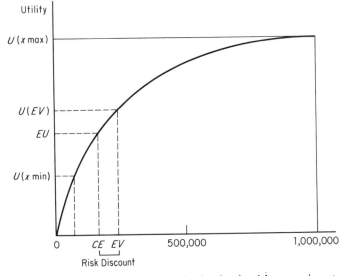

Figure 4.5 Risky investment valuation by the risk-averse investor

Not surprisingly, this amount is termed the *certainty equivalent* of that security, the number of certain dollars "in the hand" that the investor is prepared to give up in order to acquire the prospects for return offered by the security. The difference between the expected value of the security and its certainty equivalent is then the *risk discount,* the discount an investor requires in order to exchange certain dollars for expected, but risky, dollars.

We illustrate with a simple example. Suppose your total wealth is $200,000 and you have the opportunity to invest all of it in a joint venture. If successful, the venture will increase your wealth to $5 million; if it fails, however, you will lose $100,000. The probability of success is 50%. The expected value of this investment is then:

$$EV = 5,000,000 \times 0.5 + 100,000 \times 0.5 - 200,000 = 2,350,000.$$

Thus, if you were risk-neutral you would agree to participate since the expected value is positive. In fact, you would be willing to pay an additional $2,150,000 to participate.

Let us suppose, however, that you have a utility function of the form: $U(x) = \log x$, where x is your level of dollar wealth and log is the natural logarithm, already encountered in Section 4.1.3. As is clear from Figure 4.5, this utility function exhibits diminishing marginal utility of wealth, hence risk aversion. In this case the expected utility of the investment is:

$$EU = 0.5\log(5,000,000) + 0.5\log(100,000) - \log(200,000)$$
$$= 7.71 + 5.76 - 12.21 = 1.26.$$

In other words, the expected utility of the investment is equal to the utility levels associated with each of the possible outcomes multiplied by their respective probabilities, less the utility of the certain $200,000 or current wealth you would be giving up.

Once we have this expected utility we can calculate the amount in dollars the investment opportunity is worth to the risk-averse investor by taking the certainty equivalent. This is equivalent to finding the x such that

$$\log x = EU,$$

which may be written as

$$CE = x = e^{EU} = \$3.53$$

in our example—that is, the exponent of expected utility. In other words, an individual with a log utility function would only be prepared to pay $3.53 for the investment opportunity above.

The risk discount (RD) is then equal to the expected value (EV) less the certainty equivalent (CE):

$$RD = \$2,350,000 - \$3.53 = \$2,349,996.47.$$

The reason for this huge discount is the high disutility of losing $100,000 (half of current wealth) and the low marginal utility associated with the high dollar gains.

The preceding discussion of utility functions may raise a suspicion among many of our readers that we have entered the world of economic esoterica, beyond which only insanity lies. You are assured, however, that our feet remain firmly on the ground. To make good that assurance and in the process to demonstrate the use of an actual utility function, we base the following example on the specific utility function belonging to you, the individual reader.

First, an estimate of your net wealth is required: the total of all your assets less existing liabilities. Because its value is certain at the present moment, it should be entered in the first row of Table 4.1 under the column Certainty Equivalent. Now we offer you an investment in retailing umbrellas on New York City street corners. If it rains, you will double your wealth. If it is fine, the umbrellas may be returned

Table 4.1   Utility Function Derivation

Case	Optimistic	Pessimistic	Certainty Equivalent	% of Wealth
Net Wealth			$⬚	100
Umbrella Investment	$⬚ = 2W	$⬚ = W	$⬚	⬚
Robbery	$⬚ = W	0	$⬚	⬚
Taxation	$⬚ = 1.5 W	$⬚ = 0.5 W	$⬚	⬚

to the supplier at no loss. What is the maximum nonrefundable participation fee you would be willing to pay in order to share in this marketing venture if the probability of rain is 50%? Again, complete Table 4.1, placing the figure for double your wealth in the column designated Optimistic and your maximum participation fee plus your current wealth under the Certainty Equivalent column.

Suppose, instead, we consider the risk of robbery or fraud, which would reduce your current wealth to zero. If the probability of theft is 50%, what is the maximum one-time insurance premium you would be prepared to pay to cover you against that loss? Subtract this premium from your current wealth, and place the result in the Certainty Equivalent column.

Finally, consider the case of two taxation proposals under consideration by the federal government. Proposal 1 would lead to a reduction in the value of your current wealth of 50%, while Proposal 2 would increase it by 50%. If you believe that the proposals are equally likely to be adopted, how much, if anything, would you be prepared to pay to ensure that the whole scheme is dropped by the government? Subtract this payment from your current wealth and enter the result in the final Certainty Equivalent slot. Likewise enter the dollar values of the optimistic and pessimistic outcomes.

Now complete the final column in Table 4.1 by computing each certainty equivalent as a percentage of initial wealth.

Your utility function may then be plotted on chart paper. Take first the umbrella investment, and locate your figure for the certainty equivalent as a percentage of wealth on the horizontal axis. The first point on your utility function then lies at the intersection between a vertical line from this wealth level and the dotted line from 150 on the utility index axis. Similarly plot the intersection between your certainty equivalent as a percentage of wealth under Robbery and the utility index of 50. Finally, plot the intersection with utility index 100 and the Taxation case. Starting at the origin, fit a smooth curve through these points. Compare the result with the logarithmic utility function graphed in Figure 4.5. How does your degree of risk aversion differ? Examine your risk discount in each case, given that the expected values are 150% in the case of umbrellas, 50% for robbery, and 100% for taxation.

Now apply this certainty equivalent method to the valuation of a share.[32] Recall the dividend valuation model used in Section 4.1:

$$PV_S = \frac{div_1}{1+r} + \frac{div_2}{(1+r)^2} + \ \ldots \ + \frac{div_n + P_n}{(1+r)^n}.$$

We are now able to acknowledge explicitly that the dividends in each future period are uncertain, depending on the performance of the company, its opportunities for new investment, financing decisions, and so on. If we could estimate the range of possible dividend outcomes, the probabilities associated with each, and the investor's utility function, we could calculate the certainty equivalent of the dividend possibilities in each period, giving:

$$PV_S = CE \times \frac{D_1}{1+r} + CE \times \frac{D_2}{(1+r)^2} + \ldots + CE \times \frac{D_n + P_n}{(1+r)^n}.$$

Since we have already converted the relevant cash flows (numerator) to dollar certainty equivalents, the relevant comparison must be with a "default-free" asset. For this purpose it is customary to use U.S. government bonds that have a certain nominal dollar return if held to maturity.[33] Hence the "required" rate of return r used to discount the certainty equivalents of future dividends will be the yield on such a default-free asset.

The process of valuing a share would have us

1. Estimate a range of dividend outcomes for each period
2. Attach a probability to each outcome
3. Compute the certainty equivalent for each period
4. Discount these CEs back to present value at the risk free rate

From a theoretical standpoint, this is the correct method of pricing a stock. In practice, it presents a number of significant problems. The first is clearly the specification of the individual's utility function. Of course we could go through a more detailed version of the process used to construct Table 4.1, but doing so is clearly cumbersome. It also prevents us from developing any more general method of share valuation that might be independent of the individual's utility function. Researchers have therefore searched for a workable mathematical approximation.

One of the earliest suggestions was made by the Swiss mathematician Bernoulli (1730), who proposed a logarithmic specification corresponding to the solid curve in Figure 4.4: $U(W) = a\log W + b$, where $U(W)$ is the utility of wealth and W is the dollar value of an individual's net assets. Perhaps there were some similarities to your actual utility function charted from Table 4.1; if not, don't worry: Logarithmic utility is merely a convenient example. The Bernoulli utility function exhibits risk aversion due to diminishing marginal utility of wealth because the slope becomes smaller as wealth increases. Since $\log(1) = 0$, the curve intersects the horizontal axis at some point to the right of zero determined by the value of b, but it cannot intersect the vertical axis.

At the same time, the log function has some questionable properties as a representation of utility. As wealth approaches zero, for instance, it implies that utility approaches negative infinity. Moreover, log functions display what is called "constant relative risk aversion." This term refers to the ratio of an individual's risk discount (as defined earlier) to his or her wealth being constant for any level of wealth. It seems more plausible, however, that as individuals become wealthier they also become less risk-averse.

One major alternative class of functions suitable for the representation of utility are quadratics, where $U(W) = a + bW + cW^2$. Such a function demonstrates both increasing utility with higher wealth and risk aversion when the coefficients are such that b is positive and c is negative. While retaining these basic properties, it has the advantage of more flexibility than the log function in the sense that its specific slope is quite malleable, allowing it to fit the substantial variety of risk aversion profiles we might expect to observe in practice. It has an important flaw, however: The quadratic function implies that individuals have increasing relative risk aversion: That is, an individual's risk discount as a percentage of wealth increases as wealth increases. This is a doubtful proposition in practice. We cannot avoid the conclusion, therefore, that the specification of utility presents a significant difficulty in implementation of the certainty equivalent approach.

The second obstacle to practical implementation is simply that the process of calculating the certainty equivalent is cumbersome: The number of possible outcomes is likely to be large, requiring an equally large number of probability estimates. Fortunately, the whole process can be considerably simplified, albeit at the expense of some practical, but not always fully justified, assumptions.

Specifically, if investors are assumed to have quadratic utility functions or if the probability distribution of returns is assumed to approximate the "normal" (Gaussian) distribution, then all of the relevant information about risk and return can be summarized into two measures: the expected value (equivalent to the mean) and the variance of the distribution of returns. In that case, by estimating the mean and variance associated with returns on a security directly, we can avoid the cumbersome process of listing all possible returns and their respective probabilities.

The advantages are obvious, but just how onerous are the necessary assumptions? The assumption of quadratic utility has some acceptable features, but as already noted its usefulness is limited by the implication of increasing relative risk aversion. The validity of the alternative—namely, that the returns on securities are normally distributed—is essentially an empirical issue. A number of researchers have examined the question, concluding that while the actual distribution tends to display the bell-shaped form of the Gaussian curve, there appear to be too many large positive or negative values and there may also be too many values near the mean.[34]

Nevertheless, the use of mean-variance analysis remains a worthwhile approach to the demand for securities and ultimately their valuation. The reason is simply that a more realistic approach does not yet exist. Accepting the premises of the conventional approach, the next step is to develop a method by which direct estimates of the mean and variance of returns on securities can be obtained (see Section 4.2.4).

Before proceeding, we recall that returns are the sum of dividends and price changes. Since dividends evolve fairly smoothly over time, the distribution of returns is effectively determined by the distribution of price changes. The actual distribution of day-to-day changes in the Standard & Poor 500 index over the years 1969 through 1990 is shown in Figure 4.6.[35]

The most conspicuous feature of Figure 4.6 is its asymmetry; that is, there

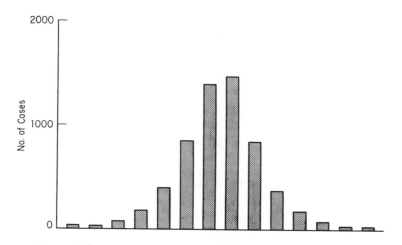

Figure 4.6   The distribution of daily changes in the S&P500 stock index. *Note:*   Except for those at the extreme left and right, each of
the fourteen bars corresponds to an interval with a width of one-half
of the standard deviation; the mean itself is located between the sev-
enth and eighth bars. The bars at the extreme left and right correspond to open-ended intervals more than 3 standard deviations away
from the mean. The mean was about 0.02% per day, equivalent to
an average increase of about 5% per year, and the standard deviation was a little less than 1% per day. The length of each bar is proportional to the number of cases in the corresponding interval; thus
there were 1,379 days in the tallest bar (out of a total of 5,558
days) and about 25 in each of the shortest bars.

are more small price increases (relative to the mean, which is also positive) than
there are small price decreases. This skewness is confirmed by the third moment
around the mean, which is negative. Less visible but more important is the relative abundance of large positive and negative price changes compared to the
normal distribution. According to tables of the normal distribution there should
be about seven cases in each of the "tails" (the extreme left-hand and right-hand
bars); actually there are more than three times as many. The distribution of stock
price changes is therefore "fat-tailed," meaning that calculations of risk based on
the normal distribution may be misleading. The same phenomenon has been
observed in other financial instruments, particularly futures contracts.

4.2.4 Estimating the Mean and Variance of Returns

The first method of estimation that might be considered is simply to compute the
mean and variance of the actual returns on a stock over its past history. Thus
the return in any year, quarter, and so on, may be computed as:

$$R_t = \frac{div_t + P_{t+1}}{P_t} - 1,$$

where div_t is the dividend paid during the period and P_{t+1} and P_t are the prices of the share at the end and beginning of the period, respectively. The sample mean is then simply

$$R* = \frac{1}{n} \sum_{t=1}^{n} r_t,$$

where n is the number of periods in the sample, and the sample variance is

$$\sigma^2 = \frac{1}{n-1} \sum_{t=1}^{n} (R_t - R*)^2.$$

This approach may provide a useful starting point for the analysis. Indeed, in the case of the variance it may be the best estimate we have available to us in practice. Looking to the past, however, does ignore the basic fact that the mean and variance of a stock's return will depend on the performance of the firm in the markets of the future, in the face of competition, technological change, and shifts in the demand for its products over coming years. Past performance will be a poor guide if the markets in which it operates change fundamentally. Thus, if we have any information at all about the likely future competitiveness and growth or decline of the firm whose stock we are valuing, we should attempt to explicitly incorporate that into our estimation of the mean and variance of its future returns.

In fact, this is primarily what the large research staffs retained by many of the leading stockbrokers and mutual funds aim to do. They take information on past performance obtained from the annual reports of individual companies and various other sources of data and they comment on trends in supply, demand, and competition within that firm's markets. Drawing on specialist knowledge gained by observing an industry over a long period, they produce forecasts of the mean or "expected" earnings for a number of periods in the future. This important topic of *fundamental analysis* (so termed because it attempts to use data on likely future earnings to derive a "fundamental" value of the stock, which may differ from its current market value) is discussed in Chapter 7.

4.2.5 Conditional Probabilities and Expected Values

We now introduce an important refinement of the concepts of probability and expected value (this will be used again in Chapter 5). Suppose you own some bonds in the PQR corporation, which has just reported a large loss. Given this loss you would like to know the probability that PQR will default on its bonds within a certain period, say 1 year from now. This probability may be written

Prob $(D|L)$, Where D represents default on the bonds and L the known loss. This is a *conditional probability* with L as the condition under which the probability of the outcome D is to be evaluated. We are not now concerned with the actual evaluation of Prob$(D|L)$, only with the concept.

To take another example, let it be known that the stock market went up today, a fact we shall denote by U_t. What is the probability of the outcome U_{t+1}, which means that the market will also rise tomorrow? The latter probability may be expressed as Prob$(U_{t+1}|U_t)$.

Conditional expected values are defined similarly. For instance, if dp_t is today's change in some stock market index and dp_{t+1} is tomorrow's change, then $EV(dp_{t+1}|dp_t)$ is the conditional expected value of tomorrow's change given today's change. As we will see in Chapter 5, this conditional expected value plays a key role in defining market efficiency.

The expression appearing after the vertical bar in the preceding formulas may involve more than one condition. Thus $EV(dp_{t+1}|dp_{t-1}, dp_t)$ represents the expected value of tomorrow's price change conditional not only on today's but also on yesterday's price change. Clearly this idea can be extended to any number of conditions.

4.3 THE PORTFOLIO COMPLICATION

The more sophisticated analyses of demand for goods and services examine the problem of consumer choice not in terms of demand for a good per se but as a combined set of demands for the individual attributes it embodies. Choosing a particular wine, for example, is actually the choice of the bottling that offers the combination of color, bouquet, taste, alcohol content, and so on that most closely approximates the exact mix of these attributes the purchaser desires. The extent to which the mix of attributes embodied in a particular bottling or brand matches the buyer's "ideal" bundle of attributes, in turn, has important implications for the shape of its demand curve. Specifically, the better the match, the higher the relative price the purchaser is prepared to pay before he or she will be induced to shift to an alternative brand.

This analysis applies equally to the investor's choice between the many securities offered in the market. It is unlikely that any security alone will have the exact mix of attributes that the investor desires. He or she will therefore demand the security that appears to come closest to this ideal. (We say "appears" because the "labeling" on securities is often more difficult to decipher and interpret than that on wine!) In addition, investors have the possibility of mixing different securities together in the form of a portfolio in order to come closer to their desired bundle of attributes. The first task in analyzing the demand for securities is therefore to define the relevant attributes involved.

Suppose you have a portfolio of securities, the overall return on which fluctuates over successive business cycles. You are then offered the chance to purchase an additional security that, while very volatile in terms of its returns overall, tends to fluctuate countercyclically. It should be obvious that by adding this countercyclical security to the portfolio, the overall return can be stabilized. Even if that security viewed in isolation is highly risky, it would be strongly favored by a risk averter as part of a portfolio due to its stabilizing influence.

Although this is an extreme example, it illustrates the more general point that the true measure of a security's risk is not its own variance but the amount of additional volatility introduced into an investor's portfolio by including it. This condition leads us to an important distinction between systematic and unsystematic risk.[37] That part of the volatility in a security's return that is positively correlated with the other securities in the portfolio will serve to exacerbate the fluctuations in the overall return on the portfolio. This "correlated" element is known as *systematic risk*. That part of a security's return volatility that is independent of fluctuations in the return on other securities in the portfolio will tend to "wash out" as we put a large number of securities together. In other words, this uncorrelated or *unsystematic* portion of a security's volatility can be diversified away by spreading one's investment over a large portfolio of securities.

Our conclusion, therefore, is that the critical measure of mean and variance from the investor's standpoint are those of the portfolio. To understand the variance of a portfolio, in turn, we must examine the split between systematic and unsystematic risk, hence the correlations between returns on different securities over different states of the world.

In order to gain an appreciation of these relationships, we begin with the two security case. Using the techniques discussed in Section 4.2.4, suppose we have computed expected returns for each of the two stocks (ER_1 and ER_2) for our relevant investment horizon, and that past experience has provided us with estimates of the variance of the returns on each (var_1 and var_2).

By examining past returns we can also estimate the correlation between the returns on the two stocks (ρ_{12}) as follows. First we take the actual returns on the two stocks for various periods:

$$R_{11} \ldots R_{1t} \ldots R_{1n}$$
$$R_{21} \ldots R_{2t} \ldots R_{2n}$$

where $t = 1, \ldots, n,$ and compute the means R_1^* and R_2^*. The covariance between return on the two stocks is then:

$$\text{cov}_{12} = \frac{1}{n-1} \sum_{t=1}^{n} (R_{1t} - R_1^*)(R_{2t} - R_2^*).$$

This statistic is then usually scaled to between -1 and $+1$ for ease of interpretation by computing the correlation coefficient:

$$\rho_{12} = cov_{12}/\sqrt{var_1 var_2}$$
$$= \frac{cov_{12}}{\sigma_1 \sigma_2}.$$

A value of 1 indicates that fluctuations in returns are perfectly synchronized, while a value of -1 indicates exactly opposite movements, and a value of zero, that the fluctuations in returns on two stocks are independent of each other.

From these basic statistics the mean and variance of different portfolio combinations can be computed. If the proportion of our total investment in security 1 is a fraction denoted a, then the remaining fraction $(1-a)$ is the proportion invested in security 2.[38] The *expected return* on the portfolio is then

$$ER_{pf} = aER_1 + (1-a)ER_2.$$

The variance of the portfolio is given by:

$$var_{pf} = a^2 var_1 + (1-a)^2 var_2 + 2a(1-a)\rho_{12}\sigma_1\sigma_2.$$

where σ_1 and σ_2 are the standard deviations of returns on the two individual securities.

The most interesting aspect of this formula is the way the variance of the portfolio as a whole changes with the degree of correlation between fluctuations in the returns on each security, as measured by the correlation coefficient ρ_{12}. Let us look more closely at the third term on the right in the equation, namely: $2a(1-a)\rho_{12}\sigma_1\sigma_2$. Notice that, when the two standard deviations are given, the smaller ρ_{12} becomes, the smaller is this component of the portfolio variance so that the overall var_{pf} declines. When the returns on the two securities fluctuate completely independently of each other, this third term disappears altogether, causing var_{pf} to decline still further. Obviously a negative correlation could reduce var_{pf} even below this level.

This formula expresses what we described earlier as the benefits of portfolio diversification. These benefits accrue even when we have only two securities from which to chose provided that movements in their returns are not perfectly positively correlated. We can illustrate with a simple numerical example.

Suppose the expected return on security 1 $R_1 = 10\%$ with a standard deviation of $\sigma_1 = 4\%$, and similarly $R_2 = 20\%$ and $\sigma_2 = 7\%$, and we mix the two on a 50:50 basis. Computing σ_{pf} for different possible values of the correlation coefficient ρ_{12} gives the values shown in Table 4.2. In each case a 50:50 portfolio has the following expected return: $R_p = (0.5*10) + (0.5*20) = 15\%$.

Table 4.2 Correlation vs. Portfolio Standard Deviation

ρ_{12}	1.0	0.5	0.0	-0.5	-1.0
σ_{pf}	5.5	4.82	4.03	3.04	1.5

What does this analysis imply about the risk-return trade-off? If we computed R_{pf} and σ_{pf} for different portfolio mixes along the spectrum from investment of our entire portfolio in the low-risk security 1, through the 50:50 split, to the other extreme of placing our entire investment in the higher risk, higher return security 2 we would come up with a risk-return trade-off. The shape of this trade-off would differ depending on the degree of correlation ρ_{12} between returns on the two securities. The resulting trade-offs for five sample levels of correlation are shown in Figure 4.7.

Notice that as the correlation between returns on our sample stocks declines from its maximum of 1, we have the opportunity of ever lower risk for any given level of expected return provided we mix the two securities so as to take advantage of the benefits of diversification. In the extreme case of two securities that are perfectly negatively correlated, it is possible to eliminate the volatility of return on the portfolio altogether by choosing the appropriate combination.

It is a relatively straightforward matter to go beyond two securities and generalize the model to any number of stocks. For some total number of stocks available in the market, call it n, the formulas for a portfolio's expected return, variance and standard deviation, become:

$$R_{pf} = \sum_i a_i R_i$$

$$\sigma_{pf} = \sqrt{\sum_i \sum_j a_i a_j \rho_{ij} \sigma_i \sigma_j},$$

where a_i is the proportion of an individual security i in the portfolio.

Testing different portfolio mixes (different sets of a_i), we can then generate

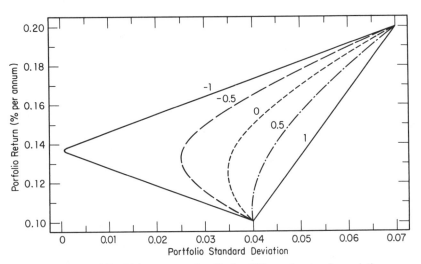

Figure 4.7   Risk return trade-offs for different levels of correlation

an opportunity set of available portfolio risk-return combinations. Any such combination is "inefficient" if there exists a better portfolio combination (i.e., one that either offers higher return for the same level of risk or a lower risk for the same return). These inefficient portfolios fail to exploit the potential for diversifying away unsystematic risk and will not be selected by an astute investor. After eliminating the inefficient portfolios, the investor is left with the "efficient" ones, all of which can be optimal for some desired combination of risk and return. The actual choice among the efficient portfolios depends on the risk-return preferences of this particular investor.[39]

Once the desired risk-return combination is decided upon, the portfolio structure (i.e., the proportions invested in individual securities) is then determined by optimal diversification alone. This result serves to reemphasise the point made earlier that, given the importance of the correlation between returns on securities in determining the real level of risk associated with an individual stock, the decision of how much of a particular security to buy is unavoidably part of a wider portfolio choice. It cannot be viewed in isolation from an individual's other investments.

Finally, a word of caution is in order. Although diversification is a powerful device for achieving a desired risk-return combination, it is not always optimal. Consider the case of a small businessman who enjoys an annual return of 20% on the capital invested in his firm, but with a high variance σ_B^2. The alternative investments available to him in the market all have returns well below 10%, though most of them have much lower variances than σ_B^2 and some of them even have negative covariances with his business income. By investing in some of these alternatives he could certainly reduce the variance of his portfolio, but his return would also be much smaller. Consequently, he may decide not to diversify and to be content with his high return despite its large volatility. This decision would be all the more compelling if credit for his firm is difficult to obtain or very expensive, in which case he could not withdraw money from the firm without endangering its viability.

Diversification, in fact, is common but by no means universal in the management of capital. It is distinctly uncommon in other important markets, particularly the labor market. Some people invest considerable time and money to become doctors or lawyers. These occupations are not riskfree, yet it is rare for someone to qualify herself or himself for a second occupation just in case the chosen one does not work out. The small-business example just discussed is actually on the borderline between the capital market and the labor market because going into small business is tantamount to choosing an occupation. The idea of diversification embodies the popular wisdom of "not putting all your eggs in one basket," but sometimes it is better to "put all your eggs in one basket and watch that basket."

5

Securities Markets and Their Efficiency

Imagine a situation where shares are sold in much the same way as used cars, with prices set through a haphazard system of bargaining between individual buyers and sellers, and with information about the different items on offer transmitted through a variety of channels from "for sale" or "wanted" notices to newspaper advertisements or dealer displays. Under such a regime, reliable and reasonably precise information about the value of your shares would be very difficult to obtain. The cost of searching for a potential trading partner with a matching desire to sell or buy a particular stock would in many cases make trading prohibitively expensive,[1] as would the cost of verifying that the seller had a valid title to the stock being delivered and that the buyer has the funds with which to pay.

We are so used to the existence of organized exchanges, where millions of securities change hands every hour, that it is easy to take for granted their contribution to the ease with which securities can be traded. The discussion in this chapter therefore begins with an analysis of the economics of securities trading and the rationale for brokers and central trading places. In the following section we take a closer look at the types of orders buyers or sellers may place in the market and the way these are executed. This topic leads to a discussion of the system of "specialists" commonly found on the stock exchanges designed to provide a smooth and continuous market for individual stocks. Having outlined the mechanics of securities trading in some detail, we proceed to examine the implications of central exchanges where information flows rapidly between participants for the efficiency of the stock market as a whole and, in particular, the "random walk" behavior of share prices.

5.1 CENTRAL TRADING PLACES

Some of the problems that would arise if stocks and bonds were traded in the same way as assets such as used cars have already been alluded to. The first important steps toward removing those impediments is the interposition of brokers as intermediaries between potential buyers and sellers.

The role of the broker is basically to collect information about supply (specifically, the characteristics of the goods being offered, quantities, prices asked, and the integrity of those desiring to sell) and corresponding information about demand from those wishing to buy. The broker has lower costs than any individual buyer or seller because he or she can spread fixed search costs over a large number of transactions. In addition, the broker benefits from accumulated experience of how and where to obtain reliable information. Some of these economic benefits are absorbed in the broker's profits, while the remainder are passed on to customers in the form of better information and lower transactions costs.[2]

The market for real estate is a classic example where brokers trade on the benefits just described. The fact that there are many independent real estate agents in most areas means that transactions costs may be higher than they could be, since search costs are duplicated by individual agents collecting essentially the same information simultaneously; the offsetting advantage, of course, is competition among brokers. The efficiency of the market can be improved by an exchange of information among brokers, as occurs in a multiple listing network.

It is this elimination of duplicated search costs that also underlies the use of a central trading place, where buyers and sellers (or the brokers who represent them) get together, exchange information about supply and demand (mostly by making bids and offers), and execute trades. In the form of open-air markets such trading places exist in many parts of the world, though they have become rare in the United States. In this book we are mostly concerned with centralized trading places in financial instruments, particularly stocks, options, and futures contracts; the latter two markets are discussed in Chapters 8 and 9, respectively.

5.1.1 Stock Exchanges

Like the real-estate market, the market in corporate securities is mostly a market in existing assets.[3] In addition, both facilitate the creation of new assets, such as newly built houses and newly issued shares. Trading in existing assets is economically important because investors would be hesitant to acquire assets if they could not sell them when they wanted to. By providing liquidity and price information, markets in existing assets encourage the purchase of newly created assets. Unlike houses, corporate securities are sufficiently homogeneous to permit a highly organized form of trading.

The physical gathering of those interested in trading securities under the now famous buttonwood tree on the Wall Street of 1790 was the origins of the

New York Stock Exchange (NYSE).[4] New York weather can be credited with its move indoors to the Tontine Cafe in 1793. Subsequently it erected buildings of its own, including the present one near the corner of Wall and Broad Streets. The move indoors made it easier to enforce agreements on standard trading times, rules of conduct, brokerage charges, and exclusivity so that trading would only take place between members. These conditions were formalized in 1817 with the NYSE's first constitution.

The institution of exclusivity arrangements has three advantages. First, it further reduces the costs of trading because the integrity (solvency and reliability in delivering on agreed trades) of the other party is ensured by membership of the exchange and hence does not need to be checked every time a trade is about to take place. Second, it allows for certain uniform rules to be agreed upon and universally adhered to. These rules mean that many of the details of the trade (such as the definition of lot sizes, delivery terms, etc.) are effectively determined by standard practice. Thus, most of the information that would normally have to be exchanged in the course of a trade is simply "understood" each time a price is quoted; as a result, transaction costs are reduced drastically. Third, it allows the exchange to invest in its own physical assets (such as buildings and quotation equipment) and operate with its own staff by levying various fees on members.[5]

From the public's point of view, however, exclusivity had an important disadvantage: It facilitated the fixing of standard fees by brokers. In fact, this anticompetitive practice became institutionalized in the NYSE rules (and those of most other exchanges) and prevailed in the United States until it was outlawed by legislation in 1975. At present, commissions (another name for brokerage charges) can be negotiated between investors and their brokers. Many "discount brokers" offer execution of orders at much lower fees than the "old-line" houses, which also provide their customers with advice and research.

Today the NYSE has 1,366 active members, a maximum that has remained constant since 1953 despite an enormous increase in the volume of trading.[6] Memberships are valuable because they give trading privileges and because they imply a share in the assets of the exchange, but these advantages are to some extent offset by the periodic dues that members have to pay. Large firms often find it convenient to own more than one membership; at the end of 1991, in fact, there were only 518 different firms owning memberships.

To become a member, certain financial and personal criteria set by the exchange must first be satisfied. Then a membership or "seat" has to be purchased from a present member. The market in which memberships are traded is known as the *seat market* (which does not mean that a busy stock exchange provides many opportunities for sitting down). Since exchanges are rarely liquidated, the price of a seat depends on the income that can be expected from exercising the trading rights that go with it. In the short run, fluctuations in seat prices reflect fluctuations in trading volume, but in the longer run, changes in competitive conditions—such as the introduction of negotiable commissions—may also be important. In April 1987, the price of an NYSE seat reached the million-dollar mark for the first time, but it has remained well below that level since "Black Monday." The value of a membership, incidentally, also serves as collateral against any claims the exchange may have on its members.

There are four main types of membership. *Floor brokers* execute orders for their individual customers or their member firms (such as Merrill Lynch or E. F. Hutton). There are also floor brokers, known as "two-dollar brokers," who are not associated with a large member firm; they accept orders from other brokers who are overloaded in peak periods (or may not wish to be identified) and execute them for a flat fee.

Floor traders, by contrast, buy or sell only against their own portfolio rather than on behalf of either a customer or another broker. Essentially, they are speculators seeking to profit from their instant access to market information by virtue of being on the trading floor, along with the fact that they avoid paying commissions by acting directly for themselves. Often floor traders buy and sell a stock within the same day, seeking to profit from very short-term fluctuations in supply and demand, an activity known as *day trading*.

Specialists constitute a category of members characteristic of U.S. stock exchanges. At present there are about 50 specialist firms on the NYSE, each with several members. Each is charged with maintaining an orderly market in a number of stocks (those in which it "specializes") that have been assigned to the firm by the exchange. A specialist acts both as a brokers' broker (executing trades for floor brokers) and as a dealer (buying and selling on his own accounts and at his own risk). When buy orders temporarily exceed sell orders, the specialist is expected to sell stock from his inventory (which may be negative) in order to equalize supply and demand. Conversely, he is expected to even out excess supply by purchasing stock for his own portfolio. In this way the specialist helps to achieve an orderly and continuously liquid market. Another important responsibility of the specialist is to handle "limit" and "stop" orders left with him by floor brokers, the mechanics of which are discussed in the next section. (See also Section 5.1.3 for more details about the operations of specialists.)

"Off-floor" members, unlike the three categories just mentioned, do not engage in appreciable activity on the exchange floor. They rely mostly on floor brokers for their transactions, but their membership gives them the option to do their own executions if it is to their advantage. The prestige conveyed by membership may be valuable to broker firms in dealing with investors, and it gives them a voice in exchange decision making.

In addition to the rules of conduct placed on members, exchanges also place requirements on the companies whose shares they trade.

1. To qualify for listing on the NYSE, the company must exceed a minimum size. Specifically, it must have at least 1 million shares outstanding with a market value (sometimes estimated on the basis of net tangible assets) in excess of $16 million, and there must be at least 2,000 holders

with 100 shares or more. This criterion excludes the vast majority of the millions of corporations that exist in the United States.

2. It must have demonstrated past earning power of at least $2.5 million profit before taxes during the past year and $2 million for each of the 2 years before that.

3. It must agree to NYSE reporting standards, including the publication of its earnings each quarter.

4. The company must maintain a share registrar and transfer agent in New York City.[7]

5. A majority of the company's directors must vote in favor of listing. This requirement means that an otherwise eligible corporation may choose to remain unlisted, thus ensuring that it will stay under private control.

Firms that are unable or unwilling to be listed on the NYSE can apply for listing on the American Stock Exchange (also located in New York), on one or more of the regional exchanges (such as those in Boston, Chicago, Los Angeles-San Francisco, and Philadelphia-Baltimore-Washington), or in the over-the-counter (OTC) market (see Section 5.2.1). The regional exchanges generally have less stringent listing requirements than the NYSE and therefore appeal to smaller companies. Large corporations are often listed on several exchanges, and most of the trading on the regional exchanges is now in securities that are also listed on the NYSE. An electronic network known as ITS (Intermarket Trading System) links the exchanges and makes it possible for orders to be executed on the exchange where the price is most favorable to the buyer or seller.

Tables 5.1 and 5.2 present information on the relative importance of the various U.S. stock exchanges in recent years; to add further perspective, the over-the-counter market (or at least that part coordinated by the National Association of Securities Dealers Automated Quotations, or NASDAQ) is also included. Looking first at exchange trading, we see that the NYSE has remained dominant during the period covered, with a 1992 market share of 81% in volume and 86% in value, compared to 80% and 84%, respectively, in 1980.[8] The regional stock exchanges have by and large held their own by these criteria. The big loser, at least in relative terms, has been the American Stock Exchange, whose share in volume declined from 11% in 1980 to 5% in 1992.

A different picture emerges when the over-the-counter market is considered. That market increased its share of total trading considerably; between 1980 and 1992 the volume share increased markedly and the value share rose even more. As a result, the NYSE handled only 43% of the total volume and 52% of the total value in 1992. The NYSE continues to be the first in equity trading, but its position is increasingly threatened by the OTC market, whose organization, as discussed in Section 5.2.1, is quite different.

While not as overwhelming as it used to be, the preeminence of the NYSE may be attributed largely to the high market liquidity it provides. Small and

Table 5.1 Annual Volume of Trading in Shares[a]
(billions of shares)

Exchange	1980	1985	1990	1992
New York	12.4	30.2	43.8	53.3
American	1.7	2.1	3.1	3.6
Midwest[b]	0.6	2.3	2.5	3.0
Pacific[c]	0.4	1.4	1.7	2.1
Other regional	0.4	1.1	2.2	3.5
ALL EXCHANGES	15.5	37.0	53.3	65.5
NASDAQ	6.7	20.7	33.4	48.5
TOTAL	22.2	57.7	86.7	113.0

[a]Including rights and warrants, but not options.

[b]The Midwest Stock Exchange was recently merged into the Chicago Stock Exchange. Value figures are not available for the (pre-merger) Chicago exchange, which is included in "other regional."

[c]Los Angeles-San Francisco.

Source: 1994 Statistical Abstract of the United States, tables 812 and 816.

Table 5.2 Annual Market Value of Trading in Shares[a]
(billions of dollars)

Exchange	1980	1985	1990	1992
New York	398	1023	1390	1757
American	35	26	36	42
Midwest[b]	21	79	74	87
Pacific[c]	11	37	45	58
Other regional	11	35	84	89
ALL EXCHANGES	476	1200	1612	2033
NASDAQ	69	234	452	1350
TOTAL	545	1434	2064	3383

[a]Including rights and warrants, but not options.

[b]The Midwest Stock Exchange was recently merged into the Chicago Stock Exchange. Value figures are not available for the (pre-merger) Chicago exchange, which is included in "other regional."

[c]Los Angeles-San Francisco.

Source: 1994 Statistical Abstract of the United States, tables 812 and 816.

medium-sized orders—say of 1 up to 100 round lots—are normally executed instantaneously without any appreciable effect on the prevailing price. Even very large orders, sometimes involving many millions of shares, can usually be executed promptly and smoothly as well.[9] Extensive use of computers has enabled the exchange to keep pace with trading volumes that frequently exceed 200 million shares in one day. The largest volume to date occurred on the Tuesday (October 20, 1987) after "Black Monday" and exceeded 600 million shares; even this volume was handled without excessive delays.

The bottom lines of Tables 5.1 and 5.2 highlight the tremendous growth of share trading in recent decades. Between 1980 and 1992, the number of shares traded multiplied nearly fivefold and their value increased more than sixfold.[10] To some extent this increase was a result of more shares being listed due to new issues and splits; thus the total number of shares listed on the NYSE went up from 22 billion in 1975 to 80 billion in 1989. In addition, shares have tended to turn over more frequently, most likely as a consequence of lower commission rates; the "turnover ratio" (shares traded as a percentage of shares listed) rose from 21 in 1975 to 52 in 1989.

5.1.2 Types of Orders and Their Execution

The simplest type of order is the *market order:* a request to the broker to buy or sell as soon as possible at the best price then obtainable on the trading floor (i.e., at the "market price").[11] Market orders have the advantage of rapid execution, which may be important in a fast-moving market. On the other hand, the "best price" is uncertain and may turn out to be disappointing, particularly in respect to an inactive stock, where it may reflect a short-term distortion or a wide spread between bid and ask prices. Sometimes the originator specifies that a market order is to be executed at a particular time rather than immediately. If the order is specified "market at close" (MOC) the execution price will be the closing price for the day.

The major alternative is a *limit order,* which will only be executed at a price no worse than the limit: that is, no higher than the limit specified by the buyer or no lower than the limit specified by the seller. Its disadvantage arises in a rapidly moving market where the price may have passed the wrong side of the limit by a small margin when the order reaches the floor. In that case it will not be executed for the time being, causing the investor to "miss the market" by as little as 1/8 of a point (equivalent to 12½ cents) per share.

A different type of limit sell order serves to provide automatic protection against loss in the case of rapid price decline. It is known as a "stop-loss order" or, more generally, as a *stop order.* In this case the investor constrains his or her maximum loss by specifying a limit price at which a market order to sell will be executed once the stock price drops to that level. Suppose that IBM is trading around 66; then an order to "sell 100 IBM at 64 on stop" will be executed only if the price drops to 64, at which time it becomes a market sell order. A stop buy order may be placed by a potential buyer (for instance, one who has previously sold the stock short); the order becomes a market buy order when the price rises to the specified limit.[12]

Since limit orders (including stop orders) may not be executed immediately, it is important to specify the time period during which they will be in force. Limit orders may be *day orders,* which automatically expire if unexecuted at the end of the day, or *open orders,* which may be entered for a week or some other period, or *good till canceled* (GTC), which are valid for 6 months unless notice is received to terminate them beforehand. Yet another type is *fill or kill* (FOK), where the order is canceled if it cannot be executed immediately.[13]

Pricing on the NYSE and most other exchanges amounts to a continuous auction in which both buyers and sellers make bids and offers all the time. The highest price offered by a prospective purchaser at any point in time becomes the "bid price," and the lowest offered among the sellers at the same time is the "ask price," which together are reported as the "bid-ask quotation." For many stocks, particularly if trading is inactive, either the bid price or the ask price (or, more rarely, both) are set by the specialist, as discussed in the next section.

When a broker receives an inquiry from a client considering the sale of IBM stock, for example, she will first ascertain the current bid-ask quotation in the market. Suppose these are 66 bid and 66¼ ask, the specialist being willing to buy at least 100 shares at 66 and sell 400 at a price of 66¼. On receiving this information, the investor decides to place a market order to sell 100 shares. The account broker then transmits this order to her firm's representative on the floor who goes to the "post" where IBM is traded and checks that the 66–66¼ quotation is still in force.

As long as the quotation remains valid, the broker knows she need not sell for less than 66 because the specialist will buy at least 100 at that price. At the same time, it is clear that there is no point in asking more than 66¼ since there are already limit sell orders unexecuted at that price. There is a chance, however, that there will be a buyer at 66⅛, with ⅛ or 12½ cents per share being the smallest increment in which bidding occurs.

The broker therefore calls out "100 at 6⅛" (the 60 is understood) to the floor, inviting another broker with an order to buy at 66⅛ to "take" the ask, in which case information would be exchanged and the trade completed. It may be, however, that the broker fails to get a "take" and so must call the next lowest ask: "100 at 6." The first response will take the deal, and this may come either from the specialist or from another floor broker at the IBM post with a limit order to buy at 66. In many cases this kind of calling auction will be unnecessary since the bid-ask spread will already be ⅛. If so, the broker might just as well go directly to the specialist and execute the trade.

Following execution, the buyer usually has 5 business days to pay and the seller has the same time to transfer the actual certificate that is evidence of ownership of the shares.[14] Two institutions have been set up to facilitate the latter process. The first is a centralized clearinghouse operated by the National Securities Clearing Corporation. A record of each transaction is transmitted to the clearinghouse, which updates the stock and cash accounts of each member broker, thereby netting out all cross transactions (e.g., avoiding certificates on the same stock flowing in both directions between two brokers over a short space of time). At the close of each day, the opposite sides of each trade are verified for consistency, each member's accounts are netted out, and the outstanding balances of cash and scrip certificates are settled.

A second system operated by the Depository Trust Company (DTC) virtually eliminates the movement of paper certificates altogether. Members of the system deposit the certificates, which are credited to their accounts. Transfers are then made in the form of electronic debits and credits to these accounts, reflecting shifting claims against this "bank" of certificates held by the DTC.

The processes we have described so far trace the path of an order once it becomes a "market order." For a limit order (including a stop order), however, this chain of events will follow only after the specified limit price has been "hit." When a limit order is initially placed with a brokerage firm, its floor broker (or a two-dollar broker) will take it to the specialist in the stock, who will then enter it into his or her "book," where all unexecuted orders are listed. If there are already other limit orders in the book at the same price, each will be executed on a FIFO (first in, first out) basis once the price is hit, until demand or supply at that price is exhausted.

5.1.3 Specialists and Market Clearing

Since orders to buy and sell stock arrive in a more or less random pattern over time, the market price will fluctuate up or down depending on whether successive orders offset or reinforce each other (i.e., on whether they are on opposite sides or on the same side of the market). These random fluctuations will occur even if there is no persistent pressure for the price to move in a particular direction.

Consequently, floor traders could profit from an ability to distinguish between random short-term fluctuations and more fundamental movements in the price. If, for example, a floor trader felt that the price had fallen simply because a few large sell orders happened to arrive together, he[15] would buy the stock and resell it shortly thereafter at a profit when some further orders to buy arrived, causing the market price to rise. If his assessment were wrong, however, and a disproportionate number of sell orders continued to come in because investors had reduced their opinion of the fundamental value of the stock, the trader would be forced to take a loss on resale.

To the extent that such speculators can accurately identify random price fluctuations caused by the coincidental arrival of buy or sell orders, their operations will tend to stabilize the market because they buy as the price begins to fall and sell as it begins to rise. This kind of short-term speculation has been institutionalized on the stock exchanges in the form of the specialists mentioned earlier, though not to the exclusion of floor traders. Together, floor traders and specialists provide greater stability and continuity to the market.

The specialist has a particular advantage in distinguishing between random fluctuation and price trend because all unexecuted limit orders are listed in his book, as are the MOC and other time-specific market orders mentioned earlier. The specialist, in effect, knows the short-run supply and demand curves for the stocks in which he specializes. The word "curve" should not be interpreted too literally, since the price usually varies in steps of $\frac{1}{8}$ rather than continuously. As a result, there may not be any price at which supply and demand balance exactly; the specialist will take up the slack.

A simple example serves to clarify the operation of a specialist's book in the absence of trading by the specialist himself and by floor traders. Suppose XYZ last traded at 11:00 A.M. at a price of 91. After that trade, the specialist in XYZ has the following unfilled limit orders in his book:

1. Buy 1,000 at 88 or better
2. Buy 200 at 88$\frac{1}{2}$ or better
3. Buy 100 at 89 or better
4. Buy 500 at 90 or better
5. Buy 200 at 90$\frac{3}{4}$ or better
6. Buy 300 at 93 on stop (i.e., buy at market if price rises to 93)
7. Buy 100 at 93$\frac{1}{4}$ on stop
8. Sell 300 at 91$\frac{1}{4}$ or better
9. Sell 800 at 92 or better
10. Sell 1,500 at 92$\frac{1}{2}$ or better
11. Sell 200 at 89 on stop (i.e., sell at market if price falls to 89)
12. Sell 200 at 87 on stop

The last market price lay between the lowest offer (91$\frac{1}{4}$) and the highest bid (90$\frac{3}{4}$) so that the book stands without further execution taking place. The stop orders are irrelevant for the time being because they will only be triggered when the current price changes.

At 11:05 A.M. a market order to sell 1,000 shares of XYZ reaches the trading post. The specialist must then look for a price that will allow the market order to be executed in its entirety, while satisfying public limit orders first.

If he were to set a price at 89, the book would provide total orders to buy of 800 (200 + 500 + 100 for the three highest buy orders outstanding), not enough to fill the new order. At that price, moreover, order no. 11 (to sell 200 at 89 on stop) would be triggered so that excess supply would be 400: 200 remaining unsold from the new market order and a further 200 from the stop order. At a price of 88$\frac{1}{2}$, order no. 2 (to buy 200 at that price) would also be activated, but this is still insufficient because of the extra supply from order no. 11.

The price must therefore be reduced to 88, at which price 1,200 shares change hands. This will leave order no. 1 (to buy 1,000 at 88 or better) only 20% filled, so the bid will now be 88. This situation illustrates the point made earlier that with a discontinuously varying price it may not be possible to match supply and demand exactly. The lowest asking price on the specialist's book remains at 91$\frac{1}{4}$ (order no. 8).[16]

It will be noticed that the arrival of the new market order, in the absence of intervention by the specialist or by floor traders, causes the market price to drop from 91 to 88 in 5 minutes. This steep decline is due not only to the relatively large size of the new order but also to the triggering of stop order no. 11. Yet the arrival of the new order could be a purely random event without significance for the underlying value of XYZ stock. It is as if a plane suddenly hits an "air pocket" and drops several feet without deviating from its set course.

It is in such circumstances that the specialist and the floor traders find their opportunity. Rather than allowing the price to be buffeted by a single market order, they may take a chance that buy orders will soon arrive to bring the price back to somewhere near its previous level. If this is their belief, they will take the opposite side of the new order, at a price well above the 88 that would emerge without their intervention. In doing so, of course, they assume a risk— namely, that additional market sell orders will arrive, forcing them take a loss on their expanded inventory. The reward for assuming this risk is that they can buy at the bid price and sell at the asking price, whereas outsiders have to buy at the asking price and sell at the bid price.[17]

The difference between floor traders and specialists is that the former can intervene at their discretion, while the latter have a definite responsibility for doing so. The specialists are charged by the exchange with maintaining a "fair and orderly" market in the stocks in which they specialize. Specialists, as we know, are also responsible for keeping the book of unexecuted orders, and this gives them a unique insight into the state of the market, particularly with respect to stop orders.

In order to fulfill their assignments, each specialist firm is required to sell from its own inventory at the current asking price so as to smooth out temporary excess demand, and to buy on its own account at the current bid price when there is excess supply. This is called "leaning against the wind." Potential traders are thus assured that at any time there is a buyer and seller in the market (continuity), and that the bid-ask spread is kept close to its minimum of $1/8$. Specialists are also required to execute all public limit orders they hold when the specified trigger price is hit, before buying or selling at that price for their own accounts.

The specialists' obligation does not apply to orders above a certain size. Currently, specialists must stand ready to fill all orders up to about 1,100 shares. In the preceding example, the specialist would actually fill the new order (to sell 1,000 shares at the market) by buying at the bid price. Since the previous trade was assumed to be at 91, and the lowest offering (order no. 8) was at $91^{1/4}$, the bid would probably be at $91^{1/8}$.[18] By taking the other side of the new order at $90^{7/8}$, the specialist would prevent the precipitous fall to 88 we found earlier.

The specialist's own inventory can be a particularly useful buffer against unnecessary short-term price fluctuation when a *block order* (involving 10,000 shares or more) reaches the market. In this case, the specialist is required to execute all public limited orders until 1,000 shares, or 5% of the block if this is larger, have been absorbed. The remainder may be taken up by the specialist, at his discretion, into inventory; if so, the decline in the market price would be arrested. The enlarged inventory is then available for subsequent sales against upward fluctuations in the market, but if these do not materialize the specialist may have to sell at a loss (after executing all outstanding public orders in the relevant price range.) The specialist's inventory, incidentally, need not be positive; he may be short, and often is.

Earlier we characterized exchange trading as a "continuous auction." Strictly speaking, this description is incorrect because the market is not open all the time; the NYSE, for instance, starts trading at 9:30 A.M. and closes at 4 P.M. (Monday through Friday).[19] Trading in any particular stock, however, does not necessarily begin at 9:30. The first task of the specialist is to determine an opening price, which will reflect the buy and sell orders that have come in before the bell, the official signal that trading is permitted. In most cases, these orders are matched closely enough so that the specialist can quote an opening price at which all the market orders (and those limit and stop orders that are triggered at the opening price) are executed, perhaps with some help from the specialist's own inventory. The opening in that stock will then occur within a few minutes after the bell.

Occasionally the preopening orders are very far from matching, for instance if there are many orders to sell and few to buy. The specialist may then be unable or unwilling to use his inventory to bring the orders into balance, and the opening is delayed. Efforts will then be made to find additional buyers (in this example) among large traders, probably at a much lower price than the previous close, until an opening price is found at which the market orders, along with the relevant limit and stop orders, can be filled. Such an "imbalance of orders" can also occur during the day, in which case trading in the stock is temporarily suspended. The exchange may also call for suspension if some important news item (for instance concerning a merger or acquisition) is pending. What all this amounts to is that the specialists' obligation to "make a market" is not absolute.

The role of the specialists is controversial because they are both officially designated market makers and businesspeople aiming for profit. Despite close regulation by the exchange, the specialists' monopoly on important market information has often been criticized. It is argued that the substantial incomes of specialists are excessive for the service they perform, and that their economic function could be carried out more efficiently by an interactive computer system that kept track of limit orders. To the extent a specialist's market operations call for the exercise of judgment, however, it may be difficult to replace him or her with a computer.[20]

The future of the specialist system in the United States, and especially on the NYSE, will depend largely on its success in keeping the stock market reasonably stable. Occasionally there have been signs that the capacity of specialists to prevent excessive price fluctuations can be strained by a large volume of trading. As mentioned earlier, the stock markets as a whole weathered the "Black Monday" upheaval fairly well, but a few specialist firms were unable to cope and had to go out of business. A few other firms failed to meet the standards by which specialists are judged, causing the NYSE to reassign some of their stocks to other specialists. Even before "Black Monday," the phenomena of "program trading" and of the "triple witching hour" (to be discussed in Chapter 9) had caused concern. If these strains persist, the solution would not be to abolish the specialist system, which on the whole has worked well; it may be preferable to increase the number of specialist firms and to introduce more competition in the process by which stocks are assigned to them.

The precipitous fall of stock prices in mid-October 1987 (including the three or four trading days preceding "Black Monday") puts the risks that specialists are expected to assume in a new perspective. During those few days, the overall price indexes lost about one-third of their value; some shares, of course, lost more than that. Is the obligation of specialists to "lean against the wind" reasonable, and indeed enforceable, in such conditions? If there were no potential buyers at anywhere near current prices, the specialists might be obliged to acquire stocks worth hundreds of billions of dollars.[21] Even if they could get the necessary credit, the resulting losses in a declining market would soon wipe out their net worth.

It might be tempting to conclude from this analysis that, if the specialists continued to perform according to the rules, they could not survive the kind of crash that occurred in 1987 (and also in 1929 and a few other years). This conclusion would be false: Specialists can protect themselves against catastrophic losses. More specifically, the introduction of stock index futures (to be discussed in Chapter 9) has made it possible for specialists and others to "hedge" their portfolios. How much use specialists make of this opportunity is a factual matter on which information is difficult to obtain.

5.2 FINANCIAL MARKETS WITHOUT CENTRAL
TRADING PLACES

The stock exchanges, on which we have focused until now, are not the only important markets in financial instruments. The organization of the other markets in the United States differs significantly from that of the stock exchanges with their central trading places and specialist systems. A brief discussion of these other markets is useful not only because they are of great interest in themselves but also because it puts the special features of the stock exchanges in perspective.

The *bond market* actually consists of several submarkets, particularly those in Treasuries, municipals, and corporate bonds; these securities were described in Chapter 3. None of them has a central trading place, and there are no specialists,[22] though there are dealers who serve as market makers. The trading is conducted by telex and telephone. The organization of the bond markets, in fact, resembles that of the over-the-counter market in stocks discussed in Section 5.2.1.

The *foreign currency* market, like the bond market, has a very large volume but no central trading place and no specialists. Most of the trading is among banks; there are also brokers. The Federal Reserve intervenes occasionally, as do the central banks of other countries. It is a typical wholesale market in which the number of participants is relatively small—a few hundred at the most. Except for some large multinational corporations, firms engaged in international trade generally arrange their foreign exchange transactions through their bankers. Participation by the general public is strongly discouraged.[23]

The *Federal Funds market,* also discussed in Chapter 3, involves banks with occasional intervention by the Federal Reserve. There is no public participation.

How can we explain this variety of organizational patterns? It would seem that there are two key factors: the number of participants and the number of different objects traded. Central trading places are economically justified when there are many participants, as is the case in equities, options, and futures; otherwise, the traders can communicate more cheaply by other means.[24] This is why there is no central trading place in currencies; the case of bonds is less clear-cut.

The number of traded objects is important in determining the viability of specialists as opposed to floor traders. The NYSE, for instance, lists more than 2,000 different shares, of which only a small fraction are actively traded during most or all of the trading hours. The specialists to whom those active equities are assigned can make handsome profits, but their economic function could arguably be performed more cheaply by floor traders or by multiple market makers competing with each other.[25] Many other stocks, by contrast, trade several dozens of round lots per day at best. Specialists are most needed in those inactive stocks, since floor traders would not find it worth their while to watch them. In the absence of specialists, the market would be thin and prices would be erratic. On the futures exchanges, the number of different instruments (i.e., futures contracts) is much smaller; the presence of floor traders is usually enough to ensure reasonable continuity of prices.

5.2.1 The Over-the-Counter Stock Market

Despite the advantages described in Section 5.1.3, by no means are all shares traded on centralized exchanges. A large number of less important stocks (and some important ones) are traded on the over-the-counter market. This market has no central trading place; for many OTC stocks somewhat the same function is performed instead by an electronic communications network known as NASDAQ. While the OTC market is especially valuable for newly established corporations without the track record required for listing on a centralized exchange, we shall see in a moment that it has retained the allegiance of certain firms that have outgrown this limitation.

The backbone of the OTC market consists of dealers who are willing to quote bid and ask prices for the stocks in which they "make a market," and who stand ready to execute at least one round lot at the quoted prices at any time.[26]

The current quotations may be called up by brokers on terminals in their own trading room. The actual transactions, however, are made by direct negotiation between the dealer and the broker, and a different price may be agreed upon for a trade of more than 100 shares.[27]

As shown in Tables 5.1 and 5.2, the OTC market has gained ground on the centralized exchanges in recent years. It is perhaps more significant that such growth companies as Apple Computer, Intel, Lotus Development, MCI Communications, and Microsoft have continued their listing on NASDAQ even though they are sufficiently large and profitable to qualify for the New York Stock Exchange. In fact, the 1990 trading volume in MCI (a telephone company) on NASDAQ exceeded that of any company listed on the NYSE. It cannot be said, therefore, that the OTC market is confined to small companies hoping to grow enough to be listed on a centralized exchange. Indeed, the large volume in the five firms just mentioned suggests that the centralized exchanges no longer have much of an advantage over the less formal trading arrangements in the OTC market.

The principal disadvantage of having multiple market makers is the possibility of conflicts of interest. Typically, the market makers on NASDAQ are stockbrokers who also deal with the public. They may be tempted to treat the positions of their customers as part of their trading inventories. As a result, the customers may not benefit from the best possible execution of their orders; sometimes selling customers, for instance, will simply receive an average price calculated at the end of the day rather than the highest bid price prevailing at the time they placed their order. Market-making brokers may also slant their investment advice to further their market-making activity. An investor in OTC equities would do well to inquire if his or her broker makes a market in the stock concerned.

Prior to the abolition of fixed commissions on organized exchanges in 1975, a further market known as the "Third Market" began to grow as large institutions sought to avoid high brokerage fees by using a nonmember broker to search for another institution with a complementary supply or demand so that the trade could occur off the central exchange. More recently, it has become common for institutional investors to dispense with brokers and exchanges entirely and deal directly among themselves (these are known as "Fourth Market" trades). This trend has been facilitated by the establishment of computer networks that are capable of providing quotation and execution directly between buyer and seller: *Instinet* in the U.S.A. and *Ariel* in London. It appears that the third and fourth markets have not captured a large part of the trading in equities, but by providing alternatives to the stock exchanges they serve to keep the latter competitive.

The basic economics of share trading, dominated by the benefits of eliminating the duplication of costly search and verification, still govern the organization of exchanges. Advances in computers and communications, however, are changing the technology by which those benefits are realized and apparently favor the OTC market. Ultimately, the result could be the replacement of central trading places with their electronic equivalent: a continuously updated, central database.[28] However, the ability of the traditional exchanges and the OTC market to cope with large volumes of trading and the lowering of brokerage charges has pushed that long-predicted development further and further into the future.

5.3 STOCK EXCHANGES IN OTHER COUNTRIES

In recent years, American investors, both institutional and individual, have increasingly recognized the potential gains from international diversification of their portfolios. Many brokers now trade for their customers 24 hours a day, following time zones around the globe. Thus they are paying increasing attention to stock markets abroad. These markets are also of interest because of the different methods of trading they follow.

The relative volumes of equities traded on the world's major stock exchanges is shown in Figure 5.1. Although volume obviously varies from year to year, we can make a number of general observations. It is clear that the NYSE and NASDAQ together account for a very substantial part of the world trade in equities. In recent years, Tokyo has grown to become a very important market in global terms. London, although less than 40% the size of the NYSE in volume terms, has the largest activity in foreign (nondomestic) stocks. It is therefore one of the most important centers for investors who wish to trade an international portfolio of equities with the convenience of dealing on a single exchange. In the remainder of this section we concentrate on the London and Tokyo markets, explaining some of the major differences in trading practices and terminology between these exchanges and those in the United States.

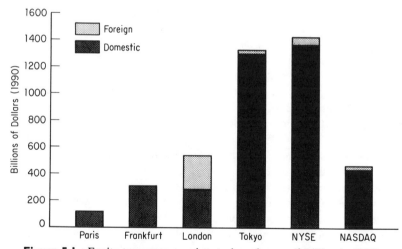

Figure 5.1   Equity turnover on major stock exchanges ($ billion in 1990). *Note:* Frankfurt and Paris have approximately $10 billion and $5 billion turnover of foreign equities, respectively. *Source:* Data from the International Stock Exchange (London), Annual Report, 1992.

5.3.1 The International Stock Exchange in London

The roots of the London Stock Exchange are to be found in the informal exchange of shares of various international trading ventures. As long ago as the late sixteenth century, when trade spread to newly discovered continents, the risks of individual voyages was increasing. Merchants sought to share the costs and potential revenues with other partners. But long periods at sea made it difficult to recruit investors without some means of selling the shares should the funds be required before the vessels returned and their cargoes were sold. Initially, this kind of trading was conducted in coffeehouses and other meeting places where entrepreneurs and investors met to raise the finance for such ventures. The formal stock exchange was constituted in 1802 to facilitate easy trading of shares and eliminate undue risk by establishing a set of recognized trading rules and a central trading place.

Over the next 100 years there was an expansion in the types of enterprises whose shares were traded on the exchange to include industrial ventures and large-scale projects such as railways. The parties operating on the exchange also became more specialized, the most important distinction being between stockbrokers and "stockjobbers." Jobbers maintained stalls, known as "pitches," on the floor of the exchange. Without disclosing whether they were buying or selling, the stockbrokers would request prices for both transactions on behalf of their clients from a number of jobbers' pitches. The broker would then undertake the transaction with the jobber who offered the best price. Having quoted a price to a broker, the jobber was obliged to undertake the trade. The jobbers were thus dealers who took ownership of the shares, albeit often for only an instant. Like the OTC market makers in the United States, they made their profits from the difference between their buying and selling prices. Brokers, in contrast, were agents obliged to get the best price for their clients. They were compensated by fixed commissions. This system, called "single-capacity dealing" because the parties were either jobbers or brokers but could not act as both, operated on the London market from 1912 to 1986.

Overnight on October 27, 1986, the London Stock Exchange underwent a major change in its trading rules, known colloquially as "Big Bang." Fixed commissions were abolished. The distinction between brokers and jobbers was dropped. Firms could now act in a "dual capacity," dealing in shares on their own behalf as market makers and also acting as brokers for their clients. In order to preserve integrity in performing two potentially conflicting roles, the new rules imposed certain restrictions. First, brokers were permitted to conduct business with their own jobber only when the in-house jobber at least matches the best price available elsewhere in the market. Second, all jobbers were required to continuously advertise their prices on the exchange's electronic price service Stock Exchange Automated Quotation (SEAQ), itself based on the NASDAQ system.

Limits on corporate ownership of the new market makers were also lifted, allowing banks and other local and foreign financial institutions to operate directly on the London exchange. In the same year, the present International Stock Exchange of Great Britain and the Republic of Ireland was formed through the merger of the domestic stock exchange with international equity dealers operating in London.

True to its name, Big Bang has initiated a great deal of change on the London market. The trading floor for shares has now disappeared.[29] Unlike the system of matching buy and sell orders used on the NYSE (an "order-driven system"), London now relies solely on the display on screens of competing buy and sell quotes for the prices and quantities in which market makers undertake to deal (a "quote-driven system"). Trading in London now takes place by computer and telephone from brokers and market-maker's offices. Using the information displayed on the SEAQ screen, the investor chooses the best price available from a range of quotes and then arranges the trade with the most competitive market maker.

The relative merits of quote-driven and order-driven systems have been hotly debated in London. One of the most important tests of the success of any securities trading system is how well it promotes market liquidity. As already mentioned, one important measure of liquidity is the bid-ask spread. An investor who purchased securities and then wished to sell them almost immediately would suffer a loss equal to the spread, even if the price of the security did not change. A large bid-ask spread indicates a less liquid market in the sense that investors cannot move between securities and cash at a low cost. Under London's quote-driven system, bid-ask spreads for most actively traded stocks narrowed somewhat after Big Bang to an average of about 1.75%, but the spreads for thinly traded shares have risen steeply to between 4% and 10% of the price of these stocks.

Some people argue that the NYSE's order-driven system with "monopoly specialists" may be superior to a quote-driven system for thinly traded securities. They point out that a monopoly can reduce search costs; potential buyers and sellers know where to go to trade. When trades are only once or twice per week it takes time and effort to match buyers and sellers. This activity becomes more difficult the more market makers there are. They also point out that the specialist system may encourage the market maker to take larger positions in particular stocks, thus increasing the ability of the market to smooth out the price fluctuations that may result from a large buy or sell order in a market where transactions are few and far between.

Opponents argue that the specialist system exposes investors to unnecessary risk of exploitation by these favored monopolists who have superior information by virtue of their privileged position. They have the full picture of the orders in the market, as well as unexecuted limit orders. Competition through alternative quotes, they argue, is the best way to minimize bid-offer spreads. This disagreement parallels the one about the role of NYSE specialists and about the relative merits of exchange trading and over-the-counter trading in the United States.

Big Bang has also affected brokers' commissions. Following the abandonment of fixed rates, commissions for execution share trades declined from almost 0.5% of the transaction value before the reforms to a current average of 0.25%. Not surprisingly, the fall in commission rates was more than the average for large deals and actively traded shares as competition for this volume business intensified. Commission rates on small, retail trades have actually risen a little, toward 2%.

The British banks and merchant banks, as well as major international companies like Merrill Lynch and Nomura (Japan's largest securities house), joined the market following Big Bang. In total, new entrants invested some $1.1 billion in former brokerage and jobbing firms. While a proportion of this money was paid to the existing partners, it also meant a large injection of capital, which market makers could draw upon to deal. Daily trading volume, although notoriously cyclical, has increased substantially, settling at almost double pre-Big Bang levels.

Another significant change since 1986 has been the increased trading of non-British shares, which now takes place on the London exchange. At present there are more than 550 equities in foreign companies listed, including many of the major American, German, French, Italian, and Dutch companies. More than $200 billion (U.S.) of foreign equities are now traded in London each year—a much higher volume of international business than any other exchange in the world. Surveys have shown that up to half the turnover in large French and Italian companies and one quarter of all trading in major German shares takes place in London. In response, other European markets have begun to deregulate commissions and change some of their ancient trading practices. The Paris bourse staged its own version of Big Bang in 1990. The previously fragmented regional exchanges in Germany have come together to form a linked Federation of German Exchanges.

A final aspect of the London Stock Exchange that differs from the NYSE (where transactions were normally settled within 5 days from the originating trade)[30] is the use of an "account period." The trading year in London is divided into a series of "accounts" that are normally 10 working days, ending on a Monday. The account periods are defined by a first day of dealings, a last day of dealings, and an account day. Shares purchased during an account (i.e., between the first and last day of dealing, both included) do not have to be paid for until after the end of the account, on the account day, which is usually the second Monday after the last day of dealings. Nor, of course, does the seller of shares obtain the proceeds of sale during an account until the following account day. Prior to the end of an account, parties are simply sent a "contract note" advising them of the details of the bargain made on their behalf.

There are also special provisions relating to shares purchased and resold during the same account. In this case, the trader does not actually have to pay for the shares at all but simply receives the net gain or pays the net loss on account day. Dealings within the same account do not attract the usual stamp duty of 0.5%. Moreover, the broker charges commission only once on the entire trade. It is also permissible to sell shares short during an account, so long as the same quantity is bought back before the end of the account. This alternative is of interest to traders who believe the price of a particular share will fall during the account period.[31]

5.3.2 The Tokyo Stock Exchange

Strong growth and heavy investment by Japanese corporations over the past 30 years have made the Tokyo Stock Exchange one of the world's most important securities markets. Several hundreds of millions of shares are now traded there each working day by both Japanese and foreign investors. In the boom before "Black Monday" in October 1987, Tokyo's most important stock index (the Nikkei 225, which covers the 225 largest Japanese corporate stocks) reached almost 28,000. These high share prices, combined with a strong yen, meant that the Tokyo exchange surpassed the NYSE as the world's largest exchange, as measured by the market capitalization of listed stocks. But the market proved volatile, and some years later, with share prices trading in a range 40% below this peak, Tokyo remains in the number two position.

Since the end of World War II, the Tokyo Stock Exchange has operated as a private, nonprofit company subject to the Securities and Exchange Law administered by the Ministry of Finance. It has two types of members: regular members and Santoris. Regular members are companies whose main activity is to buy and sell shares on the floor of the exchange. They do so both as agents for their clients and for their own account. The main activity of Santoris, by contrast, is to act as intermediaries between regular members. In some ways they are like specialists on the NYSE: They have trading posts on the floor of the exchange from which they deal in specific securities. They differ, however, in the important sense that Santoris are not permitted to trade on their own accounts; they simply keep records of orders and act as agents of the regular members for a commission. A number of American and British broking firms currently hold regular membership of the Tokyo exchange.

The marketplaces are divided between the "first trading section," comprising approximately the top 1,000 shares; the "second trading section," with around 400 shares of medium-sized companies and new issues; and the over-the-counter market, which handles trading of smaller "registered" and "subregistered" securities, as well as 95% of the trading in bonds.

Dealing arrangements are unusually complex in that there are two types of trading and four types of settlement. The *Itayose* method, used primarily for bonds, treats all orders arriving before the opening of trading as simultaneous. Before any trades are consummated, all of these orders are examined in order to set an opening price that will clear both all market orders and all limit orders to the extent they can be matched. This matching process continues as new orders arrive. Under the *Zaraba* trading method, used for most shares, an opening price is first determined as just described. Then there is an open auction for all the outstanding orders that cannot be executed at the opening price, with new bids being made, and the lowest selling price bid and highest buying price bid being executed at any point in time in a sort of "double-sided" auction.

Until 1985, this open auction system was conducted by floor traders through a mixture of frenetic hand signals and shouts, creating a scene much beloved by newspapers around the world as the image of dynamic capitalism. Part of this bustle arose because an estimated 70% of all orders on the Tokyo exchange are for less than 5,000 shares, so the ratio of orders to total trading volume is high. But now the bulk of transactions takes place by means of an electronic auction where the exchange's computers calculate the opening price and then register the subsequent bids. Only very large lot orders are still traded face-to-face on the floor and then entered into the electronic system.

Once a bargain is struck, the most common form of settlement, termed a *regular way transaction*, is through the stock exchange clearing department on the third business day following the bargain. Business days in Japan include Saturdays, except for the third Saturday in each month. Other bargains may be made for settlement the same day (*cash transactions*) or at a fixed date within 14 days (*special agreement transactions*). This latter form of settlement is now rare. It dates from a time in the past where poor transport and communications in Japan necessitated a means of allowing time for people in remote locations to settle transactions. The final settlement method, known as *when issued,* is used for new issues. As the term suggests, settlement is not made until the share scrip is actually issued.

5.4 OPERATIONAL EFFICIENCY AND THE EFFICIENT MARKET HYPOTHESIS

We now turn to the efficiency of the stock market. All major stocks, and many less important ones, are listed on exchanges or on NASDAQ. The reporting systems of these submarkets enable a large number of actual and potential investors to obtain information on prices, volume of trading, and other variables such as the dividends and reported earnings of a company. This fact has important implications for the informational efficiency of the market and, in turn, the potential to profit by trading on various types of information.

A market is said to be *informationally efficient* if at any time (assuming the market is open for trading) all information available at that time is fully reflected in current prices. The concept of informational efficiency must be sharply distinguished from another notion with which it is often confused: A market will be called *operationally efficient* if trades are executed at the lowest possible cost— that is, if transaction costs are minimal. Before exploring the profound implications of informational efficiency we must say a few words about the more mundane subject of operational efficiency.

Transaction costs can be measured as the difference between the total cost of an item to the buyer and the net proceeds from that same item to the seller. Consider a trade of 100 shares of XYZ at a price of $90 per share. Suppose the buyer and seller are each charged a commission of $75 by their respective brokers; then the buyer pays $9,075 and the seller receives $8,925, so the transaction costs are at least $150. Furthermore, there is normally a bid-ask spread of 1/4 for such a high-priced share on the stock exchange, which means either that the buyer has acquired something whose resale price is only $8,975 or the seller has given up something that it would cost him $9,025 to replace. The bid-ask spread should therefore be added to the commission for a total transaction cost of $175, or almost 2% of the nominal cost of $9,000.[32]

If there is active competition both in the stock market and among brokers, these transaction costs are presumably minimal and the market is operationally efficient. This assumption is probably satisfied at present, though it would not have been before 1975, when commissions were fixed. Moreover, 2% is not a large fraction of the nominal cost.[33]

What matters, actually, is not so much how transaction costs in the stock market compare with those in other markets but what effect they have on the frequency of trading. Clearly, a commission of $75 plus a bid-ask spread of $25 is too high to permit frequent sales and purchases of a modest number of shares. It is not surprising, therefore, that individual investors tend to keep their shares for long periods of time. Institutional investors, with their lower transaction costs—typically 3 cents per share or less on large blocks—turn over their portfolios more rapidly, while floor traders and specialists, who have the lowest transaction costs of all, are in and out of the market many times every day.

The point of the foregoing discussion is that traders with low transaction costs can respond quickly and easily to any items of information relevant to share prices that reach them. Depending on whether the news is favorable or unfavorable, they will buy or sell immediately without having to worry unduly about transaction costs. Provided there are enough traders with low transaction costs, all information available to these traders will have resulted in virtually instantaneous sales and purchases and will be reflected in current prices. The market will then be informationally efficient.

It follows that operational efficiency is a prerequisite for informational efficiency. In a market where transaction costs are relatively large, such as the housing market, we would not expect high informational efficiency. Neither would we expect the stock market to be informationally efficient if all traders had transaction costs as high as those presently affecting small investors using "full-service" brokers. Even though most important news items are widely disseminated, traders with substantial transaction costs may not find it worth their while to act on the news, or even to be "tuned in" to the news.[34] Whether the stock market is informationally efficient—that is, whether there is a sufficient number of traders with negligible transaction costs—is essentially an empirical question on which a great deal of research has been done in recent years.

According to the efficient market hypothesis (EMH), first formulated explicitly in the 1960s but implicit in earlier thinking, the stock market is informationally efficient.[35] In fact, it is often tacitly assumed that transaction costs can be ignored altogether. We first discuss the main implications of the EMH and then describe how it has been tested.

To begin with, the hypothesis implies that there is no opportunity to earn abnormal returns by investing on the basis of information already available to other market participants; if the market is efficient, this information will already be reflected in the price. In practice, this efficiency means that the market price adjusts so rapidly to new information that almost nobody can profit from it after its release, unless he or she happens to be trading right on the exchange floor.

The question to ask is then: For what types of information does this market efficiency hold? Three main variants of the EMH have been distinguished by Fama (1965):

1. The weak form, which considers only past prices
2. The semistrong form, which in addition considers publicly available information
3. The strong form, which looks also at nonpublic ("inside") information

5.4.1 The Weak Form of the EMH, and Technical Analysis

The "weak-form" hypothesis suggests that all relevant information contained in the past history of stock prices will be reflected in the current price. If this variant of the EMH were true, we could rule out so-called technical analysis as an effective method for "beating the market." Technical analysis assumes that stock price movements follow some sort of repetitive (and consequently predictable) pattern. Its devotees plot price movements on elaborate charts to determine where in the pattern the market (or a particular stock) is now; this charting is why technical analysis is also known as "chart trading." The EMH, even in its weak form, considers all this analysis a waste of time; if there were such patterns, they would have been detected long ago, and current prices would reflect this information.[36]

A great deal of research has been conducted to decide whether or not actual stock prices follow predictable cycles. Time series on stock prices, to be sure, show apparent cycles, but so do randomly generated series; if one tosses a fair coin many times, a run of heads will often be followed by a run of tails. The important distinction is that these cycles occur by chance, and so their occurrence is not predictable.[37]

One test for the presence of cycles useful in forecasting future price movements is to compute the performance of a "filter rule" of the type that technical analysts might employ. Such a rule might state, for example: "Buy a stock after it has risen 5% from a low (since this signals that an upward cycle has begun). Hold it until the price falls by 5% from its most recent peak (a sign that a downswing is under way), then make a short sale. Maintain the short position until the stock again rises by 5% from its most recent bottom, at which point a long position should again be established (to take advantage of the continued upswing)." This is a "5% filter."

Following similar work on futures prices by Houthakker (1961), Alexander (1961), and Fama and Blume (1966) tracked the performance of filter rules on data for samples of NYSE-listed equities, using filters between 0.1% and 20%. Trading rules based on filters of greater than 1.5% actually provided lower returns than a simple "buy and hold" strategy for the same stock, even before the rule's higher transaction costs were allowed for. On filters of less than 1.5% it was found that not even a floor trader with the minimum transactions cost of one-tenth of a cent per dollar transacted could net a higher return than the buy and hold strategy.

The investigation of filter rules suggests that share prices do not follow consistent cycles over time, so that future prices cannot be predicted from past history. Certain other empirical regularities, however, cannot be so easily dismissed. These center on the phenomena of seasonality.[38] The best known of them is the famous "January effect," according to which equity prices tend to rise in that month. Let us look at some data on monthly changes in the Standard & Poor 500 index—more precisely, at changes in the logarithm of the S&P500 from the end of the preceding month to the end of the current month.

Over the most recent 25 years (1968 through 1992), the January change in the S&P500 was positive thirteen times and negative twelve times, hardly the stuff from which great fortunes are made! It is true that the mean of the January changes was about 1.3%, well above the mean change of 0.5% in all months over the period of observation, but the difference between these two percentages is not significant by the usual t test. It appears that the January effect is a matter of folklore rather than of fact.[39]

The data for some other months are actually more interesting. As shown in Figure 5.1, the December changes had a higher mean than the January changes; moreover, in December there were twice as many increases as there were decreases. The largest mean change (in absolute value) occurred in September and was negative; the decreases outnumbered the increases by a wide margin. The monthly mean changes, which in Figure 5.2 were reduced by the overall mean of 0.5% mentioned earlier, are not statistically significantly different from zero by conventional criteria, but a few ratios of increases to decreases may be significant. The existence of monthly seasonality can therefore not be ruled out.

Another type of seasonality that has been investigated is weekly, particularly the "weekend effect."[40] This effect consists of a tendency for equity prices to fall on Mondays, so it is also known as the "Monday effect." The older evidence supporting the weekend effect was stronger than it was for the January effect, but here practice appears to have caught up with analysis because the weekend effect has not been visible from 1988 on. For this reason, we do not discuss it further (although other days of the week—especially Wednesdays, when prices tend to rise—may be worth another look).

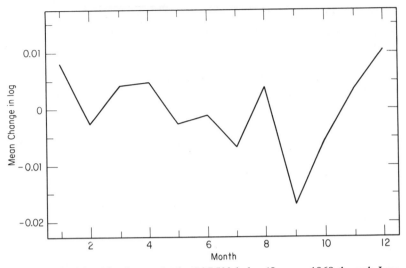

Figure 5.2 Monthly changes in the S&P500 index (January 1968 through June
1992)

While the empirical evidence on filter rules and seasonality does not cast
serious doubt on the usefulness of the weak-form EMH as a good first approximation, we cannot be dogmatic as to its validity. A major difficulty in testing
all forms of the EMH is that randomness can only be defined negatively as lack
of predictability, though the next section presents a way around this difficulty.
In a large set of data, such as daily closing prices over many years, there is an
enormous number of regularities that could possibly be used in subsequent arbitrage or speculation. Some hidden regularities may yet be brought to light. If so,
they are likely to disappear once traders turn them to their advantage, which is
apparently what happened to the weekend effect.

The reader will have gathered that we do not see much promise in technical
analysis. Nevertheless, there are two concepts from this area that are worth
knowing, if only because there are many practitioners who pay attention to them.
The first of these is known as "support." If a stock in its recent history (say a
year) has never fallen below a certain price and has tended to bounce back from
that price, technical analysts often assume that the stock will not easily fall
below it in the near future. If it does penetrate the "support"—which represents
potential buyers waiting in the wings—these analysts expect the stock to fall
further. Conversely, "resistance" is the highest price in the recent past, particularly if it was reached more than once. According to many technical analysts,
the stock will have difficulty going through the resistance level because of potential selling at that price, but if it does go through, a further rise is expected. In
practice, the determination of support and resistance levels often calls for judgment. As a result, econometric evidence on the predictive value (if any) of these
concepts is hard to find.

5.4.2 Do Equity Prices Follow a Random Walk?

If the weak form of the efficient market hypothesis holds, prices will exhibit a "random walk," an important concept of probability theory. A random variable defined at discrete times (for instance, once a day) follows a random walk if its expected value in the next period is the same as its most recent value. Referring to Section 4.2.5, this definition means that x_i, (where $i = 1, 2, \ldots, t, t+1, \ldots$) follows a random walk[41] if for all t

$$EV(x_{t+1}|x_t) = x_t. \tag{5.1}$$

For empirical testing it is convenient form to subtract x_t from x_{t+1} and x_{t-1} from x_t. Denoting the resulting differences by Δ, we then get

$$EV(\Delta x_{t+1}|\Delta x_t) = 0. \tag{5.2}$$

Furthermore, it is clear that in Equation (5.1) we may replace the x terms by their logarithms (provided x is positive) so that the Δ's in Equation (5.2) may be interpreted as logarithmic first differences. Such differences, which are approximately equal to percentage changes divided by 100, have been emphasized throughout this book.[42] In the present context, the x's are closing values of a representative price index, specifically the S&P500.

In Table 5.3, Equation (5.2) is used to test the random walk hypothesis. Trading days were grouped into three types ("fall," "flat," and "rise") according

Table 5.3 Conditional Means of Daily Changes in the S&P500 Stock Index

Period	Type[a]	No. of Observations[b]	Mean Change[c]	Standard Error	t Ratio
Jan '69–'75	Fall	775	−.00223	.00034	−6.6
	Flat	90	.00009	.00088	0.1
	Rise	768	.00217	.00031	7.0
	All	1633	−.00004	.00023	0.2
Jul '75–Jun '82	Fall	824	−.00101	.00028	−3.6
	Flat	100	.00145	.00065	2.2
	Rise	843	.00100	.00028	3.6
	All	1767	.00009	.00019	0.4
Jul '82–Jun '92	Fall	1108	.00008	.00036	0.2
	Flat	145	−.00045	.00099	0.5
	Rise	1272	.00104	.00027	3.8
	All	2525	.00053	.00022	2.4

[a]Direction of previous day's price change; "flat" means less than .0005 in either direction.

[b]Number of observations of each type.

[c]Mean change in the logarithm of the index.

to the change in the price index.[43] Then the mean price change on the next trading day was calculated for each type and divided by its standard error to obtain a t ratio. The reader will recall that a t ratio of about two—the exact value depends on the number of observations—implies that the estimated mean is significantly different from the expected value of zero at the 5% level. The table shows the relevant numbers for each of three periods; the reasons for choosing these periods will become clear in a moment.

During the first period, the 775 falls were followed by a mean change of $-.00223$, with a t ratio of 6.6, so it was highly significant: Falls tended to be followed by further falls. The 768 rises were followed by a mean change of $+.00217$ (also highly significant), so rises tended to be followed by rises. These figures show that there was considerable persistence in both rises and falls.

In the second period, rises and falls also showed significant persistence, but the conditional means and their t ratios were smaller than in the first period. During the third period, by contrast, the mean change following falls was close to zero and not significant, but the mean change following rises was still significant. However, the pattern during the third period was influenced by a marked upward trend (shown in the line labeled "all") that was not present earlier; if this trend is subtracted, the conditional mean following rises is not significant at the 5% level.

From this analysis we may conclude that the stock market, as measured by the S&P500, did not follow a random walk during the first two periods but did so in the third period. In other words, the market became more efficient over the years.

We must now discuss the rationale for the division into three periods. From 1969 through the first part of 1975, fixed commissions were in effect, causing transaction costs to be relatively high. When fixed commissions were abolished in 1975, the market came closer to a random walk, but some persistence in rises and falls remained. Finally, in 1982 another important change occurred—namely, the introduction of stock index futures (discussed in Chapter 9), which was tantamount to a further reduction in transaction costs.[44] The increase in market efficiency shown in Table 5.3 is consistent with these changes in transaction costs, though it does not prove causality.

It is somewhat ironic that in the 1970s, when the EMH gained widespread acceptance, there were significant departures from a random walk. Fortunately for financial theory—and for the functioning of our capital markets—the market now conforms closely to a random walk. Reality has caught up with theory. The recent evidence permits us to say that the weak form of the efficient market hypothesis is in general agreement with observed price behavior.

This observation does not necessarily mean that prices are constant on average. Instead, equity prices show a long-run upward trend around which they fluctuate randomly. This behavior is sometimes described as a "random walk with (positive) drift."

5.4.3 The Semistrong Form of the EMH, and Security Analysis

A more stringent hypothesis regarding efficiency is embodied in the "semistrong" form of the EMH. This form postulates that an investor cannot achieve excess returns by trading on *any* publicly available information (not just price history), because all of this information is rapidly reflected in prices after it has become available.

Efficient market theory, in this form, views stock prices as responding rapidly to the receipt by the market of new information bearing on the future returns that the stock is expected to earn. Now new information arrives randomly over time (otherwise it would be predictable and hence not really new). Since stock prices are responding to a random sequence of events, they themselves will again follow a random walk, as under the weak form.

Does this random walk imply that Wall Street's security analysts, who study the "fundamentals" of particular firms or industries, do not contribute anything in return for their handsome salaries?[45] The answer is "no." Analysts interpret information and sometimes collect new information. Many news items contain only the bare facts; their implications are often unclear, and analysts try to find them.

Suppose, for instance, that the XYZ corporation reports earnings of $2.10 per share in the first quarter of 1991 after earning $2.00 in the corresponding quarter of 1990. Is this good or bad news? It depends in part on what the firm had been expected to earn; if earnings of $2.25 had been widely anticipated, the report is disappointing. The meaning of the earnings figure also depends on how it came about. Perhaps the figure was reduced because the firm wrote off its investment in a new product that did not succeed. If so, further analysis is needed to determine its significance for future earnings.

The main business of security analysts, therefore, is to add value to raw information. By trading on this enhanced information, their customers cause it to be quickly reflected in the stock price, and they may realize some additional profit during the brief transition from the old price to the new equilibrium. Offset against this, of course, is the cost of enhancing the information. Since it is fairly easy to enter the security analysis industry, which has many participants, we would expect security analysts to earn no more than a competitive rate of return on their total investment. The existence of a security analysis industry, therefore, is not inconsistent with the impossibility of earning abnormal returns by using publicly available data, which the semistrong form hypothesizes.

Viewed in this way, fundamental analysis is not a method through which windfall profits are obtained, but a segment of the information-producing industry. Each investor must ask himself or herself whether the additional information produced by security analysts is worth its cost. The answer probably depends mostly on the investor's scale of operations. The institutional investors that now dominate the stock market can hardly afford to do without security analysts and often hire their own. For the individual investor, the answer is less clear. By using a full-service broker he or she gets access to a certain amount of "research" (essentially security and technical analysis), but at the cost of paying much higher commissions. As shown earlier in this chapter, the alternative is to rely on discount brokers who provide execution of orders but no analysis.

A large number of tests of the semistrong form of the efficient market hypothesis have been conducted by academic researchers. One of the most interesting was reported by Ball and Brown (1968). In this study, an equation was estimated to predict the earnings per share of each of 261 companies over the coming year. The forecast was based on the average trend in earnings in the past plus a deviation from this trend caused by the cycle of average corporate profitability for all other stocks. This forecast was then subtracted from the actual earnings reported at the end of the year. Firms with reported earnings greater than the forecast were placed in one group, while those reporting less than forecast were placed in another group.

Now if the stock price responds rationally to publicly reported information, we would expect the stocks in companies reporting unexpectedly high earnings to show above-average returns. Conversely, stocks reporting unexpectedly low earnings would be expected to show below-average price increases and lower returns. This pattern of rational adjustment was exactly what Ball and Brown found, but what is even more interesting is the pattern of the adjustment of share prices. Most of the good or bad information contained in the earnings reports was anticipated by the market, so that the price showed between 85% and 90% of the adjustment *before* the report was released.

The explanation of this pattern implies two conclusions about stock market behavior. First, most of the information contained in the earnings reports had already been quite accurately estimated on the basis of other data, such as macroeconomic conditions and statements by the company and its competitors. Second, the market adjusts very quickly to reflect new information in the price after receiving it. Given the number of well-informed analysts following most major stocks, this occurrence is hardly surprising. The market therefore appears to be informationally efficient in the "semistrong" sense, so that abnormally high profits cannot be made simply by collecting and analyzing publicly available information (after the cost of collection and analysis has been deducted from any gross profits).

5.4.4 How Rapidly Do Prices Adjust to News?

To conclude our discussion of the semistrong EMH, we have to mention a body of evidence that indirectly casts doubt on the assumption of rapid adjustment to publicly available news. This evidence, due mostly to Fama (1965), French (1980), and French and Roll (1986), has to do with the seemingly unrelated question of how time should be measured in the financial markets—in calendar days or in trading days. As discussed in Chapter 8, this question is relevant to the valuation of options, but it has wider implications.

The main finding of the authors just cited is that prices are much more volatile when the markets are open than when they are closed, particularly during weekends.[46] Obviously, some news is generated during weekends, as well as in the early and late hours of weekdays. Indeed, certain types of news (especially about the weather) can emerge at any time, and many government statistics and corporate earnings reports are intentionally released while the market is closed. If prices adjust as quickly to news as the weak-form EMH would have us believe, there would be little advantage in having the stock market open for 6½ hours, five days a week; it should either be open all the time or rather briefly every day. The greater volatility during trading hours implies that much of the news is not immediately translated into prices.

In discussing security analysis we saw that corporate reports often need interpretation by specialized observers. The same is true of many other kinds of news. Suppose, for instance, that a major hurricane is approaching Florida. Apart from the human suffering it will cause, this is obviously bad news for the firms that operate there and for the property insurance industry. It may be good news for home builders and furniture makers who will in due course experience increased demand. But which insurance companies, which home builders, and which furniture makers will be especially affected? This is not a simple question, and it may take many hours—perhaps days or weeks—before the hurricane's effects are fully factored into stock prices.

Another example has to do with the release of GDP data by the U.S. Department of Commerce. It might be thought that, since "a rising tide lifts all the boats," publication of a healthy growth rate in real GDP is unambiguously good news for the stock market. In reality, however, traders worry about the effect of GDP on monetary policy. If growth is too rapid, the Federal Reserve may become acutely concerned about future inflation and raise short-term interest rates, which in the past has often affected equity price adversely. As a result, the stock market has in recent years often responded favorably to modestly positive changes in real GDP but unfavorably to any news (not necessarily from the Commerce Department) suggesting that economic activity is picking up. Here again, it will take some time before the implications of new economic data are sorted out.

A further reason why the market does not respond instantaneously to news is simply that there is so much of it. The various items that come over the newswires or through the grapevine are often contradictory, leading different traders to arrive at different interpretations. The reconciliation of these conflicting views constitutes the main business of the stock market when it is open. This reconciliation appears to be the reason for the Fama-French-Roll findings that the market is much more volatile when it is open than when it is closed.

5.4.5 The Strong Form of the EMH

The "strong" form of the efficient market hypothesis goes one step further than the semistrong form by postulating that there is *no* information, publicly available or not, that will permit an investor to earn abnormal returns. In other words, it postulates that the current market price reflects *all* relevant information. Jaffe (1974) tested the strong form by collecting data on periods when there were at least three more corporate insiders selling than buying (intensive selling) and vice versa for intensive buying; such data are available from the Securities and Exchange Commission.[47] For a sample of 861 trading observations, he found that the predominant market positions being adopted by insiders outperformed the return on the market (after adjusting for the risks of the individual stocks) by 5% in the 8 months following the intensive trading by insiders.

According to this finding, then, the strong form of the EMH does not hold. If it is any consolation, you can still outperform the market for any given level of risk by trading on insider information (although your "return" may well include a prison sentence!).

5.4.6 Conclusions on Informational Efficiency

To conclude, we recapitulate a number of important points developed in the course of our discussion of informational efficiency.

There is little or no evidence that stock prices exhibit consistent cycles that could be predicted from past price movements. Prices basically follow a long-run upward trend with random fluctuations around that trend; in other words, a random walk with positive drift. This fact certainly does not imply that stock prices must be fluctuating in an irrational manner. The reason is that prices tend to respond fairly rapidly—but in many cases not instantaneously—and appropriately to new information as it becomes available. Since new information can be either good or bad and is apt to arrive randomly over time, there need not be any serial pattern in the movement of prices from day to day or from month to month.

Within this environment it is possible to realize abnormally high profits by obtaining new information and trading on it ahead of the market. To try to do so, however, is to compete in the "information producing industry" against other analysts. This industry is highly competitive, so the excess returns on producing new information are likely to be driven down to the point where they closely approximate the costs. The information generated by the industry is likely to be worth its cost to large investors, but its value to the individual investor is more doubtful.

All these arguments imply, in turn, that the informational efficiency of the market is high and that consistently outperforming it is very difficult. Indeed, it may be possible only for those with access to "inside" information. That supposition is not to suggest, of course, that investment in the stock market is not worthwhile; even without "beating the market," the investor's available return may still be quite attractive.[48]

6

The Determination
of Equity Prices

Anyone who can predict security prices with reasonable accuracy and consistency will soon be rich. From the discussion of informational efficiency in Chapter 5, it is clear that persons with this ability are rare indeed. This observation does not mean that financial success in the stock market is impossible, merely that success is less likely to be the result of superior forecasting skill than of the willingness to bear risk, of hard work, of inside knowledge, or of sheer luck.

Apart from this rather discouraging insight, does economics have anything helpful to say about the prices of shares and related securities? That is the question addressed in this chapter. We review the most important ideas suggested by economic theory in this area and assess their usefulness in the real world.

First we look at two fairly ancient but still popular models of equity prices, one of which views shares as claims to future dividends and the other as claims to the underlying net assets. For the most part, these models look at the shares of individual companies in isolation, not at the market as a whole; that is their weakness, but the asset model in particular provides important insights into aggregate equity values. As an aside to this discussion we also show that aggregate dividends have the intriguing feature of being an approximately constant percentage of National Income, which means that corporate equities offer protection (though not perfect protection) against inflation as well as participation in the real growth of the economy.

We then take up the Capital Asset Pricing Model, a discovery of the 1960s that, by considering equities in relation to each other, provided important new insights into the relation between risk and return. A more recent alternative known as Arbitrage Pricing Theory is discussed next. Finally there is a section on stock indexes.

6.1 SHARES AS CLAIMS TO FUTURE DIVIDENDS

A share in a corporation is valuable for three reasons:

1. It entitles the owner to such dividends as the corporation may declare
2. It entitles the owner to a portion of any residual value the corporation may have when it is liquidated or acquired by another corporation
3. Its market price may rise over time

The theory of share prices examined in this section focuses on the first of these considerations, while the second is the main topic of the next section. Until further notice, the dividends and liquidation value will both be taken into account. The appreciation mentioned under the third reason may to a large extent be regarded as a secondary effect—a consequence of future dividend actions rather than an independent influence; it is considered only when it is relevant.

We start with the simplest case where future dividends are known and paid annually; the time of liquidation and the liquidation value per share at that time are also known.[1] The present value of these various payments is then

$$PVDL_0 = \frac{Div(1)}{1+r_s} + \frac{Div(2)}{(1+r_s)^2} + \ldots + \frac{Div(t)}{(1+r_s)^t} + \frac{Div(T)+L}{(1+r_s)^T},$$

where $Div(t)$ is the dividend paid at time t, 0 is the present,[2] T is the time of liquidation, L is the liquidation value, and r_s is the relevant discount rate. Since in this initial example the dividends and the liquidation value are assumed to be known, the discount rate should be a default-free rate. The yield on long-term Treasury bonds is usually appropriate because equities are also long-lived securities.

Although the assumption of certainty is obviously unrealistic, it is instructive to pursue this case in more detail. To begin with, we note that if the liquidation time T is at all distant, the final term in the series will normally be small, since it is divided by a high power of the discount factor $(1+r_s)$. Thus if the risk-free rate is 5%, then for $T = 100$ the liquidation value (plus the final dividend) is divided by $(1.05)^{100} = 131.5$: Of every \$1 of liquidation value, less than 1 cent appears in $PVDL$.

It is only when the liquidation value is large and/or liquidation is expected in the near future that the actual magnitude of L makes a significant difference; in that case, the model explained in the next section is more appropriate. There we use the fact that the liquidation value vanishes when the corporation is assumed to have an infinite life.

6.1.1 Steady Growth in the Dividend

Still retaining the certainty assumption, let us look at an important special cases of the $PVDL$ equation. Instead of assuming each dividend to be known separately, it often makes more sense to postulate growth at a given rate to prevail between now and the liquidation time T, so we have

$$Div(t) = (1+g)^t Div(0). \qquad (6.1)$$

The growth rate can then be combined with the discount factor to provide an alternative equation for $PVDL$:

$$PVDL = \sum_{t=1}^{T} \left\{ \frac{(1+g)}{(1+r_s)} \right\}^t Div(0) + \frac{L}{(1+r_s)^T}, \qquad (6.2)$$

where T is again the distant time at which the company is assumed to be liquidated. It is instructive to look at the case where T approaches infinity. As pointed out earlier, the present value of L then goes to zero and only the dividends matter. The present value of all dividends (including the current one) is denoted by PVD (to indicate the suppression of L); it can be evaluated by the well-known formula for the sum of an infinite geometric series:

$$\begin{aligned} PVD &= Div(0) \sum_{t=0}^{\infty} \left\{ \frac{(1+g)}{(1+r_s)} \right\}^t \\ &= \frac{Div(0)}{1-(1+g)/(1+r_s)} \\ &= Div(0) \frac{1+r_s}{r_s-g}. \end{aligned} \qquad (6.3)$$

However, previous formulas for $PVDL$ did not include the current dividend $Div(0)$, which must therefore be subtracted:

$$Div(0) \frac{1+r_s}{r_s-g} - Div(0) = Div(0) \left(\frac{1+r_s}{r_s-g} - 1 \right) = Div(0) \frac{1+g}{r_s-g}. \qquad (6.4)$$

Clearly Equations (6.3) and (6.4) do not make sense if $g \geq r_s$, so we must assume that the growth rate is less than the discount rate. Suppose, for instance, that $r_s = 0.1$ and $g = 0.05$; then the last expression is equal to 21, so the implied stock price is 21 times the next dividend. In the financial markets it is customary to invert the price-dividend ratio, thus obtaining the "dividend yield," usually expressed as a percentage. In formula:

$$y_d = \frac{Div(0)}{PVD} = \frac{r_s-g}{1+g}. \qquad (6.5)$$

In this example the dividend yield is 4.76%, a plausible value.[3] The reader can also verify that when $g=0$ the dividend yield equals the discount rate; this case applies to a preferred share with an infinite life issued by a corporation whose survival is not in doubt. The last proviso, which applies to all the formulas in this section, is not as preposterous as it may seem, since the contribution of very distant dividends to PVD is negligible.

Figure 6.1 shows that the price-dividend ratio is quite sensitive to variations in g. For a given value of r_s, the relation between g and the yield is almost, but not quite, linear. As pointed out by Barsky and DeLong (1993), this sensitivity may explain, incidentally, why share prices fluctuate so much: Expectations of future growth rates of dividends are quite variable. If a firm comes out with disappointing quarterly earnings, for instance, this circumstance will affect the expected growth rate of dividends and will often precipitate a sharp downward correction in the stock price. It is not uncommon for an unpleasant surprise in earnings to slash the price by as much as 50% in one day.

The main implication from the steady-growth model is that the dividend yield on one company's shares will be smaller than that on another company's shares if the first company's dividend is believed to grow faster than the other dividend. Most investors, however, will be more interested in the rate of return, which is the sum of the dividend yield and the relative price change. The latter is found by observing that in Equation (6.5) the right-hand side is independent of time and that $Div(0)$ is always the most recent dividend paid, again regardless of time. Thus the equation holds just as well in 1992 as in 1993, but in 1993 the dividend is $(1+g)$ times larger than in 1992, so the 1993 price must be the same multiple of the 1992 price. The relative price change, therefore, is simply g. It follows that the rate of return equals

$$R_s = y_d + g = \frac{r_s + g^2}{1+g}. \tag{6.6}$$

Some experimentation with plausible numbers for r_s and g will show that R_s is not very sensitive to g, which means that the rate of return (unlike the dividend yield) is approximately independent of the growth rate of dividends.

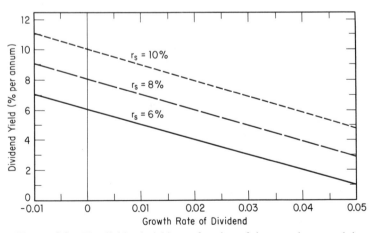

Figure 6.1   The dividend yield as a function of the growth rate and the discount factor

Before we leave the steady-growth model a word of caution is in order. In the real world, corporations and their dividends do not grow at constant rates. This fact was shown long ago by Little (1962) from a study of British companies and was confirmed by Brooks and Buckmaster (1976) for U.S. firms; it no doubt remains true today. The dividends paid by a particular corporation, or by all corporations together, may well have a statistically significant trend, but there is bound to be considerable variance around this trend. The steady-growth model does not take this variance into account—which would be mathematically possible but difficult—and is therefore too incomplete to be taken at face value. Yet the sensitivity of stock prices to expected growth (mentioned in connection with Figure 6.1) suggests that the model continues to be influential.

6.1.2 Aggregate Dividends, Earnings, and Inflation

In Chapter 2 we stressed the importance of inflation in determining the performance of the financial markets. We showed that through the "Fisher effect," bonds offer some protection against inflation, but that nevertheless the ex-post real return on government bonds has sometimes been negative. It is interesting to look at corporate equities from this point of view.

The lower curve in Figure 6.2 shows that during the period since World War II the ratio of aggregate dividends to National Income has been roughly constant at around 3% despite highly variable inflation. In that sense, corporate

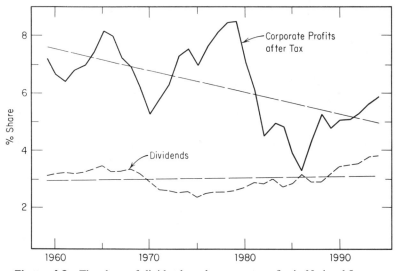

Figure 6.2   The share of dividends and corporate profits in National Income
(%). *Source:*   National Income and Product Accounts, from various issues of the *Survey of Current Business*.

equities have offered a remarkable degree of protection against inflation—more so than bonds. They have also enabled stockholders to participate more or less proportionately in the real growth of the economy.

Closer inspection reveals that the ratio of dividends to National Income declined significantly during the early 1970s but that it returned to the level of the 1950s and 1960s by the end of the period. This finding is all the more remarkable because the ratio of corporate profits after tax to National Income (represented by the top curve) was not only quite variable but also exhibited a distinct downtrend, as shown by the straight lines in the graph. These divergent trends mean that the "payout ratio" (the ratio of dividends to profits after tax) has tended to increase over time.

The contrast between the relatively smooth dividend curve and the volatile earnings curve in Figure 6.2 has another important implication. Since the correlation between aggregate profits and aggregate dividends is evidently quite low, profits have not been a good predictor of dividends, yet financial analysts pay great attention to profits. Are these analysts barking up the wrong tree? No, they are not. Given that dividends are to a large extent predetermined—even though we cannot say how—undistributed profits are used to strengthen corporate net worth. This is an argument against the basic assumption underlying this section, which was that shares are valued primarily for the dividends they are expected to pay in the future (possibly with some allowance for the liquidation value). Clearly that is not the whole story.

6.2 SHARES AS CLAIMS TO CORPORATE NET WORTH

The approach of Section 6.1 emphasized the income stream that is usually associated with share ownership; here we consider an alternative that looks at the net worth of the firm. An example introduces the basic idea.

Suppose a firm, or a group of individuals, wants to enter the supermarket business. There are two possibilities, not necessarily exclusive. One is to open a brand new supermarket, the other is to buy an existing one. The latter possibility can be realized in two ways: either by buying the store itself from its present owners or by buying the entire firm that owns it. The relative merits of these various procedures need not be analyzed here, except for one major consideration: the relative prices. Clearly, buying the firm rather than building a new one or acquiring an existing one will be the more attractive the cheaper the shares.

The same consideration is true in another example exemplified by recent takeover activity. An oil company that plans to increase its oil reserves can do so by conducting its own exploration—at great risk—or by buying an already discovered field from its owners, or by taking over another company with substantial reserves. In the case of small or middle-size oil producers,[4] oil in the ground is typically the major corporate asset. After allowing for other assets and liabilities, it is possible to calculate the valuation for oil reserves that is implicit in the market price for the shares.[5] Unless an oil company has promising exploration prospects of its own, it may well decide that buying another oil company is the cheapest method of expanding its reserves.

In an informationally efficient market, the shares of companies with valuable assets but low or negative earnings would be priced according to the former. Such companies are said to be "worth more dead than alive," and they are prime candidates for liquidation through merger or otherwise. Investors who are interested mostly in current income from dividends would not buy such companies.

The assets that put a company in this category need not be tangible. Thus some companies have tax credits (usually resulting from past losses) that they cannot use for lack of profits but that may become available to a profitable buyer. Conversely, a firm with unused tax credits may seek to take over a profitable company with a view to realizing these credits. It should be borne in mind, however, that the antitrust laws sometimes make it difficult to merge firms within the same industry, and that the Internal Revenue Service may question transactions undertaken only to make tax losses more valuable.

The *PVDL* formula stated in the beginning of Section 6.1 is sufficiently general to cover valuation of corporate equities on the basis of liquidation value rather than future dividends, though the liquidation value is only known with reasonable certainty if a takeover bid is outstanding. The argument advanced there that liquidation can normally be disregarded applies, strictly speaking, only to very large companies (such as General Motors, IBM, and Exxon), whose size makes them virtually impervious to takeover and whose voluntary liquidation is highly unlikely. In recent years, however, many smaller corporations have changed their bylaws to make themselves less vulnerable to "corporate raiders," to use one of the milder terms by which established managers describe those planning to oust them. According to the *PVDL* formula these measures tend to lower the value of the shares.

The notion that share prices are primarily determined by the net value of the underlying assets can be quantified by a ratio known as Tobin's q.[6] In its simplest form, the numerator of this ratio is the market value (*MV*) of an asset and the denominator is the replacement cost (*RC*) of that asset: $q = MV/RC$. If q is low—say, well below 1—those who want to increase their productive capacity will find it advantageous to buy existing assets, thus incidentally driving up the share prices of the companies that own these assets. A high value of q, on the other hand, means that it is cheaper to construct new capacity and to finance this investment by selling securities. The resulting interaction between real investment (that is, construction of additional productive capacity) and the financial markets acts as a self-regulating mechanism for both.

A firm's assets will have a low q if the firm does not make effective use of these assets. Thus a company that built an expensive retail facility in a low-traffic area may find it has created an asset whose market value is below its replacement cost. The same facility, however, may be worth more to another retail firm that is less dependent on traffic because its customers will seek it out wherever it is. Conversely, a well-located restaurant may be worth much more to its owners than its replacement cost, so q will exceed 1.

Pushing this analysis further we can think of q as an indicator of profitability or rate of return. Let R_a be the return on an asset valued at its replacement cost RC, and let r be the cost of capital. Then, assuming for simplicity that the asset has an infinite life, its market value is $MV = (R_a * RC)/r$, which implies $q = MV/RC = R_a/r$. Tobin's q can thus be interpreted as the rate of return on an asset relative to the owner's cost of capital. We can also write $R_a = q * r$. This rate of return R_a on the replacement cost of an asset (or group of assets) can be used in place of the conventional accounting measures of profitability, which are usually based on book value (historical cost) instead of replacement cost. McFarland (1988) simulated the behavior of a conventional accounting measure in comparison with q under different experimental growth and investment conditions. He found that R_a (as defined in the preceding text) had a much higher correlation with true profitability than the traditional measure.

When the concept of q is applied to an entire corporation rather than to specific assets, a complication arises—namely, that corporations usually have liabilities as well as assets. If TA stands for a corporation's total assets valued at replacement cost and TL for its total liabilities (excluding common stock but including preferred stock), then its net worth NW is obviously equal to $TA - TL$.[7] Suppose the market value of the firm (the price per common share multiplied by the number of shares) is MV. A prospective buyer of the entire corporation will normally have to assume the liabilities and will therefore have to pay $MV + TL$ for the assets. It follows that $q = (MV + TL)/TA$.

We may compare this calculation with the ratio of market value to net worth shown for nonfinancial corporations in Table 3.3. This ratio will be called q_1 to distinguish it from q: $q_1 = MV/NW = MV/(TA - TL)$. With a little algebra it can be shown that $q = q_1 + (1 - q_1)TL/TA$. It follows that when q_1 is less than 1 (as it has been in most years for nonfinancial corporations since World War II), q will exceed q_1, but q will also be less than 1 because TL will normally be less than TA (otherwise NW would be negative). On the other hand, if q_1 exceeds 1, it will also exceed q, but q will still be greater than 1. The reader is encouraged to verify these inequalities and to investigate the effect of changes in the ratio of total liabilities to total assets.

Both q and q_1 are useful in analyzing shares as claims to net worth. The former originated in Tobin's theory of investment and is therefore of a macroeconomic nature, while the latter is more directly relevant to the financial markets. A chart of q_1 was given in Figure 3.3. It is complemented by Figure 6.3, which refers to q, and also contains an alternative measure to be discussed in a moment. For convenience, the value 1 is added as a horizontal line.

Let us first look at the solid curve in Figure 6.3. We see that, after a strong rise in the 1950s, q fluctuated around 1 during the 1960s. It then fell, first slowly, then sharply in 1973–74 as inflation had an adverse effect on share

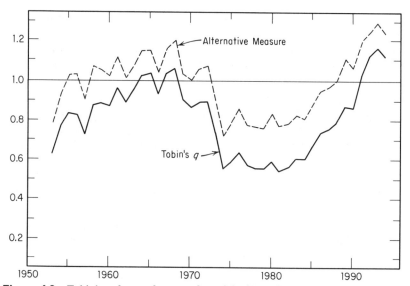

Figure 6.3 Tobin's q for nonfarm nonfinancial corporations, and an alternative measure based on historical cost. *Note:* Farm corporations, which are included in the top curve, were eliminated by assuming that they have the same q_1 as other nonfinancial corporations. Since farm corporations account for about 2% of the new worth of all nonfinancial corporations, this assumption is harmless.

prices even though it raised the underlying asset values. During the following 10 years q remained between 0.5 and 0.6, but in the middle 1980s q began to rise at an accelerating rate. At the end of 1993 q reached a record of 1.165, while q_1 was then at 1.34, also a record. During 1994 both statistics moved a little closer to 1.

What does this this story tell us about q (or q_1) as a tool for assessing aggregate share values? Although there appears to be some tendency for q to settle around 1, as happened in the 1960s and possibly in the 1990s, it cannot be very strong; otherwise it would not have taken q some 15 years to recover from the precipitous drop in 1973–74. One reason for this slow adjustment may be the inability of historical-cost accounting, as codified in the Generally Accepted Accounting Principles (GAAP), to deal with inflation. Since the data used for the solid curve in Figure 6.3 were derived from current-cost accounting, they immediately reflect the rise in asset values due to inflation. Under GAAP this rise is recognized only when the assets are replaced (see Chapter 1).

An alternative to q can be calculated from the historical cost rather than the current cost of tangible assets; it is shown as a dotted curve in Figure 6.3.[8] Since inflation was positive throughout the period of observation, the dotted curve is always above the solid curve, but it should be noted that the distance between the two curves was largest during the 1970s and early 1980s when the inflation rate was unusually high. In those years, therefore, the alternative measure was much closer to 1 than was q. Since most corporations report only according to GAAP, the historical cost of assets may have unduly influenced investors.

The downward bias of reported net worth that is inherent in GAAP was corrected in the fullness of time. The "takeover mania," as it was short-sightedly called, reflected a realization by the acquirers that other corporations were worth more than their balance sheets suggested. The large-scale share repurchases discussed in Chapter 3 reflected a similar belief on the part of managers and directors with respect to their own firms. When q returned to 1, takeovers and repurchases declined.

Some comment is needed on the historically high values of q reached in the last few years. The balance sheet data from the Federal Reserve do not take account of intangible assets, and it is conceivable that these have grown in relative importance over the years. As an example, consider the computer software industry, which hardly existed 20 years ago. A successful software firm need not have large tangible assets, while the value of its intangible assets often does not show up fully on its balance sheet. If intangible assets have in fact become more important, this may explain why at present q is well above 1.

To sum up, the idea that share prices reflect claims to net worth is to some extent supported by aggregate data. The main reason the correlation is far from perfect appears to be twofold: the undervaluation of nonfinancial assets by conventional accounting, and the slowness of the processes by which this undervaluation is eliminated.

6.3 THE CAPITAL ASSET PRICING MODEL

The most powerful framework within which to understand the pricing of shares has proven to be the Capital Asset Pricing Model (CAPM), developed by Sharpe, Lintner, and Mossin in the 1960s. Essentially it asks the following question: If all investors understand and act on the benefits of portfolio diversification and the distinction between systematic and unsystematic risk (discussed in Chapter 4), what does this imply about the prices of the securities of firms that differ in earning capacity and profit volatility?

We begin to answer this question by setting out CAPM in its most basic form. Despite the imposition of some rather restrictive initial assumptions, this approach will provide us with some important and workable results. The next subsection explores the removal of a number of these unwelcome assumptions in order to help us understand the robustness of our earlier conclusions in the more complex world of reality: when the model is applicable and under what circumstances we might need to reassess its findings.

This exploration suggests that CAPM has quite wide applicability. Our next concern is its implementation and, in particular, how an estimate of the model's key element, the β_i (beta, also called systematic risk) of each stock, may be obtained from readily available data. With theory and data in hand, we then examine the practical implications of these equity pricing results for portfolio management. In Section 6.3.5 we show, however, that despite its theoretical appeal and its importance in financial economics the empirical validity of CAPM is open to serious doubt; this discussion sets the stage for an alternative model considered in Section 6.4.

6.3.1 The Simplest Form of CAPM

In Chapter 4 we developed the concept of a set of efficient portfolios. Each portfolio belonging to this set represents the mix of individual stocks that minimizes the volatility of the return for any desired level of expected return. These efficient portfolios can be designed by taking account of the degree to which returns on the underlying securities fluctuated together versus the degree to which the fluctuation in one offset the fluctuations in another; in other words, they reflect the full benefits of diversification.

One of the central assumptions of CAPM is that the market is dominated by risk-averse investors who practice optimal diversification to stabilize their returns. The basic form of CAPM further postulates that all investors have the same expectations concerning the returns on the various securities, and concerning the variances and covariances of these returns.

It is also assumed that the market is an efficient processor of information in the sense described in Chapter 5: News that might influence the earnings of firms, or other relevant variables, is rapidly—indeed, immediately—available to all investors at negligible cost, so that it is immediately reflected in estimates of the future mean and variance of returns. Transactions costs are ignored throughout.

In its basic form, the model also abstracts from the complexities of "real-time" income and spending decisions. Its derivation is structured on the basis that all investors have the same "single-period" investment horizon over which the real interest rate is fixed. Individuals are assumed to borrow or lend at that rate at no risk regardless of the amount they need to optimize their portfolio decisions. This assumption implies that the net worth of individual investors is irrelevant; even a pennyless trader can hold a portfolio worth millions of dollars, since he or she can borrow its entire value.

The application of this final assumption provides us with an efficient portfolio frontier. By choosing a given portfolio Z, consisting of risky assets, and mixing it with varying proportions of investment in the risk-free investment, which returns the guaranteed real interest rate, an investor can achieve any desired level of portfolio risk.[9] If 100% of an investor's wealth were loaned, it would earn precisely the risk-free rate. If, on the other hand, 100% were placed in the portfolio Z, he or she would anticipate receiving the "expected return" on that portfolio as calculated in Chapter 4, but with a risk equal to the variance of the return on that portfolio.

If A represents the proportion placed in the portfolio of equities, and $1-A$ the proportion loaned out at the risk-free rate r, the expected return and risk of the joint portfolio would be:

$$E_p = (1-A)r + AE_z;$$

$$V_p = (1-A)0 + AV_z,$$

where E_z and V_z are the expected return and variance of the free-standing portfolio of risky assets, respectively. The risk-return trade-off available by choosing different proportions of risk-free lending and the equities portfolio Z are therefore shown to be the straight line rZ in Figure 6.4.

This trade-off line may be improved, however, by choosing a different portfolio (such as Y) with which to mix the risk-free investment. Here the trade-off is steeper: It offers a greater increase in expected return for every unit of additional risk. The steepest trade-off curve possible will be obtained by selecting the portfolio of risky assets that lies exactly where a line from the point r is tangent to the efficient frontier. In Figure 6.4 this portfolio corresponds to the risk-return combination M.

Suppose now that an investor wishes to accept greater volatility and higher return than is offered by placing 100% of his or her wealth in the portfolio M. The investor could choose one of the portfolios on the original efficient frontier to the right of M. A better (steeper) risk-return trade-off could be achieved,

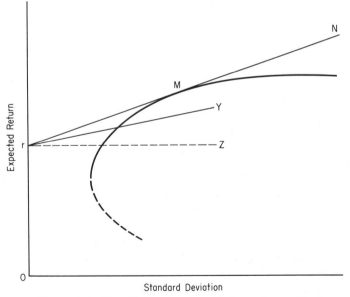

Figure 6.4   The efficient frontier with borrowing and lending

however, by borrowing money at the known interest rate and investing it in the portfolio M. In this case, the expected return and associated variance would be:

$$E_p = (1+A)E_M - Ar;$$

$$V_p = (1+A)V_M + A0,$$

where Ar is the interest payment on the borrowing while E_M and V_M are the expected return and the variance of portfolio M. These opportunities are equivalent to a rightward continuation of the straight line running through M to N.

When it is possible to borrow and lend at a known real rate of interest, the efficient portfolio frontier becomes the straight line rMN. The individual's net worth and attitude toward risk will then determine the final point he or she chooses on that line. Notice, however, that it does not influence the optimal composition of the equity portfolio M. An individual's wealth and risk preference alter the total size of his or her investment in equities relative to lending or depositing funds at risk-free interest rate, but they have no effect on the best mix of individual equities to buy. This result is known as the *separation theorem* because it implies that the decision of how much total risk to accept is separate from the decision what equities to buy.

According to this theorem, the best combination of individual stocks follows from objective [10] factors, namely, the mean and variance of expected return and the covariances between the returns on individual stocks. The subjective decision of how much total risk to accept is implemented by choosing the amount of funds invested in the fixed portfolio M rather than by varying the composition of the equity portfolio. That unique portfolio of equities M is known as the *market portfolio*.

The new "straight-line" efficient frontier derived from this analysis is known as the *capital market line* (CML). Its equation may be written as follows: $E_p = r + (E_m - r)(\sigma_p/\sigma_M)$, where σ_p and σ_M are the standard deviations of the chosen portfolio and the market portfolio, respectively.

The slope of the CML shows the compensation offered by the market (in terms of higher expected return) for bearing greater nondiversifiable risk. For any standard deviation of return (σ_p) accepted by an investor, the CML shows the highest level of expected return offered by the market, as illustrated in Figure 6.5. The slope coefficient itself is known as the *market price of risk,* or MPR for short:

$$MPR = \frac{E_M - r}{\sigma_M}.$$

In the world of CAPM, where diversification is uninhibited by transactions costs, indivisibilities, restrictions on short selling, or lack of information, any investor who fails to reap the full benefits of diversification is, quite simply, a fool. The portfolio he or she ends up with is more risky than it need be, given its expected return. According to the model, the market will pay no premium for shouldering an unnecessary burden by failing to diversify properly.

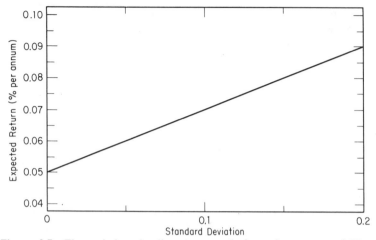

Figure 6.5   The capital market line: An example for an interest rate of 5% per annum

Let us return to the slope of the CML. Consider the following chain of logic. The CML indicates the amount of extra return offered by the market for every additional point of systematic risk in our portfolio. If we can then measure exactly how much systematic risk an individual stock adds to our portfolio, we could calculate the extra return that the market would offer us in order to buy that stock and include it in the portfolio.

What is our portfolio? If we are optimizers (and, as assumed, share the common expectations as to risk and return), we must choose market portfolio M. How much risk does an individual stock contribute to that portfolio if included in the correct proportion? Clearly the unsystematic component of its volatility will net out when mixed with the large number of other stocks in the portfolio. To the extent that it fluctuates in line with other stocks within the portfolio, however, it will exacerbate the total volatility of the portfolio.

The correct measure of how much risk a stock on net brings to the portfolio M will be proportional to the covariance between fluctuations in its return and fluctuations in the returns on all other stocks in the portfolio. Specifically, this will be measured by the covariance between an individual stock i and the portfolio M, expressed per unit of the portfolio standard deviation σ_M: cov_{iM}/σ_M. The return compensation for holding the stock will then be equal to the known interest rate r, plus the market price of risk MPR, multiplied by this index of extra portfolio risk:

$$E_i = r + MPR(\text{cov}_{iM}/\sigma_M) = r + (E_M - r)(\text{cov}_{iM}/\sigma_M^2).$$

The final expression in parentheses, a measure of the stock's systematic risk, is known to every analyst on Wall Street—and in many other parts of the world— as the beta of that stock. A beta greater than 1 identifies a stock as "aggressive"

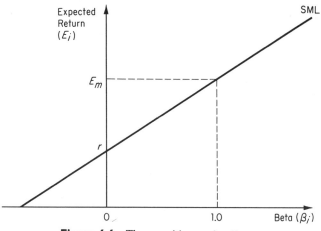

Figure 6.6 The securities market line

in the sense that it is correlated with the market portfolio in such a way that when the market moves in a particular direction, it is likely to be moving even faster in that same direction. Stocks with betas of less than 1 are "defensive" in that they move proportionately less in any particular direction than the portfolio as a whole. A stock with a negative beta actually moves countercyclically with the market portfolio.[11] The market portfolio itself moves exactly in proportion to its own fluctuations and so has a beta of 1.

These relationships are commonly expressed graphically as the securities market line (SML) shown in Figure 6.6, which has the following equation: $E_i = r + \beta_i(E_M - r)$, where β_i is the beta coefficient for stock i: $\beta_i = \text{cov}_{iM}/\sigma_M^2$. The SML therefore gives the expected return "required" by the market for holding a particular security, given the risk-free interest rate, the expected return and variance on the market portfolio, and the beta (or systematic risk) of that stock.

By providing a required rate of return for a security, CAPM also tells a good deal about how that security will be priced by the market. Suppose that a stock is expected, but far from certainly, to sell for $50 one year from now, including the value of any dividend declared but not paid. At what price should it trade on the exchange today?

The Capital Asset Pricing Model helps answer this question. First, it is necessary to obtain an estimate of the systematic risk (beta) of the stock and the expected return on the market portfolio M. Various means of constructing these estimates are discussed later in this chapter. Second, we need a measure of the relevant risk-free rate. In this case the prevailing rate on one-year Treasury securities would be appropriate. This information can then be plugged into the equation for the securities market line to produce an estimate of the required rate of return E_i. Suppose the T-bill rate is 10%, the expected return on the market portfolio is 15%, and the beta of stock i is estimated at 1.5. In that case:

$E_i = 10\% + 1.5(15\% - 10\%) = 17.5\%$. We can then use the following relation between the expected return and the current stock price: $E_i = \{E(P_1) - P_0\}/P_0$, where $E(P_1)$ is the expected price at the end of the year and P_0 is the current price.

Rewriting this equation we have: $P_0 = E(P_1)/(1 + E_i)$. In other words, the market price now should be equal to the expected future price discounted by the required rate of return (which allows for the systematic risk of the stock). Substituting the numerical values in our example, CAPM would put the current price of the stock at: $P_0 = \$50/(1 + 0.175) = \$42.55$. Note that a similar stock with higher systematic risk would have a lower current price in the market. For example, with a beta of 2.0 the corresponding values would be:

$$E_i = 10\% + 2.0(15\% - 10\%) = 20\%;$$

$$P_0 = \$50/1.20 = \$41.67.$$

It is also important to observe that the current stock price produced by this calculation depends only on the systematic risk, not on the unsystematic risk, which can be eliminated by diversification. If the "total volatility" of a security is defined as the sum of the systematic and the unsystematic risk, then it is clear that a low-beta stock may well be a highly volatile stock, and conversely. Volatility matters only to the extent it is correlated with the market portfolio.

Before leaving the basic version of CAPM just presented to explore some extensions, a comment on the concept of "market portfolio" is in order. Interestingly, it turns out that if the market prices equities according to CAPM, then the market portfolio is made up of all stocks in the market, each in proportion to the total market value of the stock in the particular company that issued it. Thus, if the total value of IBM stock accounts for 5% of the total value of all corporate stocks in the market, then 5% of the market portfolio will be in IBM. Since the market portfolio represents optimal diversification of nonsystematic risk, it follows that all individuals should allocate 5% of their total investment in equities to IBM stock, and similarly for all other stocks (at least in the strict CAPM world).

6.3.2 Extending the CAPM

As we have already noted, the basic form of CAPM involves a number of rather unwelcome assumptions in the sense that they contradict observed reality. In this section we examine a number of extensions to the basic model that allow us to relax some of those assumptions. Fortunately it can be shown that the major CAPM results remain fairly robust.

One assumption used to derive the basic CAPM is that all investors hold the same expectations about the future value of stocks and the corresponding variances of returns. Lintner (1970) has shown, however, that the model can be worked through with heterogeneous expectations among investors by expressing expected values, variances, and covariances as weighted averages of the expectations of different individuals, leaving the results essentially intact. The major departure from the basic model is that investors with different expectations will choose different portfolios rather than duplicating the same market portfolio.[12]

A second unwelcome assumption employed in the basic derivation of CAPM is the existence of a risk-free asset with a certain real interest rate at which investors could borrow or lend. As we have stressed a number of times in this book, when inflation is present there is really no such thing as a "risk-free" asset. Even money or government bonds have a risky real rate of return, given the uncertainty surrounding the future rate of inflation. The only truly risk-free instrument in this context would be an index-linked government-guaranteed bond.[13]

To overcome this difficulty, Black (1972) has presented a version of CAPM where there is no risk-free asset, yet beta remains the correct risk measure. Briefly, the risk-free asset is replaced by a "zero-beta" portfolio whose return shows no systematic correlation with the market. In reality, most stocks are positively correlated with general movements in the market to some degree. We can still construct a zero-beta portfolio, however, by selling some stocks short, so that we lose money when these stocks rise in price and gain money when their price falls. In this way, it is possible to create return streams that are negatively correlated with the market even when the stock price itself is positively correlated.

Yet another assumption that needs to be reconsidered is the requirement that investors base their decisions on a single period horizon over which the rate of interest on the risk-free asset (or the return on the zero-beta portfolio) does not vary. In reality, investors tend to have multiperiod horizons over which interest rates and expected returns may fluctuate significantly.

In an important 1973 paper, Merton tackled this problem by deriving a version of CAPM that assumed investment and trading occur continuously over time and that interest rates fluctuate. This formulation results in an equation for the required rate of return on a stock very similar to the SML, but with the addition of a second term involving another beta (β_2). A stock now has systematic risk not only to the extent that its return fluctuates in sympathy with the market portfolio (as measured by what is now called β_1), but also to the extent that it is correlated with movements in the risk-free rate. It is this second source of systematic risk that the term involving β_2 allows for.

Finally, we should mention a recent extension of CAPM that ties in with the discussion of time preference discussed in Chapter 4. The original CAPM looks at individuals only as investors who seek to maximize the return on their assets, which are assumed to be determined by factors outside the model. In reality, individuals are not merely investors; their portfolio decisions are incidental to more important decisions, such as how much to save for their old age and how to be prepared for economic uncertainties prior to retirement. What individuals and their families maximize is not primarily the return on their assets, but consumption during their lifetime (possibly augmented by intended bequests).

The consumption CAPM (CCAPM), developed by Breeden (1979), views investment in these broader terms. It considers not just the covariance between particular securities and the market portfolio but the covariance between securities and earnings from work. An automobile worker, for instance, would be ill-advised to invest in automotive shares—especially in his or her own firm—since they are likely to be depressed precisely when he or she needs cash because of layoffs or part-time work schedules. From this point of view, bonds are a better investment because interest rates are likely to fall (and hence bond prices likely to rise) during a recession.[14] Similarly, a firm that has a pension fund for its employees may not serve them well if it invested the fund in its own shares.

Although it may also be viewed as an extension of CAPM, Ross' Arbitrage Pricing Theory is sufficiently different to warrant a separate section (6.4).

6.3.3 Estimating Betas

The lynchpin of the basic CAPM and its extended versions is clearly the measure of systematic risk, beta. To make the model operational as a pricing tool, our next task must therefore be to devise a means of obtaining workable estimates of beta for individual stocks.

One widely adopted method is to estimate beta from past data on actual returns provided by a stock and the market as a whole. Returns on the stock may be calculated directly from past dividends and price movements. The return on the market is usually approximated by computing the return on some market index such as the S&P500 or Value-Line. Given these data and a measure of the risk-free rate derived from yields on government bonds, multiple regression analysis can be applied to the following form of the SML:

$$R_{it} - r_t = a_i + b_i(R_{mt} - r_t) + u_{it},$$

where R_{it} is the actual return on stock i in each past period t, R_{mt} is the actual return on a market index r_t is the yield on bonds, and u_{it} is a random error term assumed to satisfy the usual assumptions for unbiased and efficient regression estimates of a_i and b_i.

Recall that the theoretical derivation of the SML implies that $a_i = 0$ and that b_i will be a measure of systematic risk of the stock i. In fact, most empirical work finds that $a_i > 0$—that is, low beta stocks are systematically underpriced compared with what CAPM would suggest.

Overall, however, this method appears to have provided useful estimates of beta and is currently employed on a regular basis by a number of major U.S. brokerage houses. The major limitations are twofold. First, past systematic risk behavior is not necessarily a good measure of future behavior. The second, and related, problem is that actual measures of beta derived from this methodology tend to be relatively unstable from one sample period to the next. The main alternative approach is to use a number of fundamental indicators of the underlying firm's operations and financial structure in order to predict the beta of a stock. Rosenberg and McKibben (1973) provided some of the main results in this area.

In respect of one important parameter of financial structure, CAPM itself implies that the beta of a levered firm will increase linearly with the ratio of debt to equity in its balance sheet. Specifically, it can be shown that $\beta_L = \beta_U 1 + (1 - TC)(D/E)$, where β_L is the beta of a levered firm, β_U is the beta of an otherwise identical unlevered firm, TC is the corporate tax rate, and D/E is the ratio of debt to equity in the levered firm's balance sheet.

In addition to leverage, Rosenberg and McKibben identify a number of other financial and operating measures that prove useful in predicting beta for individual firms, including their level of liquidity (liquid assets over current liabilities), the importance of fixed plant in the total assets (inability to reduce capacity and fixed overhead during downswings increased the volatility of earnings), growth in total assets and sales, and so on. Once these factors are taken into account, they find that the historical beta has little additional predictive power.

Despite this work, however, the accuracy of beta forecasts remains relatively low, rendering the prediction of beta an important hurdle to implementation of the CAPM approach to equity pricing. We return to this subject in Section 6.3.5, where the validity of CAPM is considered in light of recent evidence. For the time being, however, we maintain CAPM as our working hypothesis.

6.3.4 Implications for Portfolio Management

Under the strict assumptions of CAPM, the resulting separation theorem suggests a very straightforward approach to portfolio management: Simply divide the total investment in equities according to the proportions implied in the market portfolio so as to reap maximum benefit from diversification, then mix this portfolio with an investment in the risk-free asset so as to reach the desired combination of risk and expected return. In fact, the advent of "index funds" in recent years (a way of roughly emulating the market portfolio) has come close to putting this approach into practice.

Many investors and portfolio managers, however, partly justified on the information generated by their own research operations, believe they are able to identify stocks that will outperform the market. Of course, if they could be certain of abnormally high returns from these investments, it would clearly make sense to invest their entire portfolio in such stocks. Except for insider trading, however, the most that research is likely to identify is an expectation of abnormal return (i.e., above the "required return" estimated by the SML given its beta), an expectation that itself has some degree of uncertainty. In this case, we can think in terms of an "expected abnormal return," which is the investor's best guess, and some "variance of abnormal return" around this expected value.

Placing a higher proportion of our portfolio in these "active" stocks will move us away from the optimal diversification associated with the "passive" market portfolio and thus increase the total variance of return our equity investment. In other words, it leads us to accept some unnecessary systematic risk. At the same time, because we expect some abnormal return by investing in the active stocks, the overall expected return on the unbalanced portfolio will be higher. The question then becomes, How much should we unbalance our portfolio, if we believe we can identify some stocks on which we expect abnormal returns?

To answer this question, the investor or portfolio manager must estimate the mean abnormal return he or she expects (EA_i) for each active stock i and the variance associated with this estimate (VA_i); essentially the degree of confidence about whether or not an abnormal return will eventuate.

It has been shown (Harvard Business School, 1971) that the proportion of each stock in the active portfolio (a_i) should be such that: $a_i = \lambda(EA_i/VA_i)$, where λ is a constant that will be discussed in a moment. The interpretation of this result is quite straightforward. The higher the proportion of the active portfolio placed in the ith stock is, the larger its expected abnormal return (EA_i) and the smaller the variance of this expected abnormal return (VA_i) will be; that is, the more certain the abnormal return is. The optimal split between the passive market portfolio and the active portfolio is then given by the equation

$$F = \lambda \frac{E_M - r}{\sigma_M^2} - \sum_{i=1}^{n} a_i \beta_i,$$

where F is the fraction of the total amount to be invested, which should be placed in the market portfolio. It will be noted that the beta of each active stock appears in this second formula, because the market portfolio is effectively acting as a hedge against the volatility of the active stocks. If these active stocks have high betas (i.e., move closely in sympathy with the market portfolio), then the market portfolio is a less attractive hedge, hence less of it will be held. Conversely, low betas indicate that the market portfolio is a good hedge against the volatility of the active stocks and so it will make sense to buy more of the market portfolio.

What these two equations actually define is a new CML, taking into account our expectations about abnormal returns. The only unknown that remains to be determined is λ, which indicates where we end up on the CML: how much we place in equities and how much in the risk-free asset. As before, this figure is determined by the individual's subjective risk-return preferences. Once the desired overall risk and expected value mix is chosen, we can solve for λ, which in turn may be substituted to compute the proportions F (investment in the market portfolio) and a_i (the fraction invested in each individual active stock).

An example serves to elucidate the preceding approach. Suppose you have identified three stocks, ABC, MNO, and XYZ, that you believe will outperform the market over the coming year. The unsophisticated investor may simply conclude that the entire portfolio should be placed in these stocks. As we have seen, however, this decision would involve accepting a high level of unsystematic risk

Table 6.1 Sample Assessments of Abnormal
Return

| Stock | Estimated Excess Return | | Beta |
	Mean	Variance	
ABC	5%	200	2.0
MNO	2%	80	1.0
XYZ	4%	20	0.5

Notes: Risk-free rate $= 10\%$; expected return on market
portfolio $= 15\%$; variance of return on market portfolio $= 25$.

that could otherwise be diversified away. Not surprisingly, in a highly efficient
and generally sophisticated market such as that for stocks, your belief must be
given more precise empirical form before it can be successfully put into practice.
You might produce the subjective estimates of mean abnormal return and the
variance of that return shown in Table 6.1. The next step is then to estimate or
collect from published sources values for the beta or overall systematic risk of
each of your chosen stocks, shown in the final column of the table.

By direct substitution into the equations for the a_i already shown, we are
able to produce the expressions, still containing one unknown λ, given in the
first column of Table 6.2. We can then substitute into the equation for the optimal proportion in the market portfolio:

$$F = \frac{20-10}{25}\,\lambda - (0.1\lambda + 0.025\lambda + 0.1\lambda) = 0.4\lambda - 0.225\lambda = 0.175\lambda.$$

Suppose, then, that you wish to keep a core 10% of your portfolio invested in a
"risk-free" asset such as T-bills. With this information we can use the fact that
the portfolio proportions must sum to 100% (i.e., 1.0), hence:

$$\sum_{i=1}^{n} a_i + F + RF = 1.0,$$

where RF is the proportion in the risk-free investment. Substituting the values in
Table 6.2 we have $0.275\lambda + 0.175\lambda + 0.1 = 1.0$, which implies $\lambda = 2.0$. Using

Table 6.2 Optimal Portfolio Composition

Asset	Intermediate Calculation	Optimal Proportion
ABC	0.05λ	10%
MNO	0.025λ	5%
XYZ	0.2λ	40%
Market portfolio	0.175λ	35%
T-bills	Chosen on basis of risk preference	10%

this value for λ, we can then compute the optimal proportions, completing the final column of Table 6.2. Note the high proportion placed in XYZ, reflecting the fact that a substantial abnormal return (4%) is expected with considerable certainty (a relatively low variance of 20).[15]

6.3.5 The Validity of CAPM

So far we have assumed that CAPM holds at least approximately, and we have explored its implications and ramifications. This means that we have tentatively accepted its assumptions—for the sake of argument, as it were. Any model simplifies reality in order to arrive at conclusions. If a model is to be useful, these simplifications should be relatively harmless, in the sense that minor departures from the assumptions do not seriously affect the conclusions. How do we know if CAPM is valid in the real world?

The essence of CAPM is expressed by the SML, which says that the return on any security is a linear function of its beta. In a recent paper, Fama and French (1992) looked closely at this functional relation in a large cross section of equities. Their findings can only be described as devastating: There appears to be no connection between beta and return at all. They explain the return on the securities in their sample by two other factors, namely, the size of the corporation and the ratio between market value and book value.[16] When these two factors are taken into account, beta adds nothing to the explanation. Since they deal carefully with the problems in estimating beta discussed in Section 6.3.3, their surprising results cannot be attributed to errors of measurement.

Where does this finding leave CAPM? The work of Fama and French is so recent that detailed reaction from other experts is not yet available. It is too early to assign CAPM to the scrap heap, but obviously its status as the "ruling paradigm" in financial economics has been undermined. Fortunately there is an alternative model, to which we now turn.

6.4 ARBITRAGE PRICING THEORY: AN ALTERNATIVE APPROACH

The CAPM has many attractive features and, as we have already shown, must be credited with a number of potentially useful applications in the area of securities pricing and portfolio management. At the same time it is also clear that, even in its extended form, CAPM requires some unwelcome assumptions and that the central concept of beta has not stood up in recent tests. There is also the problem, mentioned in Section 6.3.2, that when an inflationary environment renders all real returns uncertain, the model in its simplest form cannot be subjected to a decisive test of validity.

In 1976, Ross presented an alternative, more general model with a number of similarities to CAPM, which he called the "Arbitrage Pricing Theory." The name reflects the simple, yet powerful, principle on which the model is based: that a portfolio with no risk, which mixes long and short positions in such a way that it requires no net investment of wealth, must earn zero return in a market with no transactions costs. In other words, the prices of stocks in a market should be such that it is not possible to make a profit by simply arbitraging between different stocks without making any net investment or accepting any risk. If this were not the position, investors would quickly identify the opportunities to make "pure profit" and the resulting trading would cause prices to adjust until these opportunities were eliminated.

The model begins with the assumption that the actual return realized on any security is equal to its expected return plus a series of unexpected impacts on return, each of which is caused by some uncertain "risk factor" (such as inflation), each multiplied by a coefficient that reflects the systematic degree of sensitivity of the stock to that risk factor. Mathematically, this may be written as:

$$R_i = E_i + \beta_{i1}F_1 + \beta_{i2}F_2 + \ldots + \beta_{ik}F_k + u_i,$$

where R_i is the realized return on security i, E_i is its expected return, β_{ij} represents the sensitivity of the actual return on i to the jth risk factor (F_j), and u_i is a random "white noise" term that averages to zero. This β_{ij} evidently has a family resemblance to the beta of CAPM but should not be confused with it.

By combining the equation just given with the condition that there should be no opportunities for pure arbitrage profits, Ross was able to derive the following expression for the expected return on a stock:

$$E_i = \beta_0 + \beta_{i1}\alpha_1 + \beta_{i2}\alpha_2 + \ldots + \beta_{ik}\alpha_k.$$

Intuitively, this implies that the expected return on the ith security is equal to a constant return (the return on a risk-free investment), plus the sensitivity of the return on the stock to each risk factor (the β_i), times the "market price" or compensation offered by the market for accepting more exposure to that type of risk (the α_j).

Provided we have data on more stocks than there are relevant risk factors, it is possible to estimate the betas or "loadings" (from which the underlying movements in the risk factors can then be reconstructed) by a multivariate statistical technique appropriately known as "factor analysis." Tests using this methodology by Roll and Ross (1980) and Chen (1983) have found that the differences in estimated betas (sensitivities to different sources of risk) perform well in explaining variations in returns across securities and improve on those derived from CAPM.

This finding leads us to the conclusion that there are other types of systematic risk that are relevant to the determination of stock prices in addition the nondiversifiable risk associated with movements in the return on the market (which is the source of risk measured by the traditional CAPM beta). Little headway has been made in applying the APT approach, however.

The basic stumbling block is that the model does not identify the risk factors in terms of measurable variables such as inflation or GNP growth.[17] Moreover, even the actual factors estimated in empirical models do not appear to be readily recognizable in terms of such familiar variables. We are therefore unable to forecast the movements in the risk factors in a way that could make the model useful for predictive purposes. Despite its faults, CAPM thus remains the basic workhorse for computing the "required" rate of return on a stock in any period, given an estimate of its systematic risk.

6.5 APPENDIX: STOCK INDEXES

When we overhear someone in the subway saying "the market was down 10 points," most of us know which market he or she meant, and many of us also know what the "points" refer to—namely, the change in the Dow Jones Industrial index (DJI). This index is the oldest and most popular indicator of equity prices but it is not the only one and certainly not the best. Like all price indexes, the Dow is intended to summarize the diverse movements of a number of prices—in this case, the prices of the thirty stocks that are included. Since at present more than 6,000 stocks are regularly traded on exchanges or in the over-the-counter market, one may wonder how the price changes in so many equities can be adequately summarized by an index based on so few.

6.5.1 The Three Main Indexes

First look at Figure 6.7, where annual averages of three commonly used stock price indexes are plotted from 1949 to 1990. In addition to the DJI, these are the New York Stock Exchange Composite Index, covering all equities listed on that exchange, and Standard & Poor's index of 500 stocks (S&P500). The vertical scale is logarithmic; the difference between the high and low values is so large that the ordinary linear scale would not be suitable. The use of logarithms also makes it possible to show the percentage growth rates over the period, which correspond to the slopes of the three straight lines.

It is clear that the annual percentage changes in the three indexes are highly correlated and that their growth rates are very similar.[18] Actually the growth rates of the S&P500 and the NYSE Composite are virtually the same, but the growth rate of the DJI is significantly smaller: In the 1950s, the DJI was typically about eleven times the S&P500, but in the 1980s it was only about eight times the S&P500.

This difference in performance is due to two factors that cannot easily be distinguished. The first factor is the nature of the stocks covered by the two indexes: The DJI includes thirty large corporations, many of which are of the "smokestack" variety—these are in capital-intensive industries that have generally not done as well as the "high-tech" companies, of which there are relatively

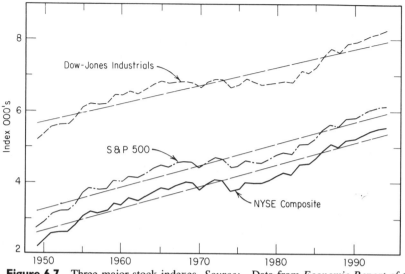

Figure 6.7 Three major stock indexes. *Source:* Data from *Economic Report of the President*, February 1995, table B-96.

more in the S&P500 (and also in the NYSE). The second factor has to do with the way the indexes are calculated and requires more detailed explanation.

Most price index numbers, including the three mentioned at this point, may be represented by the formula

$$I_t = I_0 \frac{w_1 p_{1t} + w_2 p_{2t} + \ldots + w_n p_{nt}}{w_1 p_{10} + w_2 p_{20} + \ldots + w_n p_{n0}},$$

where t is the current time period, 0 is the "base period," I_0 is the value of the index in the base period, n is the number of components (P), and w_i ($i = 1$ to n) is the relative importance or "weight" of the ith component.[19] The DJI is an "unweighted" index, which means that all of the w_i are equal to 1. In the S&P500 and the NYSE Composite, by contrast, the weight of each stock reflects the number of shares outstanding; thus large companies with many shares, such as IBM or AT&T, have a much heavier weight than other stocks.

Now we examine the effect of a stock split. Suppose Texaco, a component of all three indexes, splits 2 for 1 (as explained in Chapter 3), and suppose, furthermore, that before the split there were 10 million shares outstanding and that the price was $50 per share. After the split, there are 20 million shares outstanding and the price is $25 per share; the market value remains at $500 million.[20] In the S&P500 and the NYSE Composite, the weight of Texaco, reflecting the number of shares, will simply be doubled, thus leaving the overall value of the index unchanged, since the price of Texaco shares (both in the current and in the base period) is simultaneously reduced by one-half.

In the Dow Jones, however, the weight is always unity so it cannot be doubled. Instead, the value of I_0 in the above equation is adjusted so as to leave the value of the index unchanged. Suppose the prices of the twenty-nine other stocks in the DJI added up to 600; then the DJI was at 650 before the Texaco split. After the split, the Dow would be 625 if no adjustment were made. Consequently, Dow Jones multiplies I_0 by $650/625 = 1.04$. Somewhat confusingly, the current value of I_0 is known as the "multiplier," and we see that it changes every time a component of the DJI varies the number of outstanding shares by a stock split, stock dividend, or otherwise.[21]

The compilers of the S&P500 and the NYSE Composite also have to deal with another problem—namely, sales and purchase by a corporation of its own shares. From Chapter 3 we know that significant sales of shares are mostly associated with new issues. A stock dividend also increases the number of shares outstanding, and so does a Dividend Reinvestment Plan under which stockholders may choose to receive their dividends in the form of additional shares. Yet another possibility is that the company's convertible securities (bonds or preferred stock) or its warrants are converted into common stock.

The treatment of net issues, whether positive or negative, in the weighted stock indexes (particularly the S&P500 and the NYSE Composite) is basically simple and the same for the various possibilities discussed in the preceding paragraph. Suppose a corporation has 100 million shares outstanding and issues 10 million new shares. Its weight in the index is then increased by 10%. If instead the same corporation were to buy back 10 million shares, its weight would be reduced by 10%.

Could this straightforward procedure be a source of bias? It could be if the decision by a corporation to issue new shares, or to repurchase some of its outstanding shares, affects the market price of the stock. This effect will occur if the demand curve for the shares involved is downward sloping; in other words, if there is price elasticity.[22] A new issue will then tend to depress the market price and a repurchase will tend to enhance the market price. The magnitude of this effect will vary inversely with the price elasticity of demand for the stock; thus if a new issue raises the number of outstanding shares by 10%, then the price, everything else remaining the same, will fall by 10% divided by the price elasticity. If the price elasticity is very high (that is, if the demand curve is nearly flat), the price effect would be negligible, but if the elasticity is two, the stock price would fall by 5%. In the latter case this would be approximately equivalent to a 1.05 for one stock split, but the corresponding adjustment in the weight is not made. Under the same elasticity assumption, a repurchase of 10% would be approximately equivalent to an 0.95 for one reverse split.

Since these adjustments for implied splits are not made, it follows that corporations issuing new shares get too large a weight in the index, whereas repurchasing corporations get too small a weight. We are not proposing that such adjustments be made; that would be difficult since the relevant price elasticities are not known. It is also clear that any bias is small in the short run. It may be significant if net issues are either positive or negative over a long stretch of years, as they were in the 1980s. In any case, it should be realized that stock indexes such as the S&P500 or the NYSE Composite do not necessarily give an accurate picture of average share values in the long run.

6.5.2 Some Other Stock Indexes

None of the three indexes discussed so far covers more than a fraction of the more than 6,000 equities that are currently traded on the exchanges or over the counter. Because the prices of most equities are positively correlated, this limitation is not as serious as it may seem. Nevertheless, there is a need for more comprehensive indicators. The most comprehensive of these is called the Wilshire Associates Equity Index, though strictly speaking it is not an index number at all. It is an estimate of the total value of all stocks traded in the United States and therefore corresponds to the numerator in the preceding equation.[23] On April 12, 1991, for instance, the Wilshire "index" had a value of $3,647 billion. This value was 10% higher than a year earlier, but it is not clear that comparisons over time are meaningful. Other fairly comprehensive measures are the Value Line Index and the Russell 3,000 index.

There are also many stock indexes that cover particular classes of stocks. Thus, the NYSE Composite index has counterparts on the American Stock Exchange and on NASDAQ (the automated quotation system covering the OTC markets). Supplementing the DJI, which refers to "industrials" (rather broadly defined), Dow Jones also has indexes for transportation and for utilities. The *Wall Street Journal* (owned by Dow Jones) publishes daily indexes for a great many industries. In addition to the Russell 3,000 index just mentioned, there is a Russell 2,000 index that covers smaller companies. Recently, Standard & Poor has started publishing an index of 400 smaller stocks not included in the S&P500; it is often referred to as the "Mid-Cap" index, where "cap" is short for "capitalization."

Among foreign stock indexes, the most important ones are the *Financial Times* FT-SE100 index of 100 large shares quoted in London and the Nikkei index of Japanese shares. Since price movements on the world's stock markets are correlated, these indexes are closely watched by professional traders in the United States. Various attempts have been made to develop worldwide stock indexes, but so far none has gained general acceptance. Such indexes are of interest to investment managers because the principle of diversification (emphasized in Chapter 4) suggests that foreign equities should be included in optimal portfolios, particularly because some of them may have low correlations with domestic equities—and sometimes higher returns as well. A widely accepted international stock index would be a more meaningful indicator of investment performance than the purely domestic S&P500.

7

Security Analysis

In Chapter 5 (Section 5.3.2), we stated that security analysis is consistent with market efficiency because it interprets the news that reaches the market from firms and other sources. In this chapter we discuss in more detail how this interpretation is accomplished, drawing mostly on three sources: the economics of industrial organization, data on industry growth, and accounting.

7.1 SECURITY ANALYSIS AND MARKET EFFICIENCY

In an informationally efficient market, all publicly available information will be rapidly reflected in the market price of a security. As noted in Chapter 5, there is considerable evidence indicating that major securities markets exhibit a high degree of informational efficiency.

Does this evidence imply that security analysis is a waste of time? The answer is an emphatic "no." It is precisely because there are a large number of qualified people generating relevant information by analyzing securities and trading on the basis of this new information that the market is so efficient. As new information becomes generally known in the market, the price will adjust to reflect it, and in the process of this adjustment those with the new information early (notably those who generated it) will make money. If the new information is favorable to the stock, for example, the new market price will be higher. Those who were first to have the information will have bought early (before the rise) and thus profit as others in the market become aware and traders adjust their prices upward. If the market is efficient and adjusts quickly, all the better, since profit will come sooner.

What market efficiency does imply, however, is that if the investor is to be rewarded for time and money spent on security analysis, he or she must obtain information that is both relevant and new (i.e., not already known to the majority of active traders in the market). Clearly, security analysis is also profitable only if the value you realize from the new information exceeds what it costs you to produce it.

All of the above is just common sense, but it has important implications that are not always recognized by actual and prospective investors. These implications are best understood by likening involvement in security analysis to a firm competing in an industry, in this case an industry that produces information. As in any industry, good profits are based on having some source of advantage over competitors.

Some competitors have the advantage of rapid access to new information as it becomes available: Floor traders, for example, know almost immediately the short-term movements in the prices of the securities they follow. They can also act on this information "on the spot," causing the relevant information to be immediately incorporated into the price. It is not surprising, therefore, that so many studies have concluded that off-floor analysts gain little new information by looking at reported daily, weekly, and monthly price changes, and that technical trading rules fail to produce a net profit after transactions costs.

Other competitors, such as the large brokerage houses and mutual funds, have economies of scale in systems for rapidly collecting, processing, and distributing information on their side. The fixed costs of computerized databases, for example, can be spread by selling the information directly or indirectly (through a package of brokerage or funds management services) to a large number of customers. Yet other individuals and firms compete on the basis of superior techniques for security analysis or specialized knowledge of a particular industry. Outstanding analysts can command annual salaries in the million-dollar range.

In summary, security analysis is still useful in an efficient market and it can be the source of significant profits for the analyst (or the analyst's employer), provided she or he has some advantage that enables her or him to compete against others in what is, in fact, an information-providing industry.

7.2 A MODERN VIEW OF SECURITY ANALYSIS

The price of a security in an efficient market will be the present value of the future cash flow that it is expected to generate, discounted at a rate that corresponds to the security's beta. The objective of security analysis is basically to identify current profit and cash flow, to forecast how profit and cash flow will grow or decline in the future, and to assess the risk of fluctuations around this forecast, including the risk that the cash flow will be interrupted due to liquidation, bankruptcy, legal injunction, and the like.

During the period of relatively stable growth for most corporations in the 1960s, the emphasis was placed on projecting a firm's income statement for the current period in a roughly linear fashion, at a growth rate determined by projected growth in the economy as a whole, plus some adjustment for the particular industry in terms of demand for its class of products and sensitivity to the business cycle. At the individual firm level, attention was heavily directed toward the firm's ability to expand its physical, human, and financial resources to meet new demand, because this ability represented the most important constraints to increased value. Much of the relevant information could therefore be gleaned from the firm's existing capacity utilization, its plans for expansion, and its record of managing growth in the past.

Potential growth is still important, and it is discussed (on the industry level) in Section 7.2.2. In the more volatile economic climate of recent years, however, there have arguably been greater divergences between the performance of individual firms than can be attributed to industry growth alone. In other words, differences between the individual firms within any one industry appear to have become more significant. In response, modern security analysis has focused increased attention on the sources of competitive advantage enjoyed by the individual firm and the longer-run defensibility of those advantages, not only against established competitors but also against foreign competition and entry by firms innovating or diversifying from other industries. Analysts have increasingly looked toward theories of industrial organization and corporate strategy, combined with a detailed knowledge of recent trends in an industry to aid them in estimating companies' earnings prospects and their prospects of being taken over by other firms. Modern security analysis is thus as much a strategic assessment as it is a more traditional accounting analysis of the firm.

7.2.1 Macroeconomic Developments and Changes in Regime

Although this chapter is mainly concerned with analysis on the firm and industry level, it must be recognized that virtually all firms are affected by macroeconomic developments, particularly the real growth of the economy, the inflation rate, and the various interest rates. Some of these factors have already been discussed in Chapter 2 and elsewhere. Their impact will often differ according to the industry or industries in which the firm specializes, so we come back to this in the next section.

Furthermore, most American firms of significant size are affected by developments abroad, whether through exports or imports or because they have foreign operations. If so, their performance depends not only on economic conditions abroad but also on another set of macroeconomic factors discussed in Chapter 2, namely exchange rates. In the case of imports and exports, changes in exchange rates will alter the firm's ability to compete; an importer of Japanese cars, for instance, will be adversely affected by a rise in the yen while the same rise will help an exporter of American soybeans to Japan. Foreign operations are affected in a different way: The dollar value of earnings from abroad is converted at different rates. Thus if an American company operates in Britain, its earnings from there (or the dividends it receives from its British subsidiary, if the latter is organized as a separate corporation) will be worth more the higher the value of the British pound in terms of dollars.

Individual firms will also be influenced by what are sometimes called "changes in regime," where "regime" stands for the general rules under which all firms operate. The most important examples are the tax code and restrictions on international trade.

As regards the tax code, it is clear that a change in the rate of corporate income tax will affect all corporations.[1] Other changes in taxation may have a more selective impact, which the security analyst will have to determine. Thus an investment tax credit, permitting firms to deduct a fraction of their expenditures on capital formation from their tax bill, was in force from the 1960s to the 1980s and its reintroduction was considered by the Clinton administration. Such a credit is of special importance to capital-extensive or rapidly growing firms. Another tax change that has often been talked about is elimination of the double taxation of dividends—once under the corporate income tax and once under the individual income tax. In some countries, but not in the United States, shareholders receive an income tax credit for the corporate tax already paid on their dividends. If such an arrangement were introduced here, corporate equities would become a more attractive investment.

On the international side, the trend toward liberalization of trade and capital movements since World War II has been favorable for many American firms, the exception being those firms that saw their previous protection (in the form of tariffs or quotas) being eroded. Further progress toward free trade remains to be made, and its effect on individual companies needs to be carefully analyzed.

7.2.2 Industry Growth

As shown in Table 7.1, the major sectors of the U.S. economy have grown at quite different rates since World War II.[2] The agricultural sector stands out with the slowest growth rate. The service sector grew the fastest; other rapidly growing sectors were communications and finance (including insurance and real estate). The last column sheds light on the variability of growth in each sector. We see that growth in the agricultural and mining sectors was highly variable, while services and retail trade had much steadier growth. As one would expect, durable manufacturing, which supplies mostly investment goods and durable consumer goods, is more volatile than nondurable manufacturing.

Although a full explanation of these differences is beyond our scope, it is important to understand the main factors determining the growth rate of a sector:

    1. The *income elasticity of demand* may be defined as the percentage change

Table 7.1 Growth Rates of National Income in Major Sectors of the U.S. Economy, 1946–1989

Sector	Logarithmic Growth Rate[a]	Standard Deviation[b]
National Income[c]	0.073	0.035
Domestic sectors	0.073	0.035
Private sectors	0.072	0.039
agriculture, forestry, and fisheries	0.039	0.118
mining	0.058	0.129
construction	0.082	0.059
manufacturing	0.065	0.063
durable goods	0.068	0.081
nondurable goods	0.060	0.050
transportation and public utilities	0.070	0.035
transportation	0.060	0.050
communications	0.086	0.034
electric, gas, and sanitary	0.082	0.055
wholesale trade	0.072	0.044
retail trade	0.064	0.030
finance, insurance, and real estate	0.084	0.029
services	0.092	0.024
Government and government enterprises	0.075	0.057

[a] Mean annual change in the logarithm of each sector's contribution to National Income.

[b] Standard deviation of the logarithmic changes.

[c] Without capital consumption adjustment (see Chapter 2); includes factor payments to and from the Rest of the World, which are excluded from the other items.

Source: Calculated from NIPA table 6.03B using diskettes from Bureau of Economic Analysis.

in the consumption of a product (or group of products) associated with a 1% change in income. It is easy to show that this elasticity also equals the ratio of the growth rate of consumption of that product (or group) to the growth rate of income. Thus if the income elasticity of food demand is 0.5, then the growth rate of food consumption—everything else remaining the same—is one-half the growth rate of income. In fact, it was discovered long ago that the income elasticity of food demand is less than 1, an empirical regularity known as Engel's Law. This fact explains, at least in part, why the agricultural sector, whose main product is food, grows so slowly. Most other sectors are characterized by income elasticities of about one or greater than one, and therefore have higher growth rates.[3] Even for industries that do not sell directly to households, income elasticities are important because the demand for their products depends ultimately to a large extent on consumer demand for final products.[4]

2. *Price elasticities of demand* are defined in much the same way as income elasticities. They are important because over time the prices charged by different industries do not change at the same rate: Some products tend to become relatively cheaper, others more expensive. The relative price of household durables,

for instance, has declined over time, whereas health care has become relatively more expensive.

The principal reason for these changes in relative prices is differential growth in productivity, a measure of the efficiency with which an industry converts its inputs (especially labor) into outputs. Thus the communications sector, which consists chiefly of the telephone industry, has had a high growth rate of productivity and this has made telephone service progressively cheaper. According to econometric studies, the price elasticity of telephone demand is significantly less than zero, so households and businesses have responded to lower prices by increasing their consumption. The opposite, needless to say, has occurred in industries with low productivity growth, though it should be borne in mind that the effects of unfavorable price trends may sometimes be offset by high income elasticities (and conversely).[5] For industries with a low price elasticity of demand, or with near-average productivity growth, the effects described in this paragraph are unimportant.

3. *Changes in international competitiveness* are important for some sectors, particularly manufacturing and mining. The preceding paragraphs deal with domestic demand, some of which can be satisfied by imports. Similarly, foreign demand can be satisfied by exports from the United States. International competitiveness is determined largely by production costs here and abroad and by exchange rates; in addition, there are barriers to trade of various kinds. Rapid productivity growth in Japan and certain newly industrialized countries has made them more competitive in the U.S. market; on the other hand, the demand for American exports has benefited from growth in foreign incomes. As to exchange rates, the high value of the dollar in terms of other currencies that prevailed in the early 1980s stimulated our imports and hampered our exports. The subsequent weakening of the dollar has had the opposite effect, but the United States remains a net importer.

These differences in industry growth rates, relative prices and international competitiveness, in turn, feed through into growth in profits and dividends for firms operating in each sector (see Table 7.2).

The main defect of Tables 7.1 and 7.2 is that the major sectors it covers are too broad for security analysis. Its main purpose is to illustrate some important general principles of sectoral growth and to introduce a long-term perspective. We now proceed to the next level of detail, the major industry.[6] In line with the orientation of this book, we focus on dividends.

In Chapter 6 it was shown that over time aggregate dividends have been a roughly constant fraction of aggregate National Income, and by and large this remains true when the economy is divided into major sectors. Although the available data do not permit us to verify this for finer breakdowns, it seems plausible that this approximate constancy also holds for major industries. If so, the long-run growth of dividends in these industry is largely determined by the same factors discussed in connection with Table 7.1.

From Table 7.3 it appears that the industries with the slowest dividend

Table 7.2 Growth Rates of Corporate Profits and Dividends by Sector, 1948–1989

	Profits after Tax		Net Dividends	
Sector	Mean	S.D.	Mean	S.D.
All sectors[a]	.049	.146	.068	.050
Domestic sectors	.042	.164	.067	.060
agriculture, forestry, and fisheries	.067	[c]	.049	.460
mining	−.007	[c]	.069	[c]
construction	.075	.233	.070	.256
durable manufacturing	.038	[c]	.058	.145
nondurable manufacturing	.043	.327	.067	[c]
transportation	.028	[c]	.054	.116
communications	.091	.113	.100	.051
electric, gas, and sanitary	.059	.195	.085	.063
wholesale trade	.050	.241	.071	.099
retail trade	.050	.174	.057	.094
finance, insurance, and real estate	[b]	[c]	.049	[c]
services	.096	.187	.094	.184

[a] Mean annual change in the logarithm of each sector's contribution to National Income.

[b] Standard deviation of the logarithmic changes.

[c] Without capital consumption adjustment (see Chapter 2); includes factor payments to and from the Rest of the World, which are excluded from the other items.

Source: Calculated from NIPA table 6.03B using diskettes from Bureau of Economic Analysis.

growth were textiles and steel. These two industries were adversely affected by competition from imports, which in the case of steel was both caused and aggravated by low productivity growth. High dividend growth can be observed in the telephone and airline industries, both of which had a high growth rate of productivity and also benefited from favorable income elasticities.[7] A comparison of the airlines and the railroads suggests that some of the growth of the former was at the expense of the latter. Other industries with above-average dividend growth were electric and gas utilities and commercial banking.

In interpreting the table the following points should be borne in mind:

1. The underlying data from the National Accounts are industry totals; they are not expressed per share and have not been adjusted for inflation.[8]
2. These data are "net," which means that the dividends received by the firms in an industry have been subtracted from the dividends paid by those firms. Industries such as life insurance normally receive more dividends from their investments than they pay to their stockholders. For such industries, none of which are included in Table 7.3, net dividends are normally negative. This "netting" of dividends serves to avoid double counting.
3. Since the Rest of the World is considered a separate sector, industries with large international operations—oil and motor vehicles are conspicuous examples—may at times take in more dividends from abroad than

Table 7.3 Growth and Variability of Total Net Dividends in Selected Industries, 1948–1987

Industry	Logarithmic Growth Rate[a]	Standard Deviation[b]
Iron and steel	0.021	0.307
Nonelectrical machinery	0.051	0.135
Electrical machinery	0.078	0.228
Food processing	0.062	0.131
Textiles	0.009	0.251
Pulp and paper	0.054	0.108
Printing and publishing	0.073	0.193
Chemicals	0.077	0.162
Railroads	0.036	0.167
Airlines[c]	0.091	0.403
Telephone and telegraph	0.101	0.050
Electric and gas utilities	0.085	0.063
Retail trade	0.057	0.094
Commercial banking	0.080	0.118
ALL DOMESTIC INDUSTRIES[d]	0.067	0.060

[a] Mean annual change in the logarithm of dividends.

[b] Standard deviation of the changes in log(dividend).

[c] 1950–1987.

[d] Excluding dividends received from or paid to the Rest of the World.

Source: Calculated from NIPA table 6.22b using diskettes from the Bureau of Economic Analysis.

they pay to domestic stockholders. Their net dividends will then be negative for some years, and they had to be excluded from the table.

4. As pointed out earlier, there are millions of corporations in the United States, of which only a small fraction are listed on stock exchanges or traded with any frequency over the counter. All these corporations, whether listed or not, are covered by the National Accounts. Industries believed to consist mostly of unlisted companies (particularly in the services, in construction, in real estate, and in wholesale trade) do not appear in Table 7.3.

5. The long-term growth rates shown in Tables 7.1, 7.2, and 7.3 may mask significant changes in trend over shorter intervals.

7.2.3 International and Regional Growth

A corporation's performance and prospects depend not only on the industry (or industries) in which it operates but also on other factors, not all of them quantifiable. Here we digress briefly from industry aspects to deal with geographical factors, both international and regional.

Table 7.4 Growth Rate of Real GDP

	% per year, 1974–1993
ADVANCED INDUSTRIAL COUNTRIES[a]	2.9
United States	2.5
Canada	2.7
Europe[b]	2.1
Japan	3.8
DEVELOPING COUNTRIES	3.0
East Asia	7.5
South Asia	4.8
Latin America	2.6
Eastern Europe and former Soviet Union	1.0
Sub-Saharan African	2.0
Middle East and North Africa	1.2

[a]Includes countries not shown separately.

[b]OECD members only.

Note: Regional data are available in great detail from the Bureau of Economic Analysis (U.S. Department of Commerce), but we cannot summarize them here. Suffice it to say that regional growth trends in the U.S. are somewhat cyclical. Sometimes one region does best for a number of years, sometimes another. Population movements, generally toward the South and the West, appear to be significant in explaining regional growth.

Source: For industrial countries: Organization for Economic Co-operation and Development (OECD); for developing countries: World Bank.

Most large U.S. corporations have international operations and/or investments in foreign affiliates; they may also export some of their domestic production, as do many smaller firms. The same applies, *mutatis mutandem,* to enterprises headquartered abroad. It is therefore important to all such firms how other parts of the world are doing. The growth rates shown in Table 7.4 are the most useful summary of general economic performance.[9]

Table 7.4 only calls for a few comments. During the two decades covered, growth in the industrial nations was fairly uniform; it was lowest in Europe and highest in Japan. Actually Japan's growth rate was very high during the second quarter of the twentieth century, but it slowed markedly thereafter and has not yet recovered.

There is much more variation among the developing areas in the bottom half of the table. East Asia, helped by strong growth in mainland China, South Korea, and Taiwan, stands out; South Asia also grew strongly. By contrast, growth in the former Soviet Union and its satellites was close to zero. These countries, now independent, are still in a difficult transition to a freer economic system. Russia's growth rate was still negative in 1994–1995, but other nations in Eastern Europe appear to have turned the corner.

Regional growth rates within the United States are important to firms that do not operate nationwide. Although a movement toward greater concentration is now in progress, the majority of American banks operate only regionally or within one state. It will be many years (if ever) before the American banking system is dominated by a few nationwide banks, as has long been the case in other industrial countries. Other regionally specialized sectors include retail chains, home builders, and health maintenance organizations. To all of these regional growth is important.

7.2.4 Industry Structure

We now return to the discussion of industry aspects. One of the most influential notions of industrial organization is the "structure-conduct-performance" framework, which postulates that the average performance (including profitability) of firms within an industry will be systematically related to the structure of the industry. Here the term "structure" refers to the state of competition within the industry, as manifested by such factors as the concentration of suppliers or the barriers to entry. These relationships will reflect both direct effects of industry structure on profitability as well as indirect effects, through which structure influences the conduct of the firms (for instance, whether they emphasize competition through price, through new products or through advertising).

If, in fact, some competitive environments offer higher profit potential for well-run firms than others, security analysis could benefit from distinguishing between favorable and less favorable industry structures in valuing the securities issued by a firm. It could also usefully deploy information about changes in industry structure to predict how the profitability and cash flow of firms in an industry might evolve in the future.

There is a considerable body of evidence to suggest that these industry structure effects are important. In studies by the Federal Trade Commission, the average profitability of some industries like breakfast cereals and pharmaceuticals are found to be consistently high. Others, such as children's outerwear and metal cans, have consistently been among the least profitable industries. In other cases, such as air transport, average profitability has seen major shifts following changes in industry structure when deregulation caused entry of new competitors followed by increasing concentration.

Porter (1980) has summarized the basic forces that should be considered as part of an assessment of a firm's long-term competitive position using the framework in Figure 7.1. These five competitive forces—threat of entry, threat of substitution by alternative products, bargaining power of buyers on one hand, and suppliers on the other, and rivalry among existing competitors—determine the long-term profitability of a firm and hence its value. By understanding these forces, the influence of transient influences—such as the current stage of the business cycle, temporary shortages of material or labor disputes, and short-lived spurts in product demand—can be seen in their proper context. The dangerous

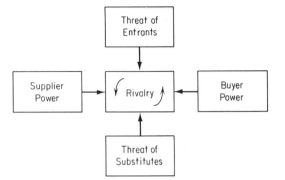

Figure 7.1 The "five forces framework." *Source:*
Based on M. E. Porter, *Competitive
Strategy,* Free Press, 1980.

temptation to project recent growth and profit performance linearly into the future can be avoided because the likely responses of potential entrants, buyers,
suppliers, and competitors, all of which can greatly alter any profit and growth
scenario, are always considered early in the analysis (Hay and Williamson, 1991).

While it is not possible here to go into the details of industry and competitive analysis, it is worthwhile to expand briefly on the five forces just listed to
see how these concepts might be used in security analysis. In Section 7.3 we
discuss how an understanding of the industry structure might be merged with
analysis of published accounts in the course of valuing a security.

1. The *threat of entry* to a firm's industry is a particularly important determinant of its future profitability. Entry, whether by new firms or through diversification or acquisition of existing ones, tends to force reductions in an existing company's market share, often causing price reductions and increases in the costs of
raw materials or labor in the process. The valuation of Apple Computer, with its
early dominance of the personal computer market, was a classic example of the
need to take entry into account. Allowing for the impact of the threat of entry on
the value of a security involves an assessment of both how easy it is for new competitors to enter (i.e., the height of barriers to entry) and the likely reaction of the
firm and existing competitors should entry occur. The most important barriers to
entry that might protect a firm's existing high profit stream into the future are:

- Economies of scale, which may mean that new entrants face higher costs
  compared with existing firms with large production
- Product differentiation in the form of brand recognition, loyalty of consumers or distributors, all of which may take entrants a great deal of time
  or costly advertising to break down
- Proprietary technology or product design.

Other barriers can arise from high costs of switching from one supplier to another (e.g., retooling or resistance from operating staff), access to distribution channels (thus unproven brands often have difficulty competing for shelf space in retail stores), access to the best locations or raw materials if these are already controlled by existing firms, and government restrictions on new entry through licensing laws.

2. The *pressure from substitute products* may also have a significant influence on future profitability. If certain substitutes will improve their future price or performance in the same function as a firm's product, its past record will be a poor guide to the long-term value of its shares. Such improvements in the competitiveness of substitutes may come from technological change, but this is far from the only source. Major entry into the industry producing a substitute, for example, may cause a large fall in price and hence encourage many customers to switch towards it at the expense of the firm under review. The introduction of hand-held electronic calculators, for instance, doomed the slide-rule industry to extinction. This threat of substitution underlines the need for security analysts to understand not only the industry in which a firm operates but also industries producing functional substitutes for its products, some of which may not pose an immediately obvious threat.

3. The next force to be considered consists of possible changes in the *bargaining power of buyers* of the firm's products. Such factors as exit, mergers or acquisitions, or the emergence of a few dominant producers may lead to concentration of power into a smaller number of buyers (each purchasing substantial volumes compared with a firm's total sales) and result in a long-term decline in price. It may also lead to higher production costs as buyers use their greater bargaining power to pressure for higher quality or more support services. Such buyer pressure will have particularly adverse effects when the buyers can easily switch to another supplier, while the costs borne by the seller in adjusting to a different set of customers are high.

4. Possible future changes in the *bargaining power of suppliers* need to be taken into account. As in the case of buyers, developments that concentrate power in the hands of a small number of suppliers are likely to adversely affect a firm's profitability as suppliers demand a bigger share of the overall margin in the chain between final product price and the costs of producing basic raw materials.

5. Finally, the analyst must consider possible future changes in the *pattern of rivalry between existing competitors*. The current profitability of a firm, in part, reflects the behavior of its current competitors. In many industries with relatively small numbers of participants, there exists an "equilibrium" in which firms, recognizing their mutual interdependence, avoid actions (such as "price wars") that would lead to a general reduction in profit margins. Several kinds of developments may upset this cozy equilibrium. A decline in industry growth may cause competitors to scramble for share and impair unit margins. Industries where there is a high component of fixed costs and/or substantial barriers to exit (e.g., specialized equipment with low resale value) are especially prone to this scenario; airlines are a case in point. Conversely, in industries where capacity must, by technical necessity, be added in large increments, future growth may

lead to recurring periods of overcapacity and price warfare. Entry of new firms, increases in imports, or takeovers may also disturb the competitive equilibrium in an industry and leave margins permanently impaired even when the industry settles down again (Williamson and Hu, 1994). Likewise, technological change can be a source of changed behavior of competitors with strong impacts on firm profitability.

In predicting the implications of these changes in rivalry, an analyst needs to know whether the growth rates, pricing, and marketing strategies of the main competitors in the industry are consistent with trends in the market as a whole. In other words, he or she must ask, "Is each firm's planned growth consistent with the growth rate of demand across the market as a whole, or will it set off a struggle for market share?"[10]

7.2.5 Firm-Specific Factors

So far we have considered a framework for analyzing the impact of industry structure and growth on the profitability of firms, and hence the value of their securities. However, it is not generally true that "industry is destiny." Some firms manage to report high profits in industries that look unattractive in respect of structure or growth. A good example is the Crown Cork & Seal company, which achieved profitability of three or four times the average of its industry (metal cans) over a long period. Other firms produce poor profits despite operating in industries where the profit potential should be high given favorable industry structure and growth rate.

Probably the most extensive analysis of whether there are persistent differences between the profitability of individual firms and the average profitability of their respective industries was undertaken in a comparative study spanning the mid-1960s to the early 1980s for samples of firms in Britain, Canada, France, Germany, Japan, and the United States (Mueller, 1990).

The first important finding of this study was that the average coefficient of variation of firm profitability (measured by accounting return on assets) within an industry was around 0.5. In other words, the dispersion of return across individual firms in an industry was quite substantial with a standard deviation close to one half of the mean. Interestingly, this dispersion became wider in years with low profitability for most Canadian, French, German, and Japanese industries. This suggests that in these countries firms differed substantially in the extent to which they were affected by bad times in an industry. In Britain and the United States, the dispersion narrowed in low profit years, suggesting that the differences between firms were more closely related to their ability to take advantage of buoyant periods.

A second key result was that there were persistent differences in the profitability of individual firms within an industry over long periods of time. There was a tendency for the competitive dynamics in a market to drive the profitability of individual firms up or down toward some long-run industry average determined by the structural features of the industry described above. However, this process was found to be both slow and incomplete. Therefore the most profitable firms in the initial period tended to have above-average profitability throughout the period. The opposite was true for the least profitable firms. Moreover, the variation between firms often dwarfed the variation in profits over time exhibited by the average firm in an industry. These results suggest that profitability differences between firms are based on structural factors associated with a firm's tangible and intangible assets and the barriers to imitation that protect its strategy from erosion by "copy cat" competitors.[11] Security analysis, therefore, must not only concern itself with industry differences, but also try to understand the aspects of a firm's strategy and asset base, which help it achieve sustainable advantage over its competitors.

While definition of a firm's strategy involves many complex factors, higher profit must ultimately stem from either lower costs or higher prices (or for outstanding firms, perhaps both). This fact has led analysts to identify three basic sources of potential long-run advantage: cost advantages, differentiation, and focus.

Cost advantages, as the phrase suggests, are aspects of a firm's strategy that help it achieve consistently lower final product costs than its competitors. This position might be achieved by building large-scale plants, by pursuing volume more aggressively (which has led to greater accumulated experience than smaller competitors), by developing proprietary systems for tight cost control and inventory minimization, by using cash flow to continually invest in efficient state of the art equipment, by spreading fixed costs by sharing facilities or marketing distribution systems with other products, and so on.

Even if rivalry drives prices down to competitors' break-even levels, a firm with overall cost leadership can still make good profits. Its lower costs are a source of extra profit margin at any given industry price. Similarly, it still has room for profits even if the force of substitute products or powerful buyers squeezes competitors to the brink of bankruptcy.

Differentiation involves developing some aspect of a product in a way that makes the firm's offering unique in a way that is valued by customers. This uniqueness may be achieved by different physical or performance characteristics of the product (its "quality"), by the way it is marketed or distributed (often termed the "informational" characteristics of the product). The use of brand names and of after-sales service may foster customer loyalty. Innovative product or process technology may help a firm maintain differentiation of its product offering against imitation by competitors.

Differentiation of a type valued by the customer results in a price premium that, depending on the costs of differentiating the product, can enhance the firm's margins compared with competitors. Developing customer loyalty helps shelter the firm if substitutes become cheaper. Since the buyer of a differentiated product loses something by shifting to another supplier, differentiation will often constrain buyer power in forcing lower margins. Thus the firm with a well-conceived differentiation strategy will have advantages in competitive rivalry.

Focus is the third general source of advantage. A firm may gain advantages over its competitors by concentrating on a particular customer group, a specialist item within a product line, or a particular geographic area. The advantages may stem from cost leadership in serving that focused segment (for instance, cost advantages in distributing to concentrations of customers in a small area), or from differentiation in the eyes of that segment (as with salespeople who have special knowledge of the insurance needs of doctors and dentists).[12]

All three sources of advantage are subject to erosion over time. Technological change may eliminate cost leadership, or a competitor may build a larger-scale plant with a new, even lower cost structure. Competitors may imitate the characteristics, distribution methods, or product image that previously differentiated a product.[13] Market segments on which a focused strategy was built may be invaded by competitors using national advertising or introducing multipurpose products.

Having identified the sources of a firm's competitive advantage, the security analyst must therefore give careful consideration to the robustness or "defensibility" of that strategy against future moves by competitors, buyers, suppliers, or producers of substitutes. He or she must ask, "What are the future weak points of the strategy?" The answer to this question will determine the strength of tomorrow's cash flows and hence the current value of the firm's stock.

In today's uncertain economic environment, this type of strategic assessment is one of the prerequisites for informed judgments about a firm's future growth in sales, profit performance, and need for additional capital. The next challenge for the analyst is to express those judgments in a quantitative way that can be meaningfully compared with the current stock price.

7.3 THE ROLE OF FINANCIAL STATEMENT ANALYSIS

Financial statement analysis has two main functions in the more general task of security analysis:

· To measure the past and present performance of a firm's strategy
· To provide a framework for quantifying judgements about the future performance of a firm's strategy and the risks associated with it

The principal ingredients of financial statement analysis have already been described in Chapter 1. They are the firm's balance sheet, its income statement, and its cash flow statement.[14] These are normally published each year in the report to the firm's shareholders, which may also be a useful source of information on management's view of the company's strategy. Greater financial detail is available in the annual 10-K reports, which public corporations are required to file with the Securities and Exchange Commission. Updated information may be obtained from the quarterly version of documents filed with the SEC (Form 10-Q).[15]

In using these statements to assess the past performance of a firm's strategy, the analyst's main approach is to compute various ratios of the reported variables; the ratio of sales to total assets, sometimes called the "asset turn," is an example. Each ratio means little taken in isolation. Ratios are instructive only when compared with those of competitors or the ratios achieved by the firm in earlier time periods. In making these comparisons, great care must be taken to check the "notes to the accounts" for differences in the accounting conventions adopted that could distort the interpretation if not allowed for (for instance, straight line versus declining balance methods of depreciation).[16]

When a significant difference in a ratio is identified, the analyst must consider whether this results from different performance or a different choice of strategy. Since failure to make this distinction has been the cause of much erroneous analysis in the past, further elaboration is worthwhile.

Take the example of two construction companies, DIY and AUO. On computing their "fixed asset turn" (sales/fixed assets), we find that DIY has a ratio of 1.5 compared with AUO at 3.0. Interpreting this difference as purely one of performance, we might conclude that DIY is plagued with low capacity utilization and idle fixed assets, whereas AUO uses its assets continuously to produce twice the revenue from every dollar of fixed assets on its books.

Interpreting the difference as one of strategy choice, we might conclude that DIY owns all of the equipment used on a job. AUO, meanwhile, rents its equipment, employs subcontractors, and owns few fixed assets itself. Certainly, AUO (Always Use Outsiders) has a much higher asset turn, but much of its sales revenue is paid out to equipment owners and subcontractors. DIY (Do It Yourself) has less sales per dollar of fixed assets, but all of that sales revenue is available to cover its internal operations.

The implications for the value of each firm's shares differ. If performance is measured by the fixed-assets turn, then AUO will be worth more until DIY gets management that attracts more sales or disposes of assets. If the difference actually reflects a strategic choice, the story could be the opposite. In profitable boom periods in construction, DIY has a guaranteed supply of equipment as a basis for accepting work and making profits. AUO may be left struggling to find subcontractors at high prices in a tight market, having to turn down work at the most profitable time. Provided the costs of holding assets in recessions are relatively low, DIY would then be the more valuable company.

Likewise, changes in ratios over time for any one company may reflect trends in performance or shifts in strategy toward the market. We now briefly discuss some of the information about performance and strategy that might be gleaned from other key ratios. The first major set of ratios focuses on the income statement and attempts to picture the division of each dollar of sales revenue between raw materials costs, production operating expenses, and the return to providers of capital (comprising interest paid to debt holders and profits to shareholders).

The *gross margin* (gross profit/net sales) can be used to provide information about both changes in demand and buyer power, and the degree to which a firm is benefiting from a differentiation strategy. Comparison of the gross margin achieved by a firm over time could, for example, point to a decline in the funds available to meet profits and operating expenses, which may in turn signal the presence of intensified competition from substitutes, growing buyer power, and so on.

By comparing gross margins across firms within an industry, meanwhile, it is possible to identify firms that are achieving higher price realization over their cost of raw materials by differentiating their product (e.g., by precision in production, by strong sales support, or by advertising).

In order to get a fuller picture of the firm's strategy and performance, however, we must examine the *net margin* (net profit before interest and taxes/net sales) in conjunction with gross margin. In the cross section context, it helps us understand whether the differentiation adopted by individual firms is really profitable; in other words, whether or not the increase in gross margin achieved through differentiation outweighs the increase in operating expenses incurred in differentiating the product.[17]

A high gross margin and low net margin compared with competitors suggest the firm is engaged in unprofitable differentiation. The question then becomes whether this is an inherent problem in pursuing a strategy of differentiation or simply poor control over the expenses involved.

A furniture company, for example, may differentiate its product by offering a wide choice of covering fabrics. If we observe a higher-than-average gross margin and a below average net margin, it may be because the price premium that consumers pay for this choice does not cover all the additional costs of carrying extra stock, disruptions to production flow involved in making to order, lower labor productivity with unfamiliar fabrics, and so on. On the other hand, it may reflect poor stock management and production scheduling compared with efficient methods. These alternative explanations have different implications for the fundamental value of the stock. If it is a basic flaw in the firm's whole approach to the market, hence costly and difficult to change, value will be lower than if the problem is one of management control (in which case the firm is probably a good candidate for takeover, replacement of management, and a substantial increase in value).

The individual *expense ratios* (e.g., selling expenses/net sales) are useful in identifying which part of the company's operations are responsible for any problems in net margin observed. This could show up either as a trend for certain expenses to absorb a higher proportion of sales revenue over time or as an expense ratio that is out of line with competitors. Again, we must ask whether such differences in expense ratios make sense in terms of profitable differences in the firm's strategy or reflect poor performance.

A second set of ratios giving insight into the operations of the firm are those relating income statement variables to the balance sheet. We have already discussed one of these: the fixed asset turn (net sales/fixed assets). Others include *inventory turnover* (cost of goods sold/average inventory), *accounts receivable turnover* (net credit sales/average accounts receivable outstanding), and *working capital turnover* (net sales/net working capital). Both inventory turnover and accounts receivable turnover, viewed over time and across competitors, offer a way to judge the company's performance in respect to inventory control and debtor collection. As a general rule, high ratios are desirable. As always, however, allowance must be made for any differences in strategy that may underlie them, the two furniture manufacturers being a case in point.

A third important group of ratios are helpful in forming a judgment as to the firm's financial (or bankruptcy) risk. These include the *times interest earned ratio* (net profit before interest and taxes/annual interest charges), the *fixed financial charges ratio* (net profit before interest and taxes/annual fixed financial charges), the *debt-equity* or *"leverage" ratio* (current and long term liabilities/total liabilities and shareholders funds), and the *cash flow ratio* (total debt/cash surplus on operations after tax per annum).

The times interest earned ratio, sometimes termed *interest cover,* is a measure of how much the net operating profit of the firm could fall before it would be unable to meet its interest commitments. Clearly, the closer the ratio falls toward 1.0, the smaller the reduction in earnings the firm can tolerate before serious financial problems arise, and thus the greater the risk.

The fixed financial charges ratio is an analogous extension. It recognizes that there may be other fixed financial claims against a firm's income that could result in bankruptcy if not met. The most important of these is lease commitments, which are therefore added into the denominator.

The debt/equity or leverage ratio is probably the most widely used of all measures of financial risk. Provided the liquidation value of the company's assets is correctly reflected in the accounts, it reflects the percentage loss in asset value (either as the result of future trading losses or extraordinary items such as the writeoff of a large bad debt) that the company could buffer with its equity before the creditors began to lose their capital. If, for example, a firm has $100 million of assets and a leverage ratio of 0.5, it could afford to take losses equal to an average of 50% on all assets before the creditors would face a serious loss of principal. This may seem unlikely, but we should recall that a number of large banks—with heavy loan exposure in real estate and developing countries—and high leverage have recently faced the prospect of almost completely wiping out their total equity base with loan writeoffs. In the early 1980s, the Chrysler Corporation had to be "rescued" from a similar fate, in this case because of trading losses.

In addition to protecting their capital, another concern of creditors is the liquidity of a firm. The cash flow ratio is one indicator. When a firm has a low ratio of short-term debt to cash surplus on operations, it will have better options for repaying some of these loans when credit markets become very tight, thus presenting difficulties in rollover or refinancing of loans during the squeeze. From a long-term perspective, the ratio of total debt to cash surplus on operations is used as an indicator of the company's ability to repay its existing loans without recourse to refinancing, allowing future borrowing to be directed toward new investment and growth.

Before leaving the topic of ratio analysis, we should mention two other measures that are in common use but have some significant problems: the *current ratio,* which is also known as the *working capital ratio* (current assets/current liabilities), and the *quick asset* or *"acid test" ratio* (current assets less inventories/current liabilities).

These ratios purport to show a company's ability to repay its short-term debts. To answer this question, we really want to know whether cash on hand plus expected inflow of cash from sales, collection of receivables, and rundown of inventories will exceed the forecast need for cash to repay maturing liabilities, make new investments to maintain production, and pay ongoing expenses. Instead, these ratios tell us how big the stock of current assets is relative to the existing current liabilities. That is only one small part, the base point in a sense, of understanding the firm's future cash position. Moreover, the working capital ratio could be high, for example, because the firm's inventory is poorly managed so that current assets are excessive.

These examples illustrate two problems with ratio analysis in general: They are really measures of past strategy and performance when what we need is an explicit forecast of the future; and they fail to highlight the interrelationships between the firm's strategy, operations, and financing.[18] Using ratios in a way that helps to overcome these deficiencies is the subject of the next two sections.

7.3.1 The Adjustment Process of Financial Ratios

The financial ratios discussed above can be categorized into two broad types. First, there are those that relate various assets and liabilities in the firm's balance sheet to each other. These represent the inputs that the firm uses to generate its income. Economic theory tells us there is some optimal combination of these inputs that will minimize the firm's costs.[19] This means each firm will have some optimal structure of assets and liabilities that can be reflected in the ratio of balance sheet components.

At any time a firm's asset-liability structure is likely to have been displaced from this optimum by random or short-term shocks, such as an increase in inventory following an unexpected downturn in demand. The optimal structure may also be a "moving target" as changes in relative factor costs or technological improvements, for example, change the optimal mix of assets and liabilities. Management will therefore be continually adjusting these balance sheet ratios to move toward the optimal structure.

Some of the ratios we have just discussed can be readjusted quickly. The current ratio, the quick ratio, and the inventory turnover can probably be altered in a matter of months, certainly within a few years. Other ratios involving buildings, plant and equipment represented by fixed assets, and long-term liabilities and equity can be expensive to change quickly and frequently. Major changes in the debt/equity ratio, for example, are usually achieved through lengthy and infrequent processes of issuing new bonds or equity or by gradually reducing the dividend payout ratio so as to build up shareholders' equity through retained earnings. Share repurchase and redemption of bonds are also methods of adjusting the debt/equity ratio.

The second broad group of ratios, primarily those derived from the firm's income statement such as return on sales, are a reflection of management initiatives to improve performance, combined with the competitive dynamics and structural changes in the firm's product markets. Here there is not really "target ratios" as such but a competitive equilibrium level for each ratio given the structure of the industry.

Just how fast these ratios move toward equilibrium depends on the strength of market forces operating in the industry. At the same time, many management actions are aimed at improving their firm's position relative to the long run industry average, interrupting convergence to the competitive equilibrium. As shown in Section 7.2.5, some firms are quite successful in maintaining above-average performance ratios compared with their competitors over long periods, while others are chronically below average. The question for the security analyst, then, is, How fast will an individual firm be drawn to the industry average level by market forces? The answer will depend importantly on the nature of these advantages and how easily they can be replicated by competitors.

Peles and Schneller (1989) examined the adjustment process of six financial ratios for 635 U.S. corporations based on annual changes over the period 1961–1980. For all of the ratios they found a negative serial correlation of the annual changes; in other words, an increase or series of increases in a ratio in one year was more likely to be followed by a decrease in the following year or series of decreases than further increases. This result is important for security analysts seeking to forecast changes in financial ratios.

As expected, the speed of adjustment varied significantly between different ratios. Estimates of the adjustment speeds are shown in Table 7.5. The results suggest that approximately 40% of disequilibrium in "short-term" ratios like the current ratio, the quick ratio, and the inventory turnover is eliminated within one year. By contrast, the debt/equity ratio, return on assets, and the total asset

Table 7.5 Adjustment of Financial Ratios

Ratio	Adjustment per Annum (%)	Duration of Adjustment (Years)
Current ratio	40	2.5
Quick ratio	36	2.75
Inventory turnover	40	2.5
Debt/equity	12	8.5
Total asset turnover	19	5.25
Return on assets	11	8.75

Source: Peles and Schneller (1989).

turnover exhibited much slower rates of adjustment of only 12% per year for the first two and 19% per year for asset turnover.

The analyst can use these results as a guide to forecasting how fast management will realistically be able to eliminate an unwanted change in its financial structure or how long a significant change in performance might last. The results imply nothing about the level of the equilibrium or target to which the ratio might converge. Early work in this area suggested that the industry average might be used as a measure of the equilibrium or target. Figure 7.2 gives an indication of the differences in the debt/equity ratio across industries and across time.

Care must be used in employing these industry benchmarks. While a potentially useful guide, recent work (Foster 1986) suggests that the links between the industry average and adjustments in financial ratios by individual firms are not always tight. This finding underlines the need to take into account the possibility that particular firms may be able to maintain persistently different ratios from the industry average because of differences in their market strategy. For example, if a firm differentiates its offering on the basis of fast response to its customers, even at the expense of excess capacity and high inventory, then it may maintain persistently lower asset turns than its competitors. It will still be profitable if customers pay a compensating price premium for this high level of service.

7.3.2 Pro Forma Income and Cash Flow

We began this chapter with the basic proposition that valuing a security involves estimating the future cash flows it will provide and discounting these by an ap-

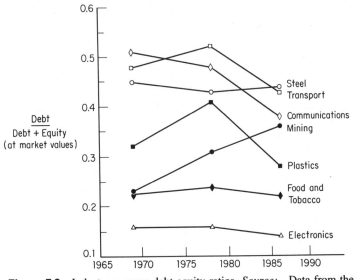

Figure 7.2   Industry average debt-equity ratios. *Source:*   Data from the Brookings Institution.

propriate rate to account for the greater value of money received sooner rather than later, and the risk that the cash flows might vary substantially from our base estimate.

The cash flow pro forma set out in Table 7.6 offers a framework for deriving estimates of the future cash flows by combining data from the last available income statement and balance sheet with an assessment of the growth and financial ratios likely to be achieved in the future. It is in the process of implementing this approach that the streams of strategic and financial analysis come together. In deciding how the ratios used in the pro forma, such as gross margin or fixed asset turnover, will change in the future, the analyst must draw on a strategic understanding of the forces of change at work in the firm's markets and its strengths and weaknesses relative to competitors. Likely changes in each of Porter's five forces bearing on the firm must be assessed and their impact on each individual ratio identified.

The next step is to go through the calculations laid out in Table 7.6, using depreciation and interest expenses based on the fixed assets and outstanding debt appearing in the latest balance sheet and current sales from the income statement. This computation results in an estimate of the net cash flow generated or required by the firm's operations during the first year (in the final row).

This net cash flow from operations can then be used to derive the debt

Table 7.6 Cash Flow Pro Forma

Item	Computation
Future Sales	Current Sales $\times$ (1 + Expected Growth)
Gross Profit	Future Sales $\times$ Expected Gross Margin
Cash Flow from Direct Operations	Gross Profit $-$ (Future Sales $\times$ Σ Nonfinancial Expense Ratios) $-$ Interest on Existing Debt $-$ Taxation Payable[a]
Increased Investment in Receivables	(Future Sales $\times$ Expected Receivables Turnover) $-$ Existing Receivables
Increased Investment in Inventories	(Future Sales $\times$ Expected Inventory Turnover) $-$ Existing Inventory
Increased Investment in Other Current Assets	(Future Sales $\times$ Expected Other Current Asset Turnover) $-$ Existing Other Current Assets
Increased Investment in Fixed Assets	(Future Sales $\times$ Expected Fixed Asset Turnover) $-$ Existing Fixed Assets
Cash Flow Generated or Required by Operations	Cash Flow from Direct Operations $-$ (Increased Investment in Receivables, Inventory, Other Current Assets and Fixed Assets)

[a]Nonfinancial ratios exclude interest and depreciation. Taxation Payable = (Cash Flow from Direct Operations $-$ Depreciation) $\times$ Expected Effective Tax Rate.

outstanding by the end of year 1 and hence the interest expense for the following year. Likewise, the depreciation expense in year 2 can be computed from the increase in investment in fixed assets. Both of these calculations are shown in Table 7.7.

With these new estimates of financing and depreciation expenses in hand, the computations set out in the cash flow pro forma (Table 7.6) can be repeated to derive the cash flow required or generated by operations in year 2, and so on. The spreadsheet software now widely available for microcomputers is well suited to this repetitive calculation.

The resulting data series can be used both in a direct calculation of security value and to compute some of the basic indicators of bankruptcy risk. In applying the standard discounted present value formula, the first problem we face arises from the fact that the shares in firm are usually regarded as perpetual securities. We could thus go on computing the cash pro forma into the hereafter. One solution is to replace the annual cash flows beyond, say, 5 years with a single "terminal value" as follows:

$$PV = \sum_{t=1}^{5} \frac{ECF(t)}{(1+r)^t} + \frac{ECT}{r(1+r)^5} \, ,$$

where $ECF(t)$ is the estimated cash flow in year t and ECT is the net annual cash flow in real terms beyond year 5. The assumption underlying this formula is that after year 5, ECT simply remains constant in perpetuity. Obviously some bias is introduced. Once we get far enough out into the future, however, the discounted

Table 7.7 Recalculation of Interest and Depreciation

Item	Computation
Cash Flow Generated or Required by Operations	From Cash Flow Pro Forma
Dividend Payments	(Cash Flow from Direct Operations − Depreciation) × Dividend Payout Ratio
Net Cash Flow	Cash Flow Generated or Required by Operations − Dividend Payments
New Debt Outstanding	Existing Debt Outstanding − Net Cash Flow
Interest Expense in Year $t+1$	New Debt Outstanding × Average Interest Rate
Depreciation Expense in Year $t+1$	(Existing Fixed Assets + Increased Investment in Fixed Assets) × Average Depreciation Rate[a]

[a]For example, a rate of 0.1 for 10-year straight-line depreciation.

present value of a dollar is so small that the resulting security value is not particularly sensitive to our assumptions and the bias they contain.

The second problem is what discount rate to use. It should be the cost of equity capital to the firm; in other words, the return that will induce investors to include the firm's shares in their portfolio. We derived a formula for this figure in Chapter 5, which uses an estimate of the firm's systematic risk or beta as follows: $r = R_f + \beta_L(R_m - R_f)$, where β_L is the firm's beta adjusted for its debt/equity ratio, also known as leverage (hence the subscript L).

Before applying this formula, however, the analyst needs to incorporate a judgment about how the firm's beta might change in the future. Again, this is where the strategic analysis of the five competitive forces acting on the firm and the strength and robustness of its competitive advantage enters into the calculation. For example, is the firm's strategy leading it to become more dependent on cyclical swings in growth of the national economy? If this were the case, we would expect its beta to increase.

We now (at last!) have a valuation of the firm's shares that reflects both the likely evolution of its cash flows and its systematic risk. It remains, then, for us to make some assessment of the changes in its risk of bankruptcy. From the cash flow pro formas we can calculate the indicator ratios mentioned in Section 7.3, such as times interest earned, leverage, and the cash flow ratio. Sufficiently serious deterioration in these indicators of bankruptcy risk would necessitate a subjective downgrading of the earlier valuation. One method would be to add a further "bankruptcy risk premium" to the discount rate used in the valuation formula.

7.3.3 Caterpiller Inc.: A Security Analysis and Valuation Example

Caterpillar is the dominant American competitor in the worldwide earth-moving equipment industry, selling its products to construction, mining, oil, and forestry companies. Despite the cyclical nature of its markets it had operated for more than 50 years up to 1980 with only a single year of loss. That year was 1932, in the worst of the Great Depression. It built an exceptional market position, attaining a share of over 50% of the world market for earth-moving equipment. It maintained this position throughout the entire decade of the 1970s and was one of a handful of companies singled out for effective management by Peters and Waterman (1982) in their popular book *In Search of Excellence*. It has long been one of the largest net exporters in the United States, with total exports in 1992 amounting to $3.33 billion.

During the 1980s, however, its performance became much less certain, as is evident from Figure 7.3. In the report to shareholders for 1990, the chairman stated: "Nineteen ninety was a disappointing year. Sales and revenues reached record levels, but profit was clearly unacceptable. Improving long-term profitability is an urgent priority, and as you'll read in this report, we're taking action

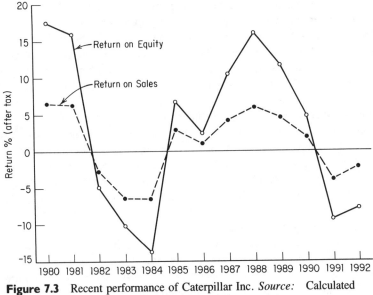

Figure 7.3 Recent performance of Caterpillar Inc. *Source:* Calculated from the company's Annual Reports.

to make Caterpillar a stronger competitor and better investment for stock-holders."

In the short term, the company went on to make losses in both 1991 and 1992. Fundamentally altering its costs and revenue streams has proved to be painful, but Caterpillar continues to adjust to the structural changes in its market and the increasing competitor strength that began to affect the firm in the early 1980s. In order to do so, it has invested more than $4.5 billion in fixed assets since 1986 as part of a program of factory modernization. In 1992 its operations generated $503 million of cash compared with $1 billion of cash needs. The valuation of its securities therefore represent a useful example of how industry, firm, and financial effects must be brought together in security analysis.

In terms of the five forces discussed in Section 7.2.4, the earth-moving equipment business had a number of attractive structural features. The market is concentrated in the hands of eight players worldwide. Both buyers and dealers are much more fragmented than the equipment suppliers, reducing their bargaining power. Likewise, parts and raw materials are generally shared with other industries (such as truck and tractor production), so they tend to be available from a number of alternative suppliers. There are substantial barriers to entry because it is difficult for dealers to divert their sales attention from proven products, train their service engineers in a new product, and duplicate their inventory of spare parts for a new product with initially small market share. The major substitute for earth-moving equipment is additional labor, which is becoming increasing expensive in real terms throughout most of the world.

On the downside, the cyclicality of the construction industry forces the earth-moving equipment producer to go through periods of excess capacity when demand falls off and suffer high costs of excess demand in boom periods. The growth in the industry is now modest in much of the developed world, with most of the growth confined to developing countries. Since labor is much cheaper there, the forces of substitution place greater limits on the prices of expensive equipment. The dealer networks of the major suppliers are less well developed in the third world, allowing better opportunities for smaller rivals or new entrants. Many of the projects are sponsored by governments who put the equipment out to competitive tender. These trends mean that the industry has become structurally less attractive since the early 1980s.

Caterpillar had maintained above-average profitability compared with its industry by differentiating its product in terms of quality (low levels of breakdown) and high levels of service through an extensive dealer network that supplied maintenance and parts as well as sales information. The costs associated with breakdown are high for many customers. In the construction industry, for example, breakdown of earth-moving equipment can delay the whole schedule and leave expensive labor and materials idle while waiting for the basic work to be completed. Thus many customers were willing to pay a substantial price premium (around 15%) for high quality and service. Caterpillar used this premium to pay its dealers attractive margins, to hold excess capacity in production with which to respond to upswings in the construction cycle, to maintain high inventories of parts that enabled it to respond quickly to breakdowns and quality problems, and last but not least to provide its shareholders with attractive returns.

Some of the competitors, notably Komatsu of Japan, had developed their product quality to close the gap with Caterpillar by the early 1980s. This competition reduced Caterpillar's ability to maintain a price premium and shifted the focus more onto competition on the basis of costs, a trend that was given further impetus by structural changes in the market. Komatsu intensified this pressure by developing ways of reducing inventory turn through modular designs, which reduced the number of different components, and employing "just-in-time" logistics systems. It also introduced more flexible manufacturing and supply chains to permit more variety to meet the precise specifications of different customers operating in different geographic environments and different user industries throughout the world. Komatsu also slowly built a substantial sales and service network. In Europe, meanwhile, mergers between French, German, and the subsidiaries of some American firms produced larger, more powerful competitors. Competitive pressure is therefore increasing in the face of an industry with modest long-term market growth.

The shift in emphasis in the market towards cost competition, combined with higher levels of variety and flexibility that make a strategy based on a price premium less viable, present long-term problems for Caterpillar. The shift requires that margins be restored primarily through reduced costs and better inventory and asset turnover. Our cash flow pro forma must therefore be driven by these ratios, rather than significantly increased prices or sustained, rapid volume growth. The key questions are, How fast can Caterpillar adjust these ratios and how much cash will be required for investment in plant modernization and development of increased variety and new products?

Figure 7.4 suggests that the management has been making some progress in improving the inventory and accounts receivable ratios in recent years. However, given the structural changes in the industry and competitive forces discussed above, it seems unlikely that accounts receivable turnover will return to the levels of the early 1980s. Continued improvements in logistics systems and modular redesign of products, on the other hand, should allow new levels of inventory turn to gradually be reached in the future. On these arguments, our pro forma calculations assume inventory turn will rise to 7 times over the next 5 years while receivables turnover will improve slightly to 5.5 times.

Some of the other critical assumptions include an average growth in sales volumes of 3% per annum over the next 5 years, in line with projected growth in the world construction industry. We assume an average 3% per annum increase in average selling prices, just below more generally projected rates of inflation. This assumption reflects the difficulties of obtaining price increases in the more competitive market described above, and the continuing shift toward smaller machines in the product mix that has characterized demand in recent years.

As indicated by management plans, we have factored in the continued need for investment in modernization at a rate close to $500 million per annum until after 1993, followed by continued investment of $300 million per annum subse-

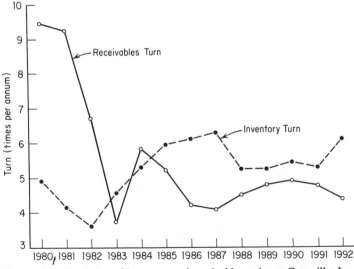

Figure 7.4 Evolution of inventory and receivables ratios at Caterpillar Inc.
Source: Calculated from the company's Annual Reports.

quently. Finally, we have based our security analysis on the average margins on sales that characterized the industry in the late 1980s, rather than the higher levels that prevailed earlier. This decision reflects an assumption that the changes in the market and competitive forces we discussed above, as well as the reduced viability of maintaining a substantial price premium through a differentiation strategy, are structural shifts. Hence they are likely to characterize conditions in the future.

Working through the pro formas set out in Tables 7.6 and 7.7, our estimates suggest that Caterpillar's ability to generate high returns for its shareholders will be held back by the interest and cash burdens associated with heavy investment in plant modernization and the need to finance rising accounts receivable, given the new realities of competition in the market. Expected improvements in inventory turnover, given the duration of adjustment, will be insufficient to offset the effects of this cash absorption.

We cannot detail all of the other assumptions inherent in the pro forma cash flow calculations for the purposes of this example. Suffice it to say that the analyst must make estimates of future interest, inflation and tax rates by working through the macroeconomic considerations described in Chapter 2. The pro forma is a way of helping to sort out their implications for a particular firm given the structure of its assets, liabilities, revenues, and costs and the market pressures upon it.

At the end of this process, we produced a series of forecasts of Caterpillar's cash flows from 1993 through 1998, after which we treated the cash stream as a perpetuity in the manner described in Section 7.3.2. When we discounted these cash flow forecasts back at an estimated cost of capital, we made allowance for the fact that Caterpillar's dependence on the construction industry tends to amplify the effects of the business cycle and give it a relatively high beta. The final result of this security analysis suggested an "inherent value" of one Caterpillar share of $58. Readers may be interested to note that during 1992 Caterpillar shares traded as high as 62⅛ and as low as 41¼. During 1993 Caterpillar's share price reached a high of 83, suggesting that the market had become much more optimistic than our security analysis would suggest was warranted. If our security analysis is at all accurate, the peak share price of $83 should have been vulnerable to disappointing earnings. This warning in fact proved correct, with Caterpillar's share price falling back to around 68 by late 1995—against the trend of a generally rising stock market.

7.4 SHORTCUTS IN SECURITY VALUATION

At this point some readers may ask, "Is all this complex analysis of financial statements, industry structure, and firm strategy really necessary; isn't there a simpler way?" They may have heard the claim that one simple rule of thumb can replace all of this security analysis: the price/earnings ratio (P/E). Perhaps less likely, they may have been impressed by the proponents of Tobin's q as a universal method of equity valuation. A brief discussion of these two concepts will be helpful.

7.4.1 Uses and Pitfalls of Price/Earnings Ratios

Price/earnings ratios are a simple way to express stock prices in terms of a common denominator. It is sometimes helpful to check whether a stock trading, say, $60 is in fact trading at a higher or lower premium than one priced at $40. If the first stock had earnings per share (*EPS*) of $6 and the second $4, then both would be trading at the same premium of 10 times earnings. If the latter stock had earnings of $8, however, its P/E multiple would be only 5.

Why might an investor be willing to pay a premium of 10 times earnings for one stock and 5 times earnings for another, or 20 for yet another? To understand, this let us return to the dividend growth valuation model discussed at the end of Section 6.1:

$$PVD = DIV(O)\,\frac{1+g_d}{r_s-g_d}\,,$$

where g_d is the assumed growth rate of dividends and r_s is the rate of return required by potential investors in this particular stock. Now the dividend in each period is equal to the earnings in each period multiplied by the dividend payout ratio:

$$d(t) = \frac{DIV(t)}{EPS(t)}\,,$$

where $EPS(t)$ stands for earnings per share. If we are prepared to assume that the dividend payout ratio $d(t)$ and the discount rate r_s remain constant over time then earnings grow at the same constant rate g_d as dividends, and the *PVD* formula also applies to earnings.[20] It can then be seen the P/E ratio reflects a combination of simplifying assumptions about the dividend payout ratio, the expected rate of growth of earnings, and the discount rate (including some allowance for risk).

This may look like a much simpler way to get an estimate of the "intrinsic" value of a stock. The problem is that those three variables—the anticipated future growth rate, the dividend payout ratio, and the discount rate—depend on all of the factors we have been discussing, including industry and firm effects and the firm's future investment needs. In a sense, the P/E ratio sweeps under the carpet many of the hypotheses one should make in order to analyze the appropriate value of a stock.

In the 1960s, a number of investigators (e.g., Whitbeck and Kisor, 1963) estimated regression equations of the form: $P/E = Y + \delta_1 g + \delta_2 d + \delta_3 \sigma$, where g

was an estimate of future growth, d was an estimate of the dividend payout ratio, and σ was a measure of risk (namely the standard deviation). Once the equation was estimated, it was then used to estimate "intrinsic P/E ratios" for individual stocks. When the actual P/E was above the estimate, the stock was said to be good value. The problem with this should be clear: Deviations from the intrinsic P/E could represent either incorrect valuation by the market or failure of the assumptions of the simplified model to capture all of the significant influences on the fundamental value of the stock. Subsequent studies of the predictive power of these models suggested that the latter explanation (incorrect model specification) was usually the cause of what were, in fact, spurious deviations from the "true values".

Although using P/E ratios in a less precise way, many commentators over the years have suggested that there is a "normal" of "sustainable" P/E for either the market as a whole or for particular stocks. Thus it was argued that in 1959 the S&P500 index, then equivalent to twenty times current earnings, was unsustainably high.

During the period since World War II, actually, the P/E ratio corresponding to the S&P500 was highly variable, ranging from a low of 5.9 in 1949 to a high of 22.4 in 1961. Nor do its movements show a neat cyclical pattern: In fact, for about a dozen years after 1959, this P/E ratio stayed fairly close to 20 (using annual data), so anyone who thought it was too high in 1959 would have needed considerable patience to profit from his foreboding. After falling sharply in the 1970s to 7.4 in 1979, it recovered again and has recently fluctuated around 15. This suggests that the P/E responds to different information and expectations about growth and the appropriate discount rates. There is conceivably a "normal" level, determined by economic growth and real interest rates in the long run, but it would be difficult to determine. To find this "normal" level for individual equities would be even more difficult. While P/E ratios have some usefulness in "scaling" stocks of different unit values, they are not a substitute for careful security analysis based on an understanding of the industry and the firm's competitive advantages within it. Their most important application, perhaps, is in valuing the equities of firms that do not pay dividends but do have earnings—or at least prospective earnings.[21] Such firms are usually fairly new and relatively small. If they have earnings at all, they often prefer to plow them back into the business, and this may indeed be the best use of these funds from the shareholders' point of view.

In a new industry, such as biotechnology, there are typically many firms with no earnings at all. Their prospects have to be assessed on the basis of technological judgments concerning the merits of their production processes, and on economic judgments about the market for their products, assuming they can actually produce them. Any P/E ratio refers to the future and is of necessity highly conjectural. Some firms will have earnings, and in a new industry the P/E ratios will usually be high, reflecting the supposed advantage of being ahead of the pack. Those firms can indeed be scaled by their P/E ratio, but one with a high ratio is not necessarily expensive; it may be that knowledgeable investors consider its prospects unusually promising. Even for those firms, consequently, the P/E ratio carries little information by itself.

7.4.2 Tobin's q as an Alternative Approach to Securities Valuation

While the P/E ratio focuses on the profit-and-loss statement of a corporation, Tobin's q (already discussed in Section 6.2 with special reference to the aggregate of all U.S. corporations) looks at its balance sheet. As we shall show, this is not the whole story, but it is a good starting point.

When we state that the value of a firm, and hence the price of its equity, is the discounted value of future dividends, it is sometimes easy to forget that any business is not a "bundle of money" but a bundle of real assets, some tangible, some intangible. If you were to ask most laymen why a firm was worth something, they would probably point to the collection of plants, distribution centers, brand names, and teams of skilled individuals as the source of intrinsic value. We should therefore have something to say about how this complex collection of assets is reflected in the price of the securities that represent claims upon it.

Suppose that a new company is set up with $1 million of equity capital. It then uses this money to construct a building on a new industrial site around which there is plenty of vacant land. What would the company—call it Specbuild Inc.—then be worth? A prospective buyer for this company might be another business wishing to move into expanded premises identical to this new building. They would have at least two alternatives. One would be to buy Specbuild Inc. lock, stock, and barrel. An alternative would be to build an exact replica on the vacant land next door. Leaving aside any differences in risk and the cost of renting other premises during construction, the value of Specbuild would therefore be equal to the replacement cost of its only asset, the building. The buyer would not want to pay more than the replacement cost, since it could avoid the premium simply by replicating the building.

One way of expressing this would be to calculate the ratio of the market value of an asset (MV) to its replacement cost (RC). This is the ratio called q by Tobin (1958). Suppose you own one of the 1 million shares in Specbuild; how much would your share be worth? We could write the share price (PS) as:

$$PS = MV/(1m) = (MV/RC)(RC/1m) = q(RC/1m),$$

where "1m" is 1 million. If Specbuild were inexperienced in the building trade and so wasted much of the materials in scrap and made poor bargains with their contractors, it may have cost them $1 million to construct a building that a more efficient company could replicate next door for only $750,000. In this case q would be 0.75 and your share would be worth 75 cents. If, on the other hand, Specbuild were efficient builders and the city government subsequently introduced a new flat rate tax of $500,000 on all new construction, the replacement cost might rise to $1.5 million, in which case your share would be worth $1.50.

More generally, this model shows how inflation in the replacement cost will increase the value of assets that are easily replicated. Whenever there is little difference between buying an existing asset or replicating it with a new one, q will remain close to 1. This is because as soon as the market value rises relative to the replacement cost, suppliers will replicate the asset, increasing the quantity available and driving the market value back into line with the replacement cost. As the time lags involved in replication increase, temporary shortages may push q well above 1. Potential buyers may be willing to pay more for the building than its replacement cost now, so as to expand their business operations immediately, rather than wait for a new one to be constructed. Clearly this would be only a temporary phenomenon.

Under what circumstances might the market value stay above the replacement cost $(q > 1)$ for a long period of time? Instead of a building, consider the problem of replicating a different kind of asset bundle, say the IBM company. Although a Herculean task, you could attempt to replicate all of IBM's tangible assets: its factories, its research laboratories, its inventories, and so on. All of this would have some total "replacement cost."

At this point, your IBM look-alike would only be worth the replacement cost of all these tangibles; q would still remain at 1. If, however, you were able to use the assets in your IBM look-alike to generate profits above your cost of capital, then this bundle of assets you put together would be much more attractive to investors and the market value would rise so that $q > 1$. Seeing a chance for capital gain by forming a bundle of assets, new entrants would spawn more IBM clones. The resulting competition in the computer market would drive your profits down, causing the market value of your company to fall back toward its replacement cost.

Yet the real IBM did for many years sustain a market value that was probably a good deal higher than the replacement cost of its tangible assets.[22] One important reason was its capacity to generate profits from its strong brand recognition, customer loyalty, and well-focused R&D, not to mention the collective know-how of its employees. By managing this complex portfolio of tangible and intangible assets in concert over a long period of time, moreover, IBM accumulated great experience in creating value for its customers and shareholders.

What makes a company really valuable is the ability to construct bundles of tangible and intangible assets that are effective in satisfying its customers and at the same time difficult for others to replicate. The company will be even more valuable if it can go on doing this over and over again by adding new assets to the bundle and replacing old ones in a cycle of investment and growth. In this case it will act as a machine for adding value to the replacement cost of its assets. Outside the firm an asset is simply worth its replacement cost, but inside the profit-generating environment of a successful firm it is worth more.

Some firms, by contrast, may have a market value that remains below the replacement cost of their assets ($q < 1$) for extended periods. An example would be a firm that invests in a plant embodying an obsolete or otherwise unsuitable technology. Similarly, a company that constructs an expensive retail outlet on a low-traffic site may find it has created an internal asset with a market value below its replacement cost. More generally, companies can get in a chronic position of $q < 1$ if they continue to invest in poor projects whose rate of return is less than the cost of capital. In this case, they will find it very difficult to raise new capital. However in some cases, management may persist in reinvesting internally generated cash flow in low-return projects for nonfinancial reasons, driving q further down. Ultimately, a very low q may encourage a takeover in which the bundle of asset is split up and sold. Even if the assets cannot be liquidated for their full replacement value, the proceeds may be greater than the current market value of the firm as a whole.[23]

As shown in Section 6.2, we can think of q as a measure of profitability or rate of return. More precisely, q can be interpreted as the ratio of the rate of return on a firm's tangible assets to its cost of capital. Using the results of Section 6.2, we can write the theoretical share price (*TP*) in terms of *RCAPS*, the replacement cost of assets per share: $TP = q * RCAPS$.[24] When $q = 1$, the company is, in effect, passively holding a bundle of assets. They may increase in value if the cost of replicating them rises, but they are unlikely to systematically increase much faster than the rate of inflation in the long run. When $q > 1$, the firm's assets are worth more than those assets would cost to replace. If the firm's strategy of asset utilization is easy to copy, new entrants will order more of these assets and use them in the same way, driving profitability and firm value down. Skilled companies, however, can find ways to bundle together their tangible assets with intangibles and accumulated skills in an operating environment, which can be very difficult to replicate. Shares in these firms will be more highly valued. If these firms can deter imitators or keep on finding new ways to utilize assets profitably, then this high value can be maintained for a long time.

Some firms, on the other hand, find that their assets are worth less than they would cost to replace. This may be because they are caught with bundles of assets designed to serve markets that are declining or to support products that are obsolete. It may reflect a series of disappointing investment decisions or a glut in the supply of certain services. Such situations will be signalled by $q < 1$ because their value has fallen to reflect their expected low returns.

We conclude that Tobin's q can, in principle, tell us a great deal about the intrinsic value of a company's shares. Its main attraction is that it puts replacement cost in the central position where it belongs. It is not a complete substitute for the detailed analysis of financial statements described in Section 7.3, but as a summary measure it appears to be superior to the price/earnings ratio. Further research is needed to see whether the promise of q theory can be realized in practice.

8

Options and Options Pricing

Many forms of option contracts are found in everyday life. These vary from the very informal to the standardized and precisely defined options traded on major options exchanges around the world. When you pay a nonrefundable deposit to reserve an outdoor tennis court for a particular day in the future, for example, you are entering into an informal options contract. You are paying a fee now in exchange for the right to buy a good or service in the future at a known price. If the day is clear, you enjoy a game of tennis. If it rains when the day arrives, or your prospective partner breaks his leg beforehand, you don't rent the court (the option is left unexercised). The most cash you can lose as a result of purchasing the option is the amount of the nonrefundable deposit, which is the price of the option.

There are two broad classes of options: puts and calls. Our example illustrates some of the important characteristics of a *call option*. It involves the right to buy a good, service, or security in the future. The buyer of the option pays a fee for this right; that fee is the *option price*. In exchange for the option price, the seller of the option agrees to provide the good, service, or security at a fixed price, called the *exercise price* or *striking price*, if the holder of the option chooses to exercise the option. In this example, the striking price is the rental payable when the tennis court is actually used. Most options are valid for a fixed period of time, after which the right to exercise the option expires. The time period for which an option remains valid is known as the *life* of the option, and the last day on which it can be exercised is its *maturity*.

The characteristics of a *put option* are virtually identical, except that the holder of the option has the right to sell a good, service, or security to the other party at an agreed exercise price until some future date, rather than to buy it. It should be noted that while the buyer of a put or call acquires a right (not an obligation), the seller of the option does incur a definite obligation. As a guarantee of his or her ability to meet this obligation, the seller may have to provide "earnest money," also called *margin*.[1]

In general, the original buyer of an option is not required to hold it until it matures. If the right embodied in the option is valuable to others, the option can be resold. Many options can be readily negotiated, which makes them financial instruments as defined in Chapter 1. Since the early 1970s, standardized options on stocks have been traded in organized markets; more recently, options on commodities, on bonds, and on futures contracts have been added to the list.

Section 8.1 discusses the basic features of option contracts, with special reference to stock options, including the way in which the contractual elements of an option (such as the maturity or exercise price) have been standardized to facilitate trading. Section 8.2 examines various methods of valuing options contracts and how the value of a option will be influenced by its maturity, striking price, market interest rates, and the price of the underlying security. It also explores the ways in which call and put options may be combined to form various types of "spreads" and "straddles," while Section 8.3 analyzes the way in which options might be used to hedge a portfolio of stocks and hence their role as a risk management tool. We then explain how the shares in a levered firm can themselves be viewed as a type of option, and the implications of this for the pricing of stocks. Finally, options on objects other than stocks are discussed in Section 8.5.

8.1 THE BASICS OF STOCK OPTIONS

In this chapter we are mostly concerned with options on stocks; other options do not come up until Section 8.5. We first discuss the organization of trading in stock options and then proceed to a preliminary economic analysis by looking at the profits and losses resulting from buying or selling these options.

8.1.1 Institutional Aspects: Exchange-Traded Stock Options

Prior to the early 1970s, options on stocks were negotiated on an individual basis between two parties, commonly matched by a broker. Since this arrangement required the identification of a buyer and a seller with complementary needs at the same point of time, the transaction costs were high and the volume of trading was severely limited. The lack of standardization and the possibility of default by individual participants made it difficult to resell options after they had been written, so the options were illiquid.

Today, puts and calls on shares are traded on most major stock exchanges in the United States and on the Chicago Board Options Exchange.[2] Similar exchanges now exist abroad, particularly in London and Amsterdam. Options on objects other than shares are discussed in Section 8.5 and in Chapter 9.

These *exchange-traded options* were made possible by standardization of the options contract in various dimensions. Instead of letting individual buyers and sellers agree on the precise terms of the contract, each exchange lists a limited number of expiration dates and striking prices. This standardization, typical of financial markets as defined in Chapter 1, served to reduce transaction costs and thus to make options readily negotiable.

Thus an option for any particular month has its maturity on the third Friday of that month. Furthermore, each option is assigned to one of three maturity cycles. Options on some stocks at first had maturities on the January-April-July-October cycle, others on the February-May-August-November cycle, and the remainder on a March-June-September-December cycle. Because interest turned out to be concentrated on nearby maturities, however, the current month and the following month have been inserted into the list in each cycle.[3] Only three maturities are listed (both for calls and for puts) at any one time; for instance, on April 24 a stock on the January cycle will have options listed for May, June, and July maturities; one on the February cycle will have May, June, and August listings; and one on the March cycle will have May, June, and September listings.[4]

Striking prices have been standardized by listing only multiples of $5.00 (except for low-priced stocks, where the multiple is $2.50). Initially, only striking prices close to the prevailing market price for the underlying security are listed; thus if at the first listing of the October option a stock trades at $57 per share, the initial striking prices will be $55 and $60. If the stock price subsequently moves significantly outside this initial range, new striking prices are listed as needed. For example, if the stock in question rises to $63, a striking price of $65 will be added to the list. The result is that toward the end of an option's life, a sizable number of striking prices may be open for trading.[5]

The number of shares per contract (100), along with rules pertaining to stock splits and dividends declared on the underlying security during the life of the option, have also been standardized by agreement among the options exchanges. In listed options, for example, the terms of the contract remain unaltered when a cash dividend is declared or paid. On the other hand, the options contract will generally be adjusted for splits and stock dividends.

Another important innovation has been the interposition of an options clearinghouse (the Options Clearing Corporation in the United States) between buyers and sellers. Once an options price has been agreed in the market, the clearinghouse acts as the seller to all buyers, and as the buyer to all sellers. This arrangement has the important effect that the clearinghouse guarantees the performance of the contract, eliminating the need for either party to check the creditworthiness of the other prior to a trade. It also means that the buyer or seller of an option can close out his position at any time by purchasing an offsetting options contract without having to locate the original counterpart to the transaction. Both aspects greatly facilitate the secondary market.[6]

Information on the prices of listed options is reported daily in the financial press. Table 8.1 reproduces listings for two stocks, showing first the name of the underlying security, with its closing price in parentheses. Then follow the volume of trading and the price (expressed on a per share basis) of each call and put currently offered.[7] The explanation of these prices is the main topic of this chapter; as regards volume of trading, it will be noted that some options do not trade at all on any given day, and that volume tends to be larger when the striking price is close to the stock price.

Some insight in the quantitative importance of trading in options on equities is provided by Table 8.2, which also shows how many options were exercised.

From this table we can draw a number of conclusions:

1. The activity in exchange-traded options, as measured by the number of contracts traded, has declined in recent years (it reached a peak in 1987). It has fallen far behind the growth in stock market volume recorded in Table 5.1.
2. The Chicago Board Options Exchange dominates the industry with roughly two-thirds of the total volume and value.
3. Only about 5% of the options traded were exercised. The options that were not exercised must either have become worthless or liquidated by an offsetting transaction prior to expiration.

Table 8.1   Sample Options Listings

	October		November		December	
	Volume	Price	Volume	Price	Volume	Price
Ford Motor (40¼)						
35 call	15	6¼	0	[a]	60	6⅝
40 call	673	1¼	94	2⅜	90	2⁹/₁₆
45 call	348	¼	55	½	97	¾
35 put	0	[a]	0	[a]	33	⁷/₁₆
40 put	284	⅞	56	1⅜	95	2⅛
45 put	20	3¾	10	4⅝	0	[a]
Data General (10)						
7½ call	0	[a]	0	[a]	276	2¹³/₁₆
10 call	25	⁹/₁₆	5	¾	624	1¹/₁₆
12½ call	0	[a]	5	¼	102	⁵/₁₆
10 put	10	½	60	¾	0	[a]
12½ put	0	[a]	0	[a]	271	2⅝

[a]No trades (see text).

Source: Investor's Business Daily, September 23, 1992 (quotations for previous day).

Table 8.2 Trading in Stock Options
(volume in millions of contracts, total value in billions of dollars)

	1985	1990	1992
VOLUME OF TRADING			
Chicago Board Options Exchange	149	130	121
American Stock Exchanges	49	41	42
Other exchanges[a]	34	39	39
ALL EXCHANGES	233	210	202
VALUE OF CONTRACTS TRADED			
Chicago Board Options Exchange	38.4	55.4	44.5
American Stock Exchanges	11.6	12.8	14.1
Other exchanges[a]	9.1	10.8	13.6
ALL EXCHANGES	59.1	79.0	72.2
Mean value in $ per option traded	254	380	357
OPTIONS EXERCISED (All exchanges)			
Number	10.5	12.1	11.6
as % of number of options traded	4.5	5.8	5.7

[a]Includes the Pacific and New York Stock Exchanges.

Source: 1994 Statistical Abstract of the U.S., table 812.

8.1.2 The Payoff from Buying and Selling Options

We now make a start with the economic analysis of puts and calls on stocks. Figure 8.1, known as a *payoff profile,* shows the profit or loss made by an investor who purchases a call option on a stock as a function of the stock price.[8] Whenever the market price of the stock (P_s) remains below the striking price stated in the option contract (P_x), the investor will not exercise the option since the stock can be procured more cheaply direct from the open market. The option is then said to be "out of the money." If an option remains out of the money until maturity, nobody will want to exercise it and it expires, worthless. The buyer will then suffer a loss equal to the price he paid for the call (P_c), plus the interest foregone on the initial outlay.

If the price of the underlying stock rises above the striking price (i.e., the option comes "into the money"), the investor will have a net payoff Z equal to the market price of the stock, less the exercise price (at which he has the option to buy the stock), less the cost of buying and holding the call option.[9] In formula $Z = P_s - P_x - P_c(1 + rT)$, where r is the short-term rate of interest and T the time interval between the acquisition of the option and its exercise, also known as the *holding period.*

This net payoff need not be positive, since the profit from exercising the option ($P_s - P_x$) may not be enough to offset the original cost of the option plus

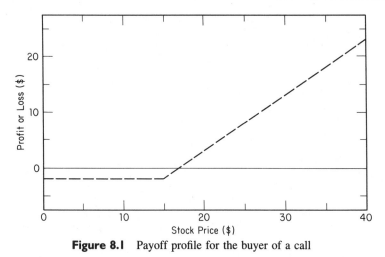

Figure 8.1   Payoff profile for the buyer of a call

interest foregone. Even if there is an overall net loss, however, it will be advantageous to exercise the option whenever P_s exceeds P_x. In practice, there may be transaction costs associated with the exercise of an option, so that P_s has to exceed P_x by more than those costs.

The relationships are reversed where the investor buys a put option. As illustrated in Figure 8.2, the option will remain unexercised if the market price of the underlying stock remains above the exercise price. This is so because it is then more profitable to sell the stock in the market than to "put" (sell) it through the option. In this case, the investor would have a loss equal to the price paid for the unexercised put (P_p) plus interest foregone. If the price of the stock were

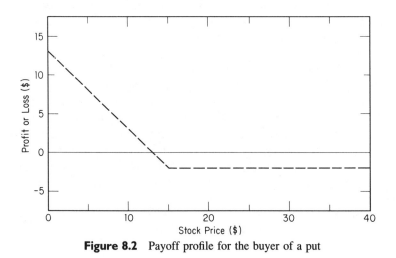

Figure 8.2   Payoff profile for the buyer of a put

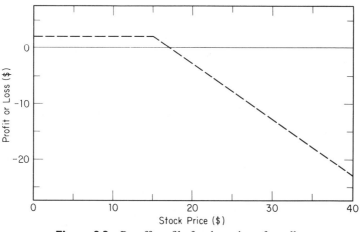

Figure 8.3 Payoff profile for the writer of a call

to fall below the exercise price, however, the net payoff Z would be given by $Z = P_x - P_s - P_p(1 + rT)$. Whether Z is positive would again depend on the cost of the option and on the interest foregone, and also on any transaction costs, as in the case of a call.

The net payoff for the seller (usually called the *writer*) of a call option is shown in Figure 8.3. Obviously, it is the mirror image of the payoff for the holder. The reader will have no difficulty in drawing a similar picture for the writer of a put option.

8.1.3 Combinations of Options

In our discussion of options so far we have looked at the pattern of profit and loss associated with the buying or selling of one put or one call considered in isolation. The buyer of a call, for example, benefits when the price of the underlying stock rises enough to move the option into the money. Similarly, the buyer of a put benefits when the stock price falls significantly. By combining options it is possible to create a different set of payoff profiles. In this section we examine the more common of these combined positions and their payoff profiles if held to maturity.

The simplest option combination is the *straddle,* in which the investor buys both a put and a call on the same stock and where both options have the same maturity and striking price. If the price of the stock remains steady throughout the life of the straddle, the investor will lose the cost of the position—that is, the price paid for the put plus the price paid for the call. Breakeven will occur when the stock price rises or falls by an amount equal to the cost of the straddle. Any larger rise or fall in the stock price at maturity then nets a dollar for dollar gain to the straddle holder. This payoff profile is charted in Figure 8.4, where the common striking price is $15, the price of the call is $2, and the price of the

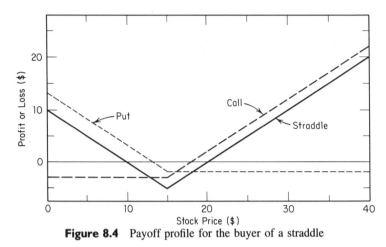

Figure 8.4 Payoff profile for the buyer of a straddle

put is $2. The figure shows both the straddle and its components; the payoff on the straddle, needless to say, is the algebraic sum of the payoffs on the components. This identity will help in drawing the payoff profiles for other combinations of options.

The reverse position of the writer of a straddle (selling the equivalent put and call simultaneously) is left for the reader to explore graphically or otherwise. In this case, the writer profits when the underlying stock price exhibits little change over the life of the straddle and loses when it moves substantially either above or below the common exercise price. A straddle, therefore, may be interpreted as a bet on the volatility of the stock price: the buyer of a straddle bets on small volatility and the writer on large volatility.

A second major set of composite positions involve the purchase or sale of a put and a call, again on the same stock and with identical maturity, but with different exercise prices (that of the put usually being less than that of the call). Such a combination is an example of an *option spread;* in this case, it may be called a *put-call spread.*

Compared with a straddle, this spread requires a larger movement in the stock price before its holder will profit, and conversely the writer can withstand a larger price movement before being forced into loss. The payoff profile for the purchaser of a spread position is again left as an exercise.

Another example of an options spread is obtained by purchasing a call at one striking price and selling a call on the same stock with the same maturity but a different striking price. Such a position is known as a *price* or *vertical* spread.[10] An investor who is mildly bullish on the price of a stock might "buy the vertical spread"; in other words, he or she might buy the option with the lower exercise price and sell the call with the higher exercise price. The total investment (maximum loss) here would be smaller than that required to buy a call alone since some of the cost of the option with the lower exercise price (which will be the more expensive) is offset by the proceeds of selling the other call.[11]

If the stock does not reach either striking price, the investor loses the difference between the original prices of the two calls. The maximum profit on the spread is also determined in advance. If the stock price rises dramatically, both options will be exercised. In that case, he or she buys at the low exercise price and sells at the higher one. The total profit will then be equal to the exercise price of the call sold less the exercise price of the call bought less the cost of call bought plus the proceeds received from the call sold.

Yet another form of spread involves simultaneously buying and selling two call options on the same stock with the same exercise price, but with different maturities. This is called a *time* or *horizontal* spread. The buyer of a horizontal spread who is bullish on the price of a stock will purchase the call with the long maturity and sell the corresponding call with a shorter maturity.

Again, the maximum loss occurs when both options remain out of the money and is equal to the difference between the price paid for the distant option and the price received for the call with shorter maturity. The maximum profit from the spread itself (assuming the longer option is sold when the nearer one matures) would occur if the stock price were exactly at the exercise price on the maturity date of the near option. In this case, the near option would be worthless to its holder but the distant option, which still has some months to run, would have a value. The profit from the horizontal spread would then be equal to the current value of the distant call plus the proceeds from sale of the near call, less the original cost of the distant call.

Numerous other possibilities are available, including selling rather than buying horizontal or vertical spreads, and *butterfly* spreads that involve buying two calls and selling two others on the same stock: one with a higher exercise price and one with a lower striking price than that of the calls originally purchased. These butterfly spreads will appeal to traders who believe that the price of the option in the middle is "out of line" with the prices of the other two. The reader is encouraged to draw the payoff profiles for such spreads.

8.1.4 Combining Options with Stocks

So far we have discussed combined positions including options only. Another important class involves combinations of a stock and options on the same stock.

A fairly common option-stock combination arises when a certain number of shares is bought and an equal number of calls is written against them.[12] This transaction is known as *writing a covered call;* an option written without an offsetting position in the underlying stock is said to be *naked*. The payoff profile is shown in Figure 8.5, where the stock component is simply a straight line with a slope of 1 going through the price of the stock when the call was written. It can easily be verified that the profile for a covered call looks identical with the one for writing a naked put.[13] As does the writer of a naked put, the writer of a

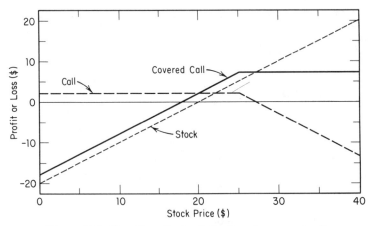

Figure 8.5 Payoff profile for the writer of a covered call

covered call runs the risk of a substantial loss if the price of the underlying stock falls by more than the call premium he or she has collected. Actually there are differences between the two transactions that are not apparent from the profiles, which lack a time dimension. Unlike a call, a stock has an infinite maturity and may earn dividends; the transaction costs, which have mostly been ignored so far, may also be different.

Another common example is buying both a stock and a put on the same stock for the same number of shares. The resulting payoff profile looks the same as that from buying a call (Figure 8.1), but again there are differences that do not show up in the profile. More generally, it should be noted that payoff profiles, while useful in explaining the basics of options, have severe limitations because they only show the initial position. In Figure 8.5, for instance, the broken line for the call is not really correct: If the market price were to fall below its initial value, the call would be worth less, as explained in Section 8.2. The covered writer could then buy back the call for less than she had originally sold it for, thus offsetting some of her loss on the stock. Payoff profiles also fail to reflect the declining value of options as they approach maturity.

Needless to say, many other combinations of stocks and options are possible, but we cannot consider them all. Only one of these deserves separate discussion because it leads to a general proposition, derived in Section 8.1.5, concerning the relation between put and call prices. It merges the two cases just discussed.

Suppose an investor buys a stock and a put, and also sells a call; the two options, which have identical exercise prices and maturities, are for the same number of shares (say one), as the stock itself. When the payoff profile for this "balanced stock-put-call position" is drawn, it turns out to be simply a horizontal line parallel to the price axis.

A numerical example may be helpful for clarification. Let the exercise price of the two options be $50 and let the initial purchase price of the stock be $47. If the stock price is below $50 when the options mature, the investor will exercise his put at $50, thus making a profit of $3 on the stock, from which the net cost of the two options must be deducted. If the stock price is precisely $50 at maturity, neither option would be exercised and the stock could again be sold for a profit of $3. For a stock price at maturity above $50 (say $52), the investor will find that the call he has sold will be exercised by its buyer, leading to a loss of $2 on the call that should be offset against a profit of $52 − $47 = $5 on the stock. Hence in all cases the payoff is $3 (the difference between the initial market price of the stock and the exercise price of the options), less the net cost of the options.[14]

8.1.5 The Put-Call Parity Theorem

The preceding example gives rise to an important theorem first stated by Stoll (1969), though it must have been known to practitioners before then. Since the net profit or loss is independent of the ultimate market price of the stock, the position we constructed is riskless. We know from Chapter 6 that the expected profit on a riskless position must equal the return on the capital invested at the default-free interest rate. In this case the capital invested is $P_s + P_p - P_c$, where P_s is the initial market price of the stock, P_p the price of the put, and P_c the price of the call. The payoff is $P_x - P_s + P_c - P_p$, where P_x, as before, is the exercise price of the two options. Consequently we must have $P_x - P_s + P_c - P_p = rT(P_s + P_p - P_c)$, which can be simplified to $P_c - P_p = P_s - (1 + rT)^{-1}P_x$, where r is again the short-term interest rate and T the holding period (which in this case is the time interval between the present [t] and the expiration date of the option). The conclusion is known as the

Put-Call Parity Theorem
The difference between the prices of a put and a call on a nondividend paying stock, both options having the same maturity (prior to which exercise is not possible) and exercise price, must equal the current price of the stock less the present value of the exercise price.

In the preceding example, suppose the interest rate is 12% per year and the holding period three months; then $rT = 0.03$ and the present value of the striking price is $50 ÷ 1.03 = $48.54. Therefore the put price must exceed the call price by $1.54 (= 48.54 − 47.00). This stands to reason since the put is "in the money" and the call "out of the money." By contrast, if the striking price had been $45, the call price would have been $3.31 (= 47 − 45 ÷ 1.03) higher than the put price.

It also follows that if the put and the call for a certain maturity are both "at the money" (that is, at the current price of the stock), then their values are approximately equal.[15] A case in point can be found in Table 8.1 for Data General, which closed at \$10 and does not pay a dividend. We see that the last price of the October 10 call was minimally different from the last (not necessarily simultaneous) price of the October 10 put, but that for the November maturity the two prices were the same. This conclusion is useful in understanding the relation not only between puts and calls (Section 8.2.6) but also between options and futures (Section 9.1.2).

Put-call parity (PCP) is important in the theory of options because it involves very few assumptions; the critical assumption (namely, that transaction costs are zero) will be discussed at the end of this section. The simplest application of PCP follows immediately from the theorem as just stated, where the difference between the call price and the put price is given as a simple function of four parameters (the stock price, the exercise price, the interest rate, and the remaining life of the option.) Thus the put price can be found if the call price— together with the four parameters—is known; the determination of the call price is the subject of the next section. An example will be presented in a moment.

First we deal with another application of PCP, made possible by solving for rT in the last displayed equation, which leads to

$$rT = \frac{P_x - P_s + P_c - P_p}{P_x - P_c + P_p}.$$

As an illustration, consider the Data General options of Table 8.1, specifically the $12\frac{1}{2}$ options expiring in December (that is, on December 18, the third Friday in that month). The formula then tells us that $rT = 0.01538$. Since the quotations are for September 22, the options had a remaining life of 87 calendar days, equivalent to 0.2384 years, which implies $r = 6.45\%$. This "implied interest rate," incidentally, does not allow for possible compounding; to get compound rates, we should replace $(1 + rT)$ in the preceding formulas with e^{-rT}.

The numerical difference between these two expressions is quite small unless rT is large; in the present illustration, for instance, use of compound-interest formulas would lead to $r = 6.34\%$. For simplicity's sake, compounding will be ignored until further notice.

The implied interest rate that has just been calculated applies in principle to all puts and calls that are (or could be) traded on any given day. It can therefore be used to estimate the value of a December 10 put, for which there is no price in Table 8.1. The call with the same striking price traded at \$1.0625, and it follows from the theorem that $P_c - P_p = 10 - 10/1.01538 = 0.51$. Consequently, the theoretical value of the December put is $1.0625 - 0.51 = \$0.55$, or about $9/16$ in the quotation system used for stock options.

To conclude the discussion of PCP, we have to say something about its empirical validity. The main weakness of the theorem is that it neglects transaction costs, yet the riskless put-call-stock combination from which the theorem is derived involves three different transactions (two in options and one in the stock), each of which may involve a bid-ask spread and—if the arbitrage is undertaken by an outside investor—a commission. In reality, therefore, PCP is more likely to be satisfied in some average sense than exactly in all cases.

8.2 THE VALUATION OF STOCK OPTIONS

The valuation of options contracts is among the most interesting—and also the most demanding—topics to be dealt with in this book. Long before stock options had reached their present importance, scholars and financiers had wondered how their prices were determined.[16] It was commonly believed that option prices somehow depend on traders' subjective expectations and risk preferences while stock prices reflected market equilibrium. This view is not helpful since these determinants on the individual level cannot be observed directly. A breakthrough in options theory came when it was realized that stock prices and options prices depend on the same set of expectations, and that this joint dependence permits the development of explicit formulas for option prices (discussed in Section 8.2.3).

Basic to an understanding of the theory is a distinction applicable to both puts and calls: The contract may state that the holder can exercise the option (1) only on maturity, in which case it is known as a *European Option,* or (2) at any time up to maturity, in which case it is known as an *American Option.*[17] The European type happens to be easier to analyze, so we shall consider it first. Remaining on an intuitive level, we may begin by analyzing what factors might logically play an important role in determining the worth of a European option to its holder.

The first such factor is clearly the price behavior of the underlying stock. Figure 8.1 shows that the higher the stock price goes, the more valuable the call option becomes to its holder.[18] A large increase in the stock price will be more likely to occur if the stock is volatile relative to the rest of the market. The first important conclusion with regard to options, therefore, is that the call option is more valuable the more volatile the underlying stock. This is in direct contrast to the valuation of the stock itself, where (as we saw in Chapter 6) volatility tends to reduce the stock's value to risk-averse investors. The most that the holders of a call option will lose if the price of the stock declines is the price they originally paid for the call, which will then remain unexercised.

The opposite is true when a stock pays a cash dividend. The shareholders face a decline in the stock price after the dividend is declared, but this decline is offset by the dividend receipt, to varying degrees depending on their tax position, the transactions costs they face, and their income preferences. The holder of a call option, however, will almost certainly lose as the chance that the stock price will exceed its striking price declines in the wake of an outflow of dividend cash from the firm.[19] The opposite holds for a European put.

The second set of important factors in option valuation are the characteristics of the option contract itself. The higher its exercise price, the lower the value of a call and the higher the value of a put (for any given current price of the stock). A higher exercise price for a call, for instance, means a greater likelihood that the call will be out of the money at maturity and hence that it will not be exercised. Although they refer to American options, the option prices shown in Table 8.1 illustrate this point, and also the next one.

The second relevant characteristic of the option contract is its maturity, which determines its remaining life T. The longer its remaining life, the greater the chance that the stock price will rise above the exercise price.[20] Moreover, since the exercise price of a European call is the amount that must be paid on maturity, a call with a long maturity will have a lower effective exercise price when discounted back to the present. In other words, since a dollar in the future is worth less than a dollar paid now, the same exercise price is actually lower the further into the future it must be paid. The corresponding analysis for a put is left to the reader.

It follows that the final factor of importance in valuing an option is the prevailing market interest rate. In fact, it turns out to have a much more pervasive influence than simply as a determinant of the present value of the exercise price, as will become apparent. Before discussing that issue, however, let us pursue our logical intuition a little further on the case of nondividend paying European calls.

The next step toward a valuation model for these calls is to understand some simple bounds outside of which the price cannot move. The first of these stems from the fact that an option to buy one unit of a stock can never be worth more than the market price for which that stock can be resold. Algebraically $P_c(t)$, the price of the call at time t, must be less than or equal to the price $P_s(t)$ of the underlying stock at that time: $P_c(t) < P_s(t)$. If this were not the case, it would be cheaper to buy the stock directly in the market than by exercising the call, even at a zero striking price.

Secondly, it should be clear that an option to buy a worthless stock will itself be worthless, so that $P_c = 0$ if $P_s = 0$. The value of an option, however, can never be negative since its holder always has the right to leave it unexercised rather than exercise it at a loss.[21] The option holder, therefore, cannot lose more than the cost of the option.

A further boundary may be defined by considering the exercise of a European call at maturity, that is at time T_1. Since the option was established at time t and was assumed to have a remaining life of T, we have $T_1 = t + T$. On that day the price of the call must be at least equal to the difference between the price $P_s(T_1)$ of the stock and the exercise price (P_x). Consequently $P_s(T_1) - P_x$ is the profit to be made by exercising the option to buy the stock at P_x and immediately selling it in the market at $P_s(T_1)$. If this potential profit were greater than the cost of the call, arbitrageurs would be buying up calls, exercising them, and

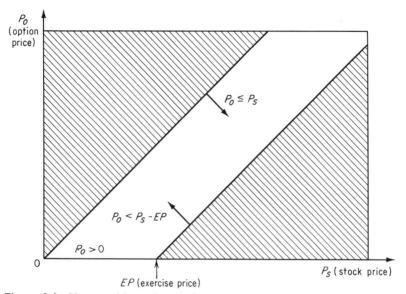

Figure 8.6 Upper and lower bounds for a European call option with no dividends

selling the stock to make a windfall gain. The resulting demand for calls would force their price P_c to rise until: $P_c(T_1) > P_s(T_1) - P_x$, and hence the potential for windfall gain would be eliminated.

Taken together, these constraints define upper and lower bounds for P_c relative to P_s forming a parallelogram of the form shown in Figure 8.6.

8.2.1 The Expected Payoff of a European Call

As just noted, the proceeds from exercising a European call at maturity T_1 equal $P_{sT} - P_x$, where $P_s(T_1)$ has been abbreviated to P_{sT}. Disregarding transaction costs, exercise will be profitable only if $P_{sT} > P_x$. The expected payoff EP may therefore be written as a conditional expectation: $EP = E(P_{sT} - P_x | P_{sT} > P_x)$, where the second expression indicates the condition under which the expectation is to be evaluated. The expectation of a difference is equal to the difference of the separate expectations, so we can also write $EP = E(P_{sT} | P_{sT} > P_x) - E(P_x | P_{sT} > P_x)$.

The first term on the right will be called E_0. In the second term on the right P_x is not a random variable but a known constant; it can therefore be put before the expectation operator and the term becomes $P_x \mathrm{prob}(P_{sT} > P_x)$, or $P_x E_1$ for short. Thus we get $EP = E_0 - P_x E_1$. The buyer of a European call, purchased at time t, has an initial investment of $P_{ct} = P_c(t)$.

The expected payoff occurs after the option has completed its remaining life

$T;$ to calculate the return on this investment, we must discount the expected payoff at an (as yet unknown) rate of r_c per annum.[22] The expected return on the investment is then

$$\{EPe^{(-r_cT)} - P_{ct}\}/P_{ct}.$$

The problem of valuing a European call has thus been reduced to determining the discount rate r_c that will bring the expected return on the call in line with alternative investments, such as buying the stock itself and holding it for the same length of time T. For this purpose we turn to the Capital Asset Pricing Model (CAPM).

8.2.2 Application of the Capital Assets Pricing Model to Options

In this section we continue to lay the groundwork for an explicit formula giving the expected value of a European call.* This formula, discussed more fully in the following section, was first derived by Black and Scholes (1973), who thereby brought a long search to a successful conclusion. Its discovery was not only an academic achievement; it has also had a major impact on the actual practice of option trading.[23]

The widespread acceptance of the Black-Scholes formula is the more remarkable because it is based on a number of simplifying assumptions whose realism is open to question. These assumptions, quoted with minor changes from the original source, are

1. The stock price follows a random walk in continuous time with a coefficient of variation[24] proportional to the stock price.
2. The coefficient of variation of the return on the stock is constant over time. This implies that the distribution of stock returns is lognormal.
3. The short-term interest rate is known and constant through time.
4. The stock pays no dividends or other distributions.
5. There are no transaction costs.

These assumptions include those underlying the CAPM, which can therefore be legitimately applied. The expected value w of a European call under these assumptions depends only on the stock price P_s and time t, and on three known parameters, namely, the interest rate r, the holding period T, and the standard deviation σ of the return on the stock. Thus we can write $E(P_c) = w(P_s,t;r,T,\sigma)$, where the parameters are separated from the principal variables by a semicolon; in fact, these parameters will usually be suppressed.

To use CAPM, we must first look at expected returns. Since by assumption the stock on which the call is written does not pay any dividend its expected return (relative to the initial investment of P_s per share) in any short time interval

---

*Readers whose knowledge of calculus stops short of partial derivatives may skip this section.

Δt is simply the expected price change $E(\Delta P_s/P_s)$ over that interval. According to CAPM, this expected return satisfies the equation

$$E\{\Delta E(\Delta P_s/P_s)\} = r\Delta t + \alpha\beta_s\Delta t, \tag{8.1}$$

where r is the return on a default-free asset, a the additional return on the market portfolio, and β_s the stock's beta. A similar equation must hold for the option, which is also a financial instrument:

$$E\{\Delta E(\Delta P_c/P_c)\} = r\Delta t + \alpha\beta_c\Delta t, \tag{8.2}$$

where β_c is the beta of the call option.

The two betas occurring in Equations (8.1) and (8.2) are obviously related to each other. To see how they are related, we consider the dependence of the call option value w on the current stock price P_s as given by the partial derivative $\partial w(P_s,t)/\partial P_s = w_1$, where the subscript reflects the position of P_s as the first argument of $w(P_s,t)$. Thus a \$1 difference in the stock price, everything else (including time) remaining the same, leads to a \$$w_1$ difference in the expected value of the option price.[25] When this relation is applied to the changes in P_s and P_c considered in the preceding paragraph, we find that $E(\Delta P_c) = w_1\Delta P_s$, from which it follows that

$$E(\Delta P_c/P_c) = (w_1 P_s/P_c)E(\Delta P_s/P_s).$$

The first factor on the right-hand side is known as the *option elasticity*. A further consequence is that

$$\beta_c = (w_1 P_s/P_c)\beta_s, \tag{8.3}$$

which is the desired relation between the two betas. Although we cannot prove it here, it is intuitively clear that the beta of a call will normally exceed the beta of the underlying stock.

The derivation of an explicit formula for the expected option value is equivalent to finding the function $w(P_s,t)$ that satisfies Equations (8.1) through (8.3). The mathematics needed for this purpose is well beyond the level assumed in this book, and we will not try to paraphrase it.[26]

8.2.3 The Black-Scholes Formula for a European Call

In its original form, the Black-Scholes formula expresses the expected value of a European call in terms of two variables (the stock price and the current date) and four parameters (the exercise price, the risk-free interest rate, the remaining life of the option, and the volatility of the underlying stock). In our notation the formula reads:

$$E\{P_c(P_s,t)\} = P_s N(d_1) - P_x e^{-r(T_1 - tN(d_2))},$$

where (repeating some of the previous definitions for convenience)

P_c = the price of a European call

P_s = the price of the underlying stock

P_x = the exercise price of the option

r = the continuously compounded annual risk-free rate of interest

T_1 = the date on which the option expires

t = the present date

$N(z)$ = the probability that a random variable will exceed z given a normal distribution with a mean of zero and a variance of 1,

$$d_1 = \frac{\log(P_s/P_x) + (T_1 - t)(r + \sigma^2/2)}{\sigma\sqrt{(T_1 - t)}};$$

$$d_2 = \frac{\log(P_s/P_x) + (T_1 - t)(r - \sigma^2/2)}{\sigma\sqrt{(T_1 - t)}};$$

σ = the standard deviation of the stock price, considered as a random variable

Since the original Black-Scholes formula is somewhat complicated, we shall now present it in a simplified appearance. The simplification is accomplished by combining the variables and parameters into only two arguments; since the process requires no additional assumptions, it does not restrict the validity of the formula in any way. The simplified Black-Scholes formula may be written

$$E(Q_c) = N(d_1) - yN(d_2), \tag{8.4}$$

where the new variables are $Q_c = P_c/P_s$, which is the ratio of the price of the call to the price of the stock, and $y = (P_x e^{-rT})/P_s$, the ratio of the present value of the exercise price to the stock price. This substitution also gives a simpler form for two components of the Black-Scholes formula:

$$d_1 = \frac{\sigma_T}{2} - \frac{\log y}{\sigma_T}$$

$$d_2 = -\frac{\sigma_T}{2} - \frac{\log y}{\sigma_T}.$$

The last two formulas involve two more new variables: $T = T_1 - t$, the remaining life of the option expressed in years, and $\sigma_T = \sigma T^{1/2}$; this is the customary standard deviation of the return on the stock multiplied by the square root of the remaining life. It corresponds to the standard deviation of the stock price during the remaining life of the option and will be called the *fractional standard deviation*.[27] Evidently if the remaining life is one year ($T = 1$), the customary and fractional standard deviation are the same, from which we see that the customary standard deviation is actually on an annual basis.

The interpretation of the simplified formula is easiest in the special case where the stock price is the same as the present value of the striking price. This is almost the same as saying that the call option is "at the money," but not quite because the striking price is discounted; when the interest rate is low or the remaining life is short, discounting will have little effect. It implies $y = 1$, log $y = 0$, and consequently

$$E(Q_c) = N(\sigma_T/2) - N(-\sigma_T/2).$$

In this particular case, the ratio of the call price to the stock price is equal to the difference between two values of the cumulative normal distribution (with zero mean and unit variance), one calculated at a point located one-half of the fractional standard deviation above the mean and the other at a point the same distance below the mean. Since the normal distribution is symmetric around the mean, the area under the normal density curve between each of these two points and the mean is the same.

We now return to the general case. As an illustration of the Black-Scholes formula, which can be easily programmed for a calculator or computer, the call option values corresponding to selected parameters (as defined above) are given in Table 8.3. The option values are given as a percentage of the stock price,

Table 8.3 Theoretical Value of a European Call as a Percentage of the Stock Price

		$\sigma = 0.2$			$\sigma = 0.3$	
T	$x =$ 0.75	1.0	1.25	0.75	1.0	1.25
			$r = .05$			
.1	25.37	2.77	0.01	25.38	4.03	0.04
.2	25.75	4.07	0.03	25.80	5.83	0.36
.3	26.12	5.12	0.13	26.30	7.27	0.89
.4	26.51	6.05	0.32	26.84	8.51	1.52
.5	26.91	6.89	0.57	27.41	9.64	2.20
.6	27.31	7.67	0.87	27.99	10.67	2.90
.7	27.73	8.42	1.20	28.58	11.63	3.60
.8	28.14	9.12	1.56	29.16	12.54	4.31
			$r = .10$			
.1	25.75	3.04	0.00	25.75	4.28	0.05
.2	26.49	4.61	0.04	26.53	6.34	0.42
.3	27.22	5.94	0.19	27.36	8.04	1.07
.4	27.96	7.15	0.46	28.22	9.53	1.84
.5	28.69	8.28	0.82	29.08	10.91	2.69
.6	29.42	9.35	1.26	29.94	12.19	3.58
.7	30.15	10.38	1.76	30.79	13.40	4.48
.8	30.87	11.37	2.30	31.63	14.56	5.38

which is equivalent to putting the stock price at $100 throughout and expressing the option value in dollars.

From this table it can be verified that the results of the Black-Scholes formula are consistent with the basic logical results presented earlier, namely, that the price of a European call option will be higher (all else equal)

- The higher the initial stock price
- The lower the exercise price
- The more volatile the price of the stock
- The longer the remaining life of the option
- The higher is the risk-free interest rate

Intuitively, the last result reflects the fact that if the risk-free rate rises, so must the required return on a perfect hedge. The achievement of this higher return implies that the investor receives a higher price for each call option sold.

8.2.4 Alternative Derivations of the Black-Scholes Formula

Although the final Black-Scholes formula is relatively simple, its derivation (given only in part) is not. More elementary proofs have been attempted, and we now present one such effort due to Cox and Rubinstein (1985).

With the earlier discussion of option-stock combinations in mind, we may think about this problem in terms of a portfolio consisting of a long position in the stock and a short position in the related call option; in other words, buying a stock while also selling one or more calls against that stock.

Suppose you paid $10 for one share and sold one European call with a striking price of $10 and a maturity of one year for $1. If at the end of the year the stock is trading in the market at a price higher than $10, the holder of the call will exercise the option requiring you to sell the stock for $10, so you wind up with gross revenue of $11. If instead at the end of the year the stock was still trading at $10, the holder would not benefit by exercising the call; you can then sell the stock on the open market for $10 while keeping the proceeds of selling the call, again leaving you with $11.

In this example of a covered call the holder of the stock is hedged against a rise in the stock price, as we know already from Section 8.1.3. If the price of the stock began to fall, however, the holder would stand to lose. She could protect herself by immediately selling more calls against her shares in order to maintain the ultimate gross revenue at $11. In deciding how many calls to sell, she would have to take into account that at the lower stock price, each call sells for less.

In a world without transactions costs, it is possible to continually readjust the ratio of calls to the price of the stock so as to protect the value of the portfolio against any changes in the stock price, thus eliminating risk altogether.

What return should an investor earn on this risk-free portfolio? The answer is the risk-free interest rate.

The reversal of this chain of reasoning allows us to derive the relationship between the price of a stock and the price of a call option on that stock. Specifically, using the requirement that a perfectly hedged portfolio must earn the risk-free rate, we can work back through the definition of the perfect hedge as a mix of a long position in the stock and a short position in the call option to derive a formula for the price of the call itself. This procedure is best illustrated by example.

Suppose there are two possible future states of the world, a boom and a recession, each with a 50% chance of occurring. If the economy goes into boom, the price of our stock will increase by $f\%$ to a new price $(1+f)P_s$.

In forming a hedged portfolio, however, we sold a number h of call options for every unit of stock we hold. Any increase in the price of the stock above the exercise price of the call option will therefore be transferred to the holder of the call at an exercise price of P_x. The total value of our hedged portfolio in a boom will therefore be $(1+f)P_s - h\{(1+f)P_s - P_x\}$: In other words, the new value of the stock, less that part of the benefit accruing to the holder of the call option multiplied by the number of calls we sold (h).

If, on the other hand, the economy goes into recession, the value of our stock will decline by $g\%$, while the calls will not be exercised, so that our portfolio will be worth simply: $(1-g)P_s$. Now if the portfolio is perfectly hedged its value must be equal whether or not the stock price rises or falls, so that $(1+f)P_s - h\{(1+f)P_s - P_x\} = (1-g)P_s$, that is, the value in boom must be the same as the value in recession.

We can use this equation to solve for the number of calls h that must be sold to achieve a perfect hedge:[28]

$$h = \frac{P_s(f+g)}{P_s(1+f)-P_x}.$$

Now recall that the amount we have invested in the hedged portfolio is equal to the amount we originally paid for the stock (P_s) less the cash we received from selling the call options (hP_c), where P_c is the price received for each call. This investment should return the risk free rate so that at the end of the period it is worth $(1+r)(P_s - hP_c)$. Equating this to the assumed value of the portfolio in a boom, we have $(1+r)(P_s - hP_c) = (1+f)P_s - h\{(1+f)P_s - P_x\}$. Substituting for the hedge ratio h, and solving this equation for the original price of the call P_c we have:

$$P_c = (r+g)\frac{(1+f)P_s - P_x}{(1+r)(f+g)}.$$

What we have then is a formula for the price of a call option in terms of the price behavior of the underlying stock, the exercise price of the call, and the risk-free rate of interest. This case is the simplest of what in the finance literature is called the *binomial option pricing formula*. Given the relevant data, it can be used to directly compute the equilibrium price of a call option. For example, suppose the present price of a stock is $50 and it is estimated to be equally likely to fall to $30 ($g = 40\%$) over the coming year as it is to rise to $80 ($f = 60\%$). If the interest rate is 10% per year, the price of a 12-month call option on that stock with an exercise price of $60 would be:

$$P_c = \frac{(0.1 + 20/50)(80 - 60)}{1.1(30/50 + 20/50)} = \$9.09.$$

It should be clear, however, that this relationship has major limitations as a satisfactory model of option pricing. Specifically, the range of stock price behavior that it can handle is very narrow, since in reality that behavior can rarely be expressed in terms of only two states of the world. A number of models incorporating richer specifications of stock price behavior have therefore been developed. Their basic logic parallels the intuitively appealing derivation we have just given. But the Black-Scholes pricing theory, thanks to its effective use of advanced mathematics, is less restrictive than any binomial-type model and continues to be most widely used.

8.2.5 Other Option Models

While a very significant improvement, the Black-Scholes model still places important restrictions on the range of stock price behavior that it can validly handle. Empirical investigations (such as Black, 1976) have concluded, for example, that the variance of returns tends to increase as the stock price declines. This condition may reflect the fact that in a levered firm with fixed interest commitments, shareholders are left with a rather erratic residual when average earnings are low.

In answer to this problem, Cox and Rubinstein (1975) proposed the constant elasticity of variance model in which the variance of returns depends on the level of the stock price. While the basic construction is similar, this requires replacement of the Black-Scholes normal distribution with an alternative statistical distribution, the gamma density function.

Finally, Merton (1976) has formulated a model in which, in addition to "normal" random fluctuations around a trend, stock prices are allowed to take discrete "jumps" that might result from events such as release of unexpected information about the firm's performance, sudden obsolescence as a result of technological breakthrough, or decisions in major lawsuits affecting the firm.

This so-called jump-diffusion model derives an adjustment to the basic Black-Scholes option price to account for the probability and size of jumps in the price of the underlying stock. Empirical evidence concerning the model's explanatory performance (e.g., Beckers, 1981) has been favorable, although the impact of jumps appears to be relatively small, particularly in a diversified options portfolio. The additional computational complexity, meanwhile, is considerable, leading most practitioners to employ the simpler binomial or Black-Scholes specifications.

8.2.6 Some Extensions of the European Call Formula

Before leaving the topic of option pricing, a number of extensions of the basic formulae to encompass dividend payments, American (flexible maturity) calls, and put options merit brief discussion.

The first approach to dividends involves an assumption that regular dividend payments are known in advance over the life of the option. In many cases such an assumption seems acceptable since the life of most options is relatively short (usually less than 9 months) and most stocks pay regular dividends that are changed relatively infrequently. In this case it is possible to allow for dividends simply by subtracting the present value of the known dividends from the stock price in our valuation equations; that is, if one dividend of D was due during the life of the option six months from now, the stock price P_s would be replaced with $P_s - De^{-r/2}$.

A similar approach is adopted when the dividends are assumed to be of uncertain size; however, in this case the certainty equivalent of the distribution of possible future dividends must be subtracted from P_s. The real problem is then to specify this distribution. Some researchers have suggested the assumption of a constant dividend yield so that the actual dollar value of dividends received varies in line with movements in the stock price. This means that P_s is replaced by $P_s e^{-d}$ where d is the constant dividend yield over the life of the option.

We now turn to the complication introduced by the right to exercise prior to maturity embodied in an American option. At the end of Section 8.2 we showed that at maturity the option cannot be worth less than the difference between the price of the stock and the exercise price; otherwise, a riskless arbitrage profit could be made simply by buying the option, exercising it, and immediately selling the stock on the market.

The counterpart of this lower boundary prior to maturity of the option will be the price of the stock at maturity less the present value of the exercise price (the amount of funds that must be invested in risk-free bonds now so that the proceeds will be sufficient to cover the exercise of the option at maturity). Figure 8.7 plots these secondary boundaries for different possible stock prices and different dates $(t_1, t_2, \ldots)$ prior to maturity.

For very high prices of the stock, the value of the option will approach the bound; in other words, it will be worth little more than the value to be derived from exercising it. This limit exists because the chance that the stock price will go even higher is very small so the additional "speculative" value that the call had at low stock prices will now be minimal.

An important point to notice from Figure 8.7 is that at any time an option

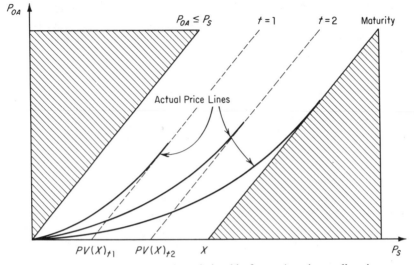

Figure 8.7   The maturity–value relationship for an American call option

will always be worth more (or, at worst, as much) left alive (unexercised) than exercised. This fact means that, in the absence of dividends, *it will never be optimal to exercise an American option prior to maturity*. The reason is that by exercising an option you forego the chance to reap the benefit of an increase in the price of the underlying stock, and it is this chance, after all, that gave the call its value in the first place.[29] It follows that the Black-Scholes formula also applies to American calls on shares without dividends.

The reason it might prove rational to exercise an American call before maturity is the right to dividends. Suppose that after some date ($t = 1$) a stock will trade in the market "ex-dividend" (i.e., a buyer after that date will not have the right to the forthcoming dividend when paid, which will instead go to the previous holder of the stock). In this situation it may be optimal for the holder of an American call option to exercise it immediately before the stock stock goes ex-dividend. Thus the holder can capture the dividend payment that he or she would lose if the option were exercised at a later date.

More precisely, it will be optimal to exercise the call if the value of the option unexercised is less than the value of exercising it at $t = 1$. The value if the option is exercised will be equal to the ex-dividend price of the stock, plus the amount of the cash dividend, less the exercise price:[30] $P_c < P_{s2} - P_x + Div_1$, where P_c is the value of the unexercised call. This value must also be based on the price at which the stock will trade ex-dividend P_{s2} along with the other pricing variables included in our valuation models such that $P_c = w(P_{s2}, r, \sigma, P_x, T)$.

Now there will be some stock price P_s^* at which a holder would be indifferent as to whether the option was exercised or not. What an American call amounts to, therefore, is a compound option which has an expected value equal to P_c multiplied by the probability that it will be optimal to leave the option unexercised, plus the value of exercising the option immediately before it is declared ex-dividend, multiplied by the probability that it will be optimal to exercise the option on that date; that is,

$$P_{0A} = QP_c + (P_{s2} - P_x + Div_1)(1 - Q).$$

The value of Q is then the probability that the ex-dividend price will be below P_{s2}^* (in which case the option will be left unexercised) and $(1 - Q)$ is the probability that the ex-dividend price is above P_{s2}^*, in which case it will be optimal to exercise the option.

Let us turn then to the issue of valuing put options. In the case of a European put, we can appeal to the put-call parity theorem, derived in Section 8.1.5, which connects the values of European puts and calls. We can then use our pricing formula for a call to determine the value of its opposite put. The formula[31] is $P_c - P_p = P_s - P_x/(1 + r)$. Utilizing this parity relationship, the value of a put can be determined directly from the value of its opposite call since $P_p = P_c + P_x/(1 + r) - P_s$.

Unfortunately, we cannot appeal to a similar parity relationship to derive a price for American puts. This is because the parity theorem assumes exercise at maturity (the only permissible exercise date for European options), yet it may be optimal to exercise an American put prior to maturity. In that case, parity with the corresponding call need not hold.

It is obvious that a put option can never be worth more than the present value of the exercise price. Once the stock price has fallen to a level well below the striking price, it is not worthwhile to wait for further declines, thereby losing interest on the accumulated profit. The put should then be exercised immediately unless dividends are due, in which case the stock may be held until they can be claimed.

The American put, therefore, presents a serious obstacle to the derivation of a pricing formula—namely, that the time when the option is exercised depends itself on the behavior of the stock price. What we have is once more a compound option consisting of an infinite series of European puts, one of which reaches maturity (hence is available for exercise) at every point in time until the expiration date of the American option itself. To date, no explicit formula for pricing this type of option has been developed. Instead, various numerical approximation procedures have been proposed; one attributed to Barone-Adesi and Whaley (1987) appears to be the most accurate.[32] As one would expect, the difference in value between American and European options is most pronounced when the options are deeply "in-the-money." For near-the-money options, the difference is generally negligible, since early exercise would not be profitable.

8.2.7 The Empirical Relevance of the Black-Scholes Formula

The Black-Scholes formula is a theorem that, like all theorems, postulates certain assumptions to yield a conclusion. Its mathematical correctness is not in doubt, but its practical relevance depends on how sensitive the conclusion is to departures from the postulates. The theorem assumes, for instance, that transaction costs are zero; this is obviously contrary to fact, yet the formula may still be substantially true in the real world. Empirical research is needed to determine whether the formula is capable of explaining option prices in the markets. Many studies (summarized in Hull [1993] and Tucker [1990]) have made such comparisons, and on the whole they have shown that the Black-Scholes formula is a useful first approximation to actual option prices, although certain systematic discrepancies have emerged.

Verifying the formula, however, is not quite as straightforward as it may seem because some of the parameters are not known with great confidence. This condition is particularly true of the variance parameter σ^2, which can be estimated from shorter or longer time series or from the value implicit in other options (with a different striking price or maturity).[34] As it happens, the option value is quite sensitive to the assumed variance. Moreover, it appears that the variances implicit in quoted options prices depend strongly on recent volatility in the underlying stock, so the variance estimated from long time series is not necessarily relevant.

One simple test of the Black-Scholes approach that does not take σ^2 as given would involve two options on the same stock (with different maturities and/or exercise prices); in theory, the variances implicit in the two option prices have to be the same. Another test would use the "delta" defined in Section 8.2.2 as the partial derivative of the option price with respect to the stock price. Because the value of delta is a byproduct of the Black-Scholes formula, it can be compared with day-to-day changes in stock and option prices. The ratio of these changes should be approximately equal to delta (which varies from day to day); an adjustment for the passage of time may also be necessary.

Pending the outcome of these more searching tests, the Black-Scholes formula and its various extensions may be accepted as a fairly reliable guide to option values.

8.3 OPTIONS AND PORTFOLIO MANAGEMENT

During the early growth of the market for exchange-traded options, some investment managers were enthusiastic about what they saw as a possibility to increase the overall return on their stock portfolio through the cash reaped by selling call options against it. In an influential article entitled "Fact and Fantasy in the Use of Options," Fischer Black (1975) helped dispel this myth by pointing out that in an efficient market, the expected return on the stock foregone by writing options against it should on average offset the proceeds received from the sale of the options.

It is clear from Figure 8.5 that writing a covered call option amounts to "selling off" the right to the upper end of the distribution of returns on the stock. When potentially high returns occur due to a large increase in the stock price, these will go to the holder of the call, which would then be exercised.

A net gain to the writer can only be expected if call options were to be systematically overpriced so that the proceeds received from the sale were large relative to the probability that the stock price would substantially exceed the exercise price during the life of the option. There is no evidence that such is the case.

Options can be of use to the portfolio manager, however, as one of the possible means of reducing the downside risk associated with a stock. Hedging a stock by selling a call against it effectively trades the upside of the distribution in exchange for the call premium, which cushions the overall portfolio return against decline or inadequate appreciation in the price of the stock itself. Depending on the risk-return preferences of investors and the transactions costs associated with other forms of risk reduction, this will occasionally provide an attractive means of risk management, but as a long-term strategy it is not promising. Neither, for that matter, is a strategy of hedging downside risk by buying puts, since their price will on the average offset the benefits of loss reduction.

To those confident of their ability to predict share prices, however, options may at times be a better vehicle than the underlying stocks because of their lower cost (more bang for the buck). No doubt much of the considerable activity in stock options is attributable to this type of trader.

8.4 CONVERTIBLE BONDS AND STOCKS AS OPTIONS

As we have already noted, options of various forms frequently arise in many quarters of everyday as well as financial life. Thus far, however, our discussion has centered on formal options listed on major world exchanges. Before concluding, we should address other contexts in which the theory of options has provided useful insights, namely, in the valuation of the shares in levered firms and convertible bonds.

A convertible bond is the most straightforward application. What it amounts to is an ordinary bond to which a call option on the firm's stock is attached.[34] The exercise price is equal to the fraction of the total value of the bond, which must be surrendered in exchange for each unit of stock.

The initial price of the call option associated with a convertible bond, meanwhile, is equal to the present value of the difference between the coupon payments accepted on the convertible and the higher coupon that would have been available on a standard bond. The maturity of the option is equal to the maturity of the bond, which may either be fixed or at the firm's discretion in the case where conversion can be forced after a certain date.

Utilizing this analogy, a convertible bond can be valued by taking the present value of its coupon payments and principal and adding to this the value of the implicit call option valued by one of the methods above. One interesting implication of viewing a convertible as an American call on a nondividend paying stock (since no dividends are received on a convertible prior to exercise of the option) is that it will never be optimal to exercise the option to convert prior to the maturity of the bond (since, as we noted above, such an option is always worth more alive than its exercise value).[35]

Conceptually, the idea that stock in a levered firm (that is, a firm with liabilities in the form of bonds, bank loans, etc.) is itself a call option may be more difficult to grasp. It follows, however, from the limited liability nature of common stock. In the process of trading, a firm may accumulate losses such that the value of its remaining assets is no longer sufficient to cover its debts to creditors and bondholders. If, in addition, its cash flow is insufficient to service these debts, it will be declared bankrupt, and the shareholders' option to participate in the assets of the firm becomes worthless. The most the shareholders can lose is the price they paid for the option to participate in the firm's assets and potential profits (i.e., the price of the shares).

In this sense the shares in a levered firm are themselves a type of call option. The underlying security is the total value of the firm's assets. The exercise price is the value of the creditors and bondholder's claims. If the price of the underlying security (the firm's assets) is higher than the price at which the creditor and bondholder claims can be satisfied (the exercise price), then the shareholders "call away" control of the assets and reap any increase in the value of those assets.

Shares, however, have two unusual elements when viewed as options. On the one hand, the option is continually being exercised until bankruptcy occurs, while other call options usually remain unexercised for most of the option's life. A second and related point is that the maturity of the option is potentially infinite.

Clearly the analogy has limitations. It does, however, have an important implication. To the extent that the common stock in a levered firm embodies a call option component, valuation theory would suggest that its price would increase the more volatile the price of the underlying security (i.e., the value of the firm's total assets). Intuitively, this implication stems from the fact that shareholders stand to gain all of the upside if the firm is successful, but just as in the case of a standard call option, their downside loss is limited by the option not to exercise. The losses associated with an asset value drawn from the lowest end of the distribution of possible asset values are ultimately absorbed by bondholders and creditors, who lose some or all of their principal.

This basic asymmetry in the returns to shareholders suggests that some degree of riskiness will increase the value of a levered firm's shares. Beyond some point, however, this effect is undone by the increased risk of bankruptcy, which makes it more and more likely that the shareholder's option will be worthless. Furthermore, the exercise price of this implicit option will then be increased by the rising cost of new debt finance.

8.5 OTHER TYPES OF OPTIONS

In this chapter we have focused on stock options, particularly on those that are traded on exchanges. There are many other kinds of options, some of great antiquity and some of recent origin.

First we mention a type of stock option that is not traded on an exchange and is called "restricted." Options of this type are frequently granted to corporate executives as a contractual supplement to their salary. Thus the president of a large firm often has the option of buying a certain number of his firm's shares at a striking price approximately equal to the market price at the time she was first employed by the firm. This call option, which often has a maturity of several years, is valuable only if the stock price rises during her presidency. The primary intention is to link the executive's total income to his performance as perceived by the stock market. In addition, there may be tax advantages to the exercise of such options as compared to an equivalent additional salary in cash.

Options are also commonly written on such underlying objects as stock indexes, commodities, bonds, and foreign currencies; these options are traded on exchanges. The most important of these are options on stock indexes (notably the S&P500 and the NYSE Composite), which have attracted a large volume of trading.[36] There are also options on futures contracts, where the relevant price is the price of the futures contract, not the price of the underlying commodity, financial instrument, or index; these options are discussed in the next chapter. The valuation formulas discussed above may need modification when the underlying object is not a stock.

9

Futures Contracts and Futures Markets

Futures trading has recently been among the fastest growing activities in the financial sector. Until the 1970s it was largely confined to agricultural commodities, and indeed only tangential to finance narrowly defined. The introduction of financial futures changed the picture drastically. First came futures in foreign exchange, then in interest rates, and most recently in stock price indexes. Several of the new futures markets have been highly successful, to the point where they have overshadowed the old-established ones in grains, metals, and the like.[1] Nevertheless, the new markets are similar in essential respects to their precursors; they differ mostly in the objects of trading. To understand financial futures, we have to consider their origin in commodity futures, which in any case are still of considerable importance.[2]

By their very nature, most financial instruments involve transactions in the future: A bond gives the right to future coupons (and, in a more remote future, redemption); a share gives the right to the future dividends of a company; an option gives the right to buy or sell a financial instrument in the future until the option expires. What sets apart a futures (note the final "s") contract is not that it involves transactions in the future; it must be something else.

At this point some definitions are in order. By the *cash market* for a commodity or financial instrument we mean the market in which actuals are traded; in other words, where title passes from seller to buyer. The cash market can be divided into the *spot market*, in which delivery is immediate, and the *forward market*, in which delivery is in some agreed future period. Conceptually distinct from the cash market is the *futures market*, whose definition is given in Section 9.3.

In this chapter we start by comparing two types of financial instrument: The forward contract and the futures contract. Both involve a contract to buy or sell a commodity or financial instrument at a predetermined price at a future date. They differ fundamentally from an option, however, because they carry the obligation to buy or sell at a future date, not simply the right.[3] In other words, a forward or futures contract must either be executed or closed out by an offsetting transaction; unlike an option, it cannot be left unexercised. Obviously this distinction alters the distribution of possible returns from the contract, as we show later in this chapter.

This is the first of two chapters dealing with futures contracts. Here we concentrate on the defining characteristics of a futures contract, on ways in which it can be settled, on types of commodities and financial instruments in which futures trading is likely to be successful, and on measures of the importance of futures markets. We also explore the exchanges on which futures contracts are traded: the history or organized markets, the role of the clearinghouses, the form of quotations, and the main market participants: hedgers, speculators, arbitrageurs, and floor traders.

In Chapter 10 we examine some of the theory and empirical evidence on the pricing of futures contracts, paralleling our discussion of stock and options prices in earlier chapters. The reader should know that some of the finer points in Chapter 9 may not be fully clear without the analysis of futures prices in Chapter 10.

9.1 FORWARD CONTRACTS

We are all familiar with forward contracts even though—as with Moliere's anti-hero who spoke prose without knowing it—the term means nothing to us. A customer who finds that the automobile he wants is not in stock may place an order for it; that is a forward contract, because the car will be delivered at some later date. An employment contract is generally also in the nature of a forward contract because the labor is to be performed during a later period. It does not matter in this context whether payment for the good or service is made immediately, upon delivery, or even later.

The terms *forward* and *future* may appear identical, and in fact they are often used interchangeably in the older literature. To grasp the nature of futures contracts, however, it is essential to distinguish them clearly from forward contracts. To sum up the following discussion, *a futures contract is a highly standardized forward contract.*[4]

In its original form, a forward contract is quite specific: It specifies not only the buyer and the seller but also the quality and location of the merchandise or service, the delivery time, and the modalities of payment; furthermore, only the buyer and the seller are responsible for its execution. Because of this heterogeneity, most forward contracts do not lend themselves to trading on an organized exchange; there are simply too many elements that have to be negotiated in each particular case. Once a forward contract is in existence, it cannot be readily resold because a third party may not like all the precise elements agreed upon by the original two. Consequently, there is no substantial secondary market, and we saw earlier that secondary trading (that is, trading in existing instruments) is the largest source of business on organized exchanges.

This rule has exceptions, however. The most important one is the London Metal Exchange, a central trading place for forward contracts in copper, aluminum, and other metals. The traders on the LME are a small number of merchants who act as principals rather than as brokers. Since there is no clearinghouse (see later), the forward contracts are merely the individual obligations of the two parties.[5] The LME contracts are partially standardized (for instance, with respect to size), but not to the point where they become futures contracts.

Although there is no central trading place and little in the way of formal organization, forward trading in foreign currencies is extremely active and highly competitive. Transaction costs are minimal because the object of trading is very homogeneous to begin with, and the amount of each transaction is large. In this market, which is conducted by computer, telephone, and telex, the traders are banks, who again operate as principals. There are also brokers, who undertake to find the best price for their customers, the banks. As we shall show, the exclusion of nonbank traders is one of the reasons why futures trading in currencies came to supplement forward trading in the early 1970s.

9.2 THE ORIGINS OF FUTURES TRADING

Commercial practices similar to present-day futures trading have been reported by economic historians in a number of countries, notably Holland and Japan, as far back as the seventeenth century. If any single city may be called the birthplace of modern futures contracts, however, it must be Chicago, where it developed in the middle of the nineteenth century. As a major transport center for American agricultural commodities, it was the natural location for merchants who engaged in the business of buying grain from farmers, arranging for shipping (often through Chicago), and selling the commodity to processors, such as flour mills.

The actual date at which the commodity (say wheat) would arrive at its destination, however, was subject to considerable uncertainty, being dependent on such exogenous factors as the date at which the grain came ready for harvest and when the Great Lakes unfroze sufficiently to permit barge traffic. This uncertainty in turn exposed the merchant to two types of risk. First, there was a price risk, since the spot price at the time of the wheat's arrival might differ substantially from that expected when the merchant originally contracted to buy the wheat. Second, since the quality of the wheat on arrival was uncertain, the merchant was subjected to a further risk as to what price his contracted consignment might fetch even if the spot price of average-quality wheat was as he expected.

Seeking to dissipate these risks, merchants began to write *to arrive* contracts) with their customers. These contracts provided a vehicle for selling the grain before it arrived in the merchant's hands: They would specify a base price for each particular grade at a standard location (Chicago, for example) to which the relevant freight charges to the final destination would be added. By means of the to arrive contract, the merchant was able to fix his selling price against his contracted buying price and lock in a more certain profit margin for his handling and agency services.

Although to arrive contracts were the forerunners of modern futures contracts, they are more properly classified as forward contracts. Forward contracts, as the name suggests, refer to delivery of a commodity or financial instrument at some point in the future. However, they are a quite specific arrangement between two identifiable parties who must agree on price, grade, and other relevant details. While to arrive contracts did not specify a precise date, they generally contained clauses that set "reasonable bounds" on the delivery period.

Following the early standardization of location and grade in the to arrive contracts, delivery dates evolved so as to focus on certain key months: May, when the lakes unfroze, permitting transport by barge; July, the beginning of the harvest season; September, the end of the harvest, and so forth. Still today, futures contracts refer to delivery within a period of about one month, the exact day being chosen by the seller. A further step involved the standardization of the quantity per contract; 5,000 bushels became the standard contract size.

The evolution of these forward contracts into a futures contract resulted from the increasing standardization of the contract terms. Ultimately a point was reached where there was no need for either party to be specific about the precise terms (except for the price), or even to know who the other party was. The first clearinghouse, founded by the Chicago Board of Trade in 1874, was originally set up to facilitate the settlement of expiring contract, but it soon assumed a wider role. By acting as seller to all buyers and as buyer to all sellers, it became the guarantor of ultimate execution (see Section 9.4). Thus contracts could be exchanged impersonally between numerous parties on both sides without each having to worry about the ability or willingness of other traders to carry out their obligations. Once impersonality was accomplished, it became possible for many traders, not necessarily professionals, to enter the market, and this in turn served to increase liquidity. When the clearinghouse assumed the function of guarantor, modern futures trading was born.

In the course of this evolution, the Chicago Board of Trade developed an elaborate set of rules to govern futures trading, especially to maintain its competitive character. It may be thought that competition is self-sustaining and needs no rules, but experience suggests the opposite. The temptation to manipulate prices by the exercise of individual market power or by collusion is always present. The occasional occurrence of "corners," discussed more fully in the chapter on regulation, threatened to discredit futures trading and was of particular concern to the exchange and to legislators. To a large extent, the history of futures trading as an institution is the history of the struggle against manipulation.

In order to make manipulation more difficult, the CBT also introduced a degree of flexibility into the contract terms, without giving up the basic principle of standardization. Having Chicago as the only delivery point sometimes enabled those holding stocks there to abuse their market power; the solution was to permit delivery at certain other locations. For the same reason, the range of deliverable grades was extended. The choice of where and what to deliver was given to the shorts, who at delivery time usually had less market power than the longs.[6] This choice is somewhat confusingly called "seller's option"; it has nothing to do with the options discussed in Chapter 8.

The development of futures trading by the CBT, which for many years specialized in grains, served as an example to exchanges dealing in other agricultural commodities and a few metals. The New York Cotton Exchange, in particular, introduced many refinements in futures trading. When financial futures made their appearance in the early 1970s, the pattern set by commodity futures was followed closely and in many cases with outstanding success. It was only in the 1980s that a significant new element (cash settlement, discussed in Section 9.3.1) was introduced.

9.3 BASIC ELEMENTS OF FUTURES CONTRACTS

As has just been noted, there are two kinds of futures contracts: those providing for delivery of the underlying object and those settled in cash. The majority of the futures contracts traded in the United States are of the first kind; these include futures in grains, in Treasury securities, in foreign currencies, and in metals. Cash-settlement contracts, found in stock indexes and Eurodollars, have also become important, but for convenience of exposition they will be discussed in a separate subsection (9.3.1).

To be classified as a futures contract in economic analysis, a contract with delivery must have the following elements:

1. A standardized *quantity* per contract (say 5,000 bushels of wheat, or Treasury bonds with a face value of $100,000)
2. A standardized *delivery period* (a month in some contracts, but shorter periods are also common)
3. A standardized *quality* or range of qualities (for instance, silver bars containing at least 99.9% silver, or corn grading No. 3 or better)
4. One or more standardized *locations* for delivery (for instance, specified grain elevators in Chicago and Buffalo, or specified banks in New York)
5. *Impersonality* on both sides of the contract through the interposition of a clearinghouse.

It should be stressed that *all* of these elements must be present.[7] The fifth one is usually the most restrictive; it means that an otherwise standardized contract issued by an individual firm (for instance, a dealer in precious metals) is not a futures contract in the economic sense.[8]

To repeat, the purpose of these five kinds of standardization is to reduce transaction costs by minimizing the number of contract elements that needs to be negotiated, and thereby to create a highly competitive market. All that buyers and sellers have to proclaim on the exchange floor is the number of contracts and the price at which they wish to buy or sell. If this purpose is achieved—we see later that newly introduced futures contracts often attract little trading, and that old-established contracts sometimes die—the futures market is likely to become the central price-determining mechanism for the commodity or financial instrument that underlies the futures contract; the cash market will then be a mere offshoot of the futures market. This relationship will be explained in more detail later.

Like many financial instruments, a futures contract is a very abstract entity. A corn futures contract is not something you can feed to hogs; in fact, it is not even a piece of paper, but merely an entry in the books of the clearinghouse and certain brokers. The abstract nature of futures has led to much misunderstanding and hostility. The fact that anyone can sell grain futures without owning any grain appeared especially sinister to many farmers and their political spokespeople, who viewed it as a city slickers' plot to deprive them of the just reward of their labor. Merchants have also occasionally opposed futures trading because it introduces a competitive element in a cozy oligopoly. Bills to prohibit futures trading have often been before Congress.[9]

Despite its abstract nature, a futures contract is real enough from an economic point of view. The reason, more fully explained in the next chapter, is that futures prices are closely correlated with cash prices (including the spot price). Far from being a mere gambling casino, the futures market has a decisive effect on the cash market and generally serves to make prices reflect supply and demand more accurately; it also can be used by producers and processors to reduce risks. In recent years, more and more farmers have overcome their traditional suspicion and taken positions in futures and futures options.

When a contract for delivery in a particular month is initially issued (commonly one or two years before maturity), it will trade at a price determined by supply and demand for the contract at that time. Assuming that the contract is settled by delivery, the buyer undertakes to take delivery of the specified quantity at the contract's maturity, and to pay for it at that time; the seller undertakes to deliver the specified quantity at maturity.[10] The price will subsequently fluctuate up or down with the market, depending on the relative strength of supply and demand for the contract over its life.

9.3.1 Delivery and Cash Settlement

Given the degree of standardization inherent in modern futures contracts, added to the fact that the bulk of the contracts written in most markets are never physically executed, one might ask whether the price of a futures contract has any relationship with the spot price of the physical commodity. While standardization makes futures contracts more readily negotiable, it also reduces their usefulness as a mechanism for buying or selling physical commodities or financial instruments. The limitations placed on location, timing, and quantity may easily conflict with the needs of an individual buyer or seller of the underlying object. This standardization is an important reason why most futures contracts are not liquidated by physical delivery but by an offsetting transaction. The buying and selling of actuals is largely confined to the cash market.

This point is reinforced when, as explained earlier, the futures contract gives a measure of discretion to the seller concerning the timing, location, and quality of the delivery. The seller, of course, will choose the cheapest method of delivery that is permissible under the futures contract. Thus the seller of an expiring cotton contract may find it most profitable to make delivery in Texas, whereas buyers may need cotton in Georgia. If there were separate futures contracts for delivery in Texas and in Georgia, the problem would not arise, but such specialization would conflict with the overriding idea of liquidity through standardization.[11]

Nonetheless, there is a direct relationship between the spot price (that is, the price of physicals for immediate delivery) and the price of a futures contract that has entered the delivery period because the *possibility* of delivery always remains. (The delivery process is described in greater detail at the end of Section 9.4.) Suppose, for instance, that an expiring coffee contract is currently quoted at $2.00 per pound and that physical coffee (of deliverable quality and location) is offered at $1.95 per pound. Anyone could then make a riskless profit of 5 cents per pound by buying the physicals, selling the expiring future, and making delivery. The opposite transaction would be profitable if physical coffee could be sold for $2.05 per pound, provided immediate delivery on the futures contract can be assumed.

This type of arbitrage ensures that the price of the futures contract at delivery time will equal the spot price of the underlying object at the location(s) and grade(s) in which deliveries are actually made.[12] It is this link between the futures market and the spot market that gives reality to futures trading.[13] In the spot market, the prices for particular grades and locations are often quoted as a difference from the relevant futures price. It is because of this feature that one of the functions of futures markets is often described as *price discovery*.

Prior to the end of the delivery period, the price of a futures contract may differ substantially from the spot price. This relative price behavior over the life of the contract is central to our discussion of the determination of futures prices in Chapter 10.

Most futures contracts are not consummated by physical delivery of the underlying object. Instead they are "closed out" by means of a reverse transaction. For example, a contract to buy May wheat at $5.00 per bushel may be closed out at any time prior to expiration by simply selling the same contract at the prevailing price, say $5.50. In this way, the holder of the contract to buy can avoid taking delivery of the wheat, realizing instead a profit of 50 cents per bushel. This profit becomes available as soon as the reverse transaction is carried out and the original long position is extinguished.

As a rule, it is inadvisable for nonprofessional traders to maintain positions in contracts that have reached the delivery stage, since they rarely know enough about the spot market to cope with delivery. There is some folklore about the housewife who speculated in egg futures and had a truckload of eggs dumped on her front lawn, but this cautionary tale is apocryphal. Merchants and other professionals, on the other hand, may find good profit opportunities during that period. In fact it is normal for some deliveries to occur on many days during the maturity of a contract; this is part of the arbitrage process that keeps spot and futures prices in line with each other.[14]

In a few of the newer financial futures markets the possibility of actual delivery has been eliminated altogether.[15] Examples include stock index futures and Eurodollar futures. Clearly the "delivery" of an actual stock index is impossible, and even the delivery of a basket of 500 stocks (in the case of the S&P), with weights corresponding to the index and a total value equal to the contract, would be cumbersome and costly.[16] Futures contracts in these types of markets have therefore been written so as to provide for cash settlement only.[17]

Under this arrangement, contracts that remain open at the end of trading are settled by a cash payment determined by the spot price of the underlying instrument at that time. Thus the Chicago Mercantile Exchange stock index futures contract has a dollar size specified at the Standard & Poor index multiplied by 500 (currently around $230,000.)[18] Accordingly, the settlement value is 500 times the level of the S&P index at the close of stock-exchange trading on the third Thursday of the delivery month. Longs who bought the contract at a lower price, or shorts who sold it at a higher price, receive a payment equal to their profit; those who find themselves on the wrong side must make a payment equal to their loss. Actually the practice of "marking to market" (see Section 9.4) means that payment of the profit or loss is spread out over the entire holding period of the contract.

Since there is no delivery in these contracts, how is the futures market related to the spot market (which in the above example consists of the stock exchanges and to some extent of the over-the-counter market)? The answer, once more, is arbitrage, but here it assumes a different form. Traders have a choice between being long in the stock index future or being long in the equities from which the index is calculated; the same choice exists on the short side. They will choose one market or the other, depending on their expectations of the value of the stock index at the expiration of the futures contract, at which time the futures price is by definition equal to the actual value of the index. In reality, most traders engaged in spot-futures arbitrage will be simultaneously long in one market and short in the other. This arbitrage, a particular form of what is known as "program trading," appears to have been highly effective in keeping the two markets in line with each other, but it has also been accused of causing excessive fluctuations in the stock market. We come back to this topic in Chapter 10.

Although cash-settlement futures have been a remarkable success in the few markets where they are traded, their scope is rather limited. This limitation is not merely because delivery futures are entrenched for historical reasons; cash-settlement futures were actually illegal until the early 1980s. The main difficulty in cash settlement is in determining the relevant spot price, or more precisely spot prices. Since spot markets are heterogeneous in respect of location and quality, there is in general no unique spot price for use in a futures market. The delivery mechanism is designed to deal with this problem, and has done so in many—by no means all—commodities and financial instruments. In the case of equities, certain indexes are accepted widely enough to serve as the criterion for cash settlement.[19] In the Treasury bond futures market—currently the most active of all futures markets—delivery continues to be required, however. It remains to be seen how many other cash-settlement contracts (in addition to those already in existence) will be viable.

9.3.2 Futures and Options

There is an important relation between futures contracts and the option contracts discussed in the preceding chapter. First recall that buying a call option gives the buyer the right, but not the obligation, to buy the underlying object at the striking price during the life of the option. Conversely, the seller of a call is obligated to sell the object at the striking price when the buyer exercises his or her right to buy. The right and obligation with respect to a put option are similar.

The payoff profiles of Chapter 8 tell us when a put or call can be profitably exercised. It is easy to see that the payoff profile for the buyer of a futures contract is simply a straight line with a slope of 45 degrees that intersects the horizontal axis at the market price (i.e., the price at which the futures contract is originally bought or sold). The same profile is obtained for an options trader who simultaneously buys a call "at the money" and sells a put at the same price. From the put-call parity theorem (Section 8.1.4) we know that at the market price, a put and a call have the same value, so the cost of buying a call (assuming there are no transaction costs) is exactly offset by the proceeds of selling a put. It follows that *buying a futures contract is equivalent to buying a call and selling a put,* both at the market price and with the same maturity as the futures contract. Similarly, selling a futures contract is equivalent to selling a call and buying a put.

The preceding argument does not mean that futures trading could be replaced by options trading. As described in Chapter 8, exchange-traded options became feasible when options of the older type were standardized with respect to striking price, maturity, and other characteristics. The hypothetical puts and calls discussed in the previous paragraph were written at the market price, which will rarely coincide with the standardized exercise price of an exchange-traded put or call. Futures trading is also based on standardization, but not with respect to the market price, which of course can vary in response to supply and demand.

Using the equivalence of options and futures it is possible to construct so-called "synthetic" options. A simple example is simultaneously buying a futures contract and selling a call with the same maturity at the market price; the reader is encouraged to verify that this leaves the trader in the same position as if he or she had sold a put at the market price. More complicated combinations of futures and options can be analyzed in the same way.

As mentioned in Chapter 8, there is considerable trading in options on futures, and we are now in a position to discuss these. In such options, as opposed to "options on physicals" (for instance, options on individual stocks or on German marks), the underlying object is a futures contract. Thus the holder of one June 400 call on S&P500 futures has the right to buy one June S&P500 futures contract at a price of 400. By exercising this right, the holder transfers his or her long position from the options market to the futures market. Moreover, the June futures option is scheduled to expire a certain number of days before the June futures contract, so the holder must then decide whether to liquidate the futures position or stay with it.[20] In most cases, no doubt, options on futures are liquidated by an opposite transaction rather than by exercise—except, of course, if they expire "out of the money," in which case no action is necessary.

Although futures contracts do not pay dividends, the Black-Scholes valuation formula in Chapter 8 needs some modification for options on futures. The main reason is that buying a futures contract, unlike buying a stock, does not require the buyer to pay or forego interest. Formulas for European futures options were derived by Black (1975). As an example, we give the one that applies to commodity futures (as opposed to financial futures):

$$E(P_c) = e^{-rT}\{P_f N(d) - P_x N(d - \sigma/\sqrt{T_1 - t})\},$$

where the notation is the same as in Section 8.2.3 except that the futures price P_f is substituted for the stock price. For financial futures it is necessary to take into account additional variables, specifically the interest rate on the instrument underlying the futures contract or—in the case of stock index futures—the dividend yield on the underlying index.

Black's formulas can be extended to American options along the lines discussed in Chapter 8.[21] As described in that chapter, it may be optimal to exercise an American put before expiration, and this is equally true for puts on futures. Unlike calls on stocks without dividends, however, early exercise of calls on futures may also be optimal. Because of the possibility of early exercise, American futures options are in general worth somewhat more—and never worth less—than European futures options with the same striking price and maturity.

In some financial instruments, particularly stock indexes and currencies, both options on physicals and options on futures are traded. The prices of these two varieties need not be equal, but they are related by arbitrage conditions. As to the relative advantages of the two types, the holder of a call on physicals, for instance, must be prepared to pay for the underlying object upon exercise, whereas the holder of a futures option need only put up the "margin" on the underlying futures contract, which is usually much less. Tax considerations may also influence the choice of options by traders.

The importance of futures options in different markets is discussed at the end of Section 9.4.3.

9.4 THE ORGANIZATION OF FUTURES MARKETS

Like the stock exchanges discussed in Chapter 5, futures exchanges are typically owned by a limited number of members, who elect a board of directors to make policy decisions and to hire staff. Every exchange has an elaborate set of rules, which is enforced by board-appointed committees and by the staff. Futures exchanges have to be licensed by the Commodity Futures Trading Commission (see Chapter 11), which exercises general supervision and has enforcement powers of its own.

In the United States, the two most important futures exchanges are located in Chicago; they are the Chicago Board of Trade (CBT) and the Chicago Mercantile Exchange (CME). Both were founded to trade in agricultural futures, but most of their business is now in financial futures. In New York there were until recently five exchanges trading mostly in such commodities as metals, petroleum and its products, cotton, and sugar; one of them offers a stock index futures contract. Unlike the Chicago exchanges, those in New York have a common trading floor in the World Trade Center. Some of the New York exchanges have recently merged, and further mergers are being considered. It appears that the New York Mercantile Exchange (NYMEX) will remain as the dominant (perhaps the only) futures market in New York. Smaller exchanges are located in Kansas City and Minneapolis. Overseas, the largest concentration of futures markets is in London, where the London International Financial Futures Exchange (LIFFE) has active trading, not only in futures on British financial instruments but also on German and other European government bonds.

A futures exchange has a separate trading area, known as a "pit," for each commodity or financial instrument; thus the CBT has a wheat pit, a bond pit, and so on. In the pit there are two types of traders: floor brokers and floor traders, sometimes known as "scalpers"; the specialists found in stock and options exchanges have no counterpart in the futures markets. In order to make competition as perfect as possible, all bids and offers have to be made by "open outcry," which means that private transactions between two traders are prohibited. Because of the resulting din, traders use a system of hand signals to clarify their intentions. At strategic locations there are exchange clerks, who keep a record of price changes and transmit them to the world at large.[22]

We stated in the preceding section that futures trading requires a *clearinghouse,* which is legally separate from the exchange and has a much smaller membership. The main function of the clearinghouse is to guarantee the execution of all outstanding futures contracts (and also futures options). It is able to do so by two devices:

1. Requiring a deposit known as *margin*[23] from each clearing member in proportion to its net position, regardless of whether that position is long or short. Clearing members are firms with substantial net worth, who (unless they trade as merchants for their own account) collect similar margins from their own customers, or from exchange members who are not clearing members. The required margin payments are calculated at the end of each trading day and due the next morning. If a clearing member has a larger deposit than is necessary under the margin rules (as will happen when prices move in its favor), the excess is returned to that member. The daily process of collecting and disbursing margin payments, known as "marking to market," is one of the ways in which futures trading differs from forward trading.

2. Calling on clearing members for additional funds in emergencies, which are rare. To be able to satisfy this contingent claim, clearing members are required to maintain a large net worth at all times. It is only when one or more clearing members fall below this capital requirement or fail to meet margin calls—usually because of trading losses—that the other members have to provide more funds. It is not possible for all clearing members to fail at the same time, for it is in the nature of futures trading that the losses of some are the profits of others. By virtue of this ultimate claim on its members' assets, a clearinghouse is said to be "good to the last drop" and able to offer a credible guarantee. No clearinghouse in the United States has ever defaulted on its obligations, though there have been defaults in other countries.[24]

To assist the clearinghouse in collecting margin payments, many exchanges put a limit on the amount by which prices can change in a day. The price of gold futures, for instance, cannot go up or down by more than $25 per ounce in one day. When this daily limit is reached in any contract month, trading in that month comes to a halt, since supply and demand can no longer be brought into equilibrium. Clearly this device impairs the usefulness of futures trading, and a sequence of "limit days" can play havoc with the normal relation between cash and futures markets. The price of the expiring future, however, is usually exempt from daily limits, which mitigates their adverse effects to some extent. Furthermore, some exchanges have a system of "expanding limits," under which the limits are widened if prices have reached the limit on two or more successive trading days.

The clearinghouse also has a central role in the delivery process. Since the exact time of delivery is chosen by each of the shorts, the process starts with the issue of "delivery notices," which also describe the quality and location of the objects to be delivered. Initially these notices are not addressed to anyone in particular, and any long who wishes to accept delivery can do so by "stopping" one or more notices. After a specified period, say one hour, the remaining notices (that is, those that have not been stopped) are allocated by the clearinghouse to the longs, those with the oldest long positions getting delivery first.[25]

9.4.1 Categories of Traders

At the beginning of this chapter, a distinction was made between the cash market (consisting of the spot market and the forward market) and the futures market.[26] This distinction is one fundamental element in the classification of traders. The other fundamental distinction is between traders whose net position (long minus short) in both markets combined is different from zero, and traders whose net position in both markets combined is zero. The former category of traders will be described as the *speculators* and the latter as the *arbitrageurs*. The arbitrageurs, needless to say, must have a long position in either of the two markets, otherwise they could be simply disregarded. We shall show that the distinction between speculators and arbitrageurs reflects the different kinds of price risks to which traders are exposed.

Combining these two distinctions we get the following basic types of traders:

1. *Spot speculators* are those who have a position in the spot market and in no other market, which in effect means those who hold inventories. A moment's reflection should convince the reader that it is not possible to be short in the spot market. Primary producers, including farmers, often belong to this type, since they tend to hold newly produced inventories.
2. *Forward speculators* have a net long or short position in the forward market and no position in the other two markets.
3. *Futures speculators* have a net long or short position in futures and no position elsewhere.
4. *Spot-forward arbitrageurs* have a spot position (necessarily long) and an equal position (necessarily short) in the forward market.
5. *Spot-futures arbitrageurs* have a spot position (again necessarily long) offset by a short position of equal size in the futures market.
6. *Forward-futures arbitrageurs* have a net long or short position in one or more forward contracts offset by an equal position of opposite sign in one or more futures contracts.
7. *Forward arbitrageurs* have a long position in one or more forward contracts offset by a short position in one or more different forward contracts.
8. *Futures arbitrageurs* have a long position in one or more futures contracts offset by a short position in one or more different futures contracts.

Some of these basic types are not of interest in what follows; others are commonly known by more familiar names. It should also be clear that some of these types are not mutually exclusive; thus a trader may be at the same time a spot speculator and a futures speculator. The main purpose of the preceding listing is to serve as a framework for further analysis.

We now look at some of the types in more detail. The threefold division of the speculators reminds us that speculators are not only found in the futures markets, as is often tacitly assumed. The spot speculators are just as exposed to price changes as the futures speculators, but the prices that matter to them are not the same: Spot prices are relevant to the former, futures prices to the latter. The arbitrageurs, by contrast, are exposed to changes in price differences; thus the spot-futures arbitrageurs bear the risk of changes in the difference between a spot price and a futures price.

These spot-futures arbitrageurs, who hold inventories and are short in futures, are especially prominent in the study of futures trading. They are more familiar under the name of *hedgers,* though this term also includes another type to be discussed in a moment. The difference between a spot price and a futures price (particularly the price of the expiring contract) is known as the *basis;* spot-futures arbitrageurs who hedge in the expiring future, therefore, run the risk of changes in the basis. The economics of hedging belongs in the next chapter, but here it should be noted that spot-futures arbitrage has been defined purely in terms of a trader's position in two markets, without any reference to motivation. In particular, it should not be assumed that hedging is the result of risk aversion.

The term *hedging* is also applied to forward-futures arbitrageurs. An example would be a trader who has sold forward contracts and is long an equal amount of futures contracts. It is customary to distinguish two kinds of hedging according to the sign of the futures position (long is positive, short is negative). According to this custom, spot-futures arbitrage is necessarily equivalent to short hedging, since the spot position must be positive. Forward-futures arbitrage may be short hedging or long hedging depending on the sign of the futures position.[27]

Finally, a word about futures arbitrageurs, who are better known as *spreaders* or straddlers.[28] There are three varieties:

1. *Intermonth spreaders* have offsetting positions in two or more maturities of the same futures contract (for instance, May silver versus July silver).
2. *Intermarket spreaders* have offsetting positions in different futures markets trading the same commodity (for instance, May Chicago wheat versus May Kansas City wheat).
3. *Intercommodity spreaders* have offsetting positions in different commodities (for instance, December gasoline versus December crude oil). By extension, this category includes spreading between different financial instruments, such as bond futures versus stock index futures.[29]

Until now, our classification of traders has referred only to their positions in the spot, forward, and futures markets, not to those in options. Instead of listing all possible positions in the four submarkets together, we shall briefly describe three important types of traders with positions in options:

Options speculators are long or short in options but not in the futures or cash markets. They differ from futures speculators not in their intention (which for both categories is to profit from the price movements they anticipate) but in their exposure to risk. The buyer of a futures contract, for instance, may incur a very large loss if the price falls, but the buyer of a call can only lose the purchase price of the option. Although quantitative evidence on this point is hard to obtain, casual observation suggests that options speculation has grown to considerable importance since the introduction of futures options in the early 1980s. In certain markets, particularly currencies and precious metals, a large part—perhaps most—of public speculative activity (as opposed to speculations by floor traders) appears to involve options rather than futures.

Cash-options arbitrageurs have spot or forward positions that are offset by options. Instead of hedging their spot inventories by selling futures, merchants or producers can cover their price risks by buying puts. Obviously these two hedging strategies are not the same: Futures hedgers give up the profit they would make in case of a price rise, but options hedgers do not. On the other hand, the latter must pay for the puts.

Options-futures arbitrageurs can engage in a variety of strategies. One is covered writing—for instance, writing calls against a long position in futures; this operation is similar to the covered writing discussed for stocks in Chapter 8. Another strategy is intended to exploit failures of put-call parity; thus, if the puts for a particular maturity and striking price are overvalued in relation to the corresponding calls, a riskless position can be established by writing puts, buying the same number of calls, and selling the same number of futures contracts. This strategy, which serves to bring the three prices (for the two options and for the future) closer to PCP, will be profitable if the transaction costs are not too large.

Unpublished research on futures options suggests that departures from PCP are quite common, but that they are rarely large enough to make options-futures arbitrage attractive to nonprofessional traders.

9.4.2 Types of Commodities and Financial Instruments Traded

In the introduction to this chapter we posed the question, Why is copper traded in futures markets while a more important commodity like steel is not?

Obviously one of the key prerequisites for a futures market in a commodity is the existence of uncertainty surrounding its price. Price uncertainty provides the impetus for buyers and sellers to hedge their future exposure by agreeing a price in advance. It also opens the way for speculators to take a position, backing their expectations against the market.

Superficially, this requirement might seem to be of little consequence. On closer examination, however, it implies that futures markets are unlikely in commodities for which the prices are "administered" in a relatively predictable way. This might be the case for commodities whose prices are subject to government regulation, pricing by a cartel (assuming it actually controls the market), or simply the controlled updating that tends to characterize pricing in many oligopolistic markets.

The second main factor bearing on the emergence of a futures market for a particular commodity is the degree of homogeneity across the individual varieties or products it covers. Since futures contracts refer to a standardized product and grade, they will be less attractive as a pricing vehicle the more the actual commodity with which the individual buyer of seller is concerned differs from this standard. A futures contract in steel, for example, would offer a poor hedge for the buyer of steel filing cabinets since fluctuations in their wholesale price may stem from a large number of factors outside the basic price of unfabricated steel.

Specifically, for a futures contract to be useful in hedging, there must be a high correlation between movements in the price of the standardized commodity specified in the contract and the price of the precise commodity in which the particular buyer or seller is exposed. These correlations will generally be higher the more standardized is the commodity.

Price correlations for different wheat shipments tend to be relatively high, although there is clearly some variation depending on grade and location compared with those specified in the standardized contract. The futures market can therefore offer a wide variety of individual buyers and sellers a satisfactory hedging mechanism. A similar argument might also be made for copper because the alloys and downstream products are relatively few and often simple transformations of the raw material—for example, copper rod, pipe, and wire.

Consider, however, the case of steel. Even at an intermediate stage of processing, there are a large number of different grades of hardness and alloy specifications, often without any close price correlation. Further downstream, the number of specific varieties increases exponentially: everything from girders, tinplate, and wire to machine tools and car bodies. This lack of homogeneity significantly reduces the usefulness of a standardized futures contract and is probably an important reason why no steel futures exists.

Finally, a futures market is more likely to emerge where there are a large number of buyers and sellers in the market for the physical commodity. Where buyers and sellers are relatively few, other methods of reducing price uncertainty (such as long-term contracting) are apt to predominate. In the limiting case, a few large vertically integrated producers will result, so that the intermediate markets between raw material producer and end user (both spot and futures) are replaced with an internal organization that agrees on transfer prices in advance.

A study by Carlton (1984) examining the evolution of futures trading in the United States found that 180 different futures markets had been launched between 1921 and 1983. No less than 40% had ceased to exist within 4 years of the start of trading. Of those markets that survived to reach the age of 6, however, more than half prospered beyond their twentieth anniversary.

Clearly, the attractiveness of futures trading in a particular commodity changes over time, reflecting changing level of supply and demand uncertainty, different pricing mechanisms in the spot market (including the breakdown of cartels), and the impact of government intervention (such as guaranteed minimum price schemes).

A large number of the new markets established in recent years have been in financial instruments rather than physical commodities.[30] An important impetus to this expansion has come from deregulation of the financial markets and the increased volatility of interest rates in an environment of high and uncertain inflation and government borrowing. The replacement of fixed by floating exchange rates in the early 1970s, for example, greatly increased interest in foreign currency futures. Futures trading in petroleum products was stimulated by the "oil shocks" of the 1970s; it was successfully extended to crude oil when the OPEC cartel lost control of the spot market around 1982, and in turn served to further weaken OPEC's market power.

Finally, the appearance of parallel markets (such as the oil futures markets just mentioned, or those in soybeans and soybean products) is worth comment. It might be argued that since the intermediate products are derived from the same raw material, a single contract in crude oil or soybeans would offer adequate hedging opportunities for processors and end users. However, the correlation among the price movements in the raw material and the intermediate products may not be very high, thus opening the door for separate futures markets. Spreading between the raw material and the products, moreover, makes it possible to hedge the processing cost. In the case of soybeans such a spread is known as a "crushing spread" and in the case of petroleum as a "refining spread."

9.4.3 Volume and Open Interest

In concluding our introduction to futures trading it remains to discuss two important measures of the size of a futures market: volume and open interest. These measures also apply to the futures options discussed in Section 9.3.2.

Volume is simply the total number of futures contracts or futures options that are bought—and consequently sold—in the market during a particular period, say one day. It is analogous to the volume of trading on the stock exchange and is reported daily in the newspapers. Volume is important as an indicator of the liquidity of the market (i.e., its ability to handle sizable orders without undue effect on the price). A low-volume market may not generate enough revenue for the exchange to cover its operating cost, so it will have to be abandoned sooner or later. If the volume is low, moreover, some floor traders will find it hard to make a living, and their departure will only aggravate the situation.

In the most active markets, volume in futures contracts may regularly exceed 100,000 contracts per day; this is the case, for instance, in the Treasury bond contract on the Chicago Board of Trade and in the Eurodollar contract on the Chicago Mercantile Exchange. Most of this volume is accounted for by transactions among floor traders rather than by outside orders. As a result, the bond pit is so crowded that traders arrive hours before the start of trading in order to secure standing room. Quite a few futures markets, however, survive on average daily volume of a few hundred contracts.

Table 9.1 provides data on the annual volume of trading in various groups of markets. It shows a very rapid growth in activity: The number of contracts

Table 9.1 Annual Volume of Trading in U.S. Futures Markets
(millions of contracts, fiscal years)

Category	1970	1980	1985	1990	1993
Grains[a]	2.2	18.3	10.7	17.0	16.0
Oilseeds and products[b]	3.7	15.7	14.9	20.4	20.7
Livestock and products[c]	3.4	11.8	7.9	8.0	5.8
Other agricultural[d]	2.0	7.8	5.1	11.0	10.6
Energy products[e]	[f]	1.1	7.0	35.2	42.8
Metals[g]	1.1	14.1	18.4	17.8	15.2
Financial instruments[h]	[f]	10.2	72.1	135.7	185.4
Foreign currencies[i]	[f]	3.7	16.4	27.2	28.8
TOTAL	12.4	82.7	152.6	272.2	325.5

[a] Mainly wheat, corn, and oats.

[b] Mainly soybeans, soybean meal, and soybean oil.

[c] Mainly live cattle and hogs, porkbellies.

[d] Mainly cotton, lumber, and orange juice.

[e] Mainly crude oil, heating oil, gasoline, and natural gas.

[f] Futures contracts introduced after 1970.

[g] Mainly copper, gold, silver, and platinum.

[h] Mainly interest rate futures (bonds, bills, etc.) and stock indexes.

[i] Mainly British pounds, Japanese yen, and German marks.

Source: 1994 *Statistical Abstract of the United States,* table 813, and earlier issues. The breakdown for 1970 may differ slightly from later years.

traded was more than twenty times as large in 1990 and 1993 as in 1970. This growth is mostly attributable to the introduction of financial futures, which have accounted for more than half of the contracts traded in recent years.

Volume in the agricultural futures rose considerably between 1970 and 1980 but has not changed much recently. Futures on energy products, introduced in the 1970s, have become prominent among the nonfinancial futures, and the crude oil contract is now the most important in that category. It should be borne in mind, however, that the money value of a financial futures contract generally exceeds $100,000, whereas the typical agricultural or energy contract is worth only about $25,000. The total money value of all futures contracts traded cannot be exactly calculated, but in recent years it has amounted to many trillions of dollars and has exceeded the annual GDP by a wide margin.

Open interest is a concept specific to the futures and options markets. It may be defined as the number of contracts outstanding in a particular maturity month at the end of a trading day. The path of open interest over time in a particular delivery month follows a more or less predictable pattern, which we describe under the assumption that ultimate delivery is required.

On the day when a futures contract (say, May wheat) is first listed for trading (typically 15 months before maturity in the case of wheat), the open interest will be zero, since there are no contracts outstanding. The first bargain between a buyer and seller will result in a tradable futures contract for May wheat, so the open interest goes to one.[31] That single contract could be traded around the market by buyers and sellers, but at some point hedgers and speculators will become more interested in May wheat; larger positions will be established, and the open interest will rise.

We know that the open interest on maturity of the contract must be physically delivered. For reasons discussed earlier, however, most speculators and many hedgers shy away from delivery.[32] This is why most contracts are offset (closed out) before maturity by means of a reverse transaction. When a contract approaches maturity, therefore, the open interest begins to fall as contracts are extinguished by offset. Typically, the open interest in any contract maturity reaches a peak two or three months before expiration. When the contract enters the delivery period, most contracts are likely to be held by professionals. The start of the delivery period is accompanied by a further large decline in the open interest, since most of the remaining shorts will make delivery as soon as possible in order to avoid further storage costs, and the remaining longs' futures position is converted into a spot position by accepting delivery. During the delivery period, whose length varies among exchanges, the open interest is typically small but not zero, for new positions can be established in an expiring contract until the final day of its life.

Knowledge of the open interest is especially important in the case of a contract that is approaching maturity (say May wheat in April). Since the contract must ultimately be settled by delivery, traders with positions in the contract watch the physical inventory (known as the "deliverable stock") that meets the requirements for delivery. If the deliverable stock is large compared to the open interest, many of the shorts are likely to deliver and this will often induce the longs to liquidate their positions, thus depressing the price.

Conversely, if the deliverable stock is relatively small, some of the shorts may not be able to deliver and will therefore have to buy back their position, which will tend to raise the price. The latter situation is most dangerous to those shorts who hold no inventory if the deliverable stock is held by one or a small number of traders, who may thus be able to operate a "corner" (see Chapter 11).

The pattern of open interest in futures contracts with cash settlement is similar in its early stages to the one just described for delivery contracts. Because there is no delivery, however, there is no pressure on nonprofessional traders to liquidate their positions. The open interest in a particular maturity may remain large until the final day, when all remaining positions are wiped out by cash settlement.

It is clear that volume and open interest are related, though the relation is not very close. We saw that the initial open interest is established by the initial volume, but subsequently trading may both increase and reduce the open interest. Generally speaking, a contract with a large open interest is likely to have

Table 9.2 Open Interest in Selected Futures Markets by Category of Trader, October 1992 through September 1993

(averages of weekly figures, in contracts)

Market	Coffee	Corn	Crude oil	T-bonds	D-mark	S&P500
TOTAL OPEN INTEREST	54172	249972	371594	360909	133491	180697
COMMERCIAL						
Long	25026	110795	263565	219710	102060	131448
Short	41210	117938	241622	225171	66657	116407
Net	− 16184	− 7143	21943	− 5462	35403	15041
NONCOMMERCIAL						
Long	9775	25796	14428	34745	9679	5935
Short	2230	13305	22518	26035	30393	21857
Net	7545	12491	− 8090	8710	− 20714	− 15921
SMALL TRADERS						
Long	16300	106637	78898	88785	19787	42610
Short	7661	111984	92752	92033	34476	41730
Net	8639	− 5348	− 13853	− 3248	− 14689	880

Note: The Total Open Interest includes spread positions, which are not included elsewhere in the table.

Source: Commodity Futures Trading Commission, *Commitments of Traders in All Futures Combined* (obtained through Pinnacle Data Corp., Webster, NY).

a large volume of trading because many traders maintain their position for a short period.[33]

In Table 9.2 we present data on open interest in six representative futures markets, three in commodities and three in financial markets. The table also shows the positions held by three categories of traders.[34] This breakdown is determined by the reporting system of the Commodity Futures Trading Commission, a regulatory agency discussed in Chapter 11. The CFTC requires daily reports concerning the futures position of large traders—those whose position exceeds a limit that varies from market to market. These traders are classified into commercial and noncommercials; the former are normally engaged in cash transactions and the latter, who are mostly futures speculators in the terminology of Section 9.4.1, are not. Most large noncommercials are believed to be commodity pool operators.

The aggregate position of small traders is calculated by subtracting the aggregate positions of the large traders from the total open interest in each futures market, which is available from the exchanges. These small traders are commercials or noncommercials with positions below the reporting limit; most of them are probably futures speculators.

Since the period covered by Table 9.2 is one year, seasonal variations are largely eliminated by averaging. Such seasonal variations are important in the analysis of futures prices, the subject of Chapter 10. Here we note that the average long or short position of large commercial traders is a large fraction (usually more than half) of the total open interest.[35] We may infer from this observation that futures markets exist primarily to serve commerce and finance; they are not mere gambling casinos. As we shall argue in more detail in the next chapter, the noncommercials contribute to this overriding purpose by accepting risk.

Table 9.2 also shows the net positions of the three groups of traders, which necessarily add up to zero. In two of the commodity markets—and also in the bond market—the average net position of the large commercials is negative (that is, they are net short in futures). Although evidently not universal since it does not hold for crude oil, this pattern is typical of commodity futures markets in general. It is consistent with the commercials being, at least on the average, short hedgers. Unfortunately, this interpretation cannot be verified directly because the table does not include positions in the spot and forward markets. Without additional analysis, which would lead us too far, nothing very illuminating can be said about the respective net positions of large noncommercials and small traders. We should mention, however, that the *Commitments of Traders* data used in Table 9.2 are in great demand from traders who believe they help in predicting prices. In fact, this is why these data, originally available only monthly, are now being released weekly. Whether they actually have predictive value is a matter on which more research is needed.

As mentioned previously, the concepts of volume and open interest also apply to futures options. Such options are traded most actively in certain financial futures markets, particularly Treasury bonds and Eurodollars. In these markets, the volume of trading in puts and calls is typically between one-third and one-half the volume in the futures themselves. In a few commodity futures markets (especially those in crude oil, soybeans, and gold), futures options have also attained considerable volume, but in most commodity markets trading in futures options is much less active than trading in futures contracts.

In this connection, a difference between futures contracts and futures options is worth noting. The open interest in futures options typically is a much larger multiple of the volume of trading than it is in futures options; in other words, futures contracts turn over much faster than futures options. In the bond market toward the end of July 1993, for instance, the daily volume in futures ran around 340,000 contracts and the open interest in futures was only slightly larger at about 365,000. By contrast, the daily volume in futures options was about 125,000 but the open interest was over 560,000, more than four times the daily volume. The lower turnover rate in options presumably reflects a larger bid-ask spread since the commissions on futures and options are much the same.

9.5 APPENDIX: THE EUROMARKETS AND
THE SWAP MARKET

For historical reasons it is natural for most of us to associate a currency with the country that issues it. The U.S. dollar has long been an important symbol of America. Many people therefore automatically assume that U.S. dollar–denominated securities are issued under U.S. regulations and traded on American exchanges. Today, however, very large amounts of deposits, bonds, and other securities denominated in U.S. dollars are created and traded without ever coming under U.S. government jurisdiction or passing through financial markets inside America. Similar offshore markets also exist for a variety of financial instruments denominated in other world currencies.

The term *Euromarkets* is used to describe these markets in financial instruments based on currency held outside its country of origin. Loans made with U.S. dollars held in Europe, for example, are termed *Eurodollar loans.* Bonds issued by governments or corporations managed by a syndicate of international banks and placed with investors worldwide are known as *Eurobonds,* even though they may be denominated in U.S. dollars, pounds sterling, deutsche marks, or yen. Paradoxically, the prefix "Euro" does not mean that these offshore securities are necessarily held in by a financial institution in Europe or traded there. The name was adopted because these markets first developed in Europe, primarily in London, and the name stuck. Today they could be U.S. dollar securities traded in Singapore or deutsche mark–denominated Eurobonds created and traded in Tokyo.

There is an important distinction between Eurobonds and other "foreign bonds" mentioned in Chapter 3. When, for example, the Swedish government bond denominated in U.S. dollars is issued and placed in the U.S. market, it is subject to all of the relevant U.S. regulations and trades like any other U.S. security. Such bonds are often give then name *Yankee bonds.* Similarly, foreign bonds issued and placed in yen under Japanese security laws are known as samurai bonds and are traded like a domestic security. Eurobonds, by contrast, remain creatures of the international capital markets, free of domestic regulation, even though they may be quoted and traded in particular local markets.

Today's Euromarkets began to emerge in the late 1950s. At that time, the U.S. government was running a sizable balance of payments deficit, paying overseas creditors in U.S. dollars rather than gold. Foreign exporters and investors who received those U.S. dollars tended to hold them in banks in Europe. A market in which these funds were exchanged between European banks and investors therefore began to emerge. Three developments fueled the growth of this infant market through the 1960s and 1970s. First, U.S. government policies, including a new Interest Equalization Tax on foreign securities in 1963, had the effect of encouraging U.S. multinationals to retain U.S. dollars abroad. Second, interest rate controls led to periods of credit rationing at home, making it attractive for U.S. companies expanding abroad to borrow Eurodollars. Third, when OPEC quadrupled the price of oil in 1973, the oil-exporting countries accumulated large amounts of dollars offshore, which were recycled through the Euromarkets.

Despite growing to serve the needs created by a particular combination of events, the Euromarkets have proven resilient. Over time they have broadened to include instruments denominated in deutsche marks, yen, Swiss francs, pounds sterling, and other national currencies as well as "currency cocktails" such as the European Currency Unit (ECU) and Special Drawing Rights (SDRs). There are active markets in Eurocurrency deposits between banks, Eurocertificates of deposit (CDs), Euro-floating rate CDs, Eurocommercial paper, and Eurobonds. Borrowers and lenders include multinational companies, sovereign states, local governments, state enterprises, and international agencies. The total size of the market is difficult to estimate due to relatively low levels of regulation, but Euromarket credits outstanding now certainly exceed U.S. $4 trillion.

London is the major Eurotrading center, accounting for around one-half of total world volume. New York, Tokyo, Frankfurt, Singapore, and Luxembourg are now also important centers of Euromarket activity. The Euromarkets, however, do not operate through a central trading place. Instead, the great majority of secondary market deals are made electronically by links between banks and other financial institutions 24 hours a day around the globe. Although there are no official specialists or nominated market makers, a number of firms act as unofficial, professional market markers, quoting prices at which they stand ready to buy or sell.

9.5.1 Rapid Innovation in Euromarket Instruments

The Euromarkets have been a source of rapid innovation with participants continually creating new types of financial instruments in the process of tailoring financial techniques to the needs of international customers. A bewildering array of new acronyms has emerged as a by-product: from FRNs, ECPs, and RUFs to NIFs and MOFs. In terms of the benefits they offer to the borrower, however, these many different instruments broadly fall into two categories: long-term and medium-term financing at variable interest rates.

The main instrument for providing long-term financing at variable interest rates is the *floating rate note* (FRN). These instruments generally have a maturity of between 5 and 15 years, but the interest rate is adjusted at regular intervals based on LIBOR (the London Interbank Overnight Rate), plus an agreed margin to reflect the particular customer's risk. LIBOR, which is effectively the rate at which banks operating in the London market will lend money to each other overnight to meet their reserve and liquidity requirements, is the pivotal interest rate on which the rates on many other financial instruments in the Euromarkets are based. Many FRNs are issued by the banks themselves. More recently, *Euro-commercial paper* (ECP), issued directly by corporations in an analogous fashion to commercial paper in the United States, has emerged in competition with FRNs.

Medium-term, variable-rate financing is provided by a series of Euromarket instruments that involve the issue of an overlapping series of short-term notes each with between 3 and 6 months duration. New notes are sold to investors to replace those that must be repaid. In order to ensure that the borrower has continuous access to funds for a number of years, banks "underwrite" the series of notes by promising to purchase any that remain unsold. For this reason, these instruments are known as *note issuance facilities* (NIFs) or *revolving underwriting facilities* (RUFs). Some borrowers may wish to have the option to change the types of notes issued (e.g., the currency or duration) as their financing needs change. In this case, the instruments are termed *multioption* facilities (MOFs).

9.5.2 The Swap Market

One of the fastest growing areas of the Euromarkets in recent years has been the area of "swaps." As late as 1985 the market in swaps was still small. By the early 1990s, total swaps outstanding were estimated to exceed several trillions of dollars.[36]

The mechanics of swap transactions can become quite complex, but the basic concept is straightforward: Swaps allow two borrowers to change the character of their existing debts. In an *interest rate swap,* for example, a borrower may convert existing debt from fixed rate to floating rate by swapping his liability with another party who wishes to fix the rate on her existing variable-rate loans. In a *currency swap,* a borrower who wants to reduce his U.S. dollar debts and replace these with a liability denominated in, say, Swiss francs, can do so by swapping with another party who wishes to convert her Swiss franc debts into a U.S. dollar liability.

The simplest form of interest rate swap is known as a "matched coupon swap." Party A has borrowed money at a floating rate of interest and would prefer to convert this to a fixed rate. Party B has borrowed money at a fixed rate of interest, but because of a change in his business or his expectations about interest rate trends, would prefer to pay a floating rate. The two borrowers retain the liability to repay the principal on their own loans when due. They swap only the "coupons"—that is, the liability to pay the interest. Therefore, Party A agrees to pay the other party's fixed interest commitment; Party B agrees to meet the floating rate interest payments on Party A's debt. By swapping the coupons in this way, Party A has effectively converted her outstanding debt to a fixed rate instrument, while Party B has converted his fixed rate of interest to a floating rate.

There are other possible reasons why such swaps might be advantageous. It may be, for example, that in some markets banks find it easier, and cheaper, to borrow fixed-rate credit than industrial companies. On the other hand, corporations often find that they can borrow competitively at floating rates. Rather than the corporation trying to borrow directly from the market with a fixed-rate instrument, there may be a margin to be gained if a bank borrows the money at a fixed rate and swaps it for a floating-rate instrument issued by the corporation. The difference between the fixed interest rate at which the bank can borrow versus the corporation going directly to the market can be shared between the two parties so that both gain. The bank for its part will take a spread for arranging the deal and lending its backing.

In other cases the benefits of a swap may arise because it helps overcome "information imperfections" in the international markets. In other words, the fact that despite increasing global integration of financial markets, some groups of borrowers and lenders know more about each other than others. For example, it may be that a U.S. company that wishes to borrow deutsche marks would be faced with paying a high interest rate because their credit risk was not well known among deutsche mark lenders. A German company, meanwhile, may wish to borrow U.S. dollars but is unknown among U.S. investors, who therefore find it difficult to make an good estimate of its credit risk. It may then be cheaper for the U.S. company to borrow in dollars and the German company to borrow in marks, using a swap agreement to exchange the funds and commit to meet each other's future interest payments.

Futures Prices

In Chapter 9 we outlined the nature of futures contracts and some of the institutional aspects of the markets in which these contracts are traded. Our task here is to analyze the forces that determine the prices of different futures contracts.

The simplest theory of futures prices holds that they are equal to the spot price expected to prevail when the futures contract becomes deliverable. By now the reader will be able to prove a proposition of this type almost automatically: If the futures price were below the expected spot price, speculators would bid for the futures contract, thus raising its price until it equals the expected spot price, and similarly if the discrepancy goes the other way. The perceptive reader will also realize that if this were the whole story, a chapter on futures prices would hardly be needed. There must be a flaw in the seemingly convincing proof just stated. This chapter exposes that flaw (particularly in Section 10.4) and develops a more satisfactory theory of futures prices.

Before doing so a brief statement of the economic functions of futures trading should be useful. They are:

- *Price discovery* (see Section 9.3.1). Since in most commodities and financial instruments the futures market is more nearly perfect than the cash market, futures prices tend to be more accurate than spot or forward prices.
- *Transfer of risk,* particularly by means of hedging. Recall that in Section 9.4.1 hedging was defined as arbitrage between the cash and futures markets. Thus merchants who hold inventories are able to shift some or all of the price risk to speculators by selling futures contracts. Whether the speculators are rewarded for assuming this risk is one of the main issues addressed in this chapter.

· *Determination of the timing of production and consumption.* For example, it will pay to postpone consumption and to speed up production if the price of a distant futures contract is well below the spot price.[1]

10.1 PROFITS AND LOSSES ON VARIOUS TRANSACTIONS

To begin with we review the financial outcome of different types of transactions. Let $s(t)$ be the spot price at time t and $f(t, u)$ the price at time t of a futures contract maturing at time u. The simplest case is that of a speculator who buys the futures contract at time 0 and sells it at time 1; his or her profit will then be $f(1, u) - f(0, u)$. A speculator who sold the contract at time 0 and covered his short position at time 1 would have a profit of $f(0, u) - f(1, u)$. The profit of a trader who buys in the spot market at time 0 and sells in the same market at time 1 is $s(1) - s(0) - z(0, 1)$, where $z(0, 1)$ is the net cost of carrying one unit in the spot market from time 0 to time 1. In general this *net carrying cost* is the algebraic sum of four components:

1. The warehouse cost (for instance, the fee charged by the owner of a storage tank for keeping a barrel of crude oil for one month).
2. The financing cost—that is, the interest paid on the amount borrowed to hold the inventory (or the interest foregone if the inventory is self-financed). The relevant interest rate is usually a short-term rate such as the repo rate or the Eurodollar rate.
3. The cost of insurance against fire and similar hazards.
4. The percentage yield on the value of the amount held. Its meaning is obvious in the case of financial instruments (see Chapters 4 and 6), and we shall show in a moment that this concept can be extended to physical commodities.

Of these four cost components, the first three are positive and the last is negative. The first component is roughly proportional to the volume or weight of the commodity, while the last three are proportional to its price. For most commodities, and for all financial instruments, the second component is the largest positive part of the net carrying cost.[2]

It follows from the last formula that *holding spot supplies is profitable only if the spot price rises by more than the net carrying cost* (or decreases by less if the latter is negative).

We now consider some more complicated transactions. A speculator who holds a futures contract until it matures at time 1 will have a profit of $s(1) - f(0,1)$, since at maturity the price of the futures contract equals the spot price and there are no carrying costs on a futures contract.[3] In the Chapter 9 a short hedger was defined as a trader who is long in the cash market and short in the futures market, say in the contract that matures at time u. A short hedge starting at time 0 and ending at time 1 therefore leads to a profit of

$$s(1) - s(0) - z(0,1) + f(0, u) - f(1, u).^4 \qquad (10.1)$$

As we know from Chapter 9, the difference between the futures price $f(t, u)$ and the spot price $s(t)$ of the standard grade (that is, the price for immediate delivery of that grade) is called the *basis*. We see then that the profit from hedging an inventory is equal to the change in the basis less the net carrying cost. Alternatively, we can say that for a short hedge to be profitable, a loss in one market (say the spot market, where it includes the net carrying cost) must be more than offset by a profit in the other market.

An important special case of formula (10.1) arises when the futures contract matures at time 1 and the long position is delivered on the futures contract. We know that the price of an expiring futures contract equals the spot price of the delivered grade {that is, $f(1, 1) = s(1)$}, so the profit on this transaction is

$$f(0, u) - s(0) - z(0, 1). \qquad (10.2)$$

10.1.1 Implied Limits on Simultaneous Price Differences

It should be noted that in formula (10.2) the prices at time 1 do not appear, from which we may infer that the transaction is riskless. Now arbitrage pricing theory (discussed in Chapter 6) tells us that the profit on a riskless transaction cannot be positive. Consequently, at time 0 the futures price for delivery at time 1 cannot exceed the spot price by more than the carrying cost between the present and the maturity of the futures contract, that is

$$f(0, u) - s(0) \leq z(0, u).$$

For example, if it costs 5 cents per bushel to carry corn for 1 month, then the price of the May future cannot exceed the spot price in January by more than 20 cents. If the difference were greater, there would be opportunities for profitable and riskless arbitrage.[5] The same argument can be used to derive an upper limit to the difference between any two futures prices $f(t, u)$ and $f(t, v)$, which cannot be greater than $z(u, v)$ (assuming that v is later than u). The proof is left to the reader.

So far, only upper limits to the differences between spot and futures prices, or between two futures prices, have been found. Can we go beyond this to find lower limits? The answer is that we can only do so in special cases discussed later, specifically in Section 10.2.1 on financial futures. In most commodities the spot price of the standard grade can exceed any futures price by an arbitrary amount; in other words, the basis can be very large.[6]

The absence of a significant upper limit to the basis does not mean that it is arbitrary. One important influence on the futures price of a particular commodity or financial instrument will clearly be the level of the spot price that is expected to prevail at the time the contract matures. The expected spot price—or the futures price that reflects it—will in turn depend on future supply and demand of the commodity or financial instrument.

The supply available at a future time is determined both by future production and consumption (or net issue in the case of financial futures) and by the inventory that is carried over (and will be carried over) from previous supply. Demand for inventories reflects, among other things, the *convenience yield* of having spot supplies available for sale or for conversion into other products.[7] Finally, the futures price will incorporate any risk premium available in the market for agreeing to a price now in the face of uncertainty concerning the spot price that will prevail later.

In addition to understanding each of these influences individually, the ways in which they interact to determine the futures price attaching to a particular contract require close attention. The importance of each factor will vary between and within the broad classes of commodities and financial instruments. Supply and demand for some commodities are strongly influenced by seasonal forces (as in the case of wheat and other fieldcrops), while others like copper display little if any seasonality. Some commodities can be stored at relatively low cost (a T-bond, for example, can be "stored" essentially at the rate of interest on overnight funds), while others such as soybean oil have limited storability. The pressure on producers or merchants to hedge their purchases or sales will be influenced by the importance of fixed costs in the production process and the prevalence of long-term fixed-price contracting arrangements for final output.

10.2 RELATIONS AMONG SPOT AND FUTURES PRICES

In light of these differences in the role of supply, demand, convenience, storage, and hedging, the discussion is divided into three main sections. We begin with futures on three important financial instruments in Section 10.2.1. The next section (10.2.2) deals with storable, essentially nonseasonal commodities like silver or crude oil. The complications associated with seasonality in supply or demand, and with the role of convenience yield and *supply of storage* in the markets for seasonal commodities, are then taken up in Section 10.2.3. Section 10.3 deals first with hedging and proceeds to analyze market equilibrium when there is an imbalance in hedging. This is followed in Section 10.4 with a discussion of expectations and their place in Keynes's theory of "normal backwardation". Finally, Section 10.5 considers some implications for investment and risk management.

10.2.1 Financial Futures

The effect of the net carrying cost on the "spreads" between different maturities and on the basis will now be illustrated by three examples that bring out different aspects and are of considerable interest in their own right. These examples cover futures in Treasury bonds, Eurodollars, and foreign currencies.

Treasury Bonds First we examine the futures market in long-term (i.e., 30-year) Treasury bonds. The return on inventory is the yield on these bonds, and the total inventory is normally large enough to make the convenience yield equal to zero. Since warehouse and insurance costs on financial instruments are negligible, the gross carrying cost is simply the cost of financing an inventory of bonds. This cost can be approximated by the rate on so-called repurchase agreements (repos for short), which applies to credit for which bonds and other default-free securities serve as collateral. As the discussion of the yield curve in Chapters 3 and 4 showed, the long-term bond rate is normally above any short-term interest rate, including the repo rate.

When the yield curve is normal, the net return from carrying long-term bonds is positive and consequently the net carrying cost is negative. This observation implies that *the prices of the more distant futures must be below those of the nearby futures by an amount corresponding to the financing cost.* Thus, if the price of the March bond contract is 100, equivalent to a yield of 8.12%, and the repo rate is 4% (1% per three months), then the price of the June contract will be 99, equivalent to a slightly higher bond yield of 8.25%.[8] Any departure from this pattern will lead to arbitrage along the lines described in Section 10.1.1. Since arbitrage involves transaction costs, which are generally very low in financial futures, it may not produce the cited numbers exactly.

Sometimes, however, the yield curve is not normal. In 1981–1982, for instance, there was a "money crunch" in which short-term rates rose far above their long-term counterparts. As a result, the net return on Treasury bonds became negative, and the distant futures rose above the near ones. The reader should have no difficulty in amending the italicized statement in the previous paragraph concerning the price of distant futures to cover this case.

The foregoing analysis also applies to futures on other fixed-interest securities. In particular, there are futures contracts on 2-year, 5-year, and 10-year Treasury notes, which together with the T-bill and T-bond futures cover most of the Treasury yield curve. With some modification, the analysis can also be applied to stock index futures, where the yield on the underlying instruments is not fixed and becomes available every day some stock included in the index pays a dividend, rather than at regular intervals.

Eurodollars A somewhat more complicated case is the subject of our second example. It involves short-term zero-coupon securities such as Eurodollars with a maturity of 3 months, in which futures trading has attained a large volume.[9] Eurodollar futures have come to dominate the short end of the interest spectrum just as T-bond futures have long dominated the long end. This dominance is one reason for looking at them in detail; another appears in Section 10.5.3, where Eurodollar futures, viewed as investments, stand out because of their high return.

To discuss this case we must first deal with some technicalities resulting from the fact that Eurodollars, T-bills, and similar financial instruments do not have coupons but are traded at a discount to their face value (i.e., the amount for which they are redeemed at maturity). For instance, the amount paid today for a newly issued T-bill with a face value of $10,000 might be $9,900, implying a 1% discount on the face value for three months, or 4% on an annual basis.

In the futures markets for these instruments, the "price" at which transactions take place is not the price of anything outside these markets; instead, it is calculated as 100 less the discount rate on an annual percentage basis. To simplify the arithmetic, however, we use decimal fractions in lieu of percentages. Measuring time in units of one quarter, let $p_1(t)$ be the quoted price (converted to a fraction) for 3-month Eurodollar deposits newly issued at time t. If that price is 0.92, anyone buying $1 worth of Eurodollars has to pay $1 less one-fourth of the annual discount of 0.08 for a net cost (ignoring commissions) of $0.98. Unlike $p_1(t)$, this $0.98 is a meaningful price, called $q_1(t)$ hereafter. If $r_1(t)$ is the annual discount (expressed as a fraction) then clearly

$$p_1(t) = 1 - r_1(t) \qquad q_1(t) = 1 - r_1(t)/4,$$

which implies

$$q_1(t) = 0.75 + p_1(t)/4. \tag{10.3}$$

We are now ready for another technicality involving Eurodollar deposits with a maturity different from 3 months, say 6 months. Such deposits can be placed in the spot market, but they can also be "synthetized" in the futures market for 3-month Eurodollars. A 6-month deposit with a face value of $1 placed today is equivalent to:[10]

1. Placing a 3-month deposit with a face value of x in the spot market, where x will be determined in a moment
2. Simultaneously buying a futures contract expiring in three months
3. Upon expiration of the futures contract (and of the initial deposit), placing another 3-month deposit at a cost of x and a face value of $1

It remains to solve for x, which can be done most easily by working backwards. Since time is measured in quarters, today corresponds to $t = 0$, 3 months from now to $t = 1$, and 6 months from now to $t = 2$. Then the cost of the second 3-month deposit (which is "locked in" by the futures contract) is $q_1(1)$.[11] This must be available upon maturity of the first 3-month deposit, and is therefore equal to x. The cost of the first deposit, which is also the cost $q_2(0)$ of the entire synthetic 6-month deposit, is then given by

$$q_2(0) = q_1(0)q_1(1). \tag{10.4}$$

For instance, if $p_1(0) = 0.97$ and $p_1(1) = 0.96$, then $q_1(0) = 0.9925$, $q_1(1) = 0.99$, and $q_2(0) = 0.982575$. The procedure used for deriving this formula can be easily generalized to maturities of any integer number of quarters:

$$q_u(0) = \prod_{t=0}^{t=u-1} q_1(t), \quad u = 1, 2, \ldots \tag{10.5}$$

where u is the number of quarters to maturity and Π denotes a product. Various extensions of Equation (10.5) are possible. One is to maturities that are fractions of quarters. Another is to synthetic futures contracts in maturities different from three months: All that is needed to obtain 6-month "futures," for instance, is to change the 0 and 1 in Equation (10.4) to 1 and 2, respectively. These exercises are again left to the reader, who is also encouraged to verify that

$$r_u(t) = \frac{4}{u}\{1 - q_u(t)\}. \tag{10.6}$$

With the aid of the preceding financial arithmetic, particularly Equations (10.3), (10.4), (10.6) and (10.5), it is in principle possible to calculate the spot discount rates $r_u(0)$ for different maturities u from the spot and futures quotations for 3-month Eurodollars. To see whether this produces realistic estimates, and to illustrate the calculation, we present Table 10.1, which refers to London Euro-dollar futures on December 15, 1992.[12]

The correspondence between the implied and actual discount rates is close— not surprisingly in view of the arbitrage that would otherwise be possible, but transaction costs may interfere with an exact fit. It follows that the spot rates for different maturities can indeed be found from the spot and futures quotations for 3-month Eurodollars. This conclusion does not necessarily mean that these spot rates are determined by the futures prices; in fact, the two sets of variables are determined simultaneously.

Table 10.1 Spot and Futures Quotations for London Eurodollars

t	Contract	Price[a]	Price[b]	u	Price[c]	Implied Rate[d]	Actual Rate[e]
0	Spot	.9644[f]	.9911	1	.9911	[g]	3.56
1	March '93	.9615	.9904	2	.9815	3.70	3.69
2	June '93	.9568	.9892	3	.9710	3.87	[h]
3	Sept. '93	.9517	.9879	4	.9592	4.08	4.12[i]

[a] $p_1(t)$.

[b] $q_1(t)$, from Equation (10.3).

[c] $q_u(0)$, from Equation (10.5).

[d] $100 * r_u(0)$, from Equation (10.6).

[e] Mean of bid and ask rate in source, except as noted. Converted to decimals.

[f] Derived from actual rate in last column.

[g] Equals actual rate by construction; see preceding note.

[h] Not available in source.

[i] Estimate; only "offered" rate of 4.19 given in source.

Source: Wall Street Journal, December 16, 1992.

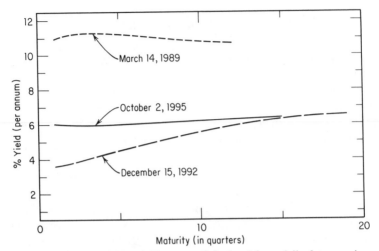

Figure 10.1 Eurodollar yield curves. Calculated from daily futures prices.

The principal conclusion from the above analysis is that the prices of Euro-dollar futures conform to certain testable restrictions involving the spot market. These restrictions are different from those found for bonds (and also from those for foreign currencies discussed next). In particular, the gross carrying cost is conspicuously absent from the equations.[13]

Using the approach of Section 4.1.3 it is also possible to calculate the yield on Eurodollars of various maturities. Since contracts as far out as 5 years are now listed in the Eurodollar futures market, a sizable part of the yield curve can be covered. This is done in Figure 10.1, where the top curve refers to March 14, 1989, and the bottom curve to December 15, 1992. On the last date, the yield curve was "normal" (that is, rising) but the earlier curve—shorter because fewer futures prices were quoted—is more or less flat with a falling tendency for longer maturities; it reflected tight monetary policy. A rising curve has usually prevailed in the 10 years since Eurodollars futures started trading, and in the spot market before then. Important implications of this phenomenon will be discussed in Sections 10.4.1 and 10.5.3.

Foreign Currencies   The third illustration is taken from futures trading in foreign currencies. A trader who is long in a foreign currency future is by impli-cation short in dollars.[14] Consider now a trader who is long June D-marks and short September D-marks. If he took delivery on his June position and delivered the D-marks so obtained in September, he would be earning a German short-term interest rate and paying a U.S. short-term rate.[15] Using the same argument as in the previous example, we conclude that the June D-mark must be above the September D-mark if the German interest rate is higher than the correspond-ing American rate, and conversely.

More precisely, *the percentage difference between the two futures prices will equal the interest differential between the two countries.* This equation is known as *interest parity theorem.* For example, if the Eurodollar interest rate is 3% per year and the Euromark rate is 9% per year, then the September D-mark contract in Chicago will be 1.5% (one-quarter of the interest differential) below the June contract. If the June–September price difference did not correspond to the interest differential, opportunities for profitable and riskless arbitrage would again emerge. The essence of this arbitrage is to borrow at the lower rate (taking into account the price change implicit in the futures quotations) and lend at the higher rate.

Thus if the price of marks for June delivery were the same as the price for September delivery, a creditworthy arbitrageur could borrow marks in June for 3 months at the German interest rate, immediately convert the marks into dollars to invest them for 3 months at the American interest rate, and in September convert the dollars back into marks (at the same exchange rate as in June) to repay the borrowed marks. He or she would then have earned the difference between the Eurodollar and Euromark rates (which is positive by assumption) without any investment. Any risk in this set of transaction, such as the risk that the conversion between marks and dollars cannot be done at the anticipated exchange rate, can be eliminated by taking appropriate futures positions. To make the transaction completely riskless, it may be necessary to operate not only in D-mark futures but also in Eurodollar and Euromark futures. These additional futures operations involve transaction costs, however, so interest parity need hold only within the narrow limits set by those costs.

The approximate prevalence of interest parity has been confirmed by considerable statistical evidence.[16] It also holds between forward contracts, and between the spot exchange rate on the one hand and the exchange rate futures (or forwards) on the other hand. Interest parity is fundamental to the understanding of exchange rates and international capital movements, subjects outside the scope of this book.

10.2.2 Nonseasonal Commodities

We now turn to the class of commodities that are produced more or less continuously throughout the year and are storable (albeit at some cost). These commodities, of which silver and gold are examples, provide the base case to which complications will subsequently be added. They have another characteristic that is pertinent to the following discussion, namely that the total inventory is so large as to make the convenience yield close to zero.

The demand for the physical form of these metals reflects some mix of demand from individual applications such as jewelry, minting of coins, chemical, electronic, and industrial uses, plus demand from investors seeking to use them as a store of value. Supply, in turn, reflects the mining capacity, and releases from inventories currently held by private investors or public bodies (such as the U.S. Treasury).

Suppose, then, that you expect a significant rise in industrial demand for silver over the coming year. If supply remains roughly constant, that implies the spot price of physical silver will be higher in 12 months than it is now. The futures price $f(0, 12)$ at which you would be willing to contract now to deliver silver to a buyer in 12 months would therefore be higher than the current spot price $s(0)$.

As we know, the difference between the futures price $f(t, u)$ and the spot price $s(t)$ of the standard grade (that is, the price for immediate delivery of that grade) is called the basis. When the futures price exceeds the current spot price (so that the basis is positive), the market is said to be in *contango*. Conversely, when the futures price is less than the current spot price, so that the basis is negative, the market is said to be in *backwardation*.[17]

To summarize so far, if future demand is expected to rise relative to supply, and hence the spot price is expected to rise, the basis will tend to be positive and the market in contango. Conversely, when future demand is expected to fall relative to supply, the basis will tend to be negative and the market will exhibit backwardation.

Suppose, then, that the futures market was exhibiting a large positive basis. In this contango market, the following opportunity for riskless arbitrage would emerge:

1. Buy spot silver of deliverable grade today at a price $s(0)$
2. Sell a futures contract to deliver silver 12 months from today at a price $f(0, 12)$
3. Pay the carrying cost $z(1, 12)$ to have it stored for 12 months [18]

These transactions would lock in a riskless profit or loss of

$$Z = s(0) - f(0, 12) - z(0, 12).$$

Should the basis move above the net carrying cost, it would be profitable for investors to engage in the arbitrage described here. As they did so, they would drive the current spot price up (by purchasing physical silver now) and drive the futures price down (by supplying futures contracts for the delivery of silver to the market) until equilibrium was again established.

Exactly the same kind of reasoning can be applied to the relationship between the price of near futures (say, 3 months) and distant futures (say, 12 months). So long as carrying costs were relatively predictable, an investor seeing a substantially higher price for 12-month contracts on silver compared with 3-month futures could profit by:

1. Purchasing a silver futures contract for delivery 3 months from today
2. Selling a silver futures contract for delivery 12 months from today
3. Taking delivery in 3 months and storing the silver during the 9-month interval

Again, therefore, arbitrage between the cash and futures markets will ensure that the relationship between the spot price and the prices of futures contracts of different maturities will be heavily influenced by the costs of carrying. The most volatile component of those carrying costs, in turn, will be the interest rate on the funds tied up in holding physical stocks.

So far we have assumed that the convenience yield is zero because the total inventory is large. This is generally true for gold and silver but not for other nonseasonal commodities such as platinum or copper.[19] In the latter commodities, inventories are held not as a store of value but for ordinary commercial purposes. Even though no significant seasonality may be present, the analysis of the following section will be applicable with slight changes.

10.2.3 Seasonal Commodities

Our discussion thus far has focused on commodities that are produced more or less continuously throughout the year. Many of the commodities on which futures contracts are traded, however, have a strong seasonal pattern in production (and sometimes consumption as well) that adds an additional complication to the analysis of futures prices. Figure 10.2 depicts the path of inventory accumulation and spot prices for a seasonal commodity over the crop year. In this example, the harvest begins to arrive in early June, with new supplies continuing through July and August. Inventory is built up in anticipation of demand later in the year and prior to the new harvest next June.

In this environment we would expect spot prices to begin to fall as new supply comes onto the market during harvest. Beyond some point the spot price is expected to rise over the remainder of the year, reflecting the cost of storing the commodity. If unit carrying costs were constant regardless of the amount stored, the price (all else equal) rises linearly in proportion to the length of time the commodity is stored. In many cases, however, unit carrying costs will rise the larger the amount to be stored. This reflects the fact that as the total volume in storage increases, more expensive methods of carrying (such as railroad boxcars) will need to be used. Costs of carrying will therefore tend to increase with volume either because of higher operating costs or because inferior methods cause greater loss and deterioration of the commodity during storage. This behavior of carrying costs will cause an additional rise in the spot price as total inventory increases, leading to the nonlinear price pattern shown by the shaded area in Figure 10.2.

We therefore consider the behavior of futures prices across a series of successive crop cycles, each showing the spot price behavior just described. The first point to note is that the futures price for a contract to buy or sell, say, March corn each year will reflect the expected supply and demand for corn each March. The supply will reflect both the size of the previous harvest and the costs of carrying, while demand will be influenced by the needs of manufacturers of corn-based products.

If the supply and demand for corn in March were the same over successive years, then the price of the March futures contract would be constant from year

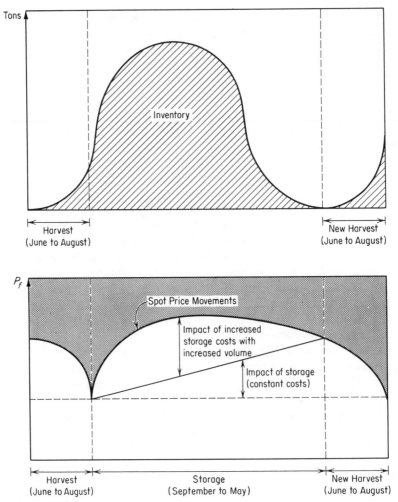

Figure 10.2 Inventory and spot price for a seasonal commodity

to year and throughout the year. The seasonality of corn has no effect on the price behavior of a particular futures contract, which is determined instead by the supply and demand and hence the spot price expected to prevail each March. On the other hand, seasonality has important effects on the relationship between the prices of futures contracts with different maturities (e.g., the price of a June contract relative to a March contract) and on the behavior of the basis over time. Figure 10.3 plots the behavior of the basis of a March corn contract where the crop cycle involves harvest beginning each September. Notice the shift between backwardation and contango over the seasonal cycle.

As has already been mentioned, seasonality influences the relationship be-

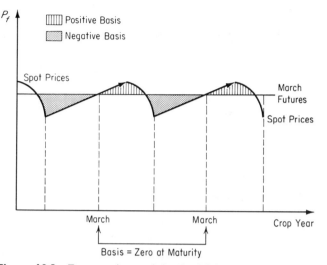

Figure 10.3 Futures prices and the "basis" in a seasonal market

tween the prices of contracts with different maturity dates. Even where supply and demand are the same from year to year, in some months "near" contracts will be more valuable than distant ones. This position will be reversed at other times in the year (see Figure 10.4).

Before leaving the issue of seasonal commodities, a closer look at the *supply curve of storage* (Working, 1949) is in order.[20] Shown in Figure 10.5, it relates the level of inventories to the basis. The underlying idea is the convenience yield

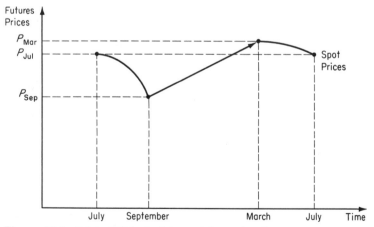

Figure 10.4 Prices of March, July, and September futures contracts for a seasonal commodity with July–August harvest

introduced in Section 10.1.1. When inventories are large, their convenience yield is zero, but there must nevertheless be an incentive to hold them. This means that the basis must equal the gross carrying cost, which as we know will itself rise as more expensive storage facilities have to be used. Even if the basis is below the gross carrying cost—and indeed if the basis is negative—some inventories will still be held by those to whom their convenience yield is sufficiently high. When inventories are close to zero, the basis will be a large negative number.[21]

10.3 HEDGERS, SPECULATORS, AND MARKET EQUILIBRIUM

An important influence on the price of futures is the risk exposure of various participants coming to the market. A producer of silver, for example, is exposed to the risk of price fluctuations on inventory of silver or silver ore held, while a manufacturer of photographic film (in which large quantities of silver halide are used) is exposed to fluctuations in the price of the raw material. We start, therefore, with an informal exploration of the circumstances under which producers or users might want to fix the price at which they buy or sell silver in advance by entering into a futures contract. A more formal model is presented in the next section.

Typically, most of a silver producer's costs will be independent of the market price of silver. Indeed, a large part of the total costs of each ounce of silver will be reflect essentially fixed costs of keeping the mine in production, costs which must be committed well before the output can be sold on the spot market. Both of these factors mean that the producer's profits are heavily dependent on the future spot price of the commodity and hence returns exposed to considerable risk.

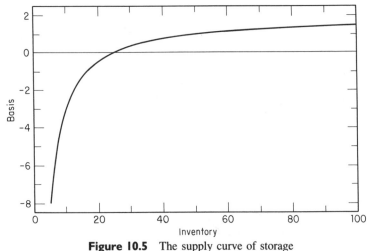

Figure 10.5   The supply curve of storage

Faced with this situation, an opportunity to fix the price in advance, and thus to guarantee a minimum return, will have considerable attraction to a risk-averse producer. Many producers will therefore seek to go short in the futures market by selling futures contracts to offset at least some of their long position in holding inventory, or their commitment to produce the physical commodity. Using the terminology of Chapter 9, this is called *short hedging*.

On the other side, consider the risk position of the manufacturer who uses the commodity (like the producer of photographic film mentioned earlier). If changes in the price of raw materials could be easily passed on in the price of the final product there would be little need for hedging by the manufacturer. However, this kind of price flexibility is often impracticable for two reasons:

1. The final product may be sold on the basis of a long-term contract according to which price is only adjusted at distant intervals. A supplier of aluminum engine mountings may, for example, contract to supply these to General Motors at an agreed price 12 months in advance, thereby exposing his profits to fluctuations in the price of aluminum.
2. The market for the final product may not sustain passing on large increases in raw material prices, either due to the availability of substitutes or hedging by major competitors. If Kodak passed on a large increase in silver prices into the price of its film while its competitors did not, Kodak's sales and profits may be severely impaired.

Risk-averse manufacturers may therefore often find it advantageous to hedge their future purchases of commodities (their short position in the physical) by contracting to buy forward at a price agreed now (going "long" in the futures market). This approach is called a *long hedge*. Entering into a long hedge in this way is an alternative to for the manufacturer to fixing the price by purchasing sufficient stocks of raw materials on the spot market now and holding the physical inventory until it was required.

10.3.1 A Portfolio Analysis of Hedging

We now develop a simplified model of a hedger—more precisely, of a trader who could turn out to be a hedger—based on Markowitz' portfolio analysis (see Chapter 4).* Assuming that there is only one futures contract, let $s(0)$ be the cash price and $f(0, 1)$ the futures price quoted at time 0 for delivery at time 1. Furthermore let $\Delta s(0)$ and $\Delta f(0, 1)$ be the changes in these prices during the next time period, and let x_0 and x_1 be the trader's position in the cash and futures markets, respectively. These two positions are the unknowns of the problem.

The random variables $\Delta s(0)$ and $\Delta f(0, 1)$ are supposed to have a (subjective) probability distribution that is normal with means μ_0 and μ_1, standard devi-

---

*This section is taken from Houthakker (1968). For a more elaborate analysis along similar lines, see Stein (1986, chapter 7).

ations σ_0 and σ_1, and correlation coefficient ρ. The trader's expected profit is then

$$Z(x_0, x_1) = x_0\mu_0 + x_1\mu_1$$

and its variance is

$$V(x_0, x_1) = x_0^2\sigma_0^2 + 2x_0x_1\rho\sigma_0\sigma_1 + x_1^2\sigma_1^2.$$

The trader is supposed to maximize $Z(x_0, x_1) - \lambda V(x_0, x_1)$, where $\lambda > 0$ is a measure of risk aversion. There are no financial or other constraints; in particular, it is not assumed that the trader's overall position is zero (which would make the trader a hedger in the sense of Chapter 8). The first-order conditions for a maximum are

$$\mu_0 = 2\lambda(x_0\sigma_0^2 + x_1\rho\sigma_0\sigma_1) \tag{10.7}$$

$$\mu_1 = 2\lambda(x_0\rho\sigma_0\sigma_1 + x_1\sigma_1^2). \tag{10.8}$$

Because these equations are linear in the unknowns, they can be solved as follows:

$$x_0 = \frac{\mu_0 - \rho\sigma_0\mu_1/\sigma_1}{2\lambda\sigma_0^2(1 - \rho^2)} \tag{10.9}$$

$$x_1 = \frac{\mu_1 - \rho\sigma_1\mu_0/\sigma_0}{2\lambda\sigma_1^2(1 - \rho^2)}. \tag{10.10}$$

These formulas can be simplified by introducing realistic approximations. Since σ_0 and σ_1 are normally close to each other, we can assume them to be equal with a common value σ. Equations (10.9) and (10.10) then reduce to

$$x_0 = \frac{\mu_0 - \rho\mu_1}{2\lambda\sigma^2(1 - \rho^2)} \tag{10.11}$$

$$x_1 = \frac{\mu_1 - \rho\mu_0}{2\lambda\sigma^2(1 - \rho^2)}. \tag{10.12}$$

Now we know that usually the cash-futures correlation ρ is close to 1, the main exception being the harvest period in agricultural commodities.[22] If so, it follows from Equations (10.11) and (10.12), which have the same denominator, that x_0 is close to being the negative of x_1, and consequently our trader is almost a hedger as defined in Chapter 9. In fact, his or her total net position is

$$x_0 + x_1 = \frac{(1 - \rho)(\mu_0 + \mu_1)}{2\lambda\sigma^2(1 - \rho^2)} = \frac{\mu_0 + \mu_1}{2\lambda\sigma^2(1 + \rho)}, \tag{10.13}$$

which for plausible values of the parameters is a small number. Whether the trader is a long hedger or a short hedger depends on μ_0 and μ_1, which reflect his or her expectations concerning the change in the spot price and the futures price, respectively. Thus, if $\mu_0 > \mu_1$, it can easily be verified that the trader will be long in the cash market and short in the futures market—that is, he or she will be a short hedger.[23]

10.3.2 Hedging Effectiveness

Since no futures market with adequate liquidity can provide a perfect hedge, the suitability of a futures market for hedging a trader's exposure to the cash market is a matter of degree. Among the measures of hedging effectiveness that have been proposed we shall present those due to Ederington (1979).

The simplest of the two Ederington measures refers to the case of "full hedging," where the futures position is the exact opposite of the cash position. The risk faced by a fully hedged trader is that the "basis" will move against him.[24] The "basis," in this case, is the difference between a particular cash price (not necessarily the one underlying the futures contract) and the price of a partic- ular futures contract (not necessarily the expiring or dominant one). Risk is mea- sured by the variance of the price in question. Then *full hedging effectiveness* (FHE) can be defined as 1 minus a ratio whose numerator is the variance of changes in the "basis" and whose denominator is the variance of changes in the cash price. If the "basis" remains constant over the time interval relevant to the hedger, its variance is 0 and the full hedging effectiveness is 1, indicating a perfect hedge. If the two variances are equal, the full hedging effectiveness is 0, so hedging is pointless.

The second Ederington measure recognizes that, as shown in Section 10.3.1, it may not be optimal to be fully hedged. If the correlation between a particular cash price and a particular futures price is less than perfect, a better combination of risk and return is obtained by "partial hedging," where the futures position is less than the cash position. The optimal ratio of the futures position to the cash position is known as the *hedge ratio* (HR). Ederington's second measure will be referred to as the *partial hedging effectiveness* (PHE); it can also be interpreted as the goodness of fit in a regression of changes in the futures price on changes in the cash price.[25] As the hedging effectiveness does for full hedging, the partial hedging effectiveness represents the reduction in risk attributable to partial hedg- ing. The three italicized concepts are not independent of each other; the inter- ested reader can verify that any one can be derived from the other two. Thus we have

$$\text{PHE} = \frac{\text{HR}^2}{2\text{HR} - \text{FHE}}.$$

As an example, let us consider the crude oil futures market in New York. The standard grade is West Texas Intermediate (WTI), an important domestic crude. The delivery point is Cushing, Oklahoma; although not known as a great center of commerce, it is where a number of pipelines connect, so that crude can be sent from there to many other points in the United States. From daily price data over a period of about 3 years ending in 1995, the FHE for WTI with respect to the expiring future is calculated to be 0.9010, a high figure that explains the wide use of New York futures by commercial traders. The hedge ratio using that future is 0.9175 and the PHE, at 0.9013, is close to the FHE.

Not all traders are interested in the expiring future, which is suitable only for hedging short-term commitments. Ederington's measures can also be calculated for more distant futures contracts. For the future that is second in order of maturity, the FHE is 0.8642, the HR is 0.8180, and the FHE is 0.8670. Going out as far as the tenth future in order of maturity, the three numbers are 0.6601, 0.5318, and 0.7009, respectively. Judging by the open interest, these FHE and PHE are still high enough to attract many hedgers.

Hedging is also possible for varieties of crude oil that are not deliverable on the New York futures contract. An example is Alaska North Slope (ANS) crude, most of which is refined in California. Price data are available for ANS delivered in Long Beach, and they imply (using the expiring New York future) an FHE of 0.7929 and a PHE of 0.7935, not much less than for WTI. Thus hedging ANS in New York futures would seem to be quite feasible, but we do not know how much of it actually occurs.

The ability of a futures contract to provide hedging for varieties other than the standard grade is important because it increases liquidity, thereby making the futures market more interesting for large traders. Thus the Brent futures market in London is used not only for hedging different North Sea crudes but also for Middle Eastern and African crudes. According to the *Commitments of Traders* data discussed at the end of Chapter 9, on the other hand, futures markets with low volume—the lumber market in Chicago is a case in point—are used by very few hedgers.

10.3.3 Market Equilibrium

The preceding argument applied to a single trader, who could turn out to be either a short hedger or a long hedger. Clearly, the total supply and demand for futures from each of the two types of hedgers can be found by aggregating over all such traders. It is also important to note that *in any futures market the net futures position of all hedgers combined is exactly offset by the net position of all speculators combined.*[26]

Now if the demand from commodity suppliers for short hedging just equalled the demand for long hedging from manufacturers and other users[27] at any future date, the futures market would simply represent an exchange of agreements between these parties at roughly the expected value of the future spot price. The net position of all hedgers combined would then be 0, as would be the net position of all speculators combined. In the process, the risk faced by suppliers and users would be eliminated, which is one of the important potential benefits of futures trading.

It has often been argued, however, that in many markets there is an inherent imbalance, due to greater underlying demand for short hedging among producers of commodities than demand for long hedging by manufacturers.[28] This imbalance might reflect the fact the producers of raw materials have very little flexibility in their cost structures—hence face high risk to profits if prices fluctuate— whereas manufacturers typically have more flexibility through their ability to pass some of the fluctuations in raw material prices on to their customers, and therefore face less risk from adverse price movements.

Such an imbalance would tend to make the futures price artificially low (relative to the expected future price) as producers of raw materials accepted less than the expected value of their commodities in an attempt to rid themselves of their high risk. On the other hand, those manufacturers who can fully pass fluctuations in raw material prices on to final customers without impairing demand for the product would only be willing to buy a futures contract at less than their expected future spot price.

Such an underlying imbalance opens up an opportunity for the entry of speculators who have neither a long nor a short position in the physical commodity to soak up the excess of demand for short hedging. The speculator's goal here would be to go long in the futures contract at a price less than the expected future spot price. If expectations were confirmed, she would reap a profit on maturity by taking delivery at the low price specified in the futures contract and reselling at the higher spot price prevailing in the future. Of course speculators may be observed on both sides of the futures market—that is, some speculators will take long positions while others take short depending on how their individual expectations differ from those of the market. If the kind of underlying imbalance just described does exist, however, the net position of all speculators combined must be long in futures.

Our reasoning up to this point may be summarized by saying that if hedgers tend to be net short in futures, then speculators must have an incentive to be net long, and this incentive consists in the futures price being less than the expected spot price in the future. Moreover, the reason the futures price can be below the expected spot price is that the hedgers will at some point prior to expiration have to cover their short positions by buying futures. When the hedgers do so, the speculators, being net long, will on the average gain. This observation leads naturally to a discussion of expectations.

10.4 THE ROLE OF EXPECTATIONS

One implication of the preceding argument is that the spot price and all the futures prices are more or less closely correlated with each other. It is not possible to maintain, therefore, that the spot price serves to equilibrate the spot market while the futures market expresses expectations concerning spot prices in the future. *If expectations matter at all, they must affect both spot and futures prices.* As Hawtrey (1939) expressed it succinctly, "The futures price equally divides the bulls and bears at the point where supply and demand balance." By the same token, anything that influences the spot price must also have an effect on the futures prices. This idea is elaborated in two stages: Section 10.4.1 sets out an important theory of futures pricing, and Section 10.4.2 resolves an apparent paradox concerning the role of carrying cost in the determination of spot and futures prices.

10.4.1 Futures Prices as Predictors of Spot Prices

In his *Treatise on Money* (1930), John Maynard Keynes took the argument regarding speculators one stage further. If speculators are to accept the risk imbalance discussed earlier, they must be rewarded for doing so.[29] That reward would comes if their long futures contracts became more valuable as they approached maturity reflecting a profit to be made by taking delivery on the contract and selling on the spot market. This profit reward will materialize if, on average, the price of a futures contract approaches the spot price on maturity from below. In other words, the basis is negative early in a contract's life {that is, $s(0) < f(t, u)$}, gradually rising toward equality with the spot price on maturity. This hypothesis about the behavior of futures prices is known as the *Theory of Normal Backwardation* because it postulates that backwardation is the normal state of the futures markets, at least in nonseasonal commodities.[30]

An example from the Chicago Eurodollar market is given in Figure 10.6, where the spot price is represented by the solid curve and a futures price (the June 1992 contract in this case) by dots.[31] It will be seen that the futures price is usually below the spot price.

Returning now to normal backwardation, we have to deal with a methodological difficulty, namely that "the" expected spot price is unobservable and indeed may not exist if expectations vary among traders, as in real life they are bound to do. Fortunately, this is less of a problem than it may seem. In purely observable terms, Keynes's theory of normal backwardation says simply that *when hedgers are net short the price of a futures contract tends to rise during the contract's life*. In that form it can be tested empirically, and there is a large but somewhat inconclusive literature devoted to such tests. Some relevant evidence will also be presented in Section 10.5.3.

10.4.2 Expectations versus Spot-Market Constraints

Apart from the validity or otherwise of the theory of normal backwardation, there is another important point to be made about expectations. In Section 10.2 we derived the relations among spot and futures prices from the carrying cost,

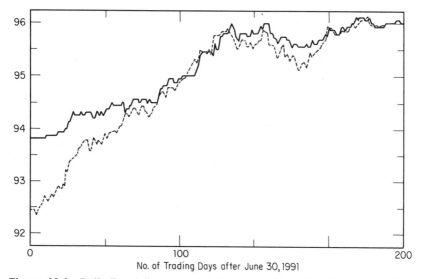

Figure 10.6   Daily Eurodollar spot and futures prices (July 1, 1991–June 30, 1992)

sometimes modified by convenience yield considerations, or (in the case of Eurodollars) from other spot-market constraints. For simplicity, the convenience yield
is eliminated until further notice by assuming that total inventories are large
enough to make it equal to zero; the Eurodollar case will also be ignored.

Even with this simplification a paradox remains. Consider, for instance, the
D-mark example used at the end of Section 10.2.1. The interest parity theorem
implies, among other things, that the spreads among futures prices for different
maturities are determined by the interest differential between Germany and the
United States. In that example the September D-mark future was 1.5% below
the June future. Now suppose that many people are convinced—because of the
monetary policies of the two countries or for other reasons—that the dollar value
of the D-mark will increase between June and September, instead of decreasing
as an interpretation of futures prices in terms of expectations would suggest.
Presumably, this conviction could lead them to buy September D-mark futures
and sell June futures. Will this transaction upset the interest-parity relation?

The answer is that such an upset is most unlikely. The covered interest
parity theorem is firmly grounded in riskless arbitrage: As soon as the June-
September spread departs significantly from interest parity, arbitrage will restore
the normal relationship.[32] What will happen is that speculation on a prospective
rise in the D-mark will cause *all* futures prices (and also the spot and forward
prices) to go up. All these prices are locked together by interest differentials,
leaving no room for expectations concerning the exact course of the exchange
rate. Anyone who believes that the D-mark will rise at some later date can of
course buy futures, but it does not matter which contracts he or she buys.

It should be noted, however, that the example just considered is not completely general because it assumed that inventories are large (as indeed they are for currencies and other financial futures). In a seasonal commodity, such as soybeans, the story is somewhat different. Suppose we are in April and the next soybean crop is due in October. An unexpected frost has damaged the newly planted soybeans, so prospects for the next crop have deteriorated. How will this affect soybean futures?

Because in this case inventories are not large (especially at the end of the crop year), the effect on old-crop and new-crop futures need not be the same. Obviously, new-crop futures will rise on the bad news; so will old-crop futures, because the carry-over from one crop to the next may have to be increased to cover some of next year's demand. Unless the next crop is believed to have failed completely (implying that current inventories have to be spread out over an additional year), the effect of the weather report on the old-crop futures is likely to be smaller than the effect on the new-crop futures. It remains true that developments seemingly affecting only one or a few futures contracts will have an impact on all.

10.4.3 Samuelson's Conjecture on Increasing Volatility

The preceding argument is relevant to a phenomenon that is of considerable interest in its own right. In a fundamental paper on market efficiency, Samuelson (1965) proved to begin with that, under standard assumptions, "correctly anticipated futures prices fluctuate randomly." This condition is essentially what has subsequently become known as the weak or semistrong form of the efficient market hypothesis, discussed in Chapter 5. Samuelson went on to argue that under the same assumptions *the prices of nearby futures contracts must be more volatile than those of more distant contracts.* In other words, the volatility (customarily measured by the standard deviation of logarithmic price differences) of a futures contract must increase as it approaches expiration. This condition is called Samuelson's conjecture.

The reasoning behind this conjecture is that the supply and demand conditions determining the price at expiration—which as we know must be equal to the spot price at that point—become clearer with the passage of time. One year before expiration these conditions would be hard to guess, but a few weeks or days before expiration they are better known, and any changes in them should have an immediate effect on the futures price because trading in the contract will soon come to an end.

The limited evidence on Samuelson's conjecture available until now is inconclusive.[33] We have therefore examined a much larger body of data, consisting of long series of daily closing prices for eleven commodities and three financial instruments.[34] The data used for Table 10.2 generally cover about 20 years ending in 1992 or early 1993; those used for Table 10.3 cover periods varying between about 10 years for crude oil and the S&P500 to more than 20

Table 10.2 Standard Deviations of Logarithmic Price Differences by Order of Maturity for Futures on Selected Food Commodities

Rank	Corn	Coffee	Cattle	Hogs	Porkbellies	Soybeans	Wheat
1	.01326	.02102	.01039	.01460	.02145	.01591	.01510
2	.01268	.01678	.01045	.01530	.02057	.01471	.01439
3	.01265	.01576	.00942	.01509	.01933	.01472	.01402
4	.01243	.01554	.00862	.01451	.01813	.01452	.01380
5	.01215	.01540	.00817	.01370	.01774	.01421	.01340
6			.00782	.01291		.01391	
7				.01244		.01340	

years for cotton. For each of these contracts the standard deviations were calculated for all futures maturing within 1 year.[35] The nearest month, whichever it is on any given data, is given rank one, the next rank two, and so on. Tables 10.2 and 10.3 give the standard deviation for all futures ranked one, two, and so on. According to Samuelson's conjecture, a lower rank implies a higher standard deviation.

Looking first at Table 10.2 we see that for the seven food commodities, Samuelson's conjecture is overwhelmingly confirmed. Indeed there are only two exceptions to the expected ranking: For cattle and hogs the standard deviation of the nearest month is slightly smaller than for the next month.

The four industrial commodities in Table 10.3 satisfy Samuelson's conjecture without exception. For the three financial instruments, however, the standard deviations are more or less the same regardless of rank. Although in all three the standard deviation for rank one is lower than for rank four, the differences are too small to be meaningful.

We cannot say, therefore, that Samuelson's conjecture holds universally. Of course, there are many more futures contracts than the fourteen shown here, but Tables 10.2 and 10.3 suggest that the conjecture is valid for physical commodi-

Table 10.3 Standard Deviations of Logarithmic Price Differences by Order of Maturity for Futures on Selected Industrial Commodities, Currencies, and Stock Indexes

Rank	Copper	Cotton	Crude	Lumber	Pound	D-mark	S&P500
1	.01593	.01476	.02473	.01556	.00718	.00684	.01342
2	.01530	.01342	.02121	.01428	.00732	.00688	.01345
3	.01500	.01287	.01985	.01293	.00740	.00687	.01339
4	.01473	.01214	.01900	.01191	.00728	.00690	.01349
5	.01450	.01130	.01840	.01126			
6	.01423		.01805	.01111			
7			.01803				
8			.01796				

ties but not for financial instruments. More research is needed to verify this tentative conclusion and to explain why the conjecture does not apply to all futures contracts.

Samuelson's conjecture, to the extent it holds, is important for three reasons:

1. It sheds further light on the relation between expectations and futures prices, already discussed in Section 10.4.1.
2. It has a bearing on the merits of futures contracts as an investment (see Section 10.5.3).
3. It casts some doubt on the realism of Black's formula for valuing futures options, discussed in Chapter 9, which assumes that the standard deviation of futures prices is constant over time. Actually Black's formula can be modified to cover this complication.

10.5 FUTURES AND PORTFOLIO MANAGEMENT

While futures may represent stand-alone investment vehicles, as shown in Section 10.5.3, much of the growing interest in futures reflects their potential for portfolio management. Futures can be used either to profit from arbitrage between a portfolio of primary securities and a related futures contract or to improve the risk-return trade-off available from a portfolio of primary securities.[36] In this section we discuss some of these uses of futures contracts, including their role in program trading and in so-called portfolio insurance.

10.5.1 Program Trading

Essentially a form of spot-futures arbitrage (see Chapter 9), program trading became important after the introduction of stock-index futures in 1982.[37] When the S&P500 spot index and the S&P500 futures get out of line with each other, profitable opportunities for "index arbitrage" emerge. "Out of line" does not necessarily mean "different"; since the futures refer to a more distant time period, their prices include an allowance for the dividends payable on the underlying stocks until the expiration of the contract and for financing costs.[38] Index arbitrage serves to keep the futures price (particularly of the nearby contract) and the spot price in proper alignment. This function is all the more important because in stock index futures there is no delivery mechanism (see Chapter 9).

Portfolio managers use stock index futures because they are highly correlated with the spot index and because it is as easy to be short the futures as it is to be long. Thus, hedging in stock index futures makes it possible to focus on particular equities without having to worry about movements in the market as a whole. These futures can also reduce the risk to underwriters in making initial public offerings, whose success often depends on general market conditions. At the same time, speculators who are so inclined can use futures to take a long or short position on the equity market as a whole without committing themselves to particular stocks.

Program trading is controversial and is sometimes blamed for the steep decline on "Black Monday."[39] To those accustomed to prefutures ways, it is a clear case of the tail wagging the dog. The question arises, however, which is the tail and which is the dog? In other markets with futures trading, price discovery takes place in the futures, and it is not obvious why stock indexes should be different. In any case, it is only the general level of share prices, not the prices of individual shares, that is influenced by index arbitrage.[40]

In response to the criticism just mentioned, the NYSE and the exchanges trading stock index futures have agreed, under congressional and regulatory pressure, to an elaborate system of "circuit breakers" and "trading halts" that would sever the link between the spot index and the futures when the spot index falls or rises by more than specified amounts. This system is somewhat similar to the daily price limits (described in Section 9.4) that exist in many other futures markets, but not in stock index futures. There is not yet enough experience to determine whether the new arrangements have increased the stability of the spot market, which is their stated purpose. So far all one can say is that, in J. Pierpoint Morgan's famous words, the stock market "continues to fluctuate."

10.5.2 Portfolio Insurance: A Postmortem

As the name suggests, portfolio insurance aims to protect the value of a portfolio against a falling stock or bond market in exchange for a small cost in terms of sacrificed potential return. This cost is sometimes believed to resemble paying an insurance premium.

At one time this idea sounded so attractive that in 1987 an estimated 6% of all American pension funds' investments (or about $80 billion) were "protected" by portfolio insurance. Actually the term *portfolio insurance* is a misnomer; in fire or collision insurance, for example, the premium is fixed ahead of time, but in portfolio insurance there is no fixed premium and the cost can only be ascertained after the damage is done. Furthermore, in ordinary insurance the insurance company maintains reserves to meet the claims of policy holders, but there is no equivalent of these reserves in portfolio insurance.

A more accurate name would be "dynamic hedging" or "dynamic risk control." Its roots go back to the hedging concept used by Black and Scholes (1973) in developing their option pricing model. As was mentioned in Chapter 8, an investor who buys the right number of put options against the shares in his or her portfolio is paying a premium—the cost of the puts—in return for eliminating the risk of loss when the market price falls below the striking price.

In practice, there turned out to be two problems. In the first place, the puts were often quite expensive. Not surprisingly, in an efficient options market the benefits from the puts seemed to be no greater than the cost of buying them. The second problem was that the options were generally not available beyond a term of 6 or 9 months, so they did not offer the long-term protection sought by institutional investment managers.

Leland (1980) and Rubinstein (1988) suggested that portfolios might be protected without using options. They argued that the same effect could be obtained by continuously adjusting the portfolio mix between equities and short-term default-free securities or bank deposits. Their idea was that in a falling stock market the investment manager would sell equities and buy T-bills (or similar securities) until the extra interest earnings on the latter would compensate for the capital loss on the remaining shares held. This dynamic hedge would be maintained by a computer program that continuously recalculates the mix between equities and T-bills.

Actually, it would be cumbersome and costly to trade blocks of equities all the time in order to keep the hedge in balance. Instead, most portfolio managers would buy and sell stock index futures contracts, which is quite similar to buying and selling the stocks themselves but saved as much as 90% of the commissions.

Portfolio "insurance" was put to the test by the "Black Monday" crash of 1987, and it failed. In a rapidly declining market it proved impossible to make the necessary adjustments in the portfolio mix. Indeed, portfolio insurance has been aptly compared to getting fire insurance when your house is already on fire! It has also been alleged that selling stock index futures in a falling market, as required by the Leland-Rubinstein theory, served by itself to aggravate the fall.

The fatal flaw in the underlying theory appears to be in the assumed distribution of price changes. If the distribution is normal or lognormal, as is usually taken for granted in financial economics, very large price changes are so unlikely that they may be ignored. We saw in Chapter 4, however, that the actual distribution of price changes is "fat-tailed": There are significantly more very large changes than normal or lognormal theory would predict.[41] One such change occurred on "Black Monday."

10.5.3 Futures Contracts as an Investment

If futures prices were unbiased forecasts of the spot price at maturity, there would be little need to consider futures contracts as an investment. For most commodities and financial instruments, however, there does appear to be a downward bias as suggested by the theory of normal backwardation. The evidence on this theory is mixed (see Section 10.4.1), but if true, it means that a long position in futures, maintained over a long period of time, will have a positive return.

Table 10.4 sheds some light on this possibility by giving the results of a simple "buy and hold" strategy for a number of commodities and financial instruments.[42] It consists of buying a futures contract when it becomes the second in order of maturity and selling it when it becomes the first in that order. Thus, in corn (which has contracts for March, May, July, September, and December), the March contract was assumed to be bought when the September contract ex-

Table 10.4 Mean Annual Results of Buy-Hold Strategy in Futures

Contract	No. of Years[a]	Unit	Result[b]
Corn	23.5	cents/bushel	−5.3
Cotton	20	cents/pound	+3.5
Crude oil	9.5	$/barrel	+1.8
German marks	17	cents/DM	−0.1
Eurodollars	8	dollars/$100 face value	+1.9
Live hogs	22.5	cents/pound	+4.5
NYSE Composite	10.25	index points	+9.9
S&P500	10.25	index points	+18.4
Treasury bills	16.5	dollars/$100 face value	+0.6
Treasury bonds	14.5	dollars/$100 face value	+1.5

[a]Period of observation always ends June 30, 1992.

[b]Total result over period divided by number of years.

pired and sold when the December contract expired; on that date, March was replaced with May. The reason for choosing this order of maturity was that in contracts with delivery the holder may not be able to keep the contract until expiration, while more distant contracts are not always available. All purchases and sales were assumed to be executed at the closing price of the relevant day, and as many years as possible were used.

It is interesting to note that eight of the ten contracts show positive results for the buy-hold strategy; the two that do not are discussed in a moment. Moreover, some of the positive results are substantial, particularly those for crude oil, Eurodollars, live hogs, and the two stock indexes. The average price of crude oil, for instance, was around $20 per barrel, so the futures appreciated at a rate of roughly 10% per year.[43] Approximately the same percentage is found for the two stock indexes and for live hogs.

The most striking finding in Table 10.4 is for Eurodollars, where the annual appreciation of the futures prices was of the order of 30%. An alternative calculation provided further insight into this phenomenon. This involved a slightly longer period starting with the introduction of Eurodollar futures in 1982, and assumed that each futures contract traded since then was bought when it began trading and held until it expired (or until June 30, 1992, if it came earlier). It turned out that of the fifty contracts traded during those 10 years no fewer than forty-three yielded a profit under this alternative strategy, and the losses on the remaining seven were relatively small. This imbalance, which can hardly have resulted from chance alone, confirms that most Eurodollars futures displayed strong backwardation during the last 10 years. The rate of appreciation under the alternative calculation, however, cannot easily be estimated.

As regards the two contracts for which Table 10.4 has a negative rate of appreciation (corn and the D-mark), the reasons for this are quite different between the two. Since D-mark futures can be used both by American firms to hedge their exposure in marks and by German firms to hedge their exposure in dollars, the explanation of normal backwardation in terms of an asymmetry in hedging does not necessarily hold. In corn, seasonal factors in the September and December contracts appear to overwhelm backwardation in the other trading months. This explanation is not wholly satisfactory, however, because distinct seasonality is also apparent in some of the other commodities shown.

Some general comments on the results in Table 10.4 are in order:

- The statistical significance of the results is difficult to assess because the underlying distributions of price changes are far from being normal. Inspection of the data suggests that the results for bonds are highly erratic and most likely insignificant. On the other hand, the alternative calculation for Eurodollars indicates that the positive results are indeed statistically significant.[44]

- To consider futures as an investment, one would of course need to know how much risk is associated with them and how they are correlated with an extended market portfolio that includes not only equities but also futures (and possibly other investments). This again raises the problem of distribution just mentioned.

- The percentage rate of appreciation should not be confused with the return on investment. In fact, the latter is difficult to evaluate because investment in futures requires only an initial margin deposit that could itself pay interest; additional margin payments may be required if the price falls (see Section 9.4). In any case, if the results in the table are statistically significant, then the return on investment for several of the contracts must be very high.

- Although in this section we have looked at the second nearest month in each contract, the discussion in Section 10.4.3 suggests that analysis of more distant months would be worthwhile.

- These results make no allowance for transaction costs, but their magnitude is generally not enough to make much difference.

- Past performance is no guarantee of future results.

11

Regulation of Financial Markets

Most financial markets are highly competitive. There are hundreds or thousands of active traders and at any time and place prices vary only within a narrow range—the bid-ask price spread. Regulation is usually associated with monopoly; thus electric utilities are regulated because each is typically the only supplier in a given area. It might seem, therefore, that regulation of financial markets is unnecessary, but why that conclusion is unwarranted is explained in Section 11.2. Then comes a discussion of the various levels of regulation: the exchanges, the regulatory commissions, and the courts. The regulation of trading in corporate shares and bonds by the Securities and Exchange Commission is the subject of Section 11.4. In Section 11.5 we show how futures markets are regulated, and finally there is a case study of an important regulatory failure, the silver manipulation of 1979–1980.

11.1 THE ETHICS OF FINANCE AND THE ECONOMIC FUNCTION OF FINANCIAL MARKETS

Before embarking on the main discussion, some brief remarks on the ethics of finance may be in order. Traditionally, financial activities have not ranked high in popular esteem. Both the Old Testament and the Koran frown on the taking of interest; the New Testament is somewhat ambiguous. Arguing from a naive labor theory of value, Karl Marx considered finance (and services in general) to be unproductive, and the resulting neglect of the financial sector in communist-controlled nations was no doubt one of the reasons for their poor economic performance. In those nations the concept of speculation was extended to include all private commercial activities, and such activities were severely punished. Even in capitalist countries, speculation is often the subject of adverse comment.[1]

These negative views have not prevented the successful development of capitalism, which could not have occurred without the simultaneous growth of the financial sector. In the developed countries, and in many developing countries, interest is generally accepted as a legitimate source of income and as the price paid for using capital. In this interpretation, interest is like any other income source or price and its existence raises no special problems of ethics.[2] This interpretation does not mean, as we shall see, that everything in the financial sector is in accordance with ethics; in particular, there is the possibility of fraud, as discussed in Section 11.2.2.

As to speculation, financial gains are usually the result of success in risk-bearing and tend to be more or less offset by losses from unsuccessful risk-bearing. In any economy there are substantial risks that in a market economy have to be borne in large part by private individuals and firms; they are willing to do so because of the possibility of speculative profits. We stated in Chapter 3 that in the United States there are no risk-free securities. Furthermore, speculation is not the easy road to riches that the uninformed believe it to be; there is some evidence that most speculators lose money.

More could be said on the subject of ethics, but instead we refer to Sen (1991) and turn to a narrower topic: the economic functions of financial markets. This discussion will clarify the problems that regulation is intended to address.

Real capital—consisting of buildings, equipment, consumer durables, and other tangible and intangible assets—is one of the three main factors of production, the other two being labor and land.[3] It is of great importance to the satisfactory performance of any economy that (1) the supply of capital be approximately equal to the demand—in other words, that there be no major shortages or surpluses—and that (2) the existing capital be allocated efficiently—more precisely, that the marginal productivity of capital be substantially the same in different uses. If these two conditions are fulfilled, the aggregate return to real capital will be maximized.

The financial markets play an essential role in the attainment of these objectives. They do so because, as stated at the beginning of Chapter 2, most real capital is financed by equities or credit, which is to say that the ultimate users of real capital rely heavily on others to provide the funds with which to acquire real capital assets. These ultimate users are usually corporations and other firms, but they also include households (for dwellings and consumer durables) and various levels of government. The providers of funds are mostly individuals and the institutional investors (such as mutual funds, pension funds, and life insurance companies) to which they have entrusted their savings. Real capital formation depends to a large extent on the availability of financing.

11.2 THE PURPOSES OF REGULATION

It follows from the preceding discussion that the regulation of financial markets has two main purposes: *maintaining competition* and *protecting investors* against fraud and similar abuses. The following subsections explain the meaning and implications of these purposes.

Before embarking on this more detailed discussion, we should point out what regulation does not try to accomplish. It is not intended to interfere with the normal working of the market mechanism; on the contrary, the main justification of well-designed regulation is that it will help the financial markets perform more efficiently. In particular, regulation does not attempt (at least in the United States) to prevent the fluctuations that have long been a feature—some would say a curse—of the financial markets. No doubt the regulators and the monetary authorities would take steps if a major financial market were to show signs of breakdown, but even in October 1987 that extreme was not reached: After the "Black Monday" crash, the stock market stabilized by itself almost immediately and soon went on to new highs.[4] In certain other countries (notably Japan and Korea), the government has at times reacted to sharp declines by ordering institutional investors to buy large blocks of shares and bonds; it is doubtful that this has had any lasting effect on the stability of the financial markets.

11.2.1 Maintaining Competition

In Chapter 1 we defined financial markets as highly competitive markets in financial instruments. This definition begs a question: What makes these markets "highly competitive"? Elementary microeconomic theory tells us that active competition is the result of four interrelated conditions:

1. The number of traders is large.
2. None of these traders has significant market power.
3. The traders act independently; that is, they do not engage in collusion with each other.
4. Entry is easy: as soon as traders on the average earn profits above the normal level (taking risk into account), other traders enter the market.

In the financial markets the first condition is usually satisfied, since the required skills are not very scarce, the earnings are competitive with those in similar occupations, and the necessary capital can usually be borrowed by otherwise qualified candidates. By the same token, the fourth condition is not very restrictive; the main barrier to entry is membership of an exchange, which can be obtained through the "seat market" (see Chapter 5). In the case of the over-the-counter market, access to NASDAQ poses no great problems, either.

The second condition is more problematic. The participants in financial trading vary greatly in size, ranging as they do from institutions with assets of many billions of dollars to individual investors with a few thousand dollars. In some financial markets, consequently, limits on the positions of traders are imposed (see Section 11.3), but in the equity markets with their numerous participants, this has not been considered advisable.

The third condition, concerning collusion, is the most difficult to enforce. Although collusion is usually against the antitrust laws (a form of regulation that applies to all business, not just finance), it is not always prosecuted with much vigor.[5] We have shown, for instance, that organized exchanges are key elements in major financial markets, and that they invariably limit membership. There are sound reasons for limiting membership to creditworthy firms, but it also opens opportunities for abuse of market power by the exchanges on behalf of their members; the fixed commissions prevalent until the middle 1970s are an example (see Chapter 5). In retrospect, the exchanges were short-sighted in keeping commissions artificially high since the volume of trading increased sharply after commissions became negotiable. Thus one cannot always count on the enlightened self-interest of these organizations and their members.

11.2.2 Preventing Fraud and Providing Information

Fraud is usually the result of a lack of information. One party to a transaction promises something, and the other party agrees, not knowing that the promise is false or seriously incomplete. This asymmetry is commonly found in the financial markets, especially in those that involve the public at large. Individual investors are sometimes lured by promises of large gain held out by professionals whose income depends more on their powers of persuasion than on their knowledge of investments.

One could argue that the market mechanism takes care of such problems without regulation. The gullible investors lose money and either become less gullible or put their remaining cash under a mattress. The fraudulent salesperson has more and more difficulty finding victims and ultimately turn to other pursuits, presumably leaving the field to more scrupulous competitors. Such was approximately the situation in the nineteenth century, when the financial markets began to assume their modern form, but it is not a desirable state of affairs. The reason is threefold:

1. The risks inherent in all trading in financial instruments are increased by the risk of fraud
2. Many potential investors are excluded from favorable opportunities because of their justified distrust
3. Transaction costs are unduly high because of the need to verify the assertions of intermediaries

We have argued throughout this book that standardization is a powerful device for reducing transaction costs, and this applies particularly to information.

If disclosure of relevant information is mandatory, investors can make their decisions with greater assurance, though complete assurance can hardly be expected.[6]

In addition to disclosure by corporations and other issuers of securities, other types of information are also important to investors. As we shall see below, regulatory agencies publish—or require exchanges to publish—statistics on the activity and positions in their respective markets. An example are data on the "short interest" in the stock market (the number of shares sold by those who did not own the shares but borrowed them). The interpretation of these data is necessarily left to investors, however. A large short interest in a particular equity can mean either that the demand for it will remain strong (since the shares sold short must ultimately be bought back) or that the outlook for it is poor (since presumably knowledgeable traders have sold it short in anticipation of an impending fall in the price).[7] In any case, such a stock is likely to be unusually volatile. Perhaps the main usefulness of the short-interest tabulation is that it warns risk-averse investors to avoid certain equities.

11.3 LEVELS OF REGULATION

Until the 1920s, when the Grain Futures Administration (later merged into the Commodity Exchange Authority) was established within the U.S. Department of Agriculture, there was no federal regulation of financial markets. Previously regulation was primarily the responsibility of the exchanges, with the possibility of appeal to the courts always present. This threefold division of regulation (the exchanges, the federal commissions, and the courts) remains in force.

The exchanges are the first level of regulation.[8] They and the clearinghouses associated with them publish extensive sets of rules that are binding on their members. These rules are enforced by exchange committees and staff by means of fines and—in serious cases—suspension or expulsion. In some circumstances, the rules also provide for restitution to other members or to customers who were damaged by violations of the rules.

The main purpose of these rules is twofold: to make sure that the members are financially able to meet their commitments, and to promote market liquidity. The financial rules are themselves essential to liquidity because they make it possible for members to trade rapidly with each other without having to worry about the creditworthiness of their counterparts. In addition, they give some assurance to investors that the intermediaries to whom they entrust their money will not vanish overnight. The need for market liquidity, however, does not end there; other rules are intended to prevent collusion among traders, to make specialists operate so as to stabilize the market (see Chapter 5), and to ensure that orders from customers get the best possible execution.

Many of the exchanges specializing in futures also attempt to prevent abuse of market power by the *position limits* mentioned earlier. Under these rules traders are not allowed to be long or short by more than a certain number of contracts, the exact number depending on the commodity or financial instrument. Such rules assume, of course, that there is no collusion among traders; we show in Section 11.6 that this assumption may be difficult to verify.

The main weakness of exchange regulation is that the members may give more weight to their parochial interests than to the public interest. Because of this danger, the rules made by exchanges have to be approved by the regulatory commissions, which may also intervene in disagreements between exchange members and their customers and among exchanges. Most disputes between brokers and customers, incidentally, are settled by arbitration.

Federal and state courts are the last resort in regulatory matters. They can overrule not only the exchanges but also the commissions, and can impose more drastic penalties and remedies than those institutions. Since court decisions (unless overturned by a higher court) carry great weight, they lead in effect to an additional set of regulations. The difficulty with going to court is that it is often costly and that it may take a long time—several years in complicated cases like the one discussed in Section 11.6—before a verdict is issued.

Not all financial markets are subject to formal regulation. An important case in point is the cash market in Treasury securities (bills, notes, and bonds). Although the Treasury exercises some control over the auctions used to sell new issues, trading in existing securities is not regulated. The spot and forward markets in foreign currencies are also unregulated, but since banks are the main participants in these markets the agencies that regulate banks (the Federal Reserve, the controller of the currency, and state commissioners) are in a position to exercise some influence.

11.4 FEDERAL REGULATION OF TRADING IN CORPORATE SECURITIES

At the federal level, trading in corporate securities is regulated by the Securities and Exchange Commission (SEC).[9] It was established in 1934 as a response to the stock market crash of 1929 and to questionable practices in the securities industry. Although the SEC has rules against manipulation—defined as causing prices to deviate from the level that would prevail in a competitive market—its principal effort has always been to prevent fraud by requiring disclosure of relevant information. We deal in particular with three areas of regulation concerning disclosure: corporate results and developments, new issues, and insider trading.

11.4.1 Reporting of Financial Results and Other Developments

It may seem obvious that corporations should disclose their financial results accurately and promptly to their shareholders, but in the past and in other countries, that has not always been the case. Since the management is judged by these results, it may be tempted to present them in an unduly favorable light, to keep shareholders in the dark over extended periods, or to slant their reports in other ways. Truthful and timely reporting is important not only to actual shareholders (and bondholders) but also to potential investors.[10] While some corporations may find it in their interest to maintain high reporting standards even if they are not required to do so, regulations on reporting have probably contributed to market efficiency.

As mentioned already, these regulations cover two aspects, of which *timeliness* is the simpler one. Firms that are listed on exchanges or on NASDAQ have to report a summary of their financial results within a specified period after the end of every quarter. In addition, these firms have to publish an annual report that usually contain more detail and, unlike quarterly reports, has to be approved by their auditors.

The question of *truth* (which includes both accuracy and completeness) in financial reporting is more complicated. It raises the further question of accounting standards, which are set by the Financial Accounting Standards Board (FASB), a private body whose rules carry authority because they are upheld by the SEC and the securities exchanges. Thus the Generally Accepted Accounting Procedures (GAAP), to which we referred in Chapter 1 and elsewhere, are laid down in FASB rules. These rules cover a great variety of subjects and are frequently updated, sometimes with considerable impact on reported corporate profits.[11] By calling for a minimal content of the published reports, these rules also aim at reasonable completeness.

Apart from financial data, corporations are also obliged to issue news releases on significant other developments such as mergers and acquisitions, changes in top management, labor disputes, lawsuits filed or decided, and patents granted or denied. Retail chains and automobile manufacturers report periodically on their sales. Oil producers have to tell the public about their drilling activities, and so on. Many of these items would no doubt become known through the grapevine in the absence of regulation, but mandatory publication serves to disseminate them more promptly, widely, and accurately.

11.4.2 New Issues

The SEC is perhaps best known for its regulations concerning public offerings of stocks and bonds. These offerings have to be accompanied by a *prospectus* providing potential purchasers with information on the issuer's business, its financial situation, its directors and officers, and the proposed use of the proceeds. The risks inherent in the securities offered have to be spelled out in considerable detail. The SEC itself looks over the prospectus, not for the purpose of approving or disapproving the new issue but to make sure that the required information is included. New issues below a certain minimum are not subject to these rules.

Because a prospectus satisfying SEC standards can be a lengthy and legalistic document, it is doubtful whether many individual investors actually read all of it, though institutional investors presumably have the staff to do so. In any case, it appears that the prospectus regulations have greatly reduced the flow of fraudulent issues, which were common before the 1930s. In this connection, it is important to know that the underwriters of public offerings also have a responsibility for truth in advertising.

11.4.3 Insider Trading

When discussing the "strong form" of the Efficient Market Hypothesis in Chapter 5, we mentioned evidence that access to nonpublic information may interfere with market efficiency and produce abnormal profits. This evidence may be cited as support for regulations against insider trading, though in fact these regulations were enacted long before the EMH was formulated. The restrictions on insider trading were originally motivated more by concern about fairness—the idea of a level playing field—than by concern about efficiency.

Insiders specifically are directors and officers of a listed corporation, as well as individuals or firms who own more than 5% of the equity; the latter are obliged to publicize their holdings.[12] Insiders are not prohibited from trading in the securities of their company, but they have to report their transactions to the SEC, which publishes a list of such transactions from time to time. If it turns out that insiders have acted on nonpublic information—for instance by selling shares prior to publication of disappointing financial results—they are subject to penalties and may have to "disgorge" their illegal gains.

It should perhaps be mentioned that insider trading can affect the market not only when it is present but also when it is absent. Selling by insiders, for instance, often takes place when beneficiaries of stock options want to have funds for consumption or alternative investments. A sudden cessation of such selling may indicate that the insiders are aware of information that has not yet reached the market.

11.5 FEDERAL REGULATION OF FUTURES MARKETS

As mentioned at the beginning of Section 11.3, federal regulation of futures trading goes back a long time. For many years it was confined to futures on domestic farm products; other futures markets (such as those in copper and coffee) were not regulated. In 1974 the Commodity Futures Trading Commission (CFTC) was founded to supervise all futures markets, including the financial futures markets that were just emerging at that time.

There are similarities between the SEC and the CFTC, but they do not go very far.[13] Both commissions, for instance, have a system for licensing professional intermediaries with a view to keeping out criminals and expelling those who commit serious violations. The main difference between the commissions is one of emphasis: The SEC stresses prevention of fraud by requiring disclosure, while the CFTC focuses on maintaining competition.

This difference reflects the nature of the markets supervised by the two agencies. Tens of millions of individual investors trade at least occasionally in the stock and bond markets or in mutual funds, which are also supervised by the SEC. If these markets were unregulated, there would be ample opportunities for taking undue advantage of investors, many of whom do not know much about what they buy. The futures markets appeal to a different type of trader; most of the trading is done by professionals who hardly need protection as long as the markets are competitive. The number of individual traders in futures is probably less—perhaps much less—than a million. These individuals can appeal to the CFTC (and to the exchanges or the courts) if they have complaints about their brokers; otherwise, they are assumed to know what they are doing. However, futures brokers are obliged to make sure that their customers have the financial ability to undertake what are often very risky transactions.

The CFTC's principal tool for maintaining competition is to require daily activity reports from large traders in futures markets. For every market there is a minimal position (that is a number of contracts held long or short) above which traders are considered "large." Most large traders are professionals, but the reporting requirements also apply to individuals and to "commodity pools," which are analogous to mutual funds. These reports are analyzed by the CFTC in order to detect attempts to exercise market power, particularly by accumulating dominant positions in delivery months that are expiring or close to expiring.[14] If two or more large traders work together, they are supposed to indicate this on their reports, but we shall see in the next section that enforcement of this provision is difficult.

While the daily reports submitted to the CFTC are confidential, summaries of them are published weekly under the title *Commitments of Traders*. In this publication, reporting traders in each futures market are classified as commercial or noncommercial; "spreading" (see Chapter 9) is identified separately. The aggregate position of the small (nonreporting) traders is found by subtracting the aggregate for the large traders from the total open interest, which is obtained from the exchanges. There are also statistics on the concentration of the open interest, particularly the percentage held by the eight largest traders combined. These data can in principle warn traders of impending squeezes or corners. The CFTC can take action against traders whose reports suggest actual or intended manipulation.[15]

The CFTC also engages in an activity that has some resemblance to the prospectus rules of the CFTC: the approval of new contracts proposed by exchanges. To get the Commission's approval, the exchange must show that the proposed contract has an "economic function," which means in practice that the contract will be used for hedging purposes. It is not clear, however, that this activity is very useful. The CFTC's consent requires a lengthy process of public comment and analysis by Commission staff that may be a significant barrier to innovation in contract design. Since contracts that do not cater to hedgers are likely to fail anyway—as new contracts do frequently even when they are approved by the CFTC—the market may well be a better judge of economic function.

11.6 A CASE STUDY: THE SILVER MANIPULATION OF 1979–1980

As an example of regulatory problems we now describe one of the most serious manipulations of an American futures market to occur in this century. For this purpose we draw on a lawsuit (*Minpeco v. Conticommodities et al.*) that resulted from the manipulation.[16] The jury found for the plaintiff on virtually all counts and the remaining defendants—most of the others had settled for payment of large damages while a few had been dismissed—did not appeal. We first summarize the relevant facts and then draw some conclusions as to the regulatory process.

11.6.1 The Silver Market

Traditionally classified as a precious metal, silver is basically an industrial raw material. Its principal use is in manufacturing photographic film; it is also used in electronics and in making jewelry and tableware. Until the 1960s silver also served in coinage, which had the important effect of fixing the nominal price of silver: Since by law a silver dollar contained about 0.775 ounces of silver, the implied price was about $1.29 per ounce without any adjustment for inflation. The U.S. Treasury had also issued "silver certificates," a form of paper money that entitled the bearer to 0.775 ounces of silver for every dollar of face value.

Because of rising industrial demand and inflation, it gradually became more difficult for the Treasury to maintain the fixed price. Silver coins disappeared from circulation, and the silver certificates were redeemed. When the use of silver coins was finally abandoned, the price became free to move in response to market factors. Futures trading in silver started in 1974; in the United States the main markets are the Commodity Exchange in New York (known as Comex) and the Chicago Board of Trade. The most commonly traded futures contract provides for the delivery of 5,000 ounces of refined silver with a purity of 99.9%; there is also a "mini-contract" of 1,000 ounces, but it is not relevant to our story.

As general background to the silver story Figure 11.1 shows monthly silver spot prices (high, low, and close) from 1975 through 1981. It is evident that something very unusual happened during most of 1979 and early 1980.

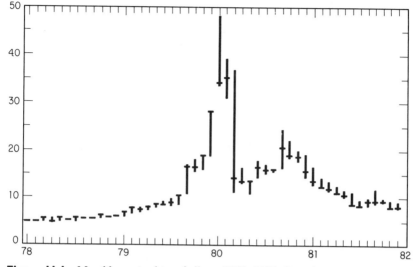

Figure 11.1 Monthly spot prices of silver, 1978–1981. Data from Handy & Harman, Inc.

11.6.2 The Manipulation

The manipulation was led by the Hunt brothers (Bunker, Herbert, and Lamar), wealthy oilmen from Dallas who speculated in futures on a large scale. Prior to their involvement in silver, Bunker and Herbert had been indicted (and later convicted) for violating the commodity laws in the soybean market. This indictment should have been a warning, but it did not deter the brothers from more serious transgressions in the silver market.

According to Fay (1982), their interest in silver was aroused by an analyst named Jerome Smith, who argued that the world was running out of silver.[17] Convinced that a major price increase was inevitable, Bunker and Herbert built up a sizable long position in silver futures, on some of which they took delivery. Unfortunately for them, the market refused to follow Smith's prediction and all they had to show for their efforts was a large stock of deliverable silver.

Toward the end of 1978 the two brothers decided that if the market would not go up by itself, it had to be pushed. Since their own resources had proved insufficient for that purpose, they formed a secret coalition with certain affluent Arabs whom Bunker had met at the race track. These new allies, who operated in part through a Swiss bank and other Swiss firms, all had accounts at the American brokerage firm Conticommodities, so they came to be known later as the Conti group.[18] The Hunts also set up a trading company named International Metals Investment Corporation (IMIC for short) with another group of Arabs whose religious scruples prevented them from speculating under their own names; Herbert became a director of IMIC.

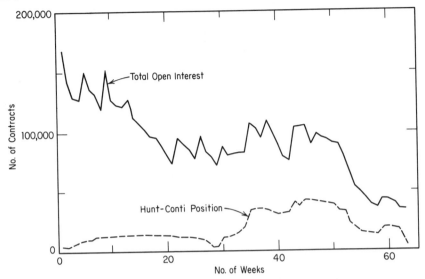

Figure 11.2   Total open interest in silver futures and the long position of the Hunt-
Conti Group, January 1979–March 1980 (in contracts, weekly data).
Source: Data for total open interest from Comex and CBT Yearbooks; data for Hunt-Conti position from discovery in Minpeco
trial.

The entire coalition (consisting of Bunker and Herbert with their several
children, Lamar, the Conti group, and IMIC) accumulated larger and larger long
positions in nearby futures (those closest to expiration), as shown in Figure 11.2.
They also took delivery on expiring contracts, thus gradually assuming control
of deliverable inventories as well (see Figure 11.3). By the middle of January
the Hunt-Conti group controlled some 70% of the relevant market, defined as
the deliverable inventory plus the open interest in the nearby futures contract. At
that time the total value of the group's position was about $7 billion, most of
which was attributable to physical silver.

This control over both expiring futures and deliverable supplies is the essence of a corner. Unlike the classical corners of the nineteenth century, which
typically lasted only for a few days or weeks prior to the arrival of a new crop,
the Hunt-Conti manipulation was aimed at a nonseasonal commodity and extended over most of a year. As in the classical corners, however, the principal
tactic was to scare the shorts, faced with large margin calls as the price soared,
into buying back their positions on terms dictated by the manipulators.[19] In line
with this tactic, a floor trader for Conticommodities made large purchases of
futures, so that after a while his mere entrance in the pit was enough to drive up
the price. Bunker Hunt, moreover, let it be known in early January 1980 that he
expected the spot price to reach $85 per ounce.

The pressure on the shorts to liquidate was all the greater because the market
became increasingly "thin" once the manipulators established control; there sim-

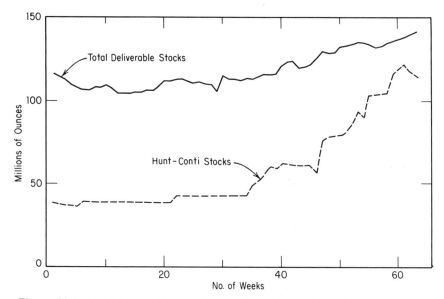

Figure 11.3   Total deliverable silver inventories and Hunt-Conti physical stocks, January 1979–March 1980 (in millions of ounces, weekly data). *Source:* Data for total deliverable stocks from Comex and CBT yearbooks; data for Hunt-Conti stocks from discovery in Minpeco trial.

ply were no offers and futures prices frequently went up by the daily limit (see Chapter 9). Indeed, between December 20, 1979, and January 18, 1980 (when trading was temporarily halted), there was only one day on which meaningful bid and ask prices could be quoted. Minpeco, the plaintiff in the lawsuit mentioned earlier, had covered its short hedges in December 1979 at a loss of about $65 million.

11.6.3 The End of the Manipulation

The manipulation came to an end for two reasons: Supply and demand began to respond—after an inevitable delay—to the artificially high prices resulting from the manipulation, and the regulators finally got their act together. The regulatory aspect is discussed more fully in Section 11.6.6; here we deal first with the economic reaction. As to supply, the public at large realized that its inventory of silver objects, such as tableware and coins, had suddenly become quite valuable. Long lines formed at precious metal dealers as housewives and others sold their silverware to be melted down and refined. Burglars neglected their usual prey and took anything made of silver. Mine production expanded. On the demand side the photographic industry announced new processes for reducing the silver content of film. These market factors in due course drove the price of silver down to a more sustainable level, though it remained relatively high for a few years.

In early January, 1980, moreover, Comex and the CFTC belatedly took a number of steps that made the manipulation more difficult. In particular, they restricted the large traders to "liquidation only," which meant that they could not increase their already huge long positions. By itself this was not enough to stop futures prices from soaring, but when the price reached $50 per ounce on January 18, 1980, trading was briefly suspended altogether. At that point the market realized that the manipulation was coming to an end and prices reversed course, falling irregularly to about $10 in March. However, most of the manipulators—including the Hunt brothers themselves—retained their long positions.

Needless to say, Bunker cried foul, maintaining that the exchange and the regulators had changed the rules in the middle of the game. Few people took these protestations seriously. From their earlier experience in soybeans Bunker and his coconspirators knew perfectly well that futures trading is subject to laws specifically designed to prevent manipulation. If in the final analysis they lost money, they had only themselves to blame. Indeed they got off relatively easily; manipulation is a criminal offense, but none of the manipulators went to jail.

11.6.4 The Other Side of the Story

Since the case against the manipulators has already been outlined, we must now say a few words about their defense. Some of their arguments, such as the assertion that no one in his right mind would try to corner a market as large as the silver market, are hardly worth discussing. Neither do we have to consider the claim of defense experts that the Hunts took large deliveries merely to take advantage of a quirk in the tax laws; the Hunts had removed any foundation for this claim by their insistence that they remembered very little about the episode. Their denials of a conspiracy did not stand up against the overwhelming evidence on that point gathered by counsel for the plaintiff.[20]

The most serious argument put forward by the defendants was that the price of silver rose sharply not because of their actions but because of political and economic developments. In this connection they pointed to the price of gold, which had risen some 300% between January 1979 and January 1980.

It is true that 1979 was a turbulent year. The taking of hostages at the American embassy in Teheran (following the fall of the shah) and the Soviet invasion of Afghanistan were no doubt disturbing to many people, as was the rise in U.S. inflation to double-digit rates. It is also likely that these developments would normally have some effect on the markets for precious metals even if they had not been manipulated. Previous episodes of turbulence, however, had been accompanied by relatively modest increases in gold and silver prices. In fact, the sharp rise in interest rates that was part of the Federal Reserve's anti-inflationary policy (adopted in August 1979) would have discouraged a flight into precious metals.

As it happens, the unusual increase in the price of gold to about $850 per ounce, instead of helping the defendants' case, was turned against them. By means of causality analysis[21] the plaintiff showed that the rise of gold was a consequence of the rise of silver, and therefore could not be used as an indicator of external political and economic developments. Needless to say, counsel for the defense tried hard to cast doubt on the validity of causality analysis, but he did not succeed.

11.6.5 The Aftermath

The end of the manipulation is not the end of the story.[22] The aftermath was more disruptive to the economy as a whole than the manipulation itself, which had affected only the silver market and to a lesser extent the market in other precious metals. When the silver price started its precipitous fall, the Hunt-Conti group found that the boot was now on the other foot: They had to put up additional margin on their enormous futures position. Furthermore the brokers, who had so obligingly lent money on unhedged physical silver, saw their collateral lose its value and pressed for repayment. Despite their great wealth the manipulators soon became unable or unwilling to provide either margin or repayment. As a result, some of their brokers, who had to settle with the clearinghouse regardless of their customers' defaults, found themselves severely strained.

The moment of truth came with the expiration of the March 1980 contract, in which the Hunts still had a large long position. Normally speculators who default on their margin payments will be "sold out" by their brokers (that is, their positions are liquidated without their consent), but even in defeat the manipulators were able to assert their market power. The liquidation of their long positions would further unsettle the silver market to the point where additional brokerage firms, and indeed the clearinghouse itself, would be threatened with insolvency. As pointed out in Chapter 9, the clearinghouses are key elements in the entire financial system; any failure would have far-reaching consequences.

To save the situation, a bank loan of about $1 billion was extended to the Hunt brothers' oil company, thus allowing them to satisfy their margin calls and to hold on to their physical silver, which at that time amounted to over 100 million ounces.[23] This was contrary to the Federal Reserve's anti-inflationary policy, which prohibited loans for speculative purposes, but the Fed made an exception. Under the terms of this loan, Bunker and Herbert had to withdraw from futures trading and to liquidate their silver inventories over a period of years. The continuing concentration of silver stocks in the brothers' hands may have served to keep silver prices above their equilibrium level for some time.

11.6.6 Regulatory Aspects

The silver manipulation of 1979–1980 was a regulatory failure of the first magnitude.[24] As we saw in the beginning of this chapter, the preservation of competitive markets is a principal purpose of regulation, yet a massive manipulation continued virtually unchecked for the better part of a year. What went wrong?

The futures exchanges are the first level of regulation, so let us first look at the two exchanges that were directly affected. The Chicago Board of Trade, which for many years specialized in agricultural futures, had successfully branched out into futures on financial instruments and precious metals in the 1970s. It is fair to say, however, that silver futures were not of great importance in its business plans. Comex, by contrast, was essentially a metals exchange; its attempts to develop financial futures had not borne fruit and its former business in some minor commodities had evaporated. This difference in the relative importance of silver futures turned out to be important in the reaction of the two exchanges.

During the manipulation of 1979–1980 the Hunt brothers and their offspring operated on both exchanges; the Conti group operated only on Comex. The Board of Trade knew from the Hunts' dealings in soybeans that they had little respect for the law, and when their trading in silver began to assume disturbing features, it did not hesitate to impose severe restrictions on the brothers, even though this meant a sharp diminution in the trading volume on that market. Comex, on the other hand, was reluctant to adopt radical measures; it may not have been displeased to see its Chicago rival reduce its role in silver futures. Comex reacted to the rise in silver prices by raising margins—a traditional reaction but one that was counterproductive in the circumstances. It was counterproductive because higher margins increased the pressure on the shorts to liquidate, while the manipulators were largely unaffected, since the price rose almost every day.

To understand these developments, one has to recall that the conspirators, fully aware that their enterprise was unlawful, were operating in secrecy. Indeed, Bunker and Herbert went so far as to maintain that they were acting independently of each other even though they had adjacent offices, saw each other all the time, and used the same bookkeeper to keep track of their positions. While the manipulation was in progress there was little or nothing—except the similarity in trading patterns—to link the Hunt brothers with the Conti group. Following standard practice, the exchanges sought and obtained assurances that the large longs would not disrupt the market by standing on delivery. Although most of these assurances were violated almost as soon as they were given, the exchanges (who were initially among the defendants in the Minpeco case) argued that they had done what they were expected to do, and the judge dismissed them from the case.

The fact remains that the exchanges—the first level of regulation—had failed to stop the manipulation. The second level, the Commodity Futures Trading Commission, turned out to be no more effective. The CFTC normally has five members, but there was a vacancy and the remaining four were equally divided; the chairman, who favored action, did not have a deciding vote. It was only in January 1980, when the price reached $40 an ounce, that the CFTC was able to exercise some of its statutory responsibility (see Section 11.6.3). The Commission also started a criminal lawsuit against some of the conspirators, but the case was so poorly prepared that no convictions ensued.

The CFTC also failed in another of its responsibilities, namely to provide information. We saw earlier that the Commission regularly publishes detailed breakdowns of the open interest in all futures markets showing the fractions held by large traders. During the period under review, however, silver was inexplicably omitted from this release. If data on silver had been published at the time, some traders would no doubt have realized that a major manipulation was under way and would not have been caught short; they could also have called for action to stop the abuse.[25] The absence of market information served only to protect the conspirators in their illegal venture.

In the end justice prevailed, at least after the fact and to limited extent. The third level of regulation (the courts) performed as it should where the other two levels had not. Although the criminal case had come to nought, the civil case mentioned earlier (*Minpeco v. Conticommodities et al.*) resulted in a final defeat for the three Hunt brothers (including Lamar, who had played a crucial role during the final stages of the manipulation) and their allies. Those defendants who stayed in the trial—several others settled when they saw the evidence and two had been dismissed—were found to have violated the antitrust laws by monopolizing and manipulating the spot and futures markets in silver. They were also found to have violated a number of other statutes, among which the RICO (Racketeer Influenced Corrupt Organizations) act was particularly important because of the triple damages for which that act provides.[26]

To conclude this section we must ask, what, if anything, has been learned from the events described? The short answer is not much. Hearings held by congressional committees uncovered many of the relevant facts but did not lead to more effective safeguards against manipulation. In fact, the financial assistance extended with official approval to the Hunt brothers after their scheme had collapsed suggests that manipulators can get away with their misdeeds if they are big enough. Ultimately—more than 8 years later—they were condemned to pay, but that may not be a sufficient deterrent. It could happen again.

11.7 REGULATION IN THE UNITED KINGDOM

In the United States the financial markets are regulated more strictly than in most other countries. Since these markets are also more highly developed than elsewhere, it would seem that regulation of the kind practiced here has on balance been helpful, or at least not harmful. In fact, the American system of regulation has served as an example to several other countries. As an illustration of regulation overseas, we now discuss the case of Britain, whose financial markets have been of international importance for many years.

Right up until the late 1980s, most financial markets in the United Kingdom had operated within a legal framework designed to prohibit fraud and certain other practices like insider trading, rather than to set down procedures to be followed. Conduct was controlled by a combination of self-regulation in the form of industry codes of practice, overseen by the Department of Trade and Industry, and a characteristically British system of "nods and winks" whereby the Bank of England exerted tight, but informal, control.

As the number and diversity of participants in the market grew and new instruments and technologies began to emerge, it was recognized that a more formal system needed to be put in place. This took the form of the Financial Services Act, which came into operation in April 1988. The act established a market watchdog in the form of the Securities and Investments Board (SIB). Any firm that wishes to do business in the area of investments or securities trading must be registered with the SIB or, more usually, with one of five "self-regulating organizations" (SROs) that the SIB recognizes. Before they can do business, firms must satisfy the SIB of their honesty, competence, and solvency. If a firm, once authorized, fails to comply with the rulebooks of the SIB and their SRO, there are three sanctions: The SIB may revoke their authorization to trade, it may bring a criminal prosecution, or they can be sued by their customers for damages (or possibly all of these). Markets must also be approved by the SIB in a similar way, becoming recognized investment exchanges.

The five SROs that are overseen by the SIB include:

- The *Securities Association* (TSA) covers dealing in British and international securities. The International Stock Exchange is itself a member as are all market makers who operate on the exchange.
- The *Investment Management Regulatory Organisation* (IMRO) is the SRO for investment managers and advisers, including managers of pension funds and unit trusts (similar to mutual funds).
- The *Financial Intermediaries, Managers & Brokers Regulatory Association* (FIBRA) covers independent intermediaries arranging deals in, and advising on, investments such as life assurance and unit trusts.
- The *Life Assurance and Unit Trust Regulatory Organisation* (LAUTRO) covers the marketing (as distinct from the managing) of life insurance and unit trust products. A rule of this organization requires agents to disclose their commissions to the public.
- The *Association of Futures Brokers and Dealers* (AFBD) sets the rules for those operating on the London International Financial Futures Exchange (LIFFE), the London Metal Exchange (LME), the London Futures and Options Exchange (FOX), the Baltic Exchange, and the International Petroleum Exchange.

Interestingly, although the SIB is accountable to the government (in the form of the secretary of state for trade and industry and the British Parliament), it is a private limited company and is financed by the financial institutions through their SROs. If a single firm is engaged in many activities, it will have to be a member of multiple SROs, which means that some firms spend up to $500,000 per year to meet their share of the costs of these regulatory bodies.

The money markets and trading in "near money" instruments are regulated directly by the Bank of England, based on its powers in the Banking Act of 1987. It has regulatory powers over banks, money markets, trading in government bonds, and foreign exchange. The Bank of England also regulates trading in gold bullion—a fact that largely reflects the historical convertibility between gold and currency in the days of the gold standard.

The main criticism of the system has been its complexity, especially the scope for overlap and inconsistency between the various regulatory bodies. The situation has been compared to "trying to play cricket with dozens of umpires all over the pitch." In an attempt to reduce these burdens, firms now deal with a "lead regulator," either an SRO, the SIB, or the Bank of England, which assumes responsibility for collecting all routine information.[27] It is too early to say whether the regulatory mechanisms introduced in 1988 will help or hurt the British financial markets.

Notes

Chapter 1. Introduction

1. If there were a single price, the market would be "perfectly competitive." The notion of perfect competition is useful in economic theory as a limiting case, but it has no counterpart in reality. This is why the term "*highly* competitive" was used in defining financial markets.

2. When the bid price and the offer price coincide, one or more transactions will take place at that single price. But this is only a temporary situation; as soon as all possible transactions have been executed, there will again be a bid price below the offer price. In Chapter 5 this process is described in detail.

3. According to data from the U.S. Internal Revenue Service, there were 2.9 million "active" corporations with assets at the end of 1983, 98.6% of which had assets under $10 million. Only about 3,000 corporations had assets of $250 million and over, but their assets were 74.7% of all corporate assets.

4. It should be clear that in this context the word "stock" is not synonymous with "equity" or "share." It is also not synonymous with "inventory," another word that is used interchangeably with "stock." Unfortunately we shall encounter many examples where the same word is commonly used with different meanings, and we shall try to warn the reader against confusion.

5. Land is used as an example because it is not normally subject to depreciation, a complication that is taken up in a moment.

6. This can be done in a number of ways. The simplest formula is "linear" depreciation; thus if the truck's salvage value is believed to be $10,000, an amount of $4,000 would be set aside each year. For tax and other reasons many firms use some form of "accelerated" depreciation, under which relatively more is set aside in the earlier years.

7. Alternatively, GAAP would value inventories at the lesser of current price and historical cost to avoid an overstatement of net worth, and other methods are also in common use. The examples of this section assume valuation of inventories at historical cost.

8. Corporations can buy back their own shares, but if they do they normally have to pay the market price regardless of the par value. The main purpose of par values, incidentally, is to prevent corporations from selling more shares without informing existing shareholders, a fraudulent practice known as "watering the stock") that was not uncommon in the nineteenth century.

9. The distinction is not always clear-cut, depending as it does on what is included in the balance sheet. Since we did not include patents in our sample balance sheet, expenditures on Research & Development appear as a current item, but it could be argued that they are an investment in future technology and as such are a capital item.

10. If the firm owns interest-earning assets, as many firms do (though not the hypothetical firm used as an example), the word "net" should be inserted before "interest paid."

11. This does not mean that the cash flow statement is unimportant. A negative Net Current Cash Flow (line 11), for example, would raise doubts about the survival of the firm if it persisted for some years.

12. For a short period centered around 1980, publicly traded corporations were mandated by the regulatory authorities to present their accounts using both historical cost and replacement cost, thus permitting a comparison. During these years the Chrysler Corporation appeared to be in good shape if one looked at its GAAP statements, but the replacement cost accounts told a very different story. In the early 1980s Chrysler, to the surprise of the stock market, had to be saved from bankruptcy by government-guaranteed loans to the tune of a billion dollars.

Chapter 2. The Place of Financial Markets in the Economy

1. See the discussion of technology and "goodwill" in Chapter 1.

2. We shall see later that corporations are treated somewhat differently in the official statistics.

3. This publication (Release C.9, published twice a year) is related to the Flow of Funds accounts discussed later in the chapter.

4. For nonfinancial corporations—not shown separately in Table 2.2—it is possible to compare the aggregate value of reproducible assets at current cost and at historical cost. Thus for plant and equipment these two figures are $3.6 trillion and $2.8 trillion, respectively.

5. The plant and equipment of this sector belongs to the nonprofit institutions, such as private universities, that are included.

6. This means, among other things, that the personal sector is not greatly affected by fluctuations in share prices, even when they are as dramatic as on "Black Monday" in October 1987. At that time many pundits predicted a repeat of the Great Depression, which is popularly believed to have been triggered by the stock market crash of September 1929—a belief, incidentally, that is not shared by most economists. The crash of 1987, though similar in magnitude to that of 1929, had little effect on the economy as a whole. The stock market itself recovered fairly soon and went on to new highs.

7. This calculation is approximate because U.S. residents owned some foreign equities and foreigners owned some U.S. equities, but the amounts involved were fairly small and largely canceled out.

8. The ratio of market value to net worth, known as Tobin's q, is discussed in Chapter 6.

9. At \$20.5t, private net worth so defined was about 3.6 times the 1991 Gross Domestic Product of \$5.7t.

10. An unknown (but probably small) percentage of the household sector's net worth was attributable to personal trusts and nonprofit institutions.

11. For 1982, when the aggregate net worth of the household sector was about \$10t, the total net worth of the 38,200 persons with net worth over \$5 million was estimated at \$413 million, or about 4% of the aggregate (from table 753 in the 1990 *Statistical Abstract of the United States*). This surprisingly small percentage is no doubt an underestimate because many wealthy people use personal trusts to avoid estate taxes.

12. From table 795 in the 1984 *Statistical Abstract of the United States*. These estimates are derived from estate tax returns. See also the more recent but less complete data in tables 759–761 of the 1991 *Statistical Abstract*.

13. From the U.S. Bureau of the Census, *Current Population Reports*, series P-70, No. 7.

14. The same applies to other industrial nations, but in Britain, France, and other countries where government-owned industries have recently been "privatized," special efforts have been made towards a wider dispersion of the resulting equities.

15. An example is the creation of money market funds in the 1970s.

16. The closely related concept of Gross National Product, which differs from GDP in its geographic coverage, was the principal concept in the U.S. National Accounts until recently. The switch from GNP to GDP brought the United States in line with international practice.

17. The U.S. National Accounts consider all government purchases of goods and services—even for such durables as highways—to be for current use; other countries do recognize government capital formation. Consumer purchases of durable goods (other than houses) are not considered investment either. Owner-occupied dwellings are considered to be held in the (unincorporated) business sector and to be rented by their owners to themselves. We shall see shortly that the Flow of Funds uses different conventions.

18. As is shown in Section 2.3.4, this is so because net imports are by definition equivalent to a flow of capital from the rest of the world. Alternatively, as is done in the National Accounts and in Table 2.4, net U.S. exports may be put on the investment side as "net foreign investment."

19. Since the fixed-weight index is not currently available for all years since 1960, the deflator was used throughout.

20. The Federal Reserve, whose policies are discussed in Section 2.4.3, has in recent years—especially after the unfortunate experience of the 1970s—put greater stress on the control of inflation than on the promotion of real growth. An acceleration in the growth of GDP therefore leads to fears of higher interest rates, which tend to affect security prices adversely. An increase in the growth rate is good news from an economic point of view, but it is not usually perceived as such by the financial community.

21. For the more correct concept of "total factor productivity," see Jorgenson et al. (1987).

22. The matrix is still published, but not as part of the regular quarterly Flow of Funds releases. It can be found, in condensed form, in the *Statistical Abstracts of the United States* and more fully in the Federal Reserve Board's *Statistical Digest*.

23. The attentive reader will no doubt wonder about the reasons for this difference in definition. We cannot provide enlightenment, but are inclined to side with the Federal Reserve.

24. In response to this concern, special tax provisions to encourage saving (Individual Retirement Accounts and Keogh plans for the self-employed) were enacted in the 1980s. These provisions no doubt led to some reshuffling of household assets, but it is not clear whether they have had any effect on aggregate saving.

25. The household sector has also steadily reduced its equity in unincorporated business, of which by definition it is the sole owner. Why this should be so is something of a mystery.

26. This phenomenon is discussed in more detail in Chapter 3.

27. The reader with some understanding of calculus will realize that exact allocation requires the evaluation of an integral over time, and that the information needed for this operation is difficult to obtain.

28. It is not necessarily equal to the current-account balance found in statistics on the balance of payments since the National Accounts, from which Table 2.7 is taken, uses somewhat different concepts.

29. On this point see also Section 2.3.1.

30. Many international economists consider the real index to be more meaningful, but the nominal index may be easier to understand.

31. A larger decline in the dollar occurred during the transition interval just mentioned. In 1969 the nominal index was 122.4, so the dollar lost nearly 20% in value between that year and the adoption of managed floating in 1973.

32. In 1985 the leading financial nations agreed on a coordinated intervention to bring the dollar down. Its success appears to have been due to good timing: market fundamentals also called for a lower dollar. Even so it took about three years before the dollar index came close to its 1980 level.

33. The reason is that the Flow of Funds accounts, unlike the National Accounts, do not provide any estimates at constant prices. Such estimates would be very useful in the analysis of financial markets.

34. Other transactions in bonds (households selling to households, for instance) are not excluded, but they would not make any difference.

35. Provided the interest rate is positive; if it were zero or negative, households would be better off hoarding the consumption good itself (assuming it is storable).

36. Strictly speaking, this is not the whole story. A strong demand for capital goods will increase employment and labor income, which will in turn increase the demand for bonds. The interested reader may like to pursue this and confirm that the basic conclusion remains valid.

37. That is, only those ovens with a sufficiently high marginal productivity could be bought.

38. This theory, developed by Robert Barro of Harvard, goes by such names as "Ricardian equivalence" and "ultrarationality." Its most important implication is that it makes no difference whether the government finances its outlays by taxes or by borrowing.

39. More recently, the German inflation rate has increased as a result of the unification of West and East Germany, while inflation in the other countries mentioned has been reduced.

40. Yet another complication is taxation. The "inflation premium" (that is, the difference between the nominal and the real interest rate) is normally taxable, so bondholders are not fully compensated for the expected fall in the purchasing power of money. It is possible to adjust the Fisher equation for taxation, but this would lead us too far.

41. The Constitution puts Congress in charge of monetary matters, but in 1913 Congress delegated this responsibility to an independent agency. In other developed countries, and in some developing countries, the central bank is also more or less independent.

42. These and other claims on financial institutions are discussed further in Section 2.6.

43. The main difficulty is the introduction of new financial instruments. Money market funds, for instance, were insignificant until the middle 1970s. Stimulated by nominal interest rates as high as 20%, they mushroomed around 1980; subsequently they have fluctuated without much of a trend.

44. The reason for using this concept—which excludes net exports, the change in business inventories, and federal purchases of goods and services—is that the U.S. money supply affects only domestic demand, not foreign demand. Federal purchases are excluded because they are largely unaffected by the money supply. The monetarist relation fits significantly better when this concept is used in lieu of GDP.

45. A more precise analysis would require the use of quarterly data and would probably involve other variables as well. In fact, most forecasters of economic activity rely on elaborate econometric models maintained by consulting firms such as Data Resources Inc. These models usually combine Keynesian and monetarist elements.

46. It is also possible that this is an example of "Goodhart's law," according to which economic relationships hold only as long as they are not used for policy making. In 1979 the Federal Reserve Board shifted to a monetarist policy of controlling the money stock rather than interest rates; although this policy was modified in 1982, monetarist influences on the board remained strong. See Evans (1987) for a discussion of this law.

47. Some monetarists go further and argue that real GDP is independent of the money supply, so that any attempt to influence GDP through the money supply would merely result in inflation or deflation. This more extreme version of monetarism does not appear to be consistent with the evidence. Changes in money supply do appear to affect real GDP, at least in the short run.

48. Keynesians did not fail to point out, however, that this policy also led to increased unemployment and could equally well be interpreted in Keynesian terms.

49. In accordance with the findings of Friedman and Schwartz cited earlier, M2 is now widely considered to be more important than M1. For the sake of simplicity, however, the discussion is confined to M1, whose meaning has remained unchanged over the years. Because of financial innovations, M2 has gradually come to include more and more financial instruments.

50. It may appear at first sight that only the buying or selling bank experiences a change in its reserves, other banks being unaffected. However, in the "federal funds" market (discussed in Chapter 3) banks can trade reserves among themselves, so that any change in total reserves is spread over the entire sector.

51. Another tool available to the Fed is the discount rate, which is the interest rate at which member banks can borrow limited amounts from the central bank. A change in the discount rate usually comes after a change in open-market policy, and therefore does not have much independent significance; it serves mainly to make a policy change official.

52. Unless stated otherwise, this term will now be used in the narrow sense of M1.

53. Extreme cases are Germany, willing to accept large unemployment as long as there is no inflation, and Brazil, which for many years appeared to be indifferent to triple-digit inflation as long as economic growth was high. Recently Brazil and other Latin American countries have adopted more orthodox monetary policies.

54. The prolonged boom of the 1980s, for instance, was accompanied by unsustainable rises in real estate prices in certain regions of the United States. In the early 1990s the chickens came home to roost, to the detriment not only of real estate owners but especially of the banks and thrift institutions that provided generous mortgages on inflated values. Since the federal government has, in effect, guaranteed these mortgages (through agencies such as the Federal Savings and Loan Insurance Corporation) the cost to taxpayers of mortgage defaults is running into many hundreds of billions of dollars. Furthermore, defaults on these and other loans weakened the capital position of many financial institutions. A movement toward greater concentration, with the stronger banks taking over the weaker ones, served to restore the strength of the American financial system.

55. The resulting wide swings in exchange rates discussed in Section 2.2.5, are themselves of great importance to the financial markets, most of which are now closely linked around the world. As shown in Table 2.3, holdings of foreign securities have risen markedly both here and abroad. Recently, securities traders have sometimes paid as much attention to the external value of the dollar as to monetary policy.

Chapter 3. The Supply of Securities

1. A mortgage on a specific property is not readily negotiable in the sense described in Chapter 1 and is therefore not a financial instrument (let alone a security) according to our definitions. Some corporate bonds are secured by real estate and in that respect are similar to mortgages. Section 3.6 shows that mortgages may also be "packaged" into securities.

2. To some extent the government can also draw down its cash balance or sell its assets.

3. Price risk can be avoided by holding a bond until it is redeemed. For this reason, it is often excluded from the definition of risk, but this exclusion can be misleading because many holders may want to sell bonds before they mature. As shown in Chapters 9 and 10, price risk can also be largely eliminated by "hedging" in futures contracts.

4. Recently, evidence has come to light of anticompetitive behavior in some of the auctions through which federal securities are first issued. It does not appear, however, that this disclosure has affected the competitive character of markets in existing (i.e., previously issued) securities.

5. As shown in Section 2.5, sales and purchases of short-term securities are also used to regulate the money supply, but that is the task of the Federal Reserve rather than the federal government as an issuer.

6. The "denomination" or "face value" is the amount that will be repaid upon maturity.

7. Occasionally bills with maturities less than 13 weeks are issued to bridge temporary fluctuations in the government's liquid assets.

8. In periods of interest rate volatility the Treasury may hold an auction, issuing the notes at a price other than par in order to match the rates being offered by competing investments.

9. As described in Chapter 5, zero-coupon bonds are also of analytical interest because their yield can be calculated more precisely than the yield on notes and bonds. The yields referred to in the present chapter are approximate.

10. Any capital gains, however, are subject to tax at the normal rate. By way of reciprocity, most states exempt interest on federal obligations from state income taxes.

11. The largest default in recent years arose in the early 1980s, when certain nuclear power projects in the Pacific Northwest had to be abandoned while still under construction. In addition, New York City was close to default during 1975 when investors were forced to accept a "restructuring" of debt, which left them with deferral of interest payments and extended maturities.

12. Foreign central banks have long held U.S. government securities as part of their international reserves rather than for investment purposes.

13. The exact figure depends not only on the maturity but also on the assumed rate of future inflation; the *Financial Times* provided yields for both 5% and 10% inflation rates. The difference in yield between these two assumptions was small. On this subject see also Woodward (1990) and the discussion of Fisher's equation in Chapter 2.

14. A business corporation (as opposed to a nonprofit corporation) must have *some* shares outstanding, so the percentage of debt cannot be 100.

15. The emergence of "junk bonds," discussed in Section 3.5.5, has created somewhat greater flexibility in this regard.

16. In some cases the preferred stockholders have priority, depending on the original agreement establishing the particular firm and on the type of preferred stock issued.

17. Bond ratings, available also for tax-exempt securities, are a long-standing feature of the U.S. financial markets. John Moody, for example, started his rating service in 1909. These rating agencies are private firms whose success depends on the credibility of their assessments.

18. Trade credit, which is credit granted by a firm to its customers in conjunction with sales of products, appears as a component of both "other assets" and "other liabilities." Trade credit granted by nonfinancial corporations to other such corporations, however, is "netted out" since the balance sheets are sector aggregates.

19. This ratio, closely related to another ratio known as "Tobin's q," is discussed further in Chapter 6.

20. There must have been sizable gains on foreign exchange during this period, but it is not clear how these are reflected in Table 3.4.

21. The purpose of par values is discussed in Chapter 1.

22. The first sale of its shares by a corporation to outsiders is known as an Initial Public Offering (IPO). It often includes both newly issued shares and existing shares offered by the company's founders.

23. The recent introduction of "shelf regulation" has increased the feasibility of smaller, more frequent share issues. Shelf regulation allows corporations to file a prospectus that remains valid for some time; the actual issue can be made whenever market conditions are favorable. Another way of issuing small amounts of new shares without undue expenses is through a "dividend reinvestment plan."

24. In the case of new issues of significant size, this is usually done by a "syndicate" of underwriters—sometimes as many as 100—organized especially for the purpose. The listing of the underwriters in the newspaper is known as a "tombstone ad."

25. Any issue of equities increases the issuer's net worth by the cash received, but in the case of a rights issue the net worth will increase by a smaller percentage than the number of shares. Thus if a corporation has one million shares outstanding and its net worth is $100 million, each share has a book value of $100. Upon issuing another million shares to current shareholders (a "1-for-1" rights issue) for a cash payment of $20 per share, the net worth becomes $120 million and the book value falls to $60 per share. This is an example of dilution.

26. The extreme form of such a defensive share repurchase is to "take the company private"—that is, to buy up all the publicly held stock and have the stock exchange listing rescinded. This also eliminates the reporting requirements imposed by stock exchanges.

27. These legislatures are often anxious to keep corporate headquarters in their state and to prevent production from being shifted elsewhere. The antitakeover laws enacted by certain states are so strict as to make large institutional investors unwilling to hold shares of corporations domiciled there.

28. This argument also applies to the "poison-pill" defense strategy, in which management arranges ahead of time for certain actions (such as selling a block of shares at a discount to a friendly party) contingent on a takeover. These devices are generally contrary to shareholders' interests.

29. One reason may be that pension funds and other large institutional investors are sometimes prohibited by law from owning low-grade bonds.

30. To some extent this may be offset by the fall in interest rates that normally accompanies a recession, as it did in the most recent one and its aftermath. Some corporations were able to call their outstanding junk bonds and issue new ones at a lower rate, thus reducing their interest burden and enhancing their credit rating.

31. An option, the main topic of Chapter 8, is the right (but not the obligation) to buy a security at a certain price.

32. In the longer run, of course, the company's common stockholders incur the additional cost of selling shares to holders of convertible bonds at below their market price.

33. The option to buy common stock at a certain price is an integral part of a convertible security. However, corporations sometimes offer such options separately, in which case they are known as *warrants* and are traded as separate securities.

34. A general reference is Scholes and Wolfson (1988). It does not deal with partnership units as such, but Thompson (1991) does.

35. This is the current situation in the United States. In many other countries, including Canada and Great Britain, the tax laws have provisions for diminishing or eliminating double taxation. Although similar provisions have long been considered in the United States, they have never been enacted. Until recently, individuals could exclude a relatively small amount of dividends from taxable income, but this exclusion is no longer available.

36. These arrangements are not to be confused with partnerships between corporations for specific purposes—often known as "joint ventures." The latter type of partnership is common, for instance, in the oil industry, where two or more firms may develop an oilfield together.

37. Similar considerations led to the creation of Real Estate Investment Trusts (REITs), which are not considered mutual funds. They were popular in the early 1970s but many of them did not survive the high interest rates that came subsequently.

38. A subspecies is unit trusts, which invest in a fixed portfolio of assets. Most mutual funds, by contrast, adjust their portfolio of primary securities frequently.

39. There are actually two kinds of load funds. Most such funds are "front-loaded," which means that the load charge is collected upon purchase. In "back-loaded" funds the load is collected upon sale, and there may be a sliding scale in which the load percentage diminishes with the number of years the fund shares are held. The discussion in the text assumes front loading.

40. There are also "dual funds" in which the shares are of two types: income shares

and capital or growth shares. Essentially the capital shares get the capital gains and the income shares receive the current earnings.

41. In fact, these studies supplied much of the evidence for the "random walk" hypothesis concerning security prices, a subject taken up in Chapter 6.

42. Stock market indexes are discussed in Chapter 6.

43. To complicate things further, the fund may be closed only to new investors, or to existing investors.

44. They do not always succeed, so small "adjustments" are occasionally necessary. Apart from these adjustments, money-market funds do not involve price risk (as defined in Section 3.2.1).

45. Many banks have responded to competition by introducing "money market accounts," but these are not MMFs.

46. In this context a foreign branch or subsidiary of a U.S. bank is considered a foreign bank.

47. To some extent they can accomplish the same purpose by trading in the Eurodollar market previously discussed.

48. Repurchase agreements, called "repos" for short, are another financial instrument whose life is typically very short. They differ from Federal Funds in being collateralized, usually by Treasury bills. The word "repurchase" reflects the legal agreement under which the borrower actually sells the underlying T-bills while retaining the right to repurchase them when the loan is due (often the next day). The Federal Reserve frequently uses repos as an intervention vehicle in the Federal Funds market.

Chapter 4. The Demand for Securities

1. Liabilities in the form of mortgages and other credit can also be useful in this rearrangement, particularly for short-term and medium-term discrepancies between income and desired consumption. It is in general more difficult, however, to rely on borrowing for retirement since the resulting debt may be uncollectible when the retiree dies. An important example of the use of liabilities in providing for retirement is to buy a house early in one's working life, finance it with a mortgage, and pay off the mortgage gradually so that the house is owned "free and clear" during retirement; this plan will reduce the income needed during retirement.

2. It might be objected that saving for retirement cannot be a major source of funds because the saving of those who are currently working is offset by the dissaving of those who are currently retired. In an economy with a growing population, however, the workers' saving is likely to outweigh the retirees' dissaving; this imbalance will be reinforced if the current workers have higher real incomes than the retirees had when they were working. Regardless of whether the flows of saving and dissaving are in balance, at any time a large stock of financial capital associated with these flows is available for investment in the securities markets.

3. The main practical problem with an annuity is that it may be overpriced from the individual's point of view. The insurance company knows that persons who believe themselves to be healthy are more likely to buy annuities than persons who believe they will die soon. To offset this self-selectivity, the company will charge more for an annuity than its actuarial value.

4. From earlier exposure to microeconomics, the reader will know that such a preference can sometimes also be expressed by means of indifference curves, but the utility

function tells us something that indifference curves do not, namely, the strength of the individual's preference for *x* over *y*. This additional feature is essential in dealing with risk, considered later in this chapter but ignored for the time being.

5. The first payment, therefore, is received when the annuity is purchased (that is, on his sixty-sixth birthday). This somewhat artificial pattern again results from the assumed timing of payments. The reader is encouraged to make the same calculation assuming that all earnings and annuity payments are received at the end of the year; in that case, some provision has to be made for Adam's consumption during his first working year.

6. We are not suggesting that savings for retirement necessarily have to be invested in securities. Apart from pension funds and the like, these savings may also be invested in real assets.

7. Since the required return on shares may differ from the required rate on bonds, a different symbol is used. The derivation of the former rate is a complex issue in itself, to which we devote a large part of Chapter 6.

8. It should also be mentioned that the present-value formula, while widely accepted, has been questioned by Scott (1985) and others as a realistic description of actual share prices.

9. In the sense that the net present value (after subtracting the cost of the investment required) is positive.

10. Congress has recently restored lower tax rates on long-term gains.

11. It does not make it impossible since we could define the time interval as being 1 day, but this makes for cumbersome expressions. With discrete time, moreover, it makes a difference whether payments (of dividends and the like) occur at the start or at the end of the period; in continuous time this is irrelevant.

12. Because of this relation, expressed in Equation 4.5, the parameter *b* is sometimes called the "force of interest."

13. In the present context "yield" and "return" are synonymous. In other contexts, "return"—also called "total return" for clarity—includes the percentage rate of change in the price of a security, whereas "yield" refers to the return from dividends or interest only.

14. It should be noted in passing that although we now work in continuous time, the year is still relevant as a conventional unit of time.

15. One might think of reinvesting the interest in another bond that has 20 years left at the time of reinvestment, but this would amount to mixing up coupon bonds of different maturity dates.

16. On this subject see also the valuable survey by Shiller (1990).

17. In an appendix to Shiller (1990), McCulloch has provided long series of zero-coupon yields, but these were laboriously derived from the prices of coupon bonds.

18. This phenomenon of an internal maximum in the yield curve can also be detected in McCulloch's table (see the preceding footnote). According to Kessel (1965), it is attributable to a difference in liquidity. In recent years the Treasury has not issued bonds with a lifetime between 10 and 30 years. The most distant maturities correspond to recently issued 30-year bonds, in which there is active trading. Bonds with a 20-year maturity, by contrast, were actually issued 10 years ago as 30-year bonds, and trading in those is much less active since many of them are held until they are redeemed. The very distant maturities, therefore, carry a "liquidity premium."

19. Interestingly enough, the first extension was in the financial area. The seventeenth century Dutch statesman Johan de Witt used probability to compare annuities with fixed-term securities, thus laying the foundation for life insurance.

20. Two such causes are the precise shape of the die and the way in which it is thrown; these should be irrelevant if the die is really fair. A recent development in this subject is "chaos theory," which emphasizes these microcauses. Peters (1991) provides an interesting introduction with special reference to financial markets. Although some chaos theorists try to dispense with the concept of probability altogether, Peters adopts a more eclectic approach. He makes a prima facie case that chaos theory is relevant to economics, but until there is more conclusive evidence we shall continue to rely on classical probability theory.

21. The elemental outcomes must be mutually exclusive (two cannot occur at the same time) and exhaustive (no possible elemental outcome is ignored). Composite outcomes may, but need not, have these properties. Although in the example the elemental outcomes are equally probable, this condition is not necessary.

22. Provided you do not run out of money in the process, a possibility known as *gambler's ruin*. A theorem in probability theory states that gambler's ruin is certain if you start out with a finite amount of capital and cannot borrow.

23. In books on statistics and probability, the terms "expectation" or "mathematical expectation" are often used as synonyms of "expected value." This usage can be confusing in the context of financial markets, where traders have "subjective" expectations that are not necessarily equal to "mathematical" expectations. In this book we therefore avoid the use of "expectation" in the mathematical sense; references to "expectations" are to be interpreted as "subjective," whereas "expected value" always refers to the mathematical concept.

24. The only difference is that the sum of the probabilities over all possible outcomes has to be replaced by the integral over the continuous variable x. In this book the use of integrals is generally avoided.

25. It should be noted that getting zero is a composite rather than an elemental outcome. There are 100 elemental outcomes, each representing the possibility that a ticket numbered from 1 to 100 gets the prize, so getting zero is a composite of 99 elemental outcomes.

26. In the case of a continuous probability distribution, some or all of the moments may not exist; that is, they are infinite. This important complication is further discussed in Section 4.2.3. From a sample of observations, the "empirical" moments can always be calculated.

27. This is more useful because the second moment depends on the mean: If each outcome value is increased by ten, for instance, the second moment is changed but the variance is not.

28. To make this independent of the units of measurement, it is customary to divide by the third power of the standard deviation.

29. Since there is only one prize, the probability of both tickets winning ($x = 500$, $y = 500$) is zero. The reader may like to contrast this with the case of owning two tickets in different lotteries.

30. If the same calculation is performed for the case mentioned in the preceding footnote, it will be found that the correlation coefficient is zero. This must clearly be so if the two lotteries are independent of each other.

31. We say "may be" because this is not the only interpretation of the buying of lottery tickets and other forms of gambling. Conceivably, gamblers get some utility from the suspense as to the outcome. A third interpretation is mentioned in a moment.

32. Actually, we use the formula for a bond because the theoretically infinite life of a share creates some complications that are not essential in the present context.

33. As shown in Chapter 3, the commonly used term "risk-free" is inappropriate because such bonds are subject to inflation risk.

34. Mandelbrot (1963) and Fama (1965) found that the actual distributions have very large variances and fourth moments, potentially tending toward infinity in the underlying theoretical distribution from which samples were being drawn. In this case, another measure of variability, such as the mean absolute deviation or the interquartile range, should be employed in lieu of the variance; these measures are discussed in statistics textbooks. Unfortunately, there is as yet no consensus on the functional form of the distribution of equity returns.

35. This and other indexes of equity prices are discussed in Chapter 6. The changes in the index are calculated as differences in the logarithm; such differences are approximately equal to one-hundredth of the percentage changes. From a computational point of view, logarithmic differences are more convenient than percentage changes.

36. It should not be confused with a bivariate probability of the kind discussed in Section 4.2.2; that is why a vertical bar is used rather than a comma.

37. The far-reaching consequences of this distinction for security pricing are examined in Chapter 6.

38. This assumes that only nonnegative amounts of each security can be held; in other words, that short selling is impossible. It is fairly straightforward to permit short selling, but this is left to the reader.

39. Portfolio selection by the method outlined here was first proposed by Harry Markowitz (1959), who was recently rewarded with the Nobel prize in economics. We recall that its optimality hinges on the assumptions of the mean-variance approach (see Section 4.3.2).

Chapter 5. Securities Markets and Their Efficiency

1. By "prohibitively expensive" we mean that it is not worth holding shares as a short- or medium-term investment if the transaction cost is too high. Cars are normally held for use rather than as an investment; consequently, the same transaction cost (in percentage terms) may not be prohibitive for cars.

2. Brokers in securities also commonly give credit to their customers, keeping the securities bought by the latter as collateral. Accounts with brokers that involve credit are known as "margin accounts." Because of fears that an excess of this type of credit may fuel unsustainable stock market booms, the Federal Reserve has been granted power to limit the percentage of securities holdings that may be financed by credit from brokers.

3. In the stock market, however, newly announced but as yet unissued securities are sometimes traded on a "when issued" basis. There is also trading in "rights" if a company chooses to issue new shares to existing shareholders rather than through underwriters (see Chapter 3).

4. The Philadelphia Stock Exchange is actually a few years older, and central trading places for securities had existed in Europe for many years.

5. Exclusivity also makes it easier for exchanges to sell the information—particularly on prices—generated on their trading floors. The supply of these "market data" to the media and to quotation networks is an important source of revenue to many exchanges.

6. The volume of trading is the total number of shares sold, which is necessarily equal to the number of shares bought. The media sometimes tell us that "the market was

driven down by heavy selling," but this cannot be literally true unless prices went to zero. For every seller there must have been a buyer.

7. The share registrar maintains the official record of share ownership, while the transfer agent (usually a bank) keeps track of sales and purchases of shares.

8. The reason the volume share and the value share differ is that relatively more high-priced shares are traded on the NYSE. The reader is encouraged to explore this difference for the other exchanges and for the over-the-counter market by dividing the volume figures of Table 5.1 into the value figures of Table 5.2.

9. In 1989, blocks of 10,000 or more shares accounted for 51% of the total volume of trading, up from 17% in 1975. The largest block trade, recorded in 1986, involved close to 50 million shares. By contrast, the percentage of transactions involving 1,000 shares or less declined from 42% in 1975 to 13% in 1989.

10. Activity in 1987, when $3 trillion worth of shares changed hands, was even greater than in 1990; after "Black Monday," trading slowed markedly, but it came close to the earlier peak in the early 1990s and exceeded it from 1993 on.

11. The seller of a security does not have to own it; the rules of most financial markets permit "short selling," where the seller (or the seller's broker) has to borrow the security until he or she evens out the position by buying it. If the "short interest" (the total number of shares in a specific company sold short) is large, such borrowing may not be possible. Orders to sell short are subject to an important restriction: They can only be executed when there is an "uptick" (an upward price movement). This restriction is intended to prevent an avalanche of sell orders from destabilizing the market.

12. A stop order need not be intended to limit the loss (or protect the accrued profit) on an existing position; it can also be used to open a position. Thus a speculator may believe that a stock is only worth buying if it rises from its current level, leading him or her to place a stop buy order at a price above the current level. This why the term "stop order" is more accurate than "stop-loss order."

13. A further variation on limit orders is to specify them as "net," which means including commission. Since commissions are negotiable, a broker may be willing to forgo some of his normal commission if the order is large enough.

14. More rarely, "next-day delivery" is arranged, but then the price may be different from the one for standard delivery.

15. Or she. Because there are few women on the exchange floor, we shall use the male pronoun to avoid prolixity without admitting gender bias.

16. The reader is encouraged to verify this outcome by calculating the total number of shares demanded or supplied at each price.

17. The minimum price change of $1/8$ (except for high-priced shares, where it is $1/4$) is known as the "tick size." It is important to specialists and floor traders because they normally make a profit of $1/8$ on every completed trade. Proposals to reduce the tick size, for instance by using decimal rather than binary fractions, threaten the profits of these traders. It can be argued, however, that the resulting reduction in transaction costs would stimulate the volume of trading, which could more than offset the lower profit per trade.

18. The asking price would then be at $90^{7/8}$, above the highest public bid of $90^{3/4}$ (order no. 5).

19. Recently the exchange has introduced after-hour trading in two "sessions." The "fixed price" session allows purchases and sales at the closing price; it has not generated much volume. The "basket" session has been somewhat more succesful; the trading there is in combinations of shares used for arbitrage with stock-index futures (see Chapter 9).

20. On the London Stock Exchange, the monopoly enjoyed by the counterpart of the specialist (called "jobber" there) has recently been removed; it is too soon to say whether this change has led to improved market efficiency.

21. On "Black Monday," actually, there were plenty of buyers; otherwise the volume of trading would not have been as large as it was. To some extent, moreover, the specialists were able to limit their purchases by widening the bid-ask spread.

22. This is not strictly true, since most of the stock exchanges also list bonds. The volume of bond trading on these exchanges, however, is quite small in relation to the overall trading in bonds. Apparently, stock-exchange procedures offer little advantage in bonds.

23. The public, however, can participate indirectly through the foreign currency futures and option markets, which do have central trading places.

24. In addition to occupying high-rent floor space, central trading places require elaborate (and expensive) reporting and display systems, as well as telephone installations through which floor personnel maintain continuous contact with the head offices of their firms.

25. Where there are no specialists, and consequently no "book," the responsibility for executing limit orders remains with the originating brokers. This is the situation on the futures exchanges discussed in Chapter 9.

26. The main differences between these market makers and the stock exchange specialists are that the former do so on their own initiative rather than by assignment, and that the bid-ask spread is often larger in the OTC market.

27. For OTC stocks not quoted on NASDAQ, indicative bid and ask prices can be obtained from the "pink sheets" published daily by the National Quotation Bureau, which collects information from wholesale OTC firms.

28. In the United States the only exchange to be fully computerized is in Cincinnati. Despite considerable pressure by the Securities and Exchange Commission to promote trading on that exchange, its volume has remained small. In Canada the Toronto Stock Exchange has a large computerized section side by side with a conventional operation in other stocks.

29. Interestingly, the full potential for electronic trading was not recognized at the time, and the exchange spent $5 million upgrading its now disused trading floor.

30. As of June 1, 1995, the settlement period on the NYSE is 3 days.

31. During the last two days of an account, special arrangements may be made to deal in "new time," in which case trades will be treated for settlement as if they had been bargains struck in the next account. By payment of a fee, investors may also be able to agree with their brokers to defer payment to the next account even outside new time. This arrangement is known as a "contango facility." Alternatively, a client who sold shares short during an account may be able to arrange with the broker to defer his or her obligation to purchase enough shares to cover a short position until the next account (called a "backwardation facility").

32. In addition, both buyer and seller have probably spent some time on this transaction and may have incurred telephone charges and the like. Although often overlooked, these are also transaction costs. Small traders who "play the market" may find that, even if they are lucky enough to make a profit, their speculations consume a disproportionate amount of time.

33. On large transactions, such as those carried out by institutional investors, the percentage is much lower; in trading real estate or used cars, for instance, it would be

considerably higher. Individual investors can reduce their transaction costs appreciably by using discount brokers (see Section 5.1.1).

34. One type of "news" that may not be widely disseminated is rumor. An old stock market maxim advises to "buy on rumor and sell on news," where the adjective "favorable" is implicit. Those with low transaction costs will therefore want to be part of the "grapevine."

35. The closely related "random-walk hypothesis" was first asserted explicitly by Kendall (1953).

36. A story told by James Duesenberry makes the point: Two economists are walking together. One says, "I see a quarter on the sidewalk." The other, a believer in the EMH, replies "Impossible. If it really were a quarter, someone would have picked it up already."

37. Statisticians have developed elaborate techniques for analyzing time series, which can also help in determining whether such series are random. These techniques are beyond the scope of this book; for a good introduction see Pindyck and Rubinfeld (1991).

38. Strictly speaking, seasonality is also a form of cyclical behavior, but it may not be always detectable by filter rules. It is not clear, in fact, how powerful these rules are in detecting cycles.

39. The reason for this negative result is not, as one might think, that the January effect was "discovered" and did not hold from that point on because too many traders tried to take advantage of it. Many of the negative changes occurred in the early part of the period of observation. We should also mention attempts to refine the January effect by confining it to small stocks or to the first week of January.

40. The empirical evidence on the January and weekend effects is surveyed in Sharpe and Alexander (1992). They also consider a modified form of the January effect that focuses on the first few trading days of the new year.

41. In a more general version of the random walk, known as a "martingale" (after an old gambling term), additional lagged terms are included after the vertical bar. Strictly speaking, the weak-form EMH—according to which there is no information in *any* past prices—implies a martingale, not merely a random walk. In this book, however, we deal only with random-walk properties.

42. They cannot be described as returns because dividends are not taken into account. Dividends are of minor importance in daily changes of broad-based price indexes such as the S&P500 or the NYSE Composite.

43. Three classes were used instead of the more usual two because very small price changes (less than 0.0005 either way) are not sufficiently different from zero to be counted as "ups" or "downs." Such small changes occur on about 5% of all trading days.

44. In fact, the commissions paid by institutions, and by individual investors using discount brokers, are now so low that the most important component of the transaction cost is the bid-ask spread.

45. Security analysis is discussed in Chapter 7. Unlike technical analysts, who look only at prices (and possibly trading volume), security analysts also consider sales, costs, orders, technological changes, competition, and other economic factors determining earnings.

46. The observant reader may wonder how price volatility can be measured when the market is closed. The answer: from the changes between each Friday's closing price and the following Monday's opening price.

47. The SEC tracks insider trading in listed securities because it is illegal for insiders

(who usually are executives and/or directors of the firm) to profit from information that is not available to the public at large. More on this in Chapter 11.

48. Studies of the long-run return on a diversified portfolio of shares—say, over a period of 50 years—suggest that it exceeds the return on any other investment in securities (though not necessarily in other assets such as real estate). This finding is true even if the period includes the Great Depression of the 1930s and the great inflation of the 1970s, both of which affected share prices adversely.

Chapter 6. The Determination of Equity Prices

1. Most publicly traded U.S. corporations pay dividends quarterly; the reader should have no difficulty in modifying the following analysis accordingly.

2. More precisely, it is the time just after payment of the dividend Div (0).

3. For more on this subject, see Sharpe and Alexander (1992).

4. As opposed to integrated companies that are also involved in transporting, refining, and marketing.

5. Estimates of this type are available from financial advisory services specializing in oil shares.

6. The theory in which q first appeared (Tobin, 1958) was a theory of investment in the nonfinancial sense of real capital formation. It said that real investment would be high when q is high, because firms would then find it cheaper to build new productive capacity than to acquire the assets of existing firms, and the opposite when q is low. Viewed in this light, the theory has not been successful, but the concept of q is nevertheless of interest in financial economics.

7. In conventional accounting, and also in the Flow of Funds data discussed in Chapters 2 and 3, liabilities are usually entered at face value. This approach may not be realistic, since the liabilities of a firm may include bonds whose market value is less than their face value, a condition that occurs if interest rates rise after the bonds are issued, or if the risk of default increases. The firm may then be able to buy its own bonds at a discount, thus raising its net worth. The argument in the text ignores this possibility.

8. The valuation of financial assets and liabilities is the same for GAAP and current-cost accounting.

9. The problems surrounding the existence of a risk-free asset, already flagged in earlier chapters, is discussed further in Section 6.3.1.

10. "Objective" in the sense of being unanimously accepted; the assumption of identical expectations—probably the most restrictive of the assumptions underlying the simple CAPM—is invoked here.

11. Such stocks are rare. Cox and Rubinstein (1985) give estimates of beta for some 375 stocks, and not one is negative; in fact, the large majority is between 0.5 and 1.5. In Chapter 8 we show that put options normally have a negative beta.

12. The main problem arising from heterogeneous expectations is that the market portfolio, as defined in the preceding section, no longer necessarily falls on the efficiency frontier. As Roll (1977) has shown, this problem renders a full empirical test of the model virtually impossible.

13. Such bonds, discussed in Chapter 3, have been issued in a number of countries but not in the United States.

14. Despite its intuitive appeal, the realism of CCAPM is questionable. One critical study (Mankiw and Shapiro, 1985) found no evidence that the covariance between security returns and earnings helps explain security prices.

15. The question arises as to whether the approach of this section is consistent with CAPM, which assumes unanimous expectations. The answer appears to be that it is consistent as long as each portfolio manager controls no more than an insignificant part of the total market value of all securities; otherwise, one would have to adopt Lintner's extension of CAPM, discussed in Section 6.3.1.

16. This ratio is close to the one examined in Section 6.2, the main difference being that Fama and French apparently used historical cost rather than replacement cost.

17. Sometimes intuition suggests that specific risk factors must be relevant to particular firms. Thus one would expect the share price of an aluminum company to be determined in part by the price of aluminum, which is determined in the world market. The work of Fama and French (see Section 6.3.5) suggests that the size of the firm and the ratio of net worth to market value are generally useful risk factors.

18. The difference in level reflects the different basis of each of the indexes. The NYSE index is relative to a base value of 50 in 1965; the S&P500 had a value of 10 in 1943. For reasons given in the following, the base value of the DJI is difficult to determine.

19. By putting t equal to zero, the value of the index number in the base period is brought out. Many well-known price indexes—for instance, the Consumer Price Index—use a base-period value of 100, but in the preceding note we saw that the S&P500 and the NYSE Composite do not. The index numbers represented by the equation are known as "fixed-weight" or Laspeyres indexes; there are other types.

20. Because stock splits are usually undertaken to improve liquidity, it is possible that the price after the split will be somewhat higher than $25, but for the sake of simplicity this slight complication will be ignored.

21. This is the reason, as noted in an earlier note, the DJI has no identifiable base-period value. It should be noted that in all three indexes, the components change from time to time, usually because a company disappears by merger or (in the case of the NYSE) because additional companies are listed. For the DJI, this is another occasion for changing the multiplier.

22. Shleifer (1986) provided evidence that the demand curves for particular stocks do have this property. Although his research did not consider new issues or repurchases, it is relevant to the general topic of stock indexes. He looked at a large number of cases where a company was first included in the S&P500, as will happen when for some reason—usually a merger—an existing component of the index is dropped. This affects the market price because index funds (discussed in Chapter 3) usually invest in all the 500 stocks in the S&P index, so they will buy the new component whenever there is a substitution. Shleifer showed that these purchases tend to increase the price of the new component. He did not estimate the elasticity, however, and subsequent attempts to do so (particularly by Loderer et al., 1991) have not been conclusive.

23. It is similar in scope to the relevant national balance sheet figure given in Chapter 2, but calculated independently.

Chapter 7. Security Analysis

1. This is true even for a firm that has no earnings and consequently pays no tax. The tax change will not only influence any future earnings but it will also affect the value a prospective buyer will attach to the firm's assets.

2. Growth is measured by each sector's contribution to National Income, which is the sum of all payments to factors of production. National Income is in current dollars,

which means it is not adjusted for inflation. It might have been more illuminating to show growth rates of GNP by industry—which is calculated at both current and constant prices and in much greater detail—but the relevant figures from the NIPAs are currently being revised and unavailable. In any case, National Income by sector is not very different from GNP by sector in current dollars.

3. Estimates of income elasticities (and also of price elasticities, considered in the next paragraph) for a large number of consumption categories can be found in Houthakker and Taylor (1970).

4. Any industry's sales can be divided into intermediate sales (i.e., sales to other industries for use as raw materials or components) and final sales. The latter can be divided into sales to households, sales to other industries for capital formation, sales to governments of all levels, and sales to the Rest of the World. Intermediate sales are the main subject of input-output analysis, also known as interindustry economics.

5. Nevertheless, industries with above-average productivity increases tend to have above-average increases in output (Houthakker, 1979). Increases in productivity, incidentally, have three sources: technological advances, economies of scale, and improvements in the quality of labor (particularly as a result of education).

6. In the Standard Industrial Classification, sectors and industries are identified by numbers with varying numbers of digits. Table 7.1 deals largely with "one-digit" industries (sectors); the next table refers to selected "two-digit" industries. For the analysis of industry structure it is often necessary to consider three-digit or four-digit industries because they are more homogeneous.

7. A remarkable contrast between these high-growth industries, both of which were subject to government regulation until the early 1980s, emerges from the standard deviations given in the last column. Dividends from airlines had the highest volatility of any industry shown, whereas telephone dividends had the lowest.

8. Attentive readers may recall the formula relating dividend growth to the price-dividend ratio at the end of Section 6.1 and wonder whether Table 7.2 can be used to calculate such ratios. The answer, unfortunately, is that it cannot. This is not only because the growth rates are not on a per-share basis, but more importantly because the formula just referred does not take account of the uncertainty expressed in the last column of the table. Adjusting the formula for uncertainty requires more advanced mathematics than is assumed in this book.

9. We also refer to the discussion of exchange rates in Chapter 2.

10. "Consistent with" does not necessarily mean "equal." Some firms in an industry may cater to a more rapidly growing segment of the market than other firms; thus some apparel retailers concentrate on the "high end" of the market whereas others supply more basic needs. When income is rising, the former will have higher growth rates than the latter, but this need not be inconsistent with competitive equilibrium.

11. It is also possible that some firms have found a fast-growing "niche" in an otherwise slow-growing industry. The demand for food as a whole has a low income elasticity, but we all know "luxury" food items with a high income elasticity.

12. The idea that focus has a positive effect is a fairly recent one. In the 1970s the formation of "conglomerates" was justified by the alleged advantages of diversification. Conglomerates included a large number of unrelated lines of business. More recently they have fallen out of favor—partly because highly diversified firms are difficult to manage and partly because diversification is more appropriately practiced by investors rather than

by firms. In many cases the former conglomerates have spun off some of their lines of business, or they have issued separate classes of common stock whose dividends reflect the earnings of a segment of the corporation. General Motors, for instance, has separate shares for its Hughes aerospace subsidiary.

13. Thus IBM, which had built up strong customer loyalty in mainframe computers and initially also in personal computers, lost its dominance of the latter market when its relatively high-priced products ceased to be sufficiently distinctive.

14. As mentioned in earlier chapters, it is highly desirable that these statements be expressed in terms of replacement cost rather than historical cost. Among other defects, the use of historical cost tends to reduce depreciation charges, thus leading to overstated earnings and a shortage of internal financing when obsolete or worn-out capacity has to be replaced.

15. Although we cannot discuss it in detail, one complication involving reported earnings has to be mentioned. Corporations will sometimes report special charges or (more rarely) special credits. The special charges are often related to restructuring or downsizing, which force the firm to write down some of its assets, or to make provisions for severance payments to redundant employees. Special credits usually arise from the profitable sale of a division or other part of the firm. Special charges reduce stockholders' equity, whereas special credits increase it.

16. It should also be borne in mind that published data on assets reflect Generally Accepted Accounting Principles, whose inadequacies from an economic point of view have been emphasized throughout this book. To be really illuminating, a security analysis should include estimates of asset values and depreciation at replacement cost.

17. Product differentiation is often accomplished at the expense of economies of scale.

18. In Section 7.2.2 we emphasized the importance of productivity growth on the industry level. It is no less important for individual firms, but the data for analyzing it are rarely available. Security analysis would be much more revealing if it could be extended to cover productivity.

19. Technically, the optimal combination will equate the ratio of the marginal products of any two inputs to the inverse of the ratio of their prices.

20. There are two complications, however. The first is that the *PVD* formula assumes that *DIV* (0) has just been paid, whereas *EPS* (0) is still accruing; the necessary adjustment is left as an exercise to the reader. The second (and more important) is that some firms have earnings but do not pay dividends. For such firms, the assumption of a constant payout ratio does not make much sense, if only because the tax code does not permit profitable firms to dispense with dividends altogether. This second complication is especially relevant to new firms, considered briefly at the end of the current section.

21. We are not discussing established firms that had to suspend their dividends because of losses. For this category, the type of competitive analysis presented in this chapter is particularly important; it should obviously include an explanation of how the firm got into its predicament and an assessment of the firm's remaining strengths on which an eventual return to profitability might be based.

22. We put this statement in the past tense because in 1992 the price of IBM shares dropped sharply when the company announced a major "restructuring," involving massive charges to the balance sheet and substantial reductions in personnel. Apparently the efficiency and market power that had made IBM highly profitable for decades—to the point

where it was considered a model for American companies—have suffered serious erosion. General Motors, another giant with rather similar characteristics, had to cope with the same problems. The strategies that enabled IBM and GM to dominate their respective industries proved to be vulnerable in the long run to new competition—from personal computers in the case of IBM and from foreign manufacturers in the case of GM.

23. Some estimates of q are worth mentioning at this point. They refer to the world's fifty largest nonfinancial corporations in 1987, as listed by *Fortune*. The five highest q's belonged to foreign companies, four of them Japanese and one German; they ranged between 2.95 and 2.34. The U.S. company with the highest q was Occidental Petroleum at 2.32; AT&T was not far behind. Only eleven of these fifty well-established companies had q's of less than 1, and only one of these (Atlantic Richfield, an oil company) was American. IBM, used as an example in the text, was slightly below the median with a q of 1.25; other American giants, such as Texaco, Ford, and General Motors, had similar q's. Among the several surprises in these estimates is that Chrysler had a distinctly higher q than its two main competitors.

24. As discussed in Section 6.2, this formula needs to be amended if the firm has liabilities such as bonds. Apart from this complication, the q-based measure overstates true profitability when intangible assets are important to the firm.

Chapter 8. Options and Options Pricing

1. In the context of options and futures, the term "margin" has nothing to do with credit, contrary to its meaning in connection with securities (see Chapter 5). The subject of margins in the present context is taken up in Chapter 9.

2. This is the only exchange specializing in options, and currently the leader in volume of trading. Originally part of the Chicago Board of Trade, it has since become independent.

3. This statement needs some qualifications. Before the third Friday, the "current" month is the calendar month, but after the third Friday the "current" month is the next calendar month.

4. Under present practice, the idea of maturity cycles applies only to the last month listed. These cycles have, in effect, become an anachronism; it would be simpler just to list the next three months for each stock. We should also mention the recent introduction of long-term options (known as "leaps"), which have maturities as long as 3 years but are not offered for every month.

5. Striking prices that have become remote from the prevailing market price, however, may be restricted to "liquidation only," which means that no new positions with these striking prices can be opened. In any case, the trading is most active in options whose striking price is close to the market price.

6. Clearinghouses, which originated in futures trading, are discussed in greater detail in Chapter 9.

7. This is the last price at which a trade took place, so the last prices of different options were not necessarily recorded at the same time. For options that were not traded, there is no last price, but normally there would still be a bid price and an asking price.

8. In the three diagrams of this section, the exercise price is $15 and the option price is $2. For typographical reasons, the slope may not appear to be 1 or -1, but by looking at the ticks on the axes the reader can convince himself that it is correct.

9. Transaction costs will be ignored for the time being, as will be dividends paid on

the stock. The figures do not show the interest foregone, which depends on the holding time of the option.

10. This term comes from the common practice of listing options with the same maturity but different exercise prices on successive lines, as was done in Table 8.1.

11. Clearly the investor gives up the chance of a large profit in case the stock were to rise sharply. That is why this spread makes sense only if the investor is mildly bullish.

12. This statement ignores the fact that exchange-traded stock options correspond to a round lot of 100 shares, not to one share; the reader will have no difficulty in correcting it. As explained in Section 8.2, the risk inherent in a call-stock combination can be reduced by writing more calls than the number of shares (in round lots) held. This is called "overwriting."

13. The reader will find it instructive to detect the numerical assumptions implicit in Figure 8.5.

14. This argument assumes that the options will only be exercised at maturity (provided it is profitable to do so). We demonstrate later that this assumption is satisfied for a call on a no-dividend stock but not necessarily for a put.

15. "Approximately" because the striking price has to be discounted. The approximation will be very close if the discount rate is low and/or the maturity of the option is nearby.

16. The subject was first seriously studied by the French mathematician Bachelier (1901, 1913). Although his first work was entitled *Theory of Speculation,* it actually dealt mostly with options, particularly on bonds.

17. However, the options currently traded on exchanges in Europe are not necessarily European options; the more flexible American type has become widely accepted. A few European options are traded on American exchanges. The distinction between European and American options is conceptual, not geographical. We should add that there are also Asian and many other types of options, very few of which are traded on organized exchanges. These "exotic" options are discussed by Hull (1993, ch. 16).

18. The opposite holds for a put option. Puts will only be mentioned explicitly when their characteristics differ from calls.

19. In the exchange-traded options on which this chapter focuses, the striking price is not adjusted for dividends.

20. It may be objected that since a European call cannot be exercised before maturity, the prior behavior of the stock price is irrelevant. However, a European option can be sold before maturity, and its price at any time will reflect, among other things, the prevailing price of the stock.

21. This is an important contrast between options contracts and the futures contracts discussed in later chapters. A futures contract must be executed or closed out by an offsetting contract even if this involves a substantial loss, whereas an option can simply be left unexercised. It should also be recalled that the writer of an option, unlike the holder, does have a definite obligation to buy or sell if the holder so desires.

22. From Section 5.3.4 we know that there is a question whether time should be measured in calendar days or trading days. For the reasons given there, trading days are usually more appropriate; see Hull (1993, 230–232) for a more detailed discussion.

23. Its publication happened to coincide with the introduction of exchange-traded options (see Section 8.1.1), and computer programs based on it are in common use.

24. The coefficient of variation is the standard deviation divided by the mean. It is independent of the units in which the random variable is expressed.

25. This partial derivative is known in the trade as the "delta" of the option. It is closely related to the "hedge ratio" mentioned in Section 8.2.4, and gives the minimum-risk combination of shares to calls in "overwriting," as defined in Section 8.1.4.

26. Apart from the classical theory of partial differential equations, the main tool is stochastic calculus, a powerful technique for analyzing random variables in continuous time. A good introduction to stochastic calculus, including many important applications to economics, is Malliaris and Brock (1981).

27. The word "fractional" is used because most options have a lifetime of less than 1 year.

28. The "hedge ratio" or "neutral hedge ratio", h, played a central part in the original derivation of option values by Black and Scholes (1973). As in earlier sections, we ignore the fact that exchange-traded calls correspond to round lots, not to single shares. The hedge ratio is relevant to overwriting (see Sections 8.1.4 and 8.2.2) because for very small changes in the stock price, the risk of a share-call combination using that ratio is zero. For larger price changes, however, the risk is positive because h depends on the stock price and other variables.

29. Another way of seeing this is to divide the value of a call option in two parts: the *exercise value* (the difference between the striking price and the current stock price, provided it is positive) and the *time value*, which reflects the probability that the option will be worth more in the future than at present. An out-of-the-money or at-the-money option, for instance, has no exercise value, but it does have a time value (see Table 8.1). Anyone who exercises an American option before maturity sacrifices the time value, which is normally positive.

30. When there are no taxes, the stock price, immediately before it goes ex-dividend, should equal the ex-dividend price plus the dividend. If some traders are subject to tax and others (foreigners, for instance) are not, this equality may not hold. In recent years Japanese investors have often bought high-yielding American equities just before the ex-dividend date, only to sell them again thereafter.

31. As was done in the early sections of this chapter, we use discrete-time instead of continuous-time discounting at this point.

32. The details of this approximation, which can also be applied to American calls on dividend-paying stocks, are beyond our scope. A useful introduction may be found in Tucker (1990, ch. 14) and a more explicit derivation in Hull (1993, 367–369).

33. Two other parameters also present some problems. There may be disagreement about the risk-free rate, but the option value is usually not very sensitive to moderate changes in that parameter. The remaining life of the option depends on whether time is measured in calendar days or in trading days; in other words, on the treatment of weekends and holidays. This treatment makes a significant difference only in options that are close to expiration, and the evidence cited in Chapter 5 suggests that trading days are the better measure.

34. Consequently, the bond and the option constitute a single financial instrument. Sometimes corporations issue separate call options on their own shares. Such options are known as *warrants;* they usually have a long life and are traded on the same exchange as the shares themselves. Some warrants were originally offered as "sweeteners" in a financial reorganization in which bondholders were forced to take a loss.

35. This proposition could be tested empirically by verifying whether holders of convertible bonds ever convert before maturity. It should also be noted that conversion on a significant scale will dilute the equity of the issuing corporation (see Chapter 3).

36. In addition to these widely used indexes, a special index of 100 stocks (known as the OEX) has been developed solely for the purpose of options trading.

Chapter 9. Futures Contracts and Futures Markets

1. Data on the activity in various groups of markets will be found in Table 9.1 near the end of this chapter.

2. The term *commodities* refers throughout to tangible commodities such as wheat, gold, and sugar, not to financial instruments. In practice, the term is often used loosely, and financial futures are usually traded through the commodity division of a brokerage house.

3. Recall, however, that it is only the buyer of a put or call who has an option to exercise, whereas the seller of an option does have a definite obligation, namely to sell to the holder of a call or buy from the holder of a put. As shown in Section 9.3.2, buying a futures contract is equivalent to simultaneously selling a put and buying a call.

4. In the finance literature, futures and forward contracts are sometimes distinguished by a different criterion. Instead of emphasizing standardization, the distinction is based there on the presence or absence of "marking to market" (see Section 9.4). Actually this feature of futures contracts is of secondary importance at best, since it is unlikely that the futures market would have evolved merely for the purpose of permitting marking to market.

5. The vulnerability of this arrangement became apparent several years ago in the case of tin, where a large trader (the International Tin Council) unexpectedly defaulted on its commitments. As a result, the LME was forced to halt forward trading in tin, and it took a few years before it could be resumed.

6. The "shorts" are those who have sold futures or forward contracts and therefore ultimately have to make delivery of the underlying commodity; the "longs," who have bought contracts, must accept delivery.

7. The observant reader may be surprised that there is no reference to an intention to make or take delivery. This omission is made in part because many futures traders have no such intention, and also because of the recent introduction of "cash settlement" contracts, discussed in Section 9.3.1.

8. Such a contract is known as a "leverage contract"; its legal status has been a matter of dispute.

9. Only one such bill has ever become law: Futures trading in onions was banned in the late 1950s, and the ban remains in effect. The introduction of new futures contracts, however, requires approval of the Commodity Futures Trading Commission (see Chapter 11).

10. No money changes hands between buyer and seller when the initial contract is established, and title to the underlying commodity or financial instrument does not pass until delivery is completed. The only way in which the buyer or seller can get out of their respective obligations is by "closing out" their contracts through an offsetting sale or purchase.

11. From time to time, commodity exchanges have introduced alternative contracts (say, for Pacific Coast wheat) calling for delivery in a different area than the main contract, but these alternatives have invariably failed for lack of business. To be successful, a futures contract must be broadly based, and if a broadly based contract does not serve the needs of professional traders (producers, processors, and merchants in the case of

physical commodities; issuers, investors, and intermediaries in the case of financial instruments), futures trading is not viable.

12. It would be simpler to say that the spot price and the futures price converge at delivery time, but that is not altogether correct when the contract permits delivery in several grades and locations. For a more detailed discussion, see Teweles and Jones (1987) or Tucker (1990).

13. By way of contrast, consider a lottery that pays off according to the final price of an expiring future: For instance, ticket 2,317 wins if the final price is 23.17. Does this lottery have any effect on the market price?

14. In addition to delivery and offset, a third method of liquidating a futures position is known as an "exchange for physicals." It involves a swap between two traders, one of whom gives up a certain number of futures contracts and the other a certain quantity of the physical commodity (not necessarily of deliverable quality).

15. See, however, note 19 below.

16. Conceivably, stock index futures could call for delivery in shares of an "index fund" (see Chapter 3). When these futures started trading in 1982, few such funds existed; since then they have become quite substantial.

17. In the United States, cash settlement is not used for any commodity futures, but in the United Kingdom, one important commodity futures contract is settled in cash, using a price index calculated by the International Petroleum Exchange: the Brent crude oil contract (named for an oil field in the North Sea), which has assumed a central place in worldwide petroleum trading. Cash settlement was adopted after physical delivery proved to be unattractive to traders. On this contract, see also Mollgaard and Phlips (1992).

18. This multiplier has nothing to do with the fact that the S&P index in question happens to cover 500 stocks. The futures contract based on the NYSE Composite Index (reflecting the prices of some 2,000 stocks) uses the same multiplier.

19. Certain other index futures have also been introduced with some success. These are a U.S. dollar index, representing the value of the dollar in relation to a basket of other currencies; an index of municipal bond prices; and two indexes of commodity futures prices.

20. If the futures contract, unlike the S&P500 contract, involved delivery, the holder or writer would run the risk of having to take or make delivery. To eliminate this risk, futures options usually expire before delivery on the underlying futures contract is possible. Because of the intimate connection between futures options and futures contracts for a particular financial instrument or commodity, the two are always traded on the same exchange; this is not necessarily true of options on "physicals" such as equities and currencies.

21. A good introduction will be found in Hull (1993, section 11.5). The discussion in Tucker (1990, ch. 19) is useful on the conceptual level, but is marred by misprints in the formulas.

22. In Section 9.3.1 we mentioned price discovery as one of the functions of futures trading. This function means that up-to-date market information is valuable and can be sold. Like the stock exchanges, the futures exchanges derive substantial revenues from the sale of "market data."

23. The same word is used on stock exchanges in connection with security credit, but in the futures context the term has nothing to do with credit and is more accurately described as "earnest money." It is sometimes argued that the stock index futures markets

have an unfair advantage over the stock exchanges because in the former the margin is usually less than 10% of the contract value, whereas in the latter buyers may have to put up as much as 50% of the value of their purchases. Actually, this comparison is meaningless since the word "margin" is used in two different senses. In the options markets, "margin" means the same as in futures markets, but it is required only from the shorts (that is, the writers of options).

24. In addition to these two mechanisms, clearinghouses can also count on credit from the Federal Reserve if all else fails. The position of the clearinghouses in the U.S. financial sector is so central that they cannot be allowed to default on their obligations.

25. Trading on and just before "first notice day," which inaugurates the delivery process, is of special importance in those futures markets that do not use cash settlement. Much of the speculation among professionals centers on how many notices will be issued and how many will be stopped; thus the prospect that many notices will not be stopped tends to depress prices. The volume of trading usually picks up during that period.

26. In addition, there are the options markets, including both options on futures and options on physicals. To keep the discussion simple, we do not consider options in this section; the interested reader will have no difficulty in taking them into account.

27. This is the economic definition of hedging; the legal definition is different in that it does not require the actual existence of forward contracts in the case of certain commercial traders. The legal definition is important because the law treats speculators more strictly than hedgers.

28. A "spread," in this context, is the difference between two futures prices.

29. Another example is known as the "ted-spread" and involves offsetting positions in T-bill futures and Eurodollar futures. The underlying financial instruments both have a life of three months, but T-bills are default-free whereas Eurodollar deposits are not. The yield on Eurodollars is typically 10% to 20% higher than the yield on T-bills; thus when the T-bill yield is 4% the Eurodollar yield is likely to be around 4.6%.

30. An even more recent development, not yet found in the United States, is futures trading in services. The only example to date involves an index of cargo freight rates, which are quite volatile. Futures on this index are traded by an affiliate of the Baltic Exchange in London, the center of world shipping.

31. The first bargain may, of course, involve more than one contract, in which case our discussion needs some obvious modification.

32. From figures in the CFTC *Annual Report* it appears that in 1989 only 4% of the average open interest in grain futures was settled by delivery. This percentage was even smaller for livestock and energy futures but somewhat larger for oilseed and metal futures.

33. The long or short position of a floor trader may exist for no more than a few minutes, but such positions are not included in the open interest, which is measured at the end of the trading day. Floor traders do not normally leave their positions open overnight.

34. These categories do not correspond to those distinguished in Section 9.4.1.

35. This is also true for most of the futures markets not covered by the table.

36. This figure may suggest an alarming risk exposure by participants, many of which are banks. Studies by the Federal Reserve suggest, however, that the exposure is not in the trillions but in the hundreds of billions, which is somewhat less alarming. The rapid growth in the swap market has posed problems not only for regulators but also for accountants, who must somehow indicate the risk exposure on the balance sheet.

Chapter 10. Futures Prices

1. This important subject is outside the scope of this book; for a thorough discussion, see Stein (1986).

2. For financial instruments the warehouse and insurance components are negligible. The net carrying cost of the bond just mentioned will be negative if its yield exceeds the financing cost. For example, if the yield is 8% then the net carrying cost to a trader who can borrow at 5% will be −3%.

3. Except for the interest foregone on the "margin" (see Chapter 9), which is generally a small amount. In fact, traders with sizable net positions are usually allowed to deposit margin in the form of Treasury bills whose yield accrues to the trader, and short hedgers may not have to deposit margin at all.

4. In this and the following example, the long position is assumed to be deliverable (see Chapter 9). Short hedging is not confined to deliverable supplies; indeed, most of it involves nondeliverable supplies, whose prices do not necessarily converge to the futures price at maturity.

5. Thus if the price difference were 30 cents it would pay to buy wheat now, sell May wheat futures, pay the storage of 20 cents per bushel, and deliver the wheat on the May contract. The profit would be 10 cents per bushel without any risk. As a result of these purchases and sales, either the spot price would rise or the May futures price would fall, or both. This arbitrage would continue until the basis is reduced to 20 cents.

6. Strictly speaking, there is a trivial limit: The basis cannot exceed the spot price itself, since the futures price cannot be negative.

7. The convenience yield (Kaldor, 1939) on a firm's inventory may be defined as the additional net profit resulting from a $1 increase in inventories at constant prices. A merchant, for instance, will be able to satisfy more customers (and hence make greater profits) if he or she has a larger assortment from which to choose. A manufacturer will have fewer interruptions in the production process if more needed inputs are on hand. The convenience yield is inversely related to the size of the inventory. When the inventory is large to begin with, an additional dollar's worth will not generate additional profits, and may indeed translate into a net loss. When the inventory is small, the convenience yield is high.

8. The futures contract on Treasury bonds assumes an 8% coupon, but other long-term bonds (within certain limits) are deliverable subject to premiums or discounts. In recent years, no T-bonds with an 8% coupon and a remaining life of 30 years have been outstanding; this means that there is no spot price for T-bonds corresponding exactly to the futures prices, and consequently no basis as defined earlier. Note also that the interest on bonds is payable twice a year, so the yield on an 8% bond trading at par is actually 8.12% (see Chapter 4).

9. The same analysis applies to T-bill futures and to the recently introduced futures markets in 1-month Eurodollars and 30-day Federal Funds.

10. In reality the size of a Eurodollar futures contract is $1 million, but the needed adjustments are left to the reader.

11. The multiplier is needed because the price is expressed in terms of a $1 face value.

12. The reason for using London futures is that the relevant spot rates are quoted only there. Although the Chicago futures market is much more active, the time differen-

tial makes it difficult to compare Chicago futures with London spot rates. The particular date was chosen (as were the dates in Figure 10.1) so as to match the spot 3-month Eurodollar contract with the futures contracts.

13. The deeper reason for this absence appears to be that the gross carrying cost is essentially the Eurodollar rate itself, so that we have to look at other segments of the spot market to find meaningful restrictions on the futures prices.

14. This is true for any futures contract, not just for foreign currency futures.

15. In practice, the relevant rates are the Eurodollar rate and the Euromark rate, both of which refer to claims and liabilities, denominated in the respective currencies, of banks with respect to each other. As shown in the previous example, there are several maturities, among which 3 months is the most actively traded; this maturity is used in the present example. The spectrum of rates is quoted every day in London, the center of Eurocurrency trading.

16. In the literature on international finance a distinction is made between "covered interest parity," where the exchange risk has been eliminated through the futures positions, and "uncovered interest parity," which holds if the return in dollars on an investment in a German financial instrument were equal to the return on the corresponding American financial instrument (and conversely for the return in marks). It can easily be verified that in the presence of futures trading these two concepts are identical.

17. The terms *contango* and *backwardation* are more commonly used in British than in American futures markets, but they are convenient for our purposes.

18. In the case of silver or any other commodity, the net carrying cost would be positive since they have no money yield.

19. In Chapter 11 we show that even in silver the basis may differ temporarily from the carrying cost if the spot and futures markets are distorted by manipulation.

20. It also applies to nonseasonal commodities in which inventories are held only for commercial reasons rather than as a store of value.

21. The axes in Figure 10.8 depend on the units of measurement. A more general formulation would express the basis as a percentage of the spot price and inventories as a percentage of annual consumption.

22. If the two standard deviations are assumed to be the same, the coefficient cannot be equal to 1 since this would cause singularity in Equations 10.7 and 10.8.

23. The portfolio analysis of this section can also be applied, with some modifications, to speculative behavior. We should add that hedging can also be explained by other models. One alternative explanation is that the profits of merchants—an important category of hedgers—vary directly with the size of their inventories, and that banks will finance a higher fraction of inventories if they are hedged. By hedging, therefore, a merchant with a given net worth can operate with a larger inventory.

24. The word "basis" is put in quotes to distinguish it from its more common meaning (also maintained elsewhere in this chapter), which is the cash price of the standard grade and location less the price of the expiring (or dominant) future.

25. The hedge ratio is the coefficient of the cash price in this regression.

26. The only qualification to this statement has to do with certain futures arbitrageurs, specifically intermarket spreaders and intercommodity spreaders (see Section 9.4.1); the intermonth spreaders' position aggregates to zero, so they do not affect the identity. To make the statement correct, we should consider the first two types of spreaders as speculators.

27. These other users could be farmers who use grain to feed their livestock, or dealers who have made forward sales without having inventories to cover them. For simplicity, they are included among the manufacturers.

28. The theoretical argument was first stated by Hicks (1946). The empirical evidence of imbalance was mostly in statistics of "Commitments of Traders," published until a few years ago by the Commodity Futures Trading Commission and its predecessors (see Chapter 11). These statistics classified large traders into speculators and hedgers, and the former were usually found to be net long. Several empirical analyses, starting with (Houthakker, 1957), were based on these data. The CFTC no longer publishes statistics with this classification; instead, it divides large traders into commercial and noncommercial, which is often considered to be similar to the old classification.

29. Keynes wrote long before the formulation of the Capital Asset Pricing Model. The discussion of CAPM in Chapter 6 showed that investors are rewarded only for assuming nondiversifiable risk. It appears, however, that the correlation between commodities and other investment assets is generally quite low, so that most of the risk in futures speculation is in fact nondiversifiable. CAPM was first applied to futures trading by Dusak (1973). However, Stein (1986, ch. 1) argued persuasively that CAPM—at least in its simplest form—does not apply to futures markets.

30. Those were the commodities that Keynes had in mind, but it does not follow that his theory is irrelevant to seasonal commodities. Although it would take us too far to pursue this case, the observable implications of normal backwardation are also found in most seasonal futures markets. We should also mention that in Keynes's time there were no true futures markets in Britain, so he did not usually distinguish between futures and forward trading.

31. We used only one, rather distant, contract because the chart would otherwise be difficult to read. The spot price may not correspond to actual transactions; it is derived by the Chicago Mercantile Exchange from earlier London quotations and subsequent changes in futures prices.

32. In the course of this arbitrage the Eurodollar and Euromark interest rates may change, but that does not affect the argument.

33. Rutledge (1976) looked at one futures contract in each of four commodities, and found that two agreed with the conjecture and two did not.

34. The most important class of financial futures, those on interest rates, could not be included because of unresolved problems created by the quotation in terms of prices rather than the rates themselves. It should also be noted that the copper contract in Table 10.3 is not the "high-grade" contract traded at present but an earlier version.

35. Except in the case of crude oil, where for technical reasons only the nearest 8 months (out of a possible 12) could be used. The situation in copper is more complicated: There are six "major" months, traded for a year or more before expiration, and six "minor" months, in which there is (not very active) trading only for a relatively short period. In Table 10.3 these minor months are ignored.

36. Primary securities are financial instruments with an identifiable issuer such as a corporation or a government; equities and bonds are the most important examples. Futures and options are sometimes called "derivative" instruments because they are derived from primary securities but do not themselves have an identifiable issuer. Swaps, discussed in Chapter 9, are also considered to be derivatives.

37. Program trading is defined by the New York Stock Exchange as the simultane-

ous sale or purchase of fifteen or more different equities with a total value of at least $1 million. Such transactions are performed by computer programs, hence the name. There are types of program trading that do not involves arbitrage against stock index futures, but only the latter type is relevant to this chapter. According to the 1993 NYSE *Fact Book,* all types of program trading accounted for 5.5% of the total volume on the exchange. Although there are other stock index futures, the S&P500 futures are believed to be the main vehicle for index arbitrage.

38. In this respect, the stock index futures are just like the interest-rate futures discussed earlier. When the dividend yield on the S&P500 exceeds the financing cost, for instance, the futures price will be below the spot index.

39. In addition, there may be some lingering concern about the "triple witching hour," the simultaneous expiration of stock index futures, stock options, and options on futures that occurs on the third Friday of March, June, September, and December. In the early days of stock index futures, before their characteristics were widely understood, this occasionally coincided with a sizable fall in share prices, but in recent years it has led to nothing more alarming than a rise in stock market volume.

40. The possibility of futures trading in individual shares has often been discussed but appears to be far from realization. The large-capitalization stocks that are candidates for futures trading would then no longer be handled by specialists, whose function in actively traded stocks is relatively minor anyway (see Chapter 5).

41. There are also more small price changes than predicted by normal or lognormal assumptions; it is the medium-sized price changes that are deficient.

42. These markets were used because of the ready availability of daily data extending to the recent past. Using them does not reflect any intention to prove a point, but their selection cannot be considered random. A more comprehensive sample could be obtained at some cost (mostly in terms of computation), and the interested reader is encouraged to explore the question with other futures contracts.

43. This happens to be the estimate given by Keynes (1923) in his original statement of the theory of normal backwardation, though it is not altogether clear how he arrived at it. Houthakker (1968) came up with similar estimates.

44. The Eurodollar results also serve to bring out an important relation: Normal backwardation implies that the yield curve (shown in Figure 10.1) is rising. This is why normal backwardation, which might seem to be relevant only to futures, plays a part in the theoretical work of Hicks (1946) mentioned earlier.

Chapter 11. Regulation of Financial Markets

1. A curious example arose in the early 1980s when stock index futures (discussed in Chapter 9) were being designed. The Dow-Jones Industrial Index is the most widely followed index and would have been the natural basis for a futures contract. Although the Dow-Jones Company could have earned large royalties if its index were so used, it refused to participate on the ground that this would encourage speculation. Presumably the company is also unhappy about purchases of its *Wall Street Journal* by speculators, but it has done nothing to stop them.

2. One aspect of interest should be mentioned because it has given rise to a considerable amount of legislation, some of which is still in the statute books. This is usury, defined as the charging of excessive rates of interest. Whether laws against usury are

desirable is a question outside our scope. It seems fair to say, however, that the need for such laws has been reduced by more active competition in the financial sector and by disclosure requirements, some of which go by the name of "truth in lending."

3. For many purposes, including the present discussion, land may be considered a particular form of capital.

4. The Federal Reserve has the power to buy almost any financial instrument (presumably including equities) in case of a financial crisis, but it has never had to exercise that power.

5. One reason is the difficulty of proving collusion: Traders may be behaving in similar fashion (many of them trying to buy or sell at the same time) without having agreed to do so. This herd behavior may be the result of a common reaction to some news item, or of widespread feelings of euphoria or despondency. It takes courage, in Kipling's words, to "keep your head while all around you are losing theirs." In some older writings on financial markets—MacKay (1841, reprinted many times) is the *locus classicus*—such phenomena were emphasized, but the Efficient Market Hypothesis that dominates contemporary thinking has no place for them. Recent theoretical work on "rational bubbles" testifies to a renewed interest in these phenomena, though relevant empirical evidence is scarce. Kindleberger (1989) deals with the same topic as MacKay but is more reliable and analytical.

6. Financial intermediaries (particularly brokers and mutual fund managers) have a fiduciary responsibility toward their customers, which means that they are supposed to take the client's best interest into account. Most intermediaries have found such a policy to be good business in the long run, but there are always some who look only for short-term profits.

7. Some of the short interest, identified as such in the statistics, is due to arbitrage and has no great significance for the future course of prices. Thus, if a Canadian stock is listed on the American Stock Exchange, there will be considerable buying and selling in both Toronto and New York aimed at profiting from temporary disparities in prices, and in the process eliminating these disparities.

8. In the over-the-counter market, where there are no exchanges, the National Association of Securities Dealers (NASD) has similar responsibilities. Its power stems in part from its automated quotation system known as NASDAQ (see Chapter 5).

9. The states also have regulatory bodies, whose role is essentially supplementary to the SEC. They tend to focus on new issues of local importance.

10. It is also required by the Internal Revenue Service, but tax returns are not normally made public.

11. A recent example has to do with the obligations of corporations to their retired employees (mostly on account of pensions and health benefits). Since these obligations are often incorporated in union contracts and other binding promises, they are in effect a liability that should appear as such on the balance sheet. Until recently, however, most corporations treated payments under this heading merely as a current expense without showing anything on their balance sheet. The FASB now requires corporations to make explicit provision for future payments to retirees. As a result, some large corporations have had to make charges of billions of dollars to their current earnings, often turning reported profits into losses.

12. More generally, an insider is anyone who possesses information that is not publicly available. A few years ago, a printer was held to have violated the rules because he

had worked on a forthcoming prospectus and had used the knowledge thus obtained to trade in the firm's shares.

13. There is some potential overlap in the jurisdiction of the two commissions, particularly in the area of options. An accord was reached some years ago under which the SEC is responsible for stock options and for those options on indexes that do not involve futures trading; the CFTC has authority over options on futures (see Chapter 9). Another potential conflict arises from stock index futures, which the SEC views with some suspicion and would like to regulate; so far, however, the CFTC has retained jurisdiction over these futures. Proposals to merge the two agencies have been considered by Congress but no action has been taken.

14. Some of this information is also available to the clearinghouses associated with the exchanges (see Chapter 9), but these organizations deal only with their own members and do not know the positions of customers of their broker-members. The exchanges and the clearinghouses do watch the delivery process rather closely.

15. The concept of manipulation is not as clear-cut as lawyers would wish; although it is a crime, prosecution is difficult. For an economic analysis of manipulation, see Pirrong (1993).

16. One of us (H. S. H.) was the principal economic witness for the plaintiff, a Peruvian company in charge of selling the output of that country's silver mines. The case was tried in the Federal District Court for the Southern District of New York. We have also relied on the informative and readable book by Stephen Fay (1982); although written before the Minpeco suit was filed, the account in that book was largely confirmed by subsequently discovered evidence. A recent book by Williams (1994) provides additional information and analysis.

17. This superficially plausible belief in the exhaustion of minerals was widespread in the 1970s. Actually, there is overwhelming evidence to the contrary. Historically, reserves and production of minerals have tended to increase and, after adjustment for inflation, most mineral prices are approximately trendless or have a downward trend. Silver has been particularly weak: Its price has recently been around $5 per ounce, well below the level prevailing in the middle 1970s, despite considerable inflation since then.

18. The Hunt brothers themselves did not use Conticommodities but divided their business among a large number of other brokers. Some of these also provided financing for the brothers' physical silver. In doing so, the lenders accepted unusual risks: Not only was the silver unhedged but also the borrowers were actually long in futures and thus doubly exposed to changes in silver prices. The lenders were in effect providing indirect assistance to the manipulation, and this is why they were included among the defendants in the Minpeco case. Most of them settled for many millions of dollars before the case came to trial.

19. In the 1979–1980 manipulation, one of these shorts was Minpeco, the plaintiff in the lawsuit mentioned earlier; its short position was a legitimate hedge against future sales from mines. We should add that in our view the manipulation was indeed a corner, but in the trial this term was largely avoided because of legal uncertainties that made monopolization and manipulation easier to prove. For a different view, see Telser (1992).

20. At the trial it was shown in great detail that Bunker and the leaders of the Conti group were in frequent contact by telephone and personal meetings. Together with the economic evidence, this proof of collusion was essential in convincing the jury that the defendants had illegally monopolized the silver market.

21. Causality analysis, introduced by Granger (1969), is a statistical technique in which two variables, x and y, are each regressed on their own past values and on past values of the other variable. If past values of x contribute significantly to the explanation of y but not conversely, then x is said to "Granger-cause" y. By thus defining causality as relative predictability, precision is added to the usual concept of causality, which is somewhat vague.

22. The following was not covered in the Minpeco trial; our account is based on Fay (1982) and government reports.

23. The total deliverable stock at that time was about 120 million ounces, but some of the Hunts' silver may not have been deliverable.

24. It was not the only major failure in recent decades. A few years before the silver manipulation, two potato merchants from the Pacific Northwest accumulated a large short position in Maine potato futures, ostensibly as a hedge against their inventories of Idaho potatoes. As they must have known, these potatoes were not deliverable, and at delivery time they defaulted. The effect of this default was to destroy the potato futures market, which may have been the two merchants' intention all along—the prohibition of futures trading in onions (see Chapter 9) also appears to have been instigated by merchants. These events occurred before the CFTC was organized; potato futures were regulated by its predecessor.

25. Some of these data were later published in a congressional report.

26. The total damages awarded against the defendants exceeded a quarter of a billion dollars. Bunker and Herbert Hunt maintained they were unable to pay and declared bankruptcy.

27. A somewhat similar system exists in the United States, where firms with memberships in two or more exchanges report their financial condition to only one of these. The exchange that receives these reports has to notify the other exchanges immediately if there is a problem.

Bibliography

Chapter 1. Introduction

Allen, M., et al., 1989, "International Capital Markets: Developments and Prospects," *International Monetary Fund Staff Papers.*

De Villiers, J. U., 1989, "Inflation, Asset Structure and the Discrepancy between Accounting and True Return," *Journal of Business Finance and Accounting* 16(4):493.

Dhaliwal, D. S., 1988, "The Effect of the Firm's Business Risk on the Choice of Accounting Methods," *Journal of Business Finance and Accounting* 15(2, summer):289.

Gilpin, A., 1986, *Dictionary of Economics and Financial Markets,* 5th ed., London: Butterworth.

Gordon, L. A., 1974, "Accounting Rate of Return vs. Economic Rate of Return," *Journal of Business Finance and Accounting* 1(3, autumn):343–356.

Gordon, L. A., and A. W. Stark, 1989, "Accounting and Economic Rates of Return: A Note on Depreciation and Other Accruals," *Journal of Business Finance and Accounting* 16(3):425.

Moore, B. J., 1975, "Equities, Capital Gains and the Role of Finance in Accumulation," *American Economic Review* 65:872–886.

Ross, S. A., 1989, "Presidential Address: Institutional Markets, Financial Marketing, and Financial Innovation," *Journal of Finance* 1(3):541–556.

Valentine, S., 1988, *International Dictionary of the Securities Industry,* 2d ed., London: Macmillan.

Chapter 2. The Place of Financial Markets in the Economy

Andersen, L., and J. Jordan, 1968, "Monetary and Fiscal Actions: A Test of Their Relative Importance in Economic Stabilization," *Federal Reserve Bank of St. Louis Review* 50(3, November):11–24.

Anderson, R., A. Ando, and J. Enzler, 1983, "Interaction between Fiscal and Monetary Policy and the Real Rate of Interest," *American Economic Review* 73(May):55–60.

Barro, R., 1974, "Are Government Bonds Net Wealth?" *Journal of Political Economy* 82(6):1095–1117.

Blanchard, O. J., 1981, "Output, the Stock Market and Interest Rates," *American Economic Review* 71:132–143.

Connock, M., and H. Hillier, 1987, "Long Bond Yields and Inflation Rates in OECD Countries: A Cross Section Study," *Applied Economics* 19(3, March):407–416.

Darrat, A. F., 1988, "On Fiscal Policy and the Stock Market," *Journal of Money, Credit and Banking* 29(3, August):353–363.

Demsetz, H., and K. Lehn, 1985, "The Structure of Corporate Ownership: Causes and Consequences," *Journal of Political Economy* 93:1155.

Dwyer, G. P. Jr., and R. W. Hafer, 1989, "Interest Rates and Economic Announcements," *Federal Reserve Bank of St. Louis Review* 71(2, March–April):34–46.

Evans, P., 1987, "Do Budget Deficits Raise Nominal Interest Rates? Evidence from Six Countries," *Journal of Monetary Economics* 20:281–300.

Feldstein, M., and J. H. Stock, 1994, "The Use of a Monetary Aggregate to Target Nominal GDP," in Mankiw, N. G. (ed.), *Monetary Policy*, Chicago: University of Chicago Press, 7–69.

Ferris, S. P., and A. K. Makhja, 1988, "Inflation Effect on Corporate Capital Investment," *Journal of Business Research* 16(3, May):251–260.

Fisher, I., 1930, *The Theory of Interest*, New York: Macmillan.

Friedman, M., and A. J. Schwartz, 1963, "Money and Business Cycles," *Review of Economics and Statistics* 45(suppl.) (February).

Goodhart, C. A. E., 1975, *Money, Information and Uncertainty*, London: Macmillan.

Groenewold, N., 1989, "The Adjustment of the Real Interest Rate to Inflation," *Applied Economics* 21(7):947.

Hamada, K., and K. Iwata, 1989, "On the International Capital Ownership Pattern at the Turn of the Twenty-first Century," *European Economic Review* 33:1055.

Hardouvelis, G. A., 1987, "Reserves Announcements and Interest Rates: Does Monetary Policy Matter?," *Journal of Finance* 42(2, June):407–422.

Hendershott, P. H., 1987, "A Flow-of-Funds Financial Model: Estimation and Application to Financial Policies and Reform," *Understanding Capital Markets*, vol. 1, Cambridge, MA: Heath.

Hendershott, P. H., and R. C. Lemmon, 1973, "The Financial Behavior of Households: Some Empirical Estimates," *Journal of Finance* 28:839.

Kester, W. C., 1986, "Capital and Ownership Structure: A Comparison of United States and Japanese Manufacturing Corporations," *Financial Management* 15(spring):5–16.

Kim, M. K., and C. Wu, 1987, "Macro-economic Factors and Stock Returns," *Journal of Financial Research* 10(2, summer):87–98.

Mishkin, F. W., 1995, *The Economics of Money, Banking and Financial Markets*, New York: HarperCollins.

Mullins, M., and S. B. Wadhwani, 1989, "The Effect of the Tax Reform Act on Capital Investment Decisions," *European Economic Review* 33:939.

Penati, A., 1986, "The Sources of the Movements in Interest Rates: An Empirical Investigation," *Journal of Banking and Finance* 10:343.

Rose, A. K., 1988, "Is the Real Interest Rate Stable?" *Journal of Finance* 43(5, December):1095–1112.

Sametz, A. W., and P. Wachtel, eds., 1977, "The Financial Environment and the Flow of Funds in the Next Decade," in *Understanding Capital Markets,* vol. 2, Cambridge, MA: Heath.

Sims, C. A., 1972, "Money, Income and Causality," *American Economic Review* 62(4, September):540–552.

Thornton, D. L., 1988, "The Effect of Monetary Policy on Short-term Interest Rates," *Federal Reserve Bank of St. Louis Review* 70(3, May-June):3–18.

Viren, M., 1989, "The Long-run Relationship between Interest Rates and Inflation: Some Cross-country Evidence," *Journal of Banking and Finance* 13(4–5, September):571–588.

Chapter 3. The Supply of Securities

Allen, D. S., R. E. Lamy, and G. R. Thompson, 1987, "Agency Costs and Alternative Call Provisions: An Empirical Investigation," *Financial Management* 16(winter):37–44.

Altman, E. I., 1987, "The Anatomy of the High-yield Bond Market," *Financial Analysts Journal* 43(July–August):12–25.

Altman, E. I., 1989, "The Convertible Debt Market: Are Returns Worth the Risk?" *Financial Analysts Journal* 45(July–August):23–31.

Ang, J. S., and J. H. Chua, 1982, "Mutual Funds: Different Strokes for Different Folks?" *Journal of Portfolio Management* 8(2, winter):43–50.

Blume, M. E., and D. B. Keim, 1987, "Lower-grade Bonds: Their Risk and Returns," *Financial Analysts Journal* 43(July–August):76–80.

Brauer, G. A., 1988, "Closed-end Fund Shares' Abnormal Returns and the Information Content of Discounts and Premiums," *Journal of Finance* 43(1, March):113–128.

Copeland, T. E., 1979, "Liquidity Changes Following Stock Splits," *Journal of Finance* 34(1, March):115–141.

Cox, W. M., and C. S. Lown, 1989, "The Capital Gains and Losses on US Government Debt: 1942–1987," *Review of Economics and Statistics* 71:1–14.

Eden, B., 1985, "Indexation and Related Issues: A Review Essay," *Journal of Monetary Economics* 16:259.

Ederington, L. H., J. B. Yawitz, and B. E. Roberts, 1987, "The Informational Content of Bond Ratings," *Journal of Financial Research* 10(3, fall):211–226.

Fama, E. F., L. Fisher, M. C. Jensen, and R. A. Roll, 1969, "The Adjustment of Stock Prices to New Information," *International Economic Review* (February):1–21.

Gatti, J. F., 1983, "Risk and Return on Corporate Bonds: A Synthesis," *Quarterly Review of Economics and Business* 23(2, summer):53–70.

Hickman, W. B., 1958, *Corporate Bond Quality and Investor Experience,* Princeton, NJ: Princeton University Press.

Hoffmeister, J. R., and P. A. Spindt, 1988, "The Micromechanics of the Federal Funds Market: Implications for Day-of-the-Week Effects in Funds Rate Variability," *Journal of Financial and Quantitative Analysis* 23(December):401.

Hsueh, L. P., and P. R. Chandy, 1989, "An Examination of the Yield Spreads between Insured and Uninsured Debt," *Journal of Financial Research* 12(3, fall):235–244.

Jorgenson, D. W., F. M. Gollop, and B. M. Fraumeni, 1987, *Productivity and Economic Growth,* Cambridge, MA: Harvard University Press.

Lakonishok, J., 1981, "Performance of Mutual Funds versus Their Expenses," *Journal of Bank Research* 12(2, summer).

Lown, C. S., 1987, "Money Market Deposit Accounts versus Money Market Mutual Funds," *Federal Reserve Bank of Dallas Economic Review* (November):29–38.

McCauley, R. N., and L. A. Hargraves, 1987, "Eurocommercial Paper and U.S. Commercial Paper: Converging Money Markets," *Federal Reserve Bank of New York Quarterly Review* 12(3, autumn).

Nichols, D. R., 1989, *The New Dow Jones-Irwin Guide to Zero Coupon Investments*, New York: Dow Jones-Irwin.

Park, S. Y., and M. R. Reinganum, 1983, "The Puzzling Price Behavior of Treasury Bills That Mature at the Turn of Calendar Months," *Journal of Financial Economics* 16(2, June):267–283.

Perry, K. J., and R. A. Taggart, 1988, "The Growing Role of Junk Bonds," *Journal of Applied Corporate Finance* 1(spring):37–45.

Roll, R. A., 1986, "The Hubris Hypothesis of Corporate Takeovers," *Journal of Business* 59(April):197–216.

Roulac, S. E., 1988, "Real Estate Securities Valuation," *Journal of Portfolio Management* 14(3, spring):35–39.

Scholes, M. C., and M. A. Wolfson, 1988. *Taxes and Business Strategy*, Englewood Cliffs, NJ: Prentice Hall.

Smith, C. W., Jr., 1986, "Raising Capital: Theory and Evidence," *Midland Corporate Finance Journal* 4(spring):6–22.

Thompson, S. C., 1991, "PTPs May Combine the Best of Corporate and Partnership Worlds," *Taxation for Accountants* 47(4):208–215.

Trim, T. D., ed., 1988, *The Municipal Bond Market: New Rules, New Opportunities, and New Strategies*, Washington, DC: Institute of Chartered Financial Analysts.

Wann, P., 1989, *Inside the US Treasury Market*, New York: Woodhead-Faulkner.

Woodward, G. T., 1990, "The Real Thing: A Dynamic Profile of Real Interest Rates and Inflation Expectations in the United Kingdom, 1982–1989," *Journal of Business* 63(3):373–398.

Zwick, B., 1980, "Yields on Privately-Placed Corporate Bonds," *Journal of Finance* 25(1, March):23–39.

Chapter 4. The Demand for Securities

Aivazian, V. A., 1983, "Mean-variance Utility Functions and the Demand for Risky Assets: An Empirical Analysis Using Flexible Functional Forms," *Journal of Financial and Quantitative Analysis* 18(4, December):411–424.

Ashton, D. J., 1982, "Stochastic Dominance and Mean Variance Rules in the Selection of Risky Investment," *Journal of Business Finance and Accounting* 9(4, winter):471–481.

Basu, K., 1982, "Determinateness of the Utility Function: Revisiting a Controversy of the Thirties," *Review of Economic Studies* 49:307.

Bernoulli, D., 1730, "Exposition of a New Theory on the Measurement of Risk," *Papers of the Imperial Academy of Science in St. Petersburg* 2:175–192. Translated into English by L. Sommer in *Econometrica* (January 1954):23–36.

Brookshire, D. S., M. A. Thayer, and J. Tschirhart, 1985, "A Test of the Expected Utility Model: Evidence from Earth-quake Risks," *Journal of Political Economy* 93:369.

Dialynas, C. P., 1988, "Bond Yield Spreads Revisited," *Journal of Portfolio Management* 22:305.

Fama, E. F., 1965, "The Behavior of Stock Market Prices," *Journal of Business* 38(January):34–105.

Frankfurter, G. M., and T. J. Frecka, 1979, "Efficient Portfolios and Superfluous Diversification," *Journal of Financial and Quantitative Analysis* 14(December):925.

Friedman, M., and J. L. Savage, 1948, "The Utility Analysis of Choices Involving Risk," *Journal of Political Economy* 56(August):279–304.

Green, R. C., and S. Srivastava, 1986, "Expected Utility Maximization and Demand Behavior," *Journal of Economic Theory* 38(2, April):313–323.

Kessel, R. A., 1965, *The Cyclical Behavior of the Term Structure of Interest Rates,* New York: National Bureau of Economic Research.

Levy, H., and H. M. Markowitz, 1979, "Approximating Expected Utility by a Function of Mean and Variance," *American Economic Review* 69:308–317.

Livingston, M., 1987, "Flattening of Bond Yield Curves," *Journal of Financial Research* 10(1, spring):17–24.

Machina, M. J., 1987, "Choice under Uncertainty: Problems Solved and Unsolved," *Journal of Economic Perspectives* 1(1):121–154.

Mandelbrot, B., 1963, "The Variation of Certain Speculative Prices," *Journal of Business* 36(October):394–419.

Markowitz, H. M., 1959, *Portfolio Selection: Efficient Diversification of Investments,* New York: Wiley.

Modigliani, F., and Brumberg, R., 1955, "Utility Analysis and the Consumption Function," in K. Kurihara, ed., *Post Keynesian Economics,* London: George Allen and Unwin.

Nelson, C. R., and A. F. Siegel, 1988, "Long-term Behavior of Yield Curves," *Journal of Financial and Quantitative Analysis* 23(March):105–110.

Peters, E. E., 1991, *Chaos and Order in the Capital Markets: A New View of Cycles, Prices and Market Volatility,* New York: Wiley.

Scott, L. O., 1985, "The Present Value Model of Stock Prices: Regression Tests and Monte Carlo Results," *Review of Economics and Statistics* 67(4):599–605.

Sharpe, W. F., 1967, "Portfolio Analysis," *Journal of Financial and Quantitative Analysis* 2(2, June):425–439.

Sharpe, W. F., and G. J. Alexander, 1992, *Investments,* 4th ed., Englewood Cliffs, NJ: Prentice Hall.

Shiller, R. J., 1990, "The Term Structure of Interest Rates," in B. M. Friedman and F. H. Hahn (eds.), *Handbook of Monetary Economics,* 1:627–722.

Speidell, L. S., D. H. Miller, and J. R. Ullman, 1989, "Portfolio Optimization: A Primer," *Financial Analysts Journal* 45(January–February):22–30.

Chapter 5. Securities Markets and Their Efficiency

Alexander, S. S., 1961, "Stock Prices: Random vs. Systematic Changes," *Industrial Management Review* (May):7–26.

Ashenfelter, O., 1989, "How Auctions Work for Wine and Art," *Journal of Economic Perspectives* 3(3, summer):23–26.

Ball, R. J., and P. Brown, 1968, "An Empirical Evaluation of Accounting Income Numbers," *Journal of Accounting Research* 6(autumn):159–178.

Black, F., 1971, "Implications of the Random Walk Hypothesis for Portfolio Management," *Financial Analysts Journal* 27(March–April):16–22.

Choi, J. Y., D. Salandro, and K. Shastri, 1988, "On the Estimation of Bid-ask Spreads: Theory and Evidence," *Journal of Financial and Quantitative Analysis* 23(2):219–230.

Christie, W., and P. Schultz, 1994, "Why Do NASDAQ Market Makers Avoid Odd-eighth Quotes?" *Journal of Finance* 49:1813–1840.

Controy, R. M., and R. L. Winkler, 1986, "Market Structure: The Specialist as Dealer and Broker," *Journal of Banking and Finance* 10:21.

Davidson, W. N., I. Dutia, and D. Dutia, 1989, "A Note on the Behavior of Security Returns: A Test of Stock Market Overreaction and Efficiency," *Journal of Financial Research* 12(3, fall):245–252.

Dubofsky, D. A., and J. C. Groth, 1986, "Relative Information Accessibility for OTC Stocks and Security Returns," *Financial Review* 21(1, February):6–17.

Etebari, A. J., O. Horrigan, and J. L. Landwehr, 1987, "To Be or Not to Be—Reaction of Stock Returns to Sudden Deaths of Corporate Chief Executive Officers," *Journal of Business Finance and Accounting* 14(2, summer):255–278.

Fama, E. F., 1965, "The Behavior of Stock Market Prices," *Journal of Business* 38(January):34–105.

Fama, E. F., and M. E. Blume, 1966, "Filter Rules and Stock Market Trading," *Journal of Business* (January):226–241.

French, K. R., 1980, "Stock Returns and the Weekend Effect," *Journal of Financial Economics* 8(March):55–69.

French, K. R., and R. Roll, 1986, "Stock Return Variances: The Arrival of Information and the Reaction of Traders," *Journal of Financial Economics* 17(September):5–26.

Godek, P., in press, "Why NASDAQ Market Makers Avoid Odd-eighth Quotes," *Journal of Financial Economics*.

Glosten, L. R., 1989, "Insider Trading, Liquidity, and the Role of the Monopolist Specialist," *Journal of Business* 62(2):211–236.

Glosten, L. R., and L. E. Harris, 1988, "Estimating the Components of the Bid/Ask Spread," *Journal of Financial Economics* 21:123–142.

Gross, M., "A Semi-strong Test of the Efficiency of the Aluminum and Copper Markets at the LME," *Journal of Futures Markets* 8(1, February):67–78.

Hasbrouck, J., 1988, "Trades, Quotes, Inventories and Information," *Journal of Financial Economics* 22:229.

Houthakker, H. S., 1961, "Systematic and Random Elements in Short-term Price Movements," *American Economic Review* 51(March):164–172.

Jaffe, J., 1974, "The Effect of Regulation Changes on Insider Trading," *Bell Journal of Economics and Management Science* (spring):93–121.

Kamarotou, H., and J. O'Hanlon, 1989, "Informational Efficiency in the UK, US, Canadian and Japanese Equity Markets: A Note," *Journal of Business Finance Accounting* 16(2, spring):183.

Keane, S. M., 1986, "The Efficient Market Hypothesis on Trial," *Financial Analysts Journal* 42(March–April):58–63.

Kendall, M. G., 1953, "The Analysis of Economic Time Series: Part I: Prices," *Journal of the Royal Statistical Society* 116:11–25.

Lee, M. H., and H. Bishara, 1989, "Recent Canadian Experience on the Profitability of Insider Trades," *Financial Review* 24(2, May):235–250.

Pindyck, R. S., and D. L. Rubinfeld, 1991, *Econometric Models and Economic Forecasts,* 3rd ed., New York: McGraw-Hill.

Rosenberg, B., and W. McKibben, 1973, "The Prediction of Systematic and Specific Risk in Common Stocks," *Journal of Financial and Quantitative Analysis* 8(2, March):317–334.

Rozeff, M. S., and M. A. Zaman, 1988, "Market Efficiency and Insider Trading: New Evidence," *Journal of Business* 61:25–44.

Sinclair, N. A., V. A. Fatseas, and K. T. Trotman, 1986, "Security Price Reaction to Qualitative Forecast Information," *Australian Journal of Management* 11(December):231–240.

Chapter 6. The Determination of Equity Prices

Barsky, R. B., and J. B. DeLong, 1993, "Why Does the Stock Market Fluctuate?" *Quarterly Journal of Economics* 108(2, May):291–312.

Black, F., 1972, "Capital Market Equilibrium with Restricted Borrowing," *Journal of Business* 45(3):444–455.

Blume, M. E., 1983, "The Pricing of Capital Assets in a Multiperiod World," *Journal of Banking and Finance* 7:31.

Breeden, D. T., 1979, "An Intertemporal Asset Pricing Model with Stochastic Consumption and Investment Opportunities," *Journal of Financial Economics* 7:265–296.

Brooks, L. D., and D. A. Buckmaster, 1976, "Further Evidence of the Time Series Properties of Accounting Income," *Journal of Finance* (31):1359–1374.

Chen, N-F., 1983, "Some Empirical Test of the Theory of Arbitrage Pricing," *Journal of Finance* 38(5):1393–1414.

Cox, J. C., and M. Rubinstein, 1985, *Option Markets,* Englewood Cliffs, NJ: Prentice Hall.

Elton, E. J., and M. J. Gruber, 1984, "Non-standard C.A.P.M.s and the Market Portfolio," *Journal of Finance* 39(3, July):911–924.

Estep, T., N. Hanson, and C. Johnson, 1983, "Sources of Value and Risk in Common Stocks," *Journal of Portfolio Management* 9(4, summer):5–13.

Farrell, J. L., 1985, "The Dividend Discount Model: A Primer," *Financial Analysts Journal* 41(November–December):26–34.

Harvard Business School, 1971, "Herrick Management & Research Company," Case No. 9-271-228, Boston, MA: Harvard Business School Publishing Division.

Jarrow, R. A., and A. Rudd, 1983, "A Comparison of the APT and CAPM: A Note," *Journal of Banking and Finance* 7:295.

Kraus, A., and R. H. Litzenberger, 1976, "Skewness Preference and the Valuation of Risk Assets," *Journal of Finance* 31:108.

Levy, H., 1980, "The CAPM and Beta in an Imperfect Market," *Journal of Portfolio Management* 6(2, winter):5–11.

Lintner, J., 1965, "The Valuation of Risk Assets and the Selection of Risky Investments in Stock Portfolios and Capital Budgets," *Review of Economics and Statistics* 47(February):13–37.

Lintner, J., 1970, "The Market Price of Risk, Size of Market and Investor's Risk Aversion," *Review of Economics and Statistics* 52(February):87–99.

Little, I. M. D., 1962, "Higgledy Piggledy Growth," *Oxford Bulletin of Economics and Statistics* 24:387–412.

Loderer, C., J. W. Cooney, and L. D. Van Drunen, 1991, "The Price Elasticity of Demand for Common Stock," *Journal of Finance* 46(2, June):621–651.

Mankiw, N. G., and M. D. Shapiro, 1985, "Risk and Return: Consumption Beta versus Market Beta," *Review of Economics and Statistics* 68(3):452–459.

McFarland, H., 1988, "Evaluating q as an Alternative to the Rate of Return in Measuring Profitability," *Review of Economics and Statistics* 70(November):614–622.

Merton, R., 1973, "An Intertemporal Capital Asset Pricing Model," *Econometrica* (September):867–888.

Mossin, J., 1966, "Equilibrium in a Capital Asset Market," *Econometrica* 35:768–783.

Mullins, D., 1982, "Does the Capital Asset Pricing Model Work?" *Harvard Business Review* 60(1, January–February):105–114.

Roll, R. A., 1977, "A Critique of the Asset Pricing Theory's Tests: Part I. On Past and Potential Testability of the Theory," *Journal of Financial Economics* 4(2, March):129–176.

Roll, R., and S. A. Ross, 1980, "An Empirical Investigation of the Arbitrage Pricing Theory," *Journal of Finance* 35(5, December):1073–1103.

Roll, R., and S. A. Ross, 1984, "The Arbitrage Pricing Theory Approach to Strategic Portfolio Planning," *Financial Analysts Journal* 40(May–June):14–29.

Rosenberg, B., and W. McKibben, 1973, "The Prediction of Systematic and Specific Risk in Common Stocks," *Journal of Financial and Quantitative Analysis* 8(2, March):317–334.

Ross, S. A., 1976, "The Arbitrage Theory of Capital Asset Pricing," *Journal of Economic Theory* 13(3, December):341–360.

Scott, L. O., 1985, "The Present Value Model of Stock Prices: Regression Tests and Monte Carlo Results," *Review of Economics and Statistics* 67(4):599–605.

Sharpe, W. F., 1964, "Capital Asset Prices: A Theory of Market Equilibrium under Conditions of Risk," *Journal of Finance* 19(September):425–442.

Sharpe, W. F., and G. J. Alexander, 1992, *Investments,* 4th ed., Englewood Cliffs, NJ: Prentice Hall.

Shleifer, A., 1986, "Do Demand Curves for Stocks Slope Down?" *Journal of Finance* 41(3, July):579–590.

Stultz, R. M., 1986, "Asset Pricing and Expected Inflation," *Journal of Finance* 41(1, March):209–223.

Tobin, J., 1958, "Liquidity Preference as Behaviour toward Risk," *Review of Economic Studies* 25(February):65–86.

Chapter 7. Security Analysis

Arnott, R. D., and W. A. Copeland, 1985, "The Business Cycle and Security Selection," *Financial Analysts Journal* 41(March–April):26–33.

Barnes, P., 1987, "The Analysis and Use of Financial Ratios: A Review Article," *Journal of Business Finance and Accounting* 14(4):449.

Chung, P. S., 1974, "An Investigation of the Firm Effects Influence in the Analysis of Earnings to Price Ratios of Industrial Common Stock," *Journal of Financial and Quantitative Analysis* 9(December):1009.

Ciccolo, J., and G. Fromm, 1980, "q, Corporate Investment, and Balance Sheet Behavior," *Journal of Money, Credit and Banking* 12(2, May):294–307.

Coggin, D., and J. Hunter, 1981, "Analysts' Forecasts Nearer Actual than Statistical Models," *Journal of Business Forecasting.*

Cohen, S., and D. J. Smyth, 1973, "Some Determinants of Price/Earnings Ratios of Industrial Common Stock," *Quarterly Review of Economics and Business* 13(4):49–60.

Foster, G., 1986, *Financial Statement Analysis,* 2d ed., Englewood Cliffs, NJ: Prentice Hall.

Goodman, D. A., and J. W. Peavy, 1983, "Industry Relative Price-earnings Ratios as Indicators of Investment Returns," *Financial Analysts Journal* 39(July–August):60–66.

Hassell, J. M., R. H. Jennings, and D. J. Lasser, 1988, "Management Earnings Forcasts: Their Usefulness as a Source of Firm-specific Information to Security Analysts," *Journal of Financial Research* 11(4, winter):303–320.

Hay, M., and P. J. Williamson, 1991, *The Strategy Handbook,* London: Blackwell.

Houthakker, H. S., 1979, "Growth and Inflation: Analysis by Industry," *Brookings Papers on Economics Activity* 1:241–257.

Houthakker, H. S., and L. D. Taylor, 1970, *Consumer Demand in the United States,* 2d ed., Cambridge, MA: Harvard University Press.

Kodde, D. A., and H. Schreuder, 1984, "Forecasting Corporate Revenue and Profit: Time-series Models versus Management and Analysts," *Journal of Business Finance and Accounting* 11(3, autumn):381–395.

Lindenberg, E. B., and S. A. Ross, 1981, "Tobin's q Ratio and Industrial Organization," *Journal of Business* 54(1, January):1–32.

McFarland, H., 1988, "Evaluating q as an Alternative to the Rate of Return in Measuring Profitability," *Review of Economics and Statistics* 70(November):614–622.

Montgomery, C. A., and B. Wernerfelt, 1988, "Diversification, Ricardian Rents, and Tobin's q," *Rand Journal of Economics* 19(4, winter):623.

Mueller, D. C., 1990, *The Dynamics of Company Profits: An International Comparison,* Cambridge, England: Cambridge University Press.

Nguyen, T-H., and G. Bernier, 1988, "Beta and q in a Simultaneous Framework with Pooled Data," *Review of Economics and Statistics* 70:520.

Peles, Y. C., and M. I. Schneller, 1989, "The Duration of the Adjustment Process of Financial Ratios," *Review of Economics and Statistics* (August):527–532.

Peters, T. J., and R. H. Waterman, 1982, *In Search of Excellence,* New York: Harper and Row.

Porter, M. E., 1980, *Competitive Strategy,* New York: Free Press.

Robichek, A. A., and M. C. Bogue, 1970, "A Note on the Behavior of Expected Price/Earnings Ratios over Time," *Journal of Finance* 25(June):243–274.

Schwalback, J., U. Grasshoff, and T. Mahmood, 1989, "The Dynamics of Corporate Profits," *European Economic Review* 33:1625.

Tobin, J., 1958, "Liquidity Preference as Behaviour toward Risk," *Review of Economic Studies* 25(February):65–86.

Whitbeck, V. S., and M. Kisor Jr., 1963, "A New Tool in Investment Decision Making," *Financial Analysts Journal* 19(3, May–June):55–62.

Williamson, P. J., with A. Hu, 1994, *Managing the Global Frontier,* London: Pitman.

Chapter 8. Options and Options Pricing

Bachelier, L., 1900, "Théorie de la Spéculation," in *Annales de l'Ecole Normale Supérieure,* 3 Paris: Gauthier-Villars. English translation in Cootner, P. H. (ed.), 1964, *The Random Character of Stock Market Prices,* Cambridge: MIT Press.

Barone-Adesi, G., and R. Whaley, 1987, "Efficient Analytic Approximation of American Option Values," *Journal of Finance* 42(June):301–320.

Beckers, S., 1981, "Standard Deviations Implied in Option Prices as Predictors of Future Stock Price Variability," *Journal of Banking and Finance* 5:363–382.

Bhattacharya, M., 1987, "Price Changes of Related Securities: The Case of Call Options and Stocks," *Journal of Financial and Quantitative Analysis* 22(March):1–15.

Black, F., 1975, "Fact and Fantasy in the Use of Options," *Financial Analysts Journal* 31(July–August):61–72.

Black, F., 1976, "Studies of Stock Price Volatility Changes," *Proceedings of the 1976 Meetings of the American Statistical Association, Business and Economic Statistics Section* (August):177–181.

Black, F., and M. Scholes, 1973, "The Pricing of Options and Corporate Liabilities," *Journal of Political Economy* 81(3, May–June):637–654.

Blomeyer, E. C., and H. Johnson, 1988, "An Empirical Examination of the Pricing of American Put Options," *Journal of Financial and Quantitative Analysis* 23(1, March):13–22.

Brennan, M. J., and E. S. Schwartz, 1977, "Convertible Bonds: Valuation and Optimal Strategies for Call and Conversion," *Journal of Finance* 32:1699.

Chang, J. S. K., and L. Shanker, 1987, "Option Pricing and the Arbitrage Pricing Theory," *Journal of Financial Research* 10(1, spring):1–16.

Clasing, H., 1989, *Currency Options,* New York: Dow Jones-Irwin.

Cox, J. C., and M. Rubinstein, 1983, "A Survey of Alternative Option Pricing Models," in M. Brenner, ed., *Option Pricing,* Cambridge, MA: Heath.

Cox, J. C., and M. Rubinstein, 1985, *Option Markets,* Englewood Cliffs, NJ: Prentice Hall.

Day, T. E., and C. M. Lewis, 1988, "The Behavior of the Volatility Implicit in the Prices of Stock Index Options," *Journal of Financial Economics* 22:103.

Gastineau, G. L., 1988, *The Options Manual,* 3d ed., New York: McGraw-Hill.

Geske, R., 1979, "The Valuation of Compound Options," *Journal of Financial Economics* 6(March):63–81.

Hsia, C-C., 1983, "On Binomial Option Pricing," *Journal of Financial Research* 6(spring):41–50.

Hull, J. C., 1993, *Options, Futures and Other Derivative Securities,* 2d ed., Englewood Cliffs, NJ: Prentice Hall.

Ingersoll, J. E., 1977, "A Contingent-claim Valuation of Convertible Securities," *Journal of Financial Economics* 4:289.

Johnson, H., and D. Shanno, 1987, "Option Pricing When the Variance Is Changing," *Journal of Financial and Quantitative Analysis* 22(June):143.

Jones, E. P., 1984, "Option Arbitrage and Strategy with Large Price Changes," *Journal of Financial Economics* 13(1, March):91–113.

Malliaris, A. G., and W. A. Brock, 1981, *Stochastic Methods in Economics and Finance,* Amsterdam: North Holland.

Merton, R. C., 1973, "Theory of Rational Options Pricing," *Bell Journal of Economics* 4(spring):141–183.

Merton, R. C., 1976, "Option Pricing When Underlying Stock Returns Are Discontinuous," *Journal of Financial Economics* 3:125.

Selby, M. J. P., and S. D. Hodges, 1987, "On the Evaluation of Compound Options," *Management Science* 33(3, March):347–355.

Stoll, H., 1969, "The Relationship between Put and Call Option Prices," *Journal of Finance* 24(May):319–332.

Tucker, A. L., 1990, *Financial Futures, Options and Swaps,* St. Paul, MN: West.

Chapter 9. Futures Contracts and Futures Markets

Arak, M., and L. S. Goodman, 1987, "Treasury Bond Futures: Valuing the Delivery Options," *Journal of Futures Markets* 7(3, June):269–286.

Black, F., 1975, "The Pricing of Commodity Contracts," *Journal of Financial Economics* (January–March):167–179.

Brooks, R., 1989, "Investment Decision Making with Index Futures and Index Futures Options," *Journal of Futures Markets* 9(2):143–162.

Carlton, D., 1984, "Futures Markets: Their Purpose, Their History, Their Growth, Their Successes and Failures," *Journal of Futures Markets* 4:237–271.

Danthine, J-P., 1987, "Financial and Futures Markets: Introduction," *European Economic Review* 31:1–2.

Hawtrey, R. G., 1939, "Mr. Kaldor on the Forward Market," *Review of Economic Studies,* 7(3):202–205.

Hirschleifer, D., 1988, "Risk, Futures Pricing, and the Organization of Production in Commodity Markets," *Journal of Political Economy* 96(6, December):1206–1220.

Houthakker, H. S., 1959, "The Scope and Limits of Futures Trading," in M. Abramovitz, ed., *The Allocation of Economic Resources,* Stanford, CA: Stanford University Press, 134–159.

Hull, J. C., 1993, *Options, Futures and Other Derivative Securities,* 2d ed., Englewood Cliffs, NJ: Prentice Hall.

Jarrow, R. A., and G. S. Oldfield, 1981, "Forward Contracts and Futures Contracts," *Journal of Financial Economics* 9:321.

Martell, T. F., and A. S. Wolf, 1987, "Determinants of Trading Volume in Futures Markets," *Journal of Futures Markets* 7(3, June):233–244.

Mollgaard, P., and L. Phlips, 1992, "Oil Futures and Strategic Stocks at Sea," in L. D. Taylor and L. Phlips, eds., *Aggregation, Consumption and Trade,* Dordrecht: Kluwer, 169–196.

Phlips, L., ed., 1991, *Commodity Futures and Financial Markets,* Dordrecht: Kluwer.

Schwarz, E. M., J. Hill, and T. Schneeweis, 1986, *Financial Futures: Fundamentals, Strategies and Applications,* New York: Irwin.

Stein, J. L., 1986, *The Economics of Futures Markets,* Oxford: Blackwell.

Telser, L. G., and Higinbotham, H. N., 1977, "Organized Futures Markets: Costs and Benefits," *Journal of Political Economy* 85(October):969–1000.

Teweles, R. F., and F. J. Jones, 1987, *The Futures Game,* 2d ed., New York: Wiley.

Tucker, A. L., 1990, *Financial Futures, Options and Swaps,* St. Paul, MN: West.

Chapter 10. Futures Prices

Billingsley, R. S., and D. M. Chance, 1989, "The Pricing and Performance of Stock Index Futures Spreads," *Journal of Futures Markets* 8(3, June):303–318.

Black, F., and M. Scholes, 1973, "The Pricing of Options and Corporate Liabilities," *Journal of Political Economy* 81(3, May–June):637–654.

Carter, C., G. Rausser, and A. Schmitz, 1983, "Efficient Asset Portfolios and the Theory of Normal Backwardation," *Journal of Political Economy* 91:319–331.

Castelino, M. G., 1989, "Basis Volatility: Implications for Hedging," *Journal of Financial Research* 12(2, summer):157–172.

Cox, J. C., J. E. Ingersoll, and S. A. Ross, 1981, "The Relation between Forward Prices and Future Prices," *Journal of Financial Economics* 9:321.

Dusak, K., 1973, "Futures Trading and Investor Returns: An Investigation of Commodity Market Risk Premiums," *Journal of Political Economy* 81:1387–1406.

Ederington, L. H., 1979, "The Hedging Performance of the New Futures Markets," *Journal of Finance* 34:164–170.

Finnerty, J. E., and H. Y. Park, 1988, "How to Profit from Program Trading," *Journal of Portfolio Management* 44(winter):40–46.

French, K. R., 1983, "A Comparison of Futures and Forward Prices," *Journal of Financial Economics* 12:311–342.

Garbade, K. D., and W. L. Silber, 1983, "Price Movements and Price Discovery in Futures and Cash Markets," *Review of Economics and Statistics* 65:289.

Grant, D., and M. Eaker, 1989, "Complex Hedges: How Well Do They Work?" *Journal of Futures Markets* 9(1):15–28.

Hicks, J. R., 1946, *Value and Capital,* 2d ed., Oxford: Clarendon Press.

Hirschleifer, D., 1989, "Determinants of Hedging and Risk Premia in Commodity Futures Markets," *Journal of Financial and Quantitative Analysis* 24(3, September):313–332.

Houthakker, H. S., 1957, "Can Speculators Forecast Prices?" *Review of Economics and Statistics* 39(May):143–151.

Houthakker, H. S., 1961, "Systematic and Random Elements in Short-term Price Movements," *American Economic Review* 51(March):164–172.

Houthakker, H. S., 1968, "Normal Backwardation," in J. N. Wolfe, ed., *Value, Capital, and Growth: Papers in Honour of Sir John Hicks,* Edinburgh: University Press, 195–214.

Kaldor, N., 1939, "Speculation and Economic Stability," *Review of Economic Studies* 7:1–27.

Keynes, J. M., 1923, "Some Aspects of Commodity Markets," *Manchester Guardian Commercial.*

Keynes, J. M., 1930, *A Treatise on Money,* vol. 2, London: Macmillan.

Leland, H. E., 1980, "Who Should Buy Portfolio Insurance?" *Journal of Finance* 35:581–594.

Macdonald, S. S., and S. E. Hein, 1989, "Future Rates and Forward Rates as Predictors of Nearterm Treasury Bill Rates," *Journal of Futures Markets* 9(3):249–262.

Rockwell, C., 1967, "Normal Backwardation, Forecasting and the Returns to Commodity Futures Trades," *Food Research Institute Studies* 7 (suppl.):107–130.

Rubenstein, M., 1988, "Portfolio Insurance after the Crash," *Financial Analysts Journal* 44(1):38–47.

Rutledge, D. J. S., 1976, "A Note on the Variability of Futures Prices," *Review of Economics and Statistics* 57 (February):118–120.

Samuelson, P. A., 1965, "Proof That Properly Anticipated Prices Fluctuate Randomly," *Industrial Management Review* 6:13–31.

Stein, J. L., 1986, *The Economics of Futures Markets,* Oxford: Blackwell.

Telser, L. G., 1958, "Futures Trading and the Storage of Cotton and Wheat," *Journal of Political Economy* 66(June):233–255.

Turnovsky, S., 1990, "The Determination of Spot and Futures Prices with Storable Commodities," *Econometrica* 51:1363–1387.

Working, H., 1942, "Quotations on Commodity Futures as Price Forecasts," *Econometrica* 10:30–52.

Working, H., 1949, "The Theory of Price of Storage," *American Economic Review* 39:1234–1252.

Chapter 11. Regulation of Financial Markets

Fay, S., 1982, *Beyond Greed,* New York: Viking.

Ferguson, R., 1988, "What to Do, or Not Do, about the Markets," *Journal of Political Economy* 14(4, summer):14–19.

Friend, I., 1979, "Economic Foundations of Stock Market Regulation," in J. L. Bicksler, ed., *Handbook of Financial Economics,* Amsterdam: North-Holland, 139–160.

Granger, C. W. J., 1969, "Investigating Causal Relations by Econometric Models and Cross-spectral Methods," *Econometrica* 37:428–438.

Hirschleifer, D., 1988, "Risk, Futures Pricing, and the Organization of Production in Commodity Markets," *Journal of Political Economy* 96(6, December):1206–1220.

Houthakker, H. S., 1982, "The Regulation of Financial and Other Futures Markets," *Journal of Finance* 37(2, May):481–491.

Kindleberger, C. P., 1989, *Manias, Panics and Crashes,* rev. ed., New York: Basic Books.

Langevoort, D. C., 1985, "Information Technology and the Structure of Securities Regulation," *Harvard Law Review* 98(4):747–804.

MacKay, C., [1841] 1980, *Extraordinary Popular Delusions and the Madness of Crowds,* New York: Harmony Books.

Malkiel, B. G., 1988, "The Brady Commission Report: A Critique," *Journal of Portfolio Management* 14(4, summer):9–13.

Manove, M., 1989, "The Harm from Insider Trading and Informed Speculation," *Quarterly Journal of Economics* 104(4, November):823–846.

Peck, A. E., ed., 1985, *Futures Markets: Regulatory Issues,* Washington, DC: American Enterprise Institute for Public Policy Research.

Pirrong, S. C., 1993, "Manipulation of the Commodity Futures Market Delivery Process," *Journal of Business* 66:335–369.

Roll, R., 1989, "Price Volatility, International Market Links, and Their Implications for Regulatory Policies," *Journal of Financial Services Research* 3(2–3):211–246.

Sen, A. K., 1991, *Money and Value: On the Ethics and Economics of Finance,* Rome: Edizione dell'Elefante.

Stigler, G. J., 1964, "Public Regulation of the Securities Market," *Journal of Business* 37(April):117–142.

Stoll, H. R., 1979, *Regulation of Securities Markets: An Examination of the Effects of Increased Competition,* Monograph 1979-2, Monograph Series in Finance and Economics, New York: New York University.

Telser, L. G., 1992, "Corners in Organized Futures Markets," in L. Phlips and L. D. Taylor, eds., *Aggregation, Consumption and Trade,* Dordrecht: Kluwer, 159–167.

Williams, J. C., 1994, *Manipulation on Trial: The Hunt Silver Case,* Cambridge, England: Cambridge University Press.

Author Index

Subject Index

NATIONAL UNIVERSITY
LIBRARY   SAN DIEGO

NATIONAL UNIVERSITY
SAN DIEGO
LIBRARY